TERROR TRAIN
AND OTHER STORIES

Publisher: GARY GROTH
Senior Editor: J. MICHAEL CATRON
Series Designer: JACOB COVEY
Volume Designer: JUSTIN ALLAN-SPENCER
Production: CHRISTINA HWANG, PAUL BARESH
Associate Publisher: ERIC REYNOLDS

Terror Train And Other Stories is copyright © 2020 Fantagraphics Books, Inc. All contents copyright © 2020 Fantagraphics Books, Inc. unless otherwise noted. All comics stories, illustrations, and photos herein copyright © 2020 William M. Gaines Agent, Inc. unless otherwise noted. "The Golden Age of Al Feldstein" copyright © 2020 Thommy Burns. "Al Feldstein" copyright © 2020 S.C. Ringgenberg. "Crime, Horror, Terror, Gore, Depravity, Disrespect for Established Authority — And Science Fiction, Too! The Ups and Downs of EC Comics" copyright © 2020 Ted White. All rights reserved. This is Volume 28 of The Fantagraphics EC Artists' Library. Permission to quote or reproduce material for reviews must be obtained from the publisher.

Fantagraphics Books, Inc.
7563 Lake City Way NE
Seattle WA 98115
(800) 657-1100
Fantagraphics.com • Twitter: @fantagraphics • facebook.com/fantagraphics.

Special thanks to Cathy Gaines Mifsud, Dorothy Crouch, Christopher Boyko, Thommy Burns, Grant Geissman, and John Benson.

First Fantagraphics Books edition: October 2020
ISBN 978-1-68396-329-5
Library of Congress Control Number: 2019953952
Printed in China

FIRST APPEARANCES

Guided by EC historian John Benson's research on EC release dates, we present the stories in this book in the order in which they originally appeared:

"The Treasure of Timberline Top" in *Saddle Justice* #3, Spring 1948
"The Case of the Savage Strongboy" in *War Against Crime* #3, Fall 1948
"Double-Crossed" in *Crime Patrol* #9, Winter 1948
"The Machine-Gun Mad Mobsters" in *War Against Crime* #4, Winter 1948
"Dance-Hall Racket" in *Crime Patrol* #10, February–March 1949
"The Law's Revenge!" in *War Against Crime* #5 February–March 1949
"Victor Wolf & Sam Bart: Kidnappers" in *Crime Patrol* #11, April–May 1949
"Money-Hungry" in *War Against Crime* #6, April–May 1949
"Nell Baker" in *Crime Patrol* #12, June–July 1949
"Your Newsdealer — He Is Your Friend!" (1st version) in *War Against Crime* #7, June–July 1949
"The Craig Gang" in *War Against Crime* #7, June–July 1949
"The Last Round" in *War Against Crime* #8, August–September 1949
"Your Newsdealer — He Is Your Friend!" (2nd version) in *War Against Crime* #8, August–September 1949
"The Case of the Floating Corpse!" in *Crime Patrol* #14, October–November 1949
"The Fatal Turn" in *War Against Crime* #9, October–November 1949
"Our Families Clashed!" in *Modern Love* #3, October–November 1949
"Case Number 318: Murder" in *Crime Patrol* #15, December 1949–January 1950
"Return From the Grave!" in *Crime Patrol* #15, December 1949–January 1950
"Buried Alive!" in *War Against Crime* #10, December 1949–January 1950

"I Was A 'B' Girl!" in *Modern Love* #4, December 1949–January 1950
"The Spectre in the Castle!" in *Crime Patrol* #16, February–March 1950
"The Mummy's Curse!" in *War Against Crime* #11, February–March 1950
"Death Must Come!" in *The Crypt of Terror* #17, April–May 1950
"Terror Train" in *Vault of Horror* #12, April–May 1950
"The Thing in the Swamp!" in *Haunt of Fear* #15, May–June 1950
"The Maestro's Hand!" in *The Crypt of Terror* #18, June–July 1950
"The Dead Will Return!" in *Vault of Horror* #13, June–July 1950
"Ghost Ship!" in *The Crypt of Terror* #19, August–September 1950
"The Strange Couple!" in *Vault of Horror* #14, August–September 1950
"The Love Story To End All Love Stories!" in *Modern Love* #8, August–September 1950
"Horror Beneath the Streets!" in *Haunt of Fear* #17, September–October 1950
"The Thing From the Sea!" in *Tales From the Crypt* #20, October–November 1950
"Hong Kong Intrigue!" in *Two-Fisted Tales* #18, November–December 1950
"A Shocking Way To Die!" in *Tales From the Crypt* #21, December 1950–January 1951
"Escape!" in *Vault of Horror* #16, December 1950–January 1951
"The Thing From the Grave!" in *Tales From the Crypt* #22, February–March 1951
"Reflection of Death!" in *Tales From the Crypt* #23, April–May 1951

TERROR TRAIN
AND OTHER STORIES

**ILLUSTRATED BY
AL FELDSTEIN**

WITH JOHN ALTON
WRITTEN BY AL FELDSTEIN

FANTAGRAPHICS BOOKS
Seattle

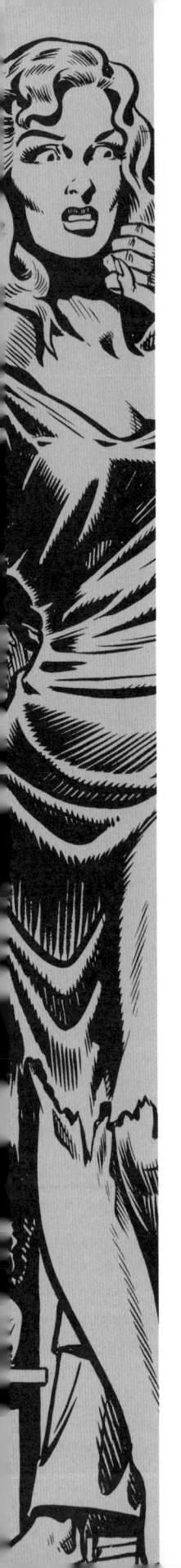

VII *The Golden Age of Al Feldstein*
Introduction by Thommy Burns

1 THE TREASURE OF TIMBERLINE TOP
script: Unknown (possibly Gardner Fox or Ivan Klapper) | art: Al Feldstein

9 THE CASE OF THE SAVAGE STRONGBOY
script: Unknown (possibly Gardner Fox or Ivan Klapper) | art: Al Feldstein

17 DOUBLE-CROSSED
script and art: Al Feldstein

26 THE MACHINE-GUN MAD MOBSTERS
script: Unknown (possibly Gardner Fox or Ivan Klapper) | art: Al Feldstein

36 DANCE-HALL RACKET
script and art: Al Feldstein

47 THE LAW'S REVENGE!
script and art: Al Feldstein

57 VICTOR WOLF & SAM BART: KIDNAPPERS
script and art: Al Feldstein

67 MONEY-HUNGRY
script and art: Al Feldstein

76 NELL BAKER
script and art: Al Feldstein

84 YOUR NEWSDEALER — HE IS YOUR FRIEND!
story: William M. Gaines, Al Feldstein | script and art: Al Feldstein

85 THE CRAIG GANG
script and art: Al Feldstein

94 THE LAST ROUND
script and art: Al Feldstein

104 YOUR NEWSDEALER — HE IS YOUR FRIEND!
story: William M. Gaines, Al Feldstein | script and art: Al Feldstein

105 THE CASE OF THE FLOATING CORPSE!
script and art: Al Feldstein

114 THE FATAL TURN
script and art: Al Feldstein

123 OUR FAMILIES CLASHED!
script and art: Al Feldstein

132 CASE NUMBER 318: MURDER
script: Unknown | art: John Alton and Al Feldstein

139 RETURN FROM THE GRAVE!
script and art: Al Feldstein

146 BURIED ALIVE!
script and art: Al Feldstein

154 I WAS A 'B'-GIRL!
script and art: Al Feldstein

161 THE SPECTRE IN THE CASTLE!
script and art: Al Feldstein

169   THE MUMMY'S CURSE!
script and art: Al Feldstein

177   DEATH MUST COME!
script and art: Al Feldstein

185   TERROR TRAIN
script and art: Al Feldstein

192   THE THING IN THE SWAMP!
story: William M. Gaines, Al Feldstein | script and art: Al Feldstein

199   THE MAESTRO'S HAND!
script and art: Al Feldstein

207   THE DEAD WILL RETURN!
script and art: Al Feldstein

215   GHOST SHIP!
script and art: Al Feldstein

223   THE STRANGE COUPLE!
script and art: Al Feldstein

230   THE LOVE STORY TO END ALL LOVE STORIES!
script and art: Al Feldstein

238   HORROR BENEATH THE STREETS!
script and art: Al Feldstein

245   THE THING FROM THE SEA!
script and art: Al Feldstein

252   HONG KONG INTRIGUE!
script and art: Al Feldstein

259   A SHOCKING WAY TO DIE!
story: William M. Gaines, Al Feldstein | script and art: Al Feldstein

267   ESCAPE!
story: William M. Gaines, Al Feldstein | script and art: Al Feldstein

274   THE THING FROM THE GRAVE!
story: Gardner Fox | script and art: Al Feldstein

282   REFLECTION OF DEATH!
story: William M. Gaines, Al Feldstein | script and art: Al Feldstein

291   *Al Feldstein*
Biography by S.C. Ringgenberg

297   *Behind the Panels*
Creator Biographies

299   *Crime, Horror, Terror, Gore, Depravity, Disrespect for Established Authority — And Science Fiction, Too!*
History by Ted White

302   *The Fantagraphics EC Artists' Library*
Titles in this Series

EC Comics did not publish writer credits, and its master records no longer exist. Based on the best information available, we believe the creator credits above to be accurate. We welcome any corrections.

WEIRD SCIENCE
CRIME SUSPENSTORIES
WEIRD
THE VAULT OF HORROR

THOMMY BURNS

THE GOLDEN AGE OF AL FELDSTEIN

"Why are we following these idiots ... Why don't we innovate, and why don't we have people follow us? ... Why don't we try horror?" — Al Feldstein to Bill Gaines, as told to S.C. Ringgenberg (*The Comics Journal Library Volume 8: The EC Artists*)

When Al Feldstein first set foot in the EC Comics offices at 225 Lafayette Street in the Little Italy section of New York, it was his reputation as an ace illustrator of "teenage books" that had gotten him there. Feldstein was illustrating *Junior* and *Sunny*, two *Archie*-type comic books for Fox Feature Syndicate and had gotten a tip from letterer Jim Wroten that EC was interested in doing a similar title. Wroten, who did the mechanical Leroy Lettering for both Fox and EC, advised Feldstein that Fox might be in financial trouble and that EC's then–business manager, Sol Cohen, was looking to do a teenage book.

Just before Valentine's Day, 1948, Feldstein met with Cohen and EC publisher Bill Gaines, who had recently, and reluctantly, inherited the business after the untimely death of his father. EC founder Max Gaines had died in a boating accident in August of 1947. Bill Gaines, unsure of how to keep the family business viable, was, at the urging of Cohen, chasing trends — "teenage books" at that moment. Cohen and Gaines were impressed with Feldstein's portfolio, and, on February 13, 1948, Gaines and Feldstein signed a contract for Feldstein to create an *Archie*-style title to be called *Going Steady With Peggy*. The contract stipulated that Feldstein would get a percentage of the profits of the book.

After Feldstein had penciled the cover and most of one story, Gaines told his new artist that he was cancelling *Peggy*, because, Gaines said, the market for teenage titles was collapsing. While this story has long been part of EC lore, Feldstein later came to have his doubts about the real reason behind Gaines's sudden change of mind, revealing to biographer Grant Geissman, "Jessie Gaines [Bill's mother] was overseeing everything her son was doing with his father's business ... I think she felt strongly that a publisher does not give a 'lowly artist' a percentage of the profits. ... I was well aware that the teenage market was not collapsing — at least not yet. But I was desperate." (*Feldstein: The Mad Life and Fantastic Art of Al Feldstein!* by Grant Geissman; IDW Publishing, 2013.) Thinking on his feet, Feldstein offered to forego payment for the work he had done and tear up the contract if Gaines would give him other regular work. Gaines agreed, and the rest is comics history.

"The Treasure of Timberline Top" (p. 1) was Feldstein's first published story for EC, appearing in the first issue of *Saddle Justice* (another trend-chasing title, piggybacking on the then-current Western comics craze). That first issue was designated #3 (don't ask) and cover-dated

---

OPPOSITE: Al Feldstein at the EC offices, in the late summer or early fall of 1950, with some of the early issues of the New Trend titles. On the rack: *Weird Science* #15 [#4], *Tales From the Crypt* #21 [#5], *Crime SuspenStories* #2, *Weird Fantasy* #16 [#4], *The Vault of Horror* #15 [#4], *Two-Fisted Tales* #18 [#1], and *Modern Love* #8 (final issue).

Spring 1948 (though its copyright registration indicates it was released in late July).

Feldstein's art is very recognizable as his, but his style had yet to develop, and it's easy to see here how he earned the early nickname of "Stiff-Figures" Feldstein. The story itself is basically a rewrite of *The Treasure of the Sierra Madre*, the film version of which had been released January 1 of that year. The script for "The Treasure of Timberline Top" was most likely written by Ivan Klapper or Gardner Fox.

"The Case of the Savage Strongboy" (p. 9) was Feldstein's next published EC story and appeared in *War Against Crime* #3 (this time, it actually was that title's third issue). Feldstein's art is still stiff, but he seems more comfortable with the crime genre, turning in some well rendered and brutally violent work. The scriptwriter is unknown, but the aforementioned Klapper and Fox are likely candidates. The story follows the classic "creation turning on its creator" plot, made explicit in the final panels, where the Strongboy is twice referred to as a "Frankenstein."

By now feeling his oats at EC, Feldstein approached Gaines and told him, "Listen, I can write my own scripts better than this" (*The Comics Journal Library Volume 8: The EC Artists*, Fantagraphics Books, 2013), so Gaines let Feldstein show what he could do.

"Double-Crossed" (p. 17) is the first EC story to be written and drawn by Feldstein. From then on, Feldstein would write almost all of the stories he drew, including, with just one or two exceptions, the rest in this collection. "Double-Crossed" appeared in *Crime Patrol*, *War Against Crime*'s sister title. The splash page informs us that "Johnny Kromer's career in crime followed a familiar pattern!" The story itself follows multiple familiar patterns and is a virtual blueprint for later Feldstein-penned yarns. Major plot elements were in fact recycled wholesale for the Wallace Wood–illustrated "Faced With Horror" (*Came The Dawn And Other Stories*, Volume 2 in this series). The lead character seems oddly like a wholesome teen character from *Junior* or *Sunny* turned psychotic, his ultra-violent acts (the sequence where he brains a woman with a piggy bank skull is especially campy) made all the more shocking by his smiling baby face. The original title of the story, revealed on a pre-publication silverprint, was actually "Angel-Face!" but the final title both foreshadows the twist ending (which the splash panel art does as well) and provides us with an early EC title pun (of which there would be many, many more to come).

ABOVE: This silverprint of "Angel-Face!" notes "title changed to Double Crossed" (upper right). Silverprints were black-and-white proofs of the original art. A color artist would paint dyes onto the silverprint and jot down codes that were unique to the comics business as a guide for the color separator. The "YR" scribbled on the man's tie and the woman's dress told the separator to use 100% yellow and 100% red (magenta) inks to get a bright red (the "Superman's cape" formula). "Y3R3B3" (the dresser drawers) calls for a combination of 50% yellow, 50% red (magenta), and 50% blue (cyan). A letter with no number indicated 100%. A letter followed by "2" meant a 25% tint, a "3" meant 50%, and a "4" meant 75%. Comics were printed using four ink colors: cyan, magenta, yellow, and black, but no tints of black were available.

"The Machine-Gun Mad Mobsters" (p. 26) is another plot that Feldstein didn't recall writing himself, so it's possible that "Double-Crossed" didn't fully convince Gaines of Feldstein's writing talent, but it's more likely that there was a backlog of material from other writers. "The

Machine-Gun Mad Mobsters" opens with a dramatic, action-packed splash panel (albeit with those "stiff figures") and then on page 2 treats the reader to a violent car crash bracketed by a couple of "headlight" panels that wouldn't be out of place in one of Feldstein's Fox teenage comics. From there, we move on to multiple shootouts (one between dueling motorboats), a cops-and-robbers beat-down, and a tear-gas smoke-out. Crime doesn't pay in the end, and we see Feldstein loosening up and finding his style.

"Dance-Hall Racket" (p. 36) is "a true crime story" with "fictitious" names and was definitely written by Feldstein, then rewritten — then rewritten again. After its initial appearance in *Crime Patrol*, it was reprinted roughly six months later in the first issue of *Modern Love* as "Dime-a-Dance Hostess" with new first and last pages (*see next spread*) that toned down the hard-boiled aspects of the story and emphasized the romance angle. It was diluted further still when, six months after that, the script was modified so it could be redrawn as a Western love story and titled "A Reno Dance-Hall Hostess!" (*see p. xii*) in the first issue of *Saddle Romances*. This time, it was billed as a "true *modern* love story" in which the names and places were "altered by the editors to conceal identities of those involved!" After three iterations — crime, romance, and Western — the identities of all involved were probably safe!

"The Law's Revenge!" (p. 47) opens with a full-page splash of an electric chair that would be reprised, with more noir panache, by Johnny Craig in "The Execution!" (*Fall Guy For Murder And Other Stories*, Volume 5). The story is, in fact, told by the electric chair, foreshadowing Feldstein's New Trend horror stories that would be narrated by shacks, steamer trunks, empty graves, and all manner of inanimate objects. The art itself is outlandish, boxy, and cartoonish, but Feldstein is really having some fun here with "a true crime story from police files!" Oh, and by the way, *"Crime doesn't pay!"* in the end.

"Victor Wolf & Sam Bart: Kidnappers" (p. 57) opens with a scene so sensational that one imagines it must have drawn attention from the early anti-comics crusaders. It's a scene that the rest of the story can't possibly measure up to — a woman is tied to a chair, breasts protruding, while a fedora-wearing thug holds a knife to her throat. As the tale unwinds, the usual beatings and robberies culminate in a kidnapping, and the rather thin plot is carried by Feldstein's over-the-top, at times even slapstick, violence, rendered in a larger-than-life comics style. By the time the FBI saves the day, we have lost interest in the story, but the art continues to engage and delight. But the story is also notable for the parody names of its title characters. Victor Fox was the publisher of *Junior* and *Sunny*, the two main books that Feldstein had worked on before coming to EC, and Sam Singer was the publisher of Say-Bart Publications. The entirety of Say-Bart's output appears to have been only a single issue of *The Adventures of Homer Cobb*,

ix

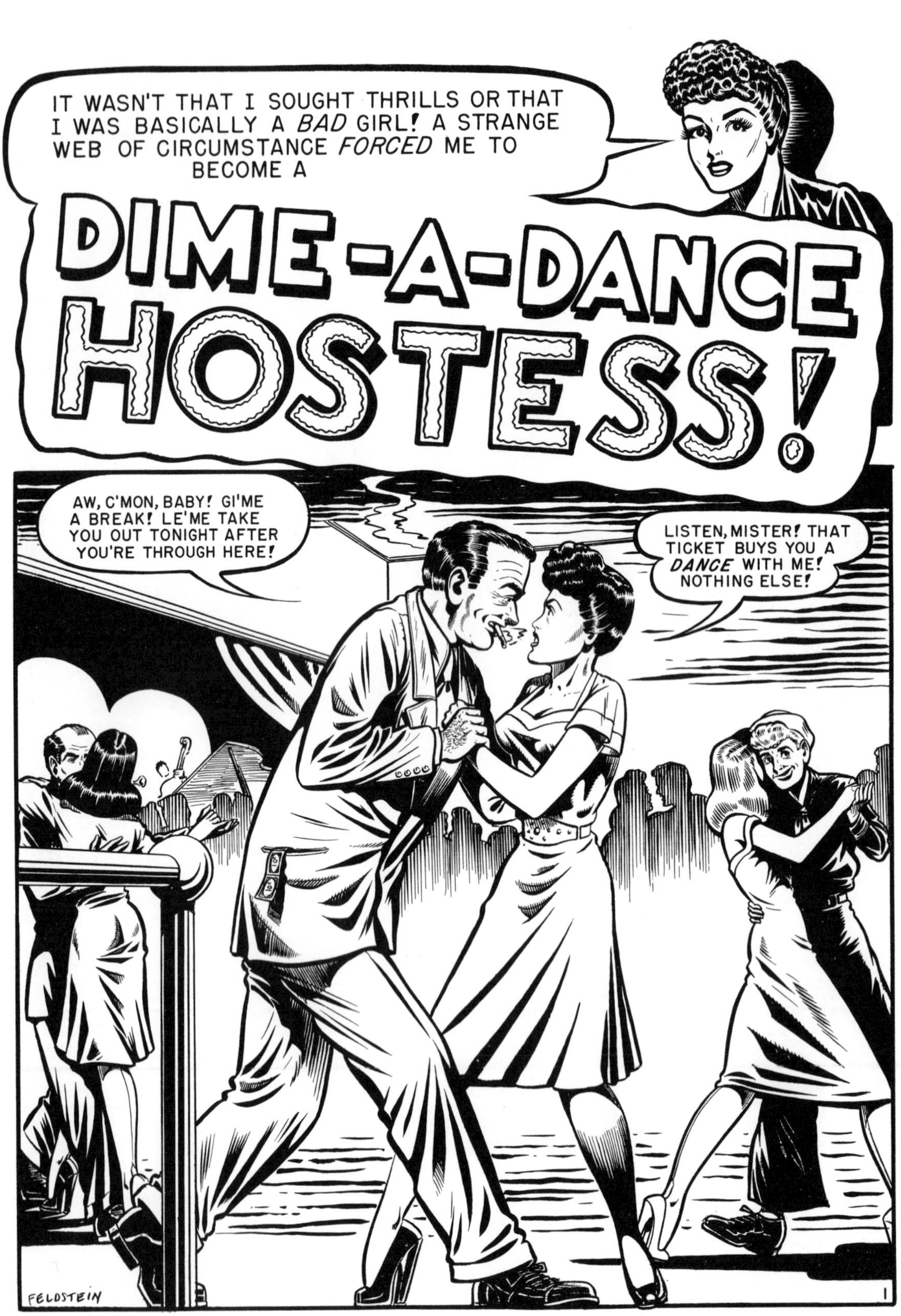
IT WASN'T THAT I SOUGHT THRILLS OR THAT I WAS BASICALLY A *BAD* GIRL! A STRANGE WEB OF CIRCUMSTANCE *FORCED* ME TO BECOME A
DIME-A-DANCE HOSTESS!
AW, C'MON, BABY! GI'ME A BREAK! LE'ME TAKE YOU OUT TONIGHT AFTER YOU'RE THROUGH HERE!
LISTEN, MISTER! THAT TICKET BUYS YOU A *DANCE* WITH ME! NOTHING ELSE!
FELDSTEIN
1

Panel 1
DAN KEPT HIS APPOINTMENT, WHILE I STAYED AT THE DANCE HALL. I WAS FRIGHTENED! I EVEN PRAYED A LITTLE! I LOVED DAN SO! IN THE PARK...

WHA...WHAT'S THE MEANING OF THIS? WHERE'S THE ...THE DAME?

SHE FORGOT THE DATE, CHUM, SO WE KEPT IT FOR HER! HAND OVER THAT LOADED WALLET, AND MAKE IT SNAPPY!

Panel 2
SURE, FELLOWS! HERE! I DON'T WANT NO TROUBLE! NOW! YOU HAVE THE TROUBLE!

WHA...?? COPS!

LET'S GET OUTTA HERE!

OKAY, CHIEF!

Panel 3
YOU SHOULDN'T HAVE PULLED THAT GUN, BENNET!

EEEEOWW!

BAMMM!

Panel 4
WE'LL, DAN! I GUESS WE CAN MARK THIS CASE CLOSED!

NOT EXACTLY, CHIEF! I HAVE SOME UNFINISHED BUSINESS BACK AT THE DANCE HALL!

Panel 5
BACK AT THE DANCE-HALL...

OH DAN, DARLING! I WAS SO WORRIED! THANK GOODNESS YOU'RE SAFE!

NINA, DEAR! I HAVE ONE MORE FAVOR TO ASK YOU! MARRY ME?

Panel 6
OF COURSE I WILL DAN, DEAREST!

LIFE HAS A MEANING FOR ME NOW---I HAVE A HUSBAND AND A HOME AND THE LOVE I SOUGHT!

Nina Foster

I HAD SPENT MY WHOLE LIFE ON A SMALL NEVADA RANCH! I WAS YOUNG AND INEXPERIENCED WHEN... OUT OF NECESSITY...I BECAME...
A RENO DANCE-HALL HOSTESS!
AN ACTUAL EXPERIENCE BY LAURIE MARLOW* AS TOLD TO THE EDITORS OF SADDLE ROMANCES
C'MON, BABY! GIVE ME A BREAK! STEP OUT WITH ME TONIGHT AFTER YOU'RE THROUGH WORKING...
LISTEN, MISTER! THAT TICKET YOU BOUGHT ENTITLES YOU TO A DANCE WITH ME... NOTHING ELSE!!!
FELDSTEIN
a true MODERN Love Story
* THE NAME LAURIE MARLOW AND ALL OTHER NAMES AND PLACES IN THIS TRUE STORY HAVE BEEN ALTERED BY THE EDITORS TO CONCEAL IDENTITIES OF THOSE INVOLVED!
MOTHER HAD BEEN AN INVALID FOR AS LONG AS I COULD REMEMBER AND... WHEN MY FATHER DIED...
I'VE GOT TO GET A JOB, MOTHER, OR ELSE WE'LL LOSE THE RANCH!
BUT, LAURIE! WHAT COULD YOU DO? YOU'VE NEVER WORKED BEFORE!
1

which apparently was mostly, if not completely, written and drawn by Feldstein.

"Money-Hungry" (p. 67) is essentially a re-write of "Savage Strongboy," but one in which the innocent shmoe who turns bad is a double-breasted suit-wearing swell and not a brutish Frankenstein. In this case, he is driven to crime by a "money-hungry" girlfriend who eventually sells him out for — you guessed it — reward money! The final page sets up a conflict that, in a later *Crime SuspenStories* comic, would have ended with the greedy dame getting hers in an ironically gruesome manner, but here the ending is pedestrian and anti-climactic. Note the address the heroine gives on page 8. 225 Lafayette Street was the real-life address of the EC offices.

"Nell Baker" (p. 76) follows its title character at a brisk pace from holdups to murder to capture, with some of the more "noir" panels (note page 5, panel 7; and page 8, panel 6) clearly influenced by Johnny Craig. The story is simple, with Nell being all bad from the first panel and no effort expended to explain how she got that way as she quickly moves from crime to crime. Readers will note a familiar face on page 7 — Feldstein has drawn his boss as a newspaper artist in panel 4, and in another sly in-joke has named him William Seniag ("Gaines" spelled backwards)!

OVERLEAF AND OPPOSITE: The crime story "Dance-Hall Racket" became the love story "Dime-a-Dance Hostess" when it was given new first and last pages. Then it was redrawn as a Western and retitled "A Reno Dance-Hall Hostess!".

"Your Newsdealer — He Is Your Friend!" (p. 84 and p. 104) came in two versions in the spring and summer of 1949. Illustrated by Feldstein, they are fairly obvious efforts to curry favor with the guys that displayed the comics!

"The Craig Gang" (p. 85) opens with a full-page splash of a gorgeous gal staring in horror (and looming above) as dapper machine-gun-toting crooks are mowed down by equally sharp, square-jawed coppers. The title is a fun example of a common EC in-joke: naming characters, businesses, and story names after each other (in this case, fellow EC artist/writer Johnny Craig). The story is another one supposedly "taken from FBI files," but it owes much more to the then-current crop of crime movies coming out of Hollywood — the remote cabin hideout, the unwitting female, and the sympathetic federal agent all being common themes. (Ironically, EC itself would soon become the subject of real-life FBI files, as detailed in *Atom Bomb And Other Stories*, Volume 26.) Feldstein's art seems to be improving with each story as he gets more comfortable with the subject matter and, presumably, his own creative freedom.

"The Last Round" (p. 94) opens with a nice full-page splash of a policeman punching an armed man in the foreground while two boxers trade their own punches in the ring illuminated in the background. The stark light and shadow, especially as it plays on the folds in the men's clothing, again betrays the influence of Craig. The story carries the "True Crime Story" tag, this time adding "As Told To A. Feldstein."

xiii

"Dreamed Up On A Deadline by A. Feldstein" was likely more accurate; the plot, as much as there is, is fairly basic (even with a primitive Feldstein "snap ending") while the boxing backstory adds some interest. How "Big Jim" fails to put two and two together as his fortunes flounder defies logic, but the piece is still enjoyable. The real saving grace here is Feldstein's art, which is worlds away from his humble EC debut roughly one year prior. When art and writing are married to subject matter he himself introduces and has more fun with, as will soon happen, a new era in comics will be born.

"The Case of the Floating Corpse!" (p. 105) finds Feldstein actually rivaling Johnny Craig in the "comics noir" department. The splash page is stunning, with a sedan's headlights illuminating the story title and casting upon a brick wall the lengthening shadow of a man dragging a body to the water even as light and shadow play upon the dingy wharf in the foreground. The second page is filled with interesting angles and more light and shadow, and in the last panel of page 4 (p. 108) we see Feldstein illustrate the effect of a blow to the head with spiraling surrealism instead of just showing the action of the blow being delivered, as he had in previous stories. He's improving by leaps and bounds now, and when his subject matter starts to equal his artistic style, the corpses in EC comics will be reanimating rather than floating! (Note that on the splash page, the story appears to be alternately titled or subtitled "The Guilty!" Feldstein would later use "The Guilty!" as the title of one of his most powerful "preachies," illustrated by Wallace Wood. See *Came The Dawn And Other Stories*, Volume 2.)

"The Fatal Turn" (p. 114) continues Feldstein's rapid development as a storyteller and artist, giving us twists and turns, both literary and literal, with ample drama, plot development, and a nice twist at the end. The insurance investigator angle is a sign that Feldstein is branching out with his plotting, and the lack of any splash panel gives him a chance to introduce the story through cinematic film-style freeze frames of the action. Note how the smoke from the wreckage of the car in panel 6 rises up through the top two tiers to the title, which is also of special note in that Feldstein has employed the exact same lettering style he would soon reprise for the *Tales From the Crypt* logo.

"Our Families Clashed!" (p. 123) is a great example of the type of story Feldstein was turning out for EC between crime dramas and a reminder that EC was throwing multiple genres at the wall to see what would stick in the days before the New Trend began. Though it's easy to simplify the history, Feldstein delivered quite a few romance and Western stories on the path from "true crime" to horror. "Our Families Clashed!" appeared in *Modern Love* less than two months before the Crypt-Keeper made his debut in the pages of *Crime Patrol*, and it dares to expose the brutal world of coal mining/farming interbreeding!

Kidding aside, given the social justice and morality tales that Feldstein would be penning within a few years, it's easy to imagine that he was really writing a story about a mixed-race or mixed-religion couple and, to skirt controversy, he substituted the livelihoods of their fathers as the central conflict. Inserting, say, a black or Hispanic boy or girl, à la *Shock SuspenStories*, would have given the story more weight, but I guarantee there would not have been a happy ending in *Shock SuspenStories* like the one we see here! Feldstein's art in this story is among his best during the pre–New Trend (Pre-Trend) era, rich with detail and very far removed from his teenage books at Fox.

"Case Number 318: Murder" (a.k.a. "The Swindle by Flame!") (p. 132) is a bit of an oddity in that it was penciled by John Alton and inked by Feldstein. Why Feldstein inked the story is unknown — Alton had done solo stories for both

Crime Patrol and *Saddle Romances* and was the only artist to span the Max and Bill Gaines EC eras, having done several "Tuffy" and "Tumbles" strips for the funny-animal title *Dandy*. Alton's work was, incredibly, even stiffer than Mr. "Stiff-Figures" himself, and Feldstein's inking surely improved the art, which, with the exception of several character faces, reads throughout as predominantly Feldstein's style. The writer is unknown, and "Case Number 318" is the last EC story Feldstein drew that was written by someone else.

"Return From the Grave!" (p. 139) is a landmark in EC history, first and foremost because it is the first story to come from "The Crypt of Terror," told by, and introducing, the Crypt-Keeper. It is the first evidence that publisher Gaines was willing to give Feldstein a chance to, in Feldstein's own words, "innovate ... have people follow us!" Gaines was not, at this point, all-in on horror, but he was willing to slip a couple of horror stories into the existing crime books as a tryout. As Feldstein recalled to S.C. Ringgenberg (*The Comics Journal Library Volume 8: The EC Artists*, Fantagraphics Books, 2013), "... we were very good friends. We used to go to roller derby together, and he used to drive me home because we both lived in Brooklyn. We'd chat on the way home, and we got to talking about what we liked when we were kids. Bill was a science-fiction and horror fan, and I was a horror movie fan, and I said, 'Why don't we try horror?' ... He said, 'OK, let's try it. Let's put one of your horror stories into *Crime Patrol*.'"

Having gone through several changes in the market, first breaking from the "educational" and funny animal fare of his father's EC, then so recently seeing the writing on the wall for teenage books, and then shifting the focus of EC's only superhero title and one of its Westerns to romance, Gaines must have been open to any new idea — but not willing to commit fully.

The Western and "true crime" markets weren't what they had been, and another business change was imminent, but, truth be told, Gaines had dipped his toes into the waters of horror before: more than a year earlier, in the spring of 1948, Sheldon Moldoff had brought Gaines a proposal for a book to be titled *Tales of the Supernatural*, and four comics stories and a one-page prose story were completed for it. Then, whether it was cold feet or cold business (like Feldstein with *Peggy*, Moldoff had been promised a percentage of the profits), Gaines changed his mind and declined to put out an all-horror book, a decision that must have been made quickly because the stories were almost immediately parceled out to various issues of EC's *Moon Girl* and *Crime Patrol*. (See *The Woman Who Loved Life And Other Stories*, Volume 25, for Johnny Craig's contribution.)

So, having already tried out horror stories in his other books, the decision to revisit the idea and allow Feldstein to give it a go couldn't have been too difficult — but this time, things were different. With the introduction of the Crypt-Keeper, "Suddenly," remembered Feldstein, "the magazine started to show a little sign of increased sales."

The first appearance of the Crypt-Keeper may be monumental, but the story itself is rather tame. It introduces what would be a recurring EC house plot wherein two business partners seek to increase their share of the profits by getting rid of a third partner — later examples include Jack Kamen's "Death's Turn" (*Daddy Lost His Head And Other Stories*, Volume 20) and Jack Davis's "What's Cookin'?" (*The Living Mummy And Other Stories*, Volume 16). "Return From the Grave!" handles this in an unusually subdued manner, and for the very first "tale from the crypt" there is little to induce actual terror. In my introduction to *The Woman Who Loved Life And Other Stories*, I suggested that Johnny Craig's offering in the same issue of *Crime Patrol* overshadowed the debut of the Crypt-Keeper — a view I maintain after re-reading "Return From the Grave!". But its historical and cultural significance cannot be understated: this is where the "New Trend" really began, and thanks to Feldstein, EC's fortunes would dramatically turn.

"Buried Alive!" (p. 146), the first story to come from "The Vault of Horror," has the edge on its rival's debut. It is well told and has more suspense and tension than "Return From the Grave!," and it is certainly the first of Feldstein's patented "psychological" horror stories. How much is in the protagonist's mind, and how much is really happening? Reality is intercut with dream sequences, and the overall effect is unsettling.

When questioned by John Benson in 1981 about his "paranoid fantasies" (*Squa Tront* #9, 1983), Feldstein said, " 'Buried Alive!' is kind of a ... personal portrait thing, yeah. ... We [Gaines and Feldstein] did these things just by the way we felt, and now to lie down on the couch of the analytical psychiatrist ... and say 'Well, I'm not sure if I had personal feelings about being locked in a coffin' or what, I mean ... I wrote a story as well as I could. While I was writing it, I tried to project myself into the story as the character would feel, whatever the plot was, and then I drew it as best I could in my particular kind of stiff, stylized style. And that was it!"

"I Was A 'B'-Girl!" (p. 154) is another example of a Pre-Trend Feldstein romance yarn, this one with a big-city nightclub setting. The art is fantastic, and as far as the plot is concerned — the art is fantastic! If nothing else, the story displayed Feldstein's ability to assume any voice for the narration — in that *Squa Tront* interview,

he said, "I wrote this as a first-person woman — now how are you going to analyze that?" Self-deprecating though he was, he deserves a lot of credit for being able to write from multiple points of view, and more often than not pull it off. The romance comics had well-paced stories with invariably sappy, happy endings, but they served Feldstein well in that variations on many of the same plots would appear in his New Trend crime stories with horribly ironic twist endings in place of the happily-ever-after.

"The Spectre In The Castle!" (p. 161) was the second outing by the Crypt-Keeper to appear in the pages of *Crime Patrol*. Feldstein is already developing the character of the Crypt-Keeper — while in his first outing he had hair covering his face (Feldstein later said that he had looked like Al Capp's Shmoo), he now grins out at the reader from his inset panel on the splash page. Also on the splash page, we see the debut of the infamous EC spelling bastardization "SuspenStory," but the story itself is far from suspenseful. The hackneyed plot is a variation on the old "spend a night in a haunted house to inherit a fortune" chestnut, but, as is often the case, Feldstein's art carries it.

Though the central couple and supporting characters could have been flown in from an issue of *Modern Love*, Feldstein is clearly having fun with the gothic haunted castle setting and seems to be feeling his horror oats. When the New Trend was in full swing, they would rarely revisit the subject of ghosts, preferring more tangible terrors, but here we sense that Feldstein is casting about, trying to settle on the identity he wanted for his horror stories. Alert readers will note a lone bisected spear sticking up in the corner of panel 6, page 5 (p. 165). The original art reveals that Feldstein had penciled a suit of armor there and forgotten to ink it.

"The Mummy's Curse!" (p. 169) borrowed its title, and much of its plot, from the Universal Pictures Mummy franchise of the early-to-mid 1940s. (Horror comics fans will note that Warren Publications did something very similar in 1964, when it published "The Mummy" in the film fan magazine *Monster World* #1 as a tryout prior to launching *Creepy*. That story was drawn by EC alumnus Wallace Wood.) This second tale from "The Vault of Horror" is further evidence of Feldstein trying to find an identity for his horror stories. Derivative as it is, he still manages to come up with some original twists and ends up with an overall successful "SuspenStory."

By now, Gaines was sufficiently impressed with the sales on the four crime issues with the Crypt-Keeper and Vault-Keeper's tales that he was ready to commit to something more long-term for the horror hosts. As Feldstein related to S.C. Ringgenberg, "Even on a basis of check-ups, not on the basis of final sales, he said, 'Let's just change the title.' ... *War Against Crime* became *The Vault of Horror*, and *Crime Patrol* became *The Crypt of Terror*, for a few issues, and then it became *Tales From the Crypt*." A "New Trend" in comics was at hand, one that would revolutionize the comics world in the early 1950s and bring about major changes for Gaines, Feldstein, EC, and the comic book industry as a whole.

"Death Must Come!" (p. 177) is the first story in the first issue of *The Crypt of Terror*. One almost senses Feldstein being taken over by the horror hosts and their tales — there is a palpable sense of enjoyment in the Crypt-Keeper's patter, the shocking details of the main character's activities as the plot unfolds, and the cruel poetic justice of the story's ending. All of these elements would be expanded on and intensified as the New Trend progressed, but the fact that they are present in all their gruesome, gleeful glory at the very start of the horror comics lines is remarkable. Feldstein would revisit the theme of two close friends making a discovery together and dealing with the unexpected consequences in his horror and science fiction stories to come. In this case, the medical breakthrough is the discovery of a gland that secretes a fluid that keeps a body young — but how to find viable youthful glands to transplant? Rest assured, grave robbing and eventual murder are involved! Even at this very early stage, Feldstein's detour into horror was not going unnoticed by those investigating the negative effects of comics on their juvenile readers — the final page of "Death Must Come!" was reproduced in full in the March 1951 Report of the New York State Joint Legislative Committee to Study the Publication of Comics.

"Terror Train" (p. 185) was Feldstein's first story to appear in the second new EC horror title, *The Vault of Horror*. "Terror Train" is an early Feldstein masterpiece, from the dynamic splash panel of a barreling steam locomotive with a looming skeletal reaper above it to the ambiguous psychological ending that foreshadows later EC "inner terror" thrillers such as "Board To Death!" (*Daddy Lost His Head And Other Stories*, Volume 20) and "Madness

xvii

THE WITCH'S CAULDRON!

ALLOW ME TO INTRODUCE MYSELF! I AM THE OLD WITCH! WHEN THE VAULT-KEEPER ASKED ME TO BREW UP A SPINE-TINGLING YARN IN MY *CAULDRON* AND PRESENT IT TO YOU IN HIS MAGAZINE, I COULDN'T REFUSE! (I AM HIS *GHOUL*-FRIEND, YOU KNOW!) THIS STORY IS ONE OF MY VERY BEST! I CALL IT...

TERROR IN THE SWAMP!

AS THE TWO MEN IN THE FLATBOTTOM BOAT GLIDE SLOWLY UPSTREAM, DEEPER AND DEEPER INTO THE HEART OF THE DREADED OKEFENOKEE SWAMP...THE DANK, MURKY STILLNESS IS SUDDENLY SHATTERED...

HU-LOO-O-O-O! YOU TWO...

LOOK, SAM! THAT OLD GUY ON THE BANK IS WAVING TO US...

COME ASHORE! DON'T GO ON ANY FURTHER! I BEG YOU...

at Manderville" (*Man And Superman And Other Stories*, Volume 27). In the *Squa Tront #9* interview, John Benson asked Feldstein if "Terror Train" was a favorite, and Feldstein responded, "Oh, yeah. It's not the best one I've done — it was OK."

"The Thing in the Swamp!" (p. 192) was Feldstein's contribution to the first issue of *The Haunt of Fear*. It was reprinted just a few months later as "Terror in the Swamp!" — with different introductory and concluding panels — in the fourth issue of *The Vault of Horror* to introduce the Old Witch, host of *The Haunt of Fear*, to the readers of the Vault-Keeper's title. The second version, with its large splash panel of the Old Witch (recycled from "Horror Beneath the Streets!", p. 238), is more engaging than the static scene of two men, viewed from behind, poling a boat through the swamp in the first version. The revised title is also more of a grabber. The dry "A Scientific SuspenStory" is dropped. For authenticity, we present the original version, but the revised panels with the Old Witch are included here for your comparison.

"The Maestro's Hand!" (p. 199) features a stunning full-page splash of the Crypt-Keeper, leering up from a book while a candle melting into the eye sockets of a skull in the foreground provides light. The skull rests on a copy of Edgar Allan Poe's "The Tell-Tale Heart," a story Feldstein would go to for plot variations on occasion. Hovering over the candlelight is a row of piano keys and the hand of the story's title. Feldstein, the self-professed "horror movie fan," drew multiple plot points from a 1924 German film, *The Hands of Orlac*, that was remade in the U.S. in 1935 as *Mad Love* starring Peter Lorre. The films concern a concert pianist whose hands are mangled in a train accident and surgically replaced with the hands of a murderer.

In Feldstein's version, the concert pianist cuts his hand badly, and it is removed by a jealous doctor friend, causing the pianist to jump

BELOW AND OPPOSITE: "The Thing in the Swamp!" (p. 192) from *The Haunt of Fear* was reprinted mere months later as "Terror in the Swamp!" in *The Vault of Horror*. The first and last pages were revised to include the Old Witch. The new splash panel was lifted from "Horror Beneath the Streets" (p. 238).

xix

in front of a train and kill himself. It is likely that Feldstein saw and remembered the 1935 version of the film, which had the love triangle/jealousy element, and the female love interest begging the doctor to operate on the pianist's hands, as happens in the Feldstein script. The departure in the EC version is the reanimated amputated hand coming back for revenge, which finally gives one of EC's "terror tales" moments of real terror — the blackened hand as it "scurries up the chimney" and "mov(es) about in the grass near the house" is the stuff of nightmares! There is a Feldstein-ian twist at the end that takes us from physical to psychological terror, and the tale stands out as one of the better early horror efforts.

"The Dead Will Return!" (p. 207) is set in a remote lighthouse where a wife and her lover murder the husband that stands in the way of their happiness — something we will see again and again in the EC horror and crime stories to follow. There is a strong suggestion that this is another psychological tale, but the story's end implies that the murdered husband has indeed returned for revenge. The fact that this takes place "off camera" leaves room for doubt, and in his closing patter, the Vault-Keeper asks: "Did Hank *really* come back ... or was it just Bert and Flo's imagination?" It wouldn't be long before Feldstein would jettison the ambiguity and unleash an army of the undead, shambling across EC's pages and performing their gory acts of revenge in plain view of the reader.

"Ghost Ship!" (p. 215) harkens back to earlier Feldstein material — the stiff figures, the cartoonishly drawn pirates that wouldn't be out of place up on Timberline Top, and a couple straight out of *Modern Love* come off as retrograde after his recent horror efforts. If it weren't for the presence of the Crypt-Keeper and the mild (very mild) horror element, one would be excused for thinking this was possibly a leftover Pre-Trend tale! But the Crypt-Keeper is indeed here, in a striking full-body splash panel that makes up for the tameness of the story to follow. EC artist Graham Ingels would come to be known for the grim mutations and perversions of nature that populated his splash panels, and Feldstein is taking tentative steps with "Ghost Ship!" to add terrifying details to his, playing it a bit safer however, with spiderwebs, bats, rats, and a skull for a doorstop. He is still hedging on the reality of the terror here, with the Crypt-Keeper (like the Vault-Keeper in the previous tale) questioning the couple's supernatural experience, saying: "What do you think happened? Was it all in their minds ... or did Don and Carol actually *sail* on a *ghost ship*?"

"The Strange Couple!" (p. 223) carries a unique credit on the first page: "Script & Art By Feldstein." At Gaines's insistence, Feldstein included this acknowledgement that he was writing as well as drawing his own stories. Gaines felt that Feldstein deserved credit, but it's the only time such a byline appeared. The story is essentially a rewrite of the Kurtzman-illustrated "Horror in the Night" (*Man And Superman And Other Stories*, Volume 27) with the roles reversed. In Feldstein's tale, a lone traveler comes upon the title couple when his car breaks down on a rainy night. In the Kurtzman version, the "strange couple" are the ones visiting, in that case, the owner of a tourist camp. The snap ending of both tales is the same — a variation of the 'was it a dream or reality?" psychological premise. "The Strange Couple!" was later redrawn by Will Elder for the 3D EC comic *Three-Dimensional Tales From the Crypt of Terror*. (Elder's version appears in *The Million Year Picnic And Other Stories*, Volume 18.)

"The Love Story to End All Love Stories!" (p. 230) was indeed the final story in the final issue of *Modern Love* and is the first of two Feldstein pieces that fictionalize the birth of the New Trend. Gaines and Feldstein appear as themselves, and the pair are convinced by publisher T. Tot (a play on Tiny Tot Publishing, one of four companies created by Gaines's father to publish EC comic book titles) to put out love comics. The market is glutted, *Modern Love* fails, and in a truly un-romantic ending, Bill and Al shoot themselves! Though outlandish and humorous (predicting the zany comics work Feldstein would write and edit for EC's *Panic* some four years later), the underlying facts of the story are, for the most part, accurate. EC was chasing trends. They started going into the red every time the market turned, and they were losing money badly on their Western, crime, and romance titles. The facts that *Modern Love* was the last holdout from the Pre-Trend era and this story appeared while the EC horror titles were already on the stands and showing signs of profitability must have made it easy for Feldstein to laugh about the change in direction, and it's easy for us to laugh, too.

"The Love Story to End All Love Stories!" far predates *Mad* and *Panic* and shows that contrary to popular opinion (and his own), Feldstein did have a sense of humor (which was fortunate for the future editor of *Mad* magazine). Due to all the principals dying at the end, the story is presented by the office boy of "T. Tot Publishing," whose sweater is monogrammed "P.K." Paul Kast was the actual office boy at EC, and it was he who masterminded the production and sale of 5"×7" photos of the Crypt-Keeper, the Vault-Keeper, and the Old Witch that were sold through the EC letters pages. The profits from those photos put him through law school.

"Horror Beneath the Streets!" (p. 238) goes hand-in-hand with "The Love Story to End All Love Stories!" in telling a fanciful fictionalized tale of the transition from romance to horror at EC. The first page has Gaines and Feldstein wrapping up a day at the office, with Feldstein saying " '*Modern Love*' is finally finished!" which was true in more ways than one. As they walk down the accurately rendered seventh floor hallway, Feldstein comments, "Pretty eerie around here at night, eh, Bill?" As they get into the elevator, Gaines suggests, "Eerie — terror — horror! Boy! That would be *terrific*! *Horror* in comics!"

Why Feldstein, knowing that it was his idea to try horror, wrote the story this way is anyone's guess, but humility, embarrassment, or reluctance to take full credit are all possibilities. As the fictional Bill and Al walk down the street, they discuss whether or not their readers would "go for *horror stories*!" While hashing it over, they realize they are being followed. They attempt escape by clambering down into a sewer, where they meet up with none other than the Crypt-Keeper and the Vault-Keeper, who force them to sign contracts.

"I guess we'll *have* to publish their stuff!" Gaines says with a shrug, standing knee-deep in flowing sewage.

As the story closes, the Old Witch informs us that it was she who "followed the two editors and forced them to enter that horrid sewer!" She got her own contract upon releasing them, and the EC horror comic books were born. As fanciful as the tale is, it represents the beginning of something that would elevate EC above other publishers and foster a feeling of belonging among its readers — maintaining the illusion that the horror hosts, or "GhouLunatics" as they came to be affectionately known, were real people, that they shared a bizarre relationship with EC's editors, and that EC's loyal following was in on the gag. The feeling of belonging and being "in on it" would drive tremendous loyalty over the course of the New Trend — and far beyond — among the "EC Fan-Addicts."

"The Thing from the Sea!" (p. 245) drew plot inspiration from "The Upper Berth" by Francis Marion Crawford. Here, a word about how Gaines and Feldstein came up with their story plots is in order. "Bill had gotten really excited about starting to plot stories when he realized I could write them," Feldstein told S.C. Ringgenberg in 1994. "He wanted to get into the plotting end of it. He had trouble sleeping because he was constantly dieting and taking Dexedrine ... it would keep him awake at night, so he'd read. He would come in in the morning ... with what he called 'springboards,' which were little notes about some of the stories or things he had read. ... And, of course, we would try very hard not to steal the story completely, you know, but they would become springboards.

We would chat about what to do with that kind of idea, and we would try and do variations, and eventually we started to plot." They would spend the morning plotting, then go for lunch at Patrissy's, a favorite Italian restaurant. Then in the afternoon, Feldstein would write the story. He wrote four stories every week, and on the fifth day, he and Gaines would edit.

"The Thing from the Sea!" follows its springboard very closely. Crawford's "The Upper Berth" was first published in 1894 and concerns a passenger on an ocean liner who relates to fellow guests a fantastic tale: on a previous voyage, he was assigned the lower berth in a stateroom, only to witness the occupant of the upper berth run from the room in terror on the first night. Inquiries to the captain reveal that the room has a notorious history of such disturbances, and the passenger is advised to stay with the captain; he refuses. On the second night, he awakes to find the porthole open and the smell of seawater and decay in the room. Upon reaching into the upper berth, he feels "something in the shape of a man's arm, but was smooth, wet, and icy cold." Then "the creature sprang violently forward against me, a clammy, oozy mass," and ran from the room. On the third night, the passenger urges the captain to stay with him so they can get to the bottom of what is going on. The men witness the apparition, which assaults them both and exits through the open porthole. Feldstein's version deviates in minor details: the number of the stateroom is changed from 105 to 13, the framing device of a passenger relating the tale over wine and cigars is removed, and a twist is added to the ending to give the story a revenge angle.

"Hong Kong Intrigue!" (p. 252) stands out as an oddity in the New Trend era: the voluptuous girl in a torn dress, the stereotypical Chinese villain, and the dashing hero of the splash panel would not be out of place in any of Feldstein's Pre-Trend crime stories. "Hong Kong Intrigue!" appeared in the first issue of Harvey Kurtzman's *Two-Fisted Tales* and betrays an almost comical lack of understanding on Gaines and Feldstein's part of what Kurtzman envisioned for the title. In a 1973 interview with John Benson (published in *Squa Tront* #9, 1983), Gaines recalled that "when Harvey made the suggestion that he do an adventure book ... I didn't know what the hell he meant by adventure. I remember the first and only adventure story that Al and I ever wrote, or attempted to write, 'Hong Kong Intrigue!' It was the most dreadful, horrible, stupid story ... From then on, Harvey handled his books by himself simply because I didn't have the faintest idea what the hell he was getting at."

When placed alongside Feldstein's Pre-Trend output, as it is in this collection, "Hong Kong Intrigue!" fares a bit better than it did sandwiched between the Kurtzman and Wallace Wood pieces in the first issue of *Two-Fisted Tales*.

"A Shocking Way To Die!" (p. 259) is the second of only two *Tales From the Crypt* stories to have the heading "The Crypt-Keeper's Tale" rather than "The Crypt of Terror," and it displays striking similarities to the 1936 Boris Karloff film *The Walking Dead*. Both stories involve a man executed in the electric chair who is revived by a doctor performing life-and-death experiments and then goes on to take revenge on those who had him killed. The big difference in the plots is that the Karloff character was framed for murder by gangsters and takes his revenge on them, while the Feldstein version has a justly executed mobster taking revenge on the jury that found him guilty.

"Escape!" (p. 267) is a fantastic early example of a Feldstein ironic twist ending, something EC readers came to love and anticipate. Part of the fun of reading an EC comic became trying to guess what the snap ending would be. In his *Squa Tront* #9 interview, Feldstein, while looking at the story, said, "This was when we were getting into the little shock endings, you know, the twists, which of course became our 'signature.' I always loved twist endings and poetic justice, and guys who screwed other people and then got screwed by them or screwed themselves."

"The Thing From the Grave!" (p. 274) is an absolute EC classic, the quintessential walking-dead revenge story, a virtual blueprint for countless EC and non-EC horror stories to follow. While fully realized in this version written and illustrated by Feldstein, the story has its origins in a short prose piece originally written for Sheldon Moldoff's aborted *Tales of the Supernatural* project in 1948. "Out of the Grave" (*The Thing From The Grave And Other Stories*, Volume 19) is believed to be written by Gardner Fox, and while *Tales of the Supernatural* was never published, the story did appear as a text piece in *Moon Girl Fights Crime* #7 in 1949. It was reprinted in the first issue of *Haunt of Fear* in 1950, with two new illustrations by Feldstein, before it was fully developed as a lead story 8-pager for *Tales From the Crypt*. Joe Orlando illustrated a new version for *Three Dimensional Tales From the Crypt of Terror* (also featured in *The Thing From The Grave And Other Stories*, Volume 19), and in 1990, it was faithfully adapted for the second season of the HBO *Tales From the Crypt* TV series.

"Reflection of Death!" (p. 282) is another story with a traceable "springboard," in this case a brief anecdote in Bennett Cerf's *Try and Stop Me*, a favorite book of Gaines's. The short piece appears on pages 275-276 of Cerf's book, in the "Trail of the Tingling Spine" chapter, a particularly rich source of Gaines's "springboards." In this case, it is fairly obvious that Feldstein didn't read the story himself (he noted to John Benson in the *Squa Tront* #9 interview, "I wasn't doing very much reading in those days," prompting Benson to observe that "your point about not reading the stories that Bill gave you the springboards from is fairly obvious, because the EC story is so different in style ...").

The Cerf anecdote involves a man who finds himself walking up the avenue with no memory of how he got there. He is confused by the reactions of all he encounters: they scream in horror, recoil in terror, and otherwise avoid him. Upon calling home, he is told that his mother is out — she is at his funeral; he was mangled to death in a workplace accident the day before. Only the barest of those elements are used in "Reflection of Death!", and it's easy to imagine Gaines presenting Feldstein with a scrap of paper simply saying something like "man has no memory, everyone he sees is horrified, turns out he's dead." Feldstein fleshed out the springboard to include a terrible car crash, multiple encounters with terrified strangers, mounting clues to the horrible truth, and a "dream within a dream" ending à la "The Strange Couple."

Feldstein has grown considerably as an artist by this time, and "Reflection of Death!" is a tour de force of terrifying imagery from the exquisite Crypt-Keeper splash page populated with shrunken heads, ghouls, ghosts, werewolves, and mummies to the utterly ghastly rotting corpse, shown in glorious close-up in panels 5, 6, and 7 on page 6 of the story (p. 287).

"Reflection of Death!" is a wonderful final horror tale for Feldstein as artist and is rightfully recognized as one of the great EC horror stories. George Evans redrew it as "picto-fiction" in *Terror Illustrated* #2, Gaines selected it as a personal favorite for a 1964 Ballantine paperback collection of EC horror stories, and it was one of five stories filmed for the feature-length 1972 *Tales From the Crypt* movie. Though he continued scripting for other artists and doing covers throughout the New Trend era, Feldstein's increasing duties as writer and editor of multiple titles (see his cartoon, p. 295) caused him to give up illustrating full stories by mid-1951.

The five stories that Feldstein collaborated on with Johnny Craig (combining their names and initials as "F.C. Aljon") can be found in *The Woman Who Loved Life And Other Stories* (Volume 25). Feldstein also wrote and drew science fiction stories for *Weird Science* and *Weird Fantasy*, all of which can be found in *Child of Tomorrow And Other Stories* (Volume 6). All were produced during the same time period as the stories in this volume.

There was a golden age of movies, there was a golden age of radio, there was a golden age of television, and there was a golden age of comic books. But these years, from 1948 to 1951, were the golden age of Al Feldstein as writer and artist.

In this collection, we have the extremely pleasurable opportunity of seeing Al Feldstein develop as an artist and a writer, gaining confidence, maturing, and exploring an artistic freedom that he was happy to extend to his fellow EC artists in his role as editor. Publisher Russ Cochran noted in his *EC Portfolio Three* (1973) "the artwork of Al Feldstein personifies those early days of the New Trend comics. His bold, stylistic approach is perhaps the most 'comic-booky' of all the EC artists." Wallace Wood said in *EC Lives!*, the 1972 EC Fan-Addict convention program book, "He was one helluva good writer ... especially for the horror. Al's Shock and Crime stories were the best ever done!"

Jack Davis said in the same convention book that Feldstein was "One of the greatest editors of any magazine anywhere! He holds everything together. He's a good man besides." Davis would know: he took over the covers and lead stories for *Tales From the Crypt* in 1952, was by far the most prolific EC artist of the New Trend, and continued for decades with *Mad* magazine, which Feldstein edited until his retirement in 1984.

Al Feldstein is deservedly revered as a creative powerhouse, and this collection of his early EC work is filled with reasons why.

THOMMY BURNS *is the founding administrator of the EC Fan-Addict Club on Facebook and frequently speaks on EC at comic book conventions. He has written about EC Comics for Fantagraphics and for the Society of Illustrators Press. He lives in Southern California with his wife, their cats, and his ever-growing EC collection.*

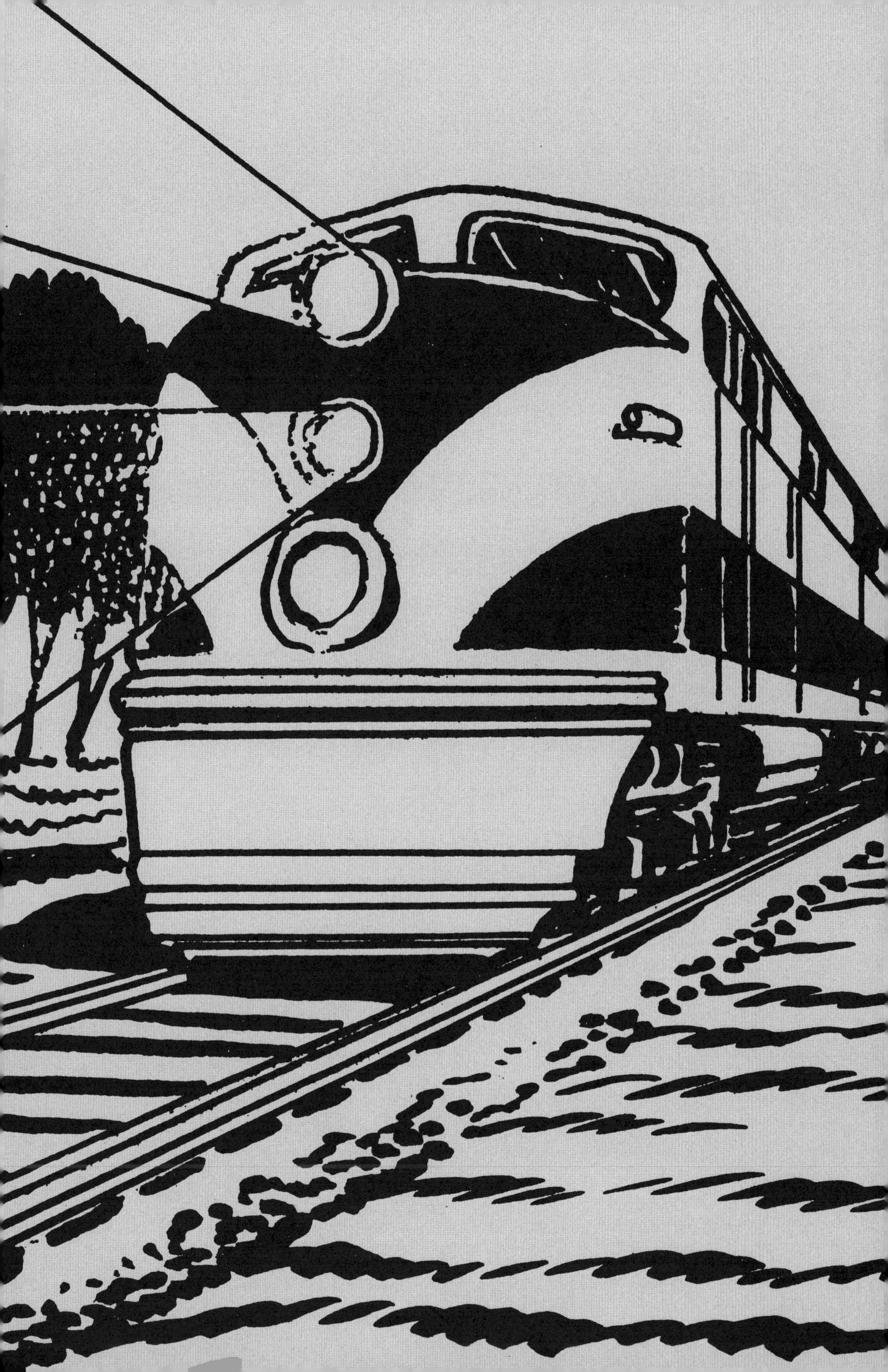

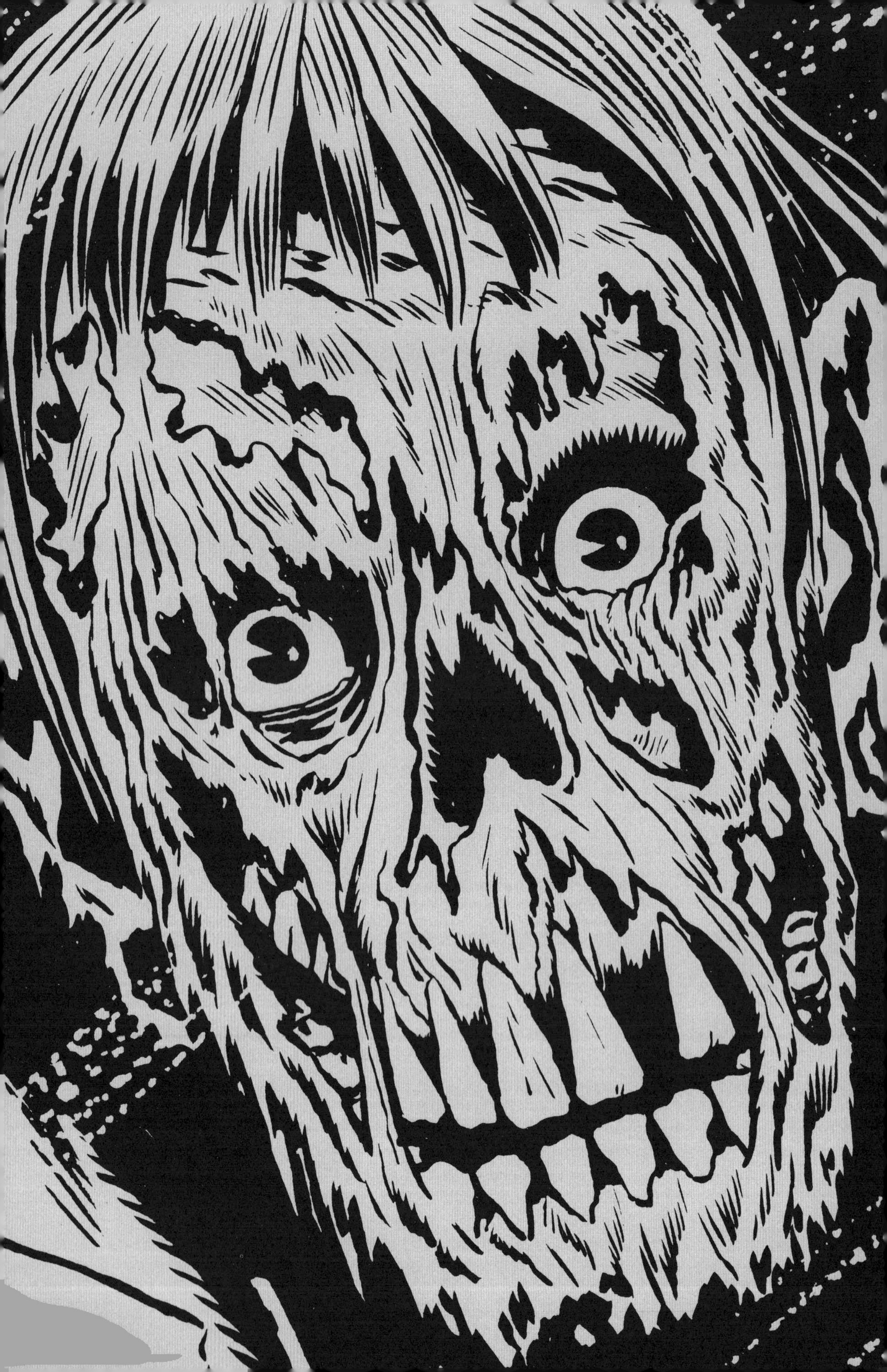

the TREASURE of TIMBERLINE TOP

THE OLD WEST IS RICH IN TALES OF LOST TREASURE. BUT ONE OF THE MOST FABULOUS, AS WELL AS ONE WITH THE BLOODIEST HISTORY, CAME UP OUT OF MEXICO OVER FOUR HUNDRED YEARS AGO. GOLD! DIAMONDS! RARE STATUES! RUBIES!

AND THE MEN WHO WERE TO WRITE ITS STORY, WHO WERE TO AMASS IT AND THEN LOSE IT, GAVE THEIR HEART'S BLOOD FOR A MERE LOOK AT—

"THE TREASURE OF TIMBERLINE TOP."

IT WAS A FEW MINUTES PAST MIDNIGHT ON A JULY MORNING IN 1556 THAT A CONQUISTADORE GASPED AND CONVULSED BEFORE A HUGE OAKEN DOORWAY IN WHAT IS NOW MEXICO CITY...

MMMMPPFF...

ROT MY LIFE AWAY HERE? THAT IS NOT FOR DON MIGUEL!

CRAAACCCK!

THE TREASURE OF TIMBERLINE TOP

THE TREASURE OF TIMBERLINE TOP

AS THE THIN LINE OF MEN AND ANIMALS WENT DEEPER INTO THE BARREN LANDS, A VOICE WHISPERED OVER AND OVER AGAIN TO ROCKY PARKER...
FIVE MEN? IT AIN'T BIG ENOUGH FOR FOUR MEN! ONE OF US HAS GOTTA...DIE! THIRDS! THAT'S WHAT I WANT. A THIRD OF THE TREASURE...
JIM—WATCH OUT! I'VE LOST MY BALANCE!
HUH?
THERE IS A DULL, MUFFLED ROAR AS ROCKY PLUNGES ACROSS THE FIRE AND ONTO HIS PARTNER...
BAROOOOM!
JIM! JIM! I WARNED YUH! YUH SHOULD'VE DROPPED YORE SHOOTIN' IRON!
'TWAREN'T YORE FAULT, ROCKY!
SURE. I HEARD YUH YELL!
HIGH INTO THE RARIFIED AIR OF TIMBERLINE TOP CLIMB THE THREE LONGRIDERS...
AIN'T FAR AHEAD NOW! WE OUGHT TO FIND IT RIGHT SOON!
JUMPIN' JEHOSEPHAT! HERE SHE IS!
WHOOPEEE!
YAHOOOO!
YIPPEEE!
4

RECKON ONE MAN'D BE ABOUT THE RICHEST WADDY IN THE WORLD IF HE HAD ALL THIS-- FOR HIMSELF!
SO LONG, PARTNERS!
BLAMM! BLAMM!
BLAMMM!
I'LL TAKE SOME OF THESE SPARKLERS TO KEEP ME IN FOOD AND REDEYE. RECKON I CAN BRING SOME PEONS TO ACT AS BEARERS AN' CART THE REST OF THE STUFF OUT...
THAT WAY THE HULL TREASURE'LL BE ALL MINE! I WON'T HAVE NOBODY TO SHARE IT WITH. AN' WHEN THE PEONS DO THEIR JOB...I'LL HAVE A BULLET FER EACH ONE OF 'EM!
SOME MONTHS LATER, ROCKY PARKER PULLED INTO THE FRONTIER TOWN OF TUCSON, JUST AS A RIFLE ROARED...
SOMEBODY NEARLY CREASED YUH THAT TIME, FRIEND!
IT'S SQUINTY HALL! HE'S AFTER ME!
RECKON I DON'T HOLD MUCH WITH DRYGULCHIN'!
SALOON-
BAMMM!
YUH DID ME A FINE TURN, STRANGER! LIGHT DOWN AN' JOIN ME IN A SHOT OF REDEYE!
GLAD TO!
5

LOOKIN' AROUND FUR SOME PEONS TO HELP ME. KNOW WHERE I CAN HIRE ANY ?
WHY, SHORE-
WHAT—!
I OUGHTA GUN YUH, YUH DRUNKEN BUM! INSTEAD--
SPLAATT!
TARNATION! DIAMONDS!
PRETTY STONES YUH GOT, ROCKY!
LET THEM--STONES? OH, YEAH! HEH! HEH! STONES!
SOME HOURS LATER, RED JAKE ROLLINS WAS SPEAKING IN HARSH, EXCITED WHISPERS TO A PRETTY DANCE HALL GIRL NAMED SELMA...
I TELL YUH THEM WAS DIAMONDS. I PLAYED DUMB IN FRONT OF HIM, SO'S HE WOULDN'T BE SUSPICIOUS!
A BAG FULL OF DIAMONDS! THAT RANNY COULD BUY AND SELL THE WHOLE TOWN!
WHATTA YUH SAY, BABY? DO YUH AN' ME WORK HIM OVER? DO WE FIND OUT WHETHER HE'S GOT MORE OF THEM STONES?
YOU BET WE DO, JAKE! I'LL KEEP AN EYE ON HIM TONIGHT!
THAT NIGHT IN THE SMOKE-FILLED ROOM OF THE GOLDEN NUGGET SALOON...
I'LL BET YOU'RE A GOOD DANCER!
BE RIGHT WITH YUH, HONEY! LUCK'S PLAYIN' MY WAY TONIGHT...WITH THE CARDS, AN' WITH YUH!
6

THERE'S A NICE VIEW OF THE TOWN ON THE BACK PORCH!
THAT'S FOR ME, BABY! LET'S GO TAKE A LOOK!
GOT 'IM! FIND THE BAG, SELMA!
ZUNNGG!
I'LL BE—!
WHEW—HERE'S A TREASURE MAP. TIMBERLINE TOP! TARNATION! I'VE HEARD TELL O' THAT! THIS IS OUR LUCKY NIGHT, SELMA!
SOME MILES OUTSIDE TUCSON...
NOBODY'LL EVER FIND HIM IN THAT QUICKSAND BOG!
THE DIAMONDS AND THE TREASURE ARE ALL OURS, JAKE!
EARLY NEXT MORNING, RED JAKE WAS MILES AWAY AND RIDING FAST...
NO SENSE SPLITTING THE SWAG WITH SELMA! I'LL JUST KEEP THE MAP AN' DIAMONDS FOR MYSELF!
HE HIGHTAILED IT OUT OF HERE LESS THAN AN HOUR AGO! I HAD TO WAIT FOR YOU TO COME IN FROM THE RANCH!
OKAY, SIS! WE'LL GO AFTER JAKE! WE'LL KEEP THE MAP IN THE FAMILY!
THERE'S THE COYOTE NOW!
WE'LL CATCH HIM IN LESS'N AN HOUR!
7

THE TREASURE OF TIMBERLINE TOP

THE CASE OF THE SAVAGE STRONGBOY

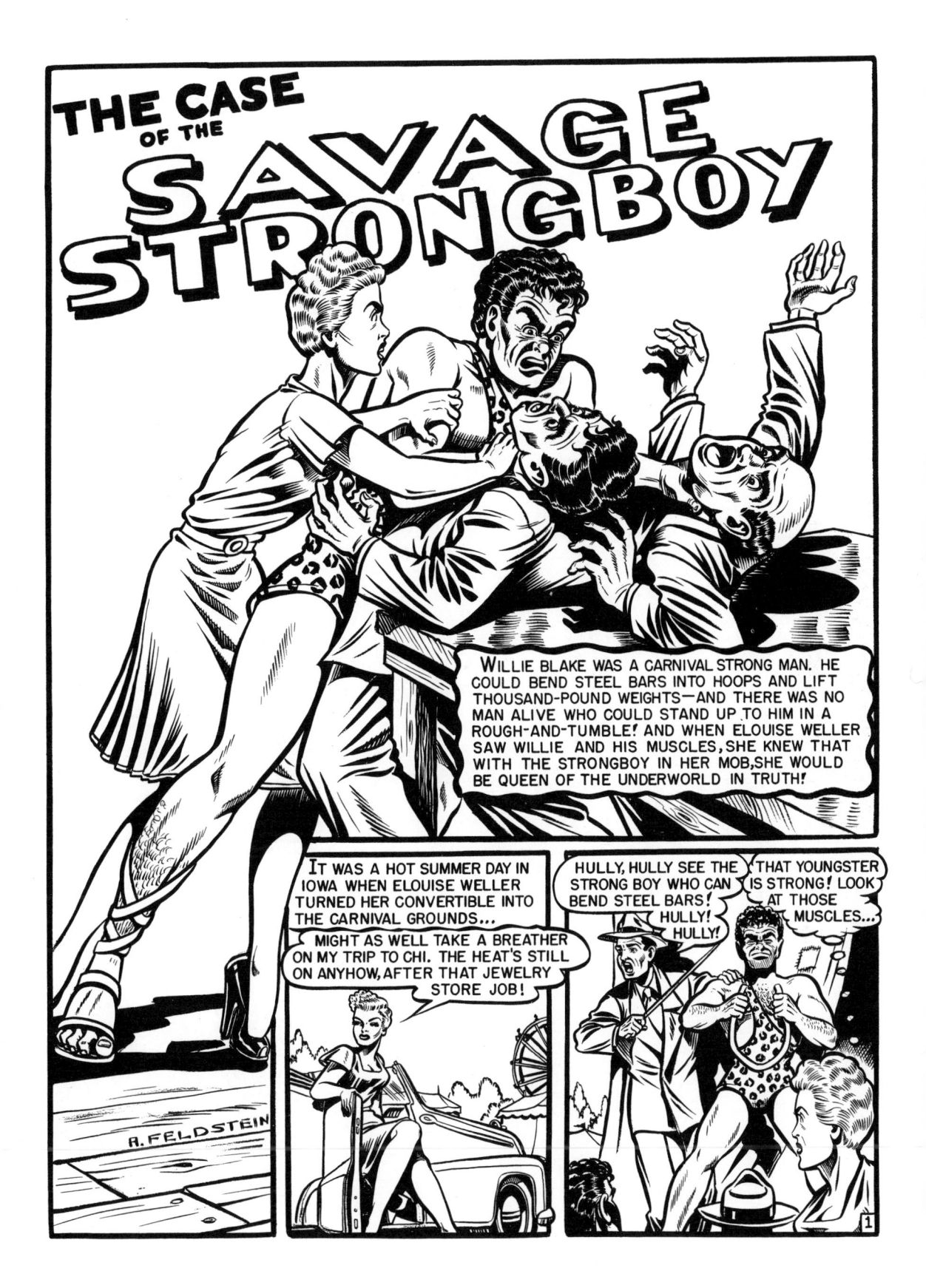

WILLIE BLAKE WAS A CARNIVAL STRONG MAN. HE COULD BEND STEEL BARS INTO HOOPS AND LIFT THOUSAND-POUND WEIGHTS—AND THERE WAS NO MAN ALIVE WHO COULD STAND UP TO HIM IN A ROUGH-AND-TUMBLE! AND WHEN ELOUISE WELLER SAW WILLIE AND HIS MUSCLES, SHE KNEW THAT WITH THE STRONGBOY IN HER MOB, SHE WOULD BE QUEEN OF THE UNDERWORLD IN TRUTH!

A. FELDSTEIN

IT WAS A HOT SUMMER DAY IN IOWA WHEN ELOUISE WELLER TURNED HER CONVERTIBLE INTO THE CARNIVAL GROUNDS...

MIGHT AS WELL TAKE A BREATHER ON MY TRIP TO CHI. THE HEAT'S STILL ON ANYHOW, AFTER THAT JEWELRY STORE JOB!

HULLY, HULLY SEE THE STRONG BOY WHO CAN BEND STEEL BARS! HULLY! HULLY!

THAT YOUNGSTER IS STRONG! LOOK AT THOSE MUSCLES...

SAY...MAYBE I COULD USE A GUY LIKE THAT IN MY MOB! WITH THOSE MUSCLES, HE COULD KEEP ORDER WITHOUT USIN' A GUN!
THAT NIGHT, AS WILLIE SAT ON THE PORCH OF HIS PORTABLE HOME...
HELLO, THERE! THOUGHT I'D DROP BY AND SEE WHAT A HUSKY FELLA LIKE YOU DOES WITH HIS EVENINGS!
OHH..HELLO. I-I GUESS I SIT AROUND AND TALK. MAYBE DO SOME EXERCISES. KEEP IN SHAPE, YOU KNOW!
BET THEY PAY YOU A FORTUNE! YOU MUST BE THE STAR OF THE SHOW!
TWENTY BUCKS A WEEK. THAT'S WHAT I MAKE. IT AIN'T MUCH BUT IT'S A LIVING!
YOU OUGHT TO GET WISE, KID. LOOK AT THIS ROLL. YOU OUGHT TO HAVE A ROLL LIKE THAT...
-GULP- I NEVER SAW SO MUCH MONEY IN MY LIFE!
FOR AN HOUR, ELOUISE WELLER TALKED TO THE STRONG BOY AND WHEN SHE LEFT...
I'LL BE READY AT DAWN. I AIN'T GOT MUCH TO PACK!
GOOD BOY! REMEMBER— YOUR STARTING SALARY IS SEVENTY-FIVE BUCKS A WEEK!
ON THE WAY TO CHICAGO, THE NEXT DAY...
YOU KNOW WHAT TO DO?
LEAVE HIM TO ME!
GAS
I'LL HANDLE THIS BABY SO THERE WON'T BE NO NOISE AT ALL!
I'LL CHECK THE CASH REGISTER!
2

THREE HUNDRED AND TEN BUCKS, WILLIE! WE SPLIT FIFTY-FIFTY! HOW DO YOU LIKE YOUR NEW JOB?
IT'S WONDERFUL! BOY, A HUNDRED AND FIFTY BUCKS—ALL MINE!
GAS
THAT WAS FAST WORK, WILLIE! YOU GRABBED THAT ATTENDANT SO QUICK HE DIDN'T SEE YOU! SAY... THAT'S AN IDEA! WITH YOU PULLING THE STRONG-ARM STUFF, WE COULD MAKE A NICE TEAM!
I FIGURED IF HE DIDN'T SEE ME, HE WOULDN'T BE ABLE TO TELL THE COPS WHAT I LOOKED LIKE!
IN A LITTLE ROOMING HOUSE, ELOUISE WELLER LAID OUT THE PLANS FOR THEIR FUTURE JOBS...
IT'S A FOOLPROOF SCHEME! THE GUYS WE MUG CAN'T SNITCH IF THEY DON'T KNOW WHAT TO TELL THE COPS. HONEY, WHAT A BREAK! YOU AN' I ARE GOIN' PLACES!
ON A SIDE STREET IN DAVENPORT...
UGGGH!
I GOT HIS ROLL, WILLIE. OKAY... LET HIM GO, AND SCRAM!
IN URBANA, ILLINOIS...
THE COAST'S CLEAR! STORE'S EMPTY!
GOT IT, BIG BOY! LET'S BLOW!
THUDD!
3

WORKING QUICKLY, EFFICIENTLY AND RUTHLESSLY, ELOUISE WELLER AND WILLIE BLAKE MADE THEIR WAY TO CHICAGO AND TO THE GIRL'S APARTMENT...
WE'RE A SUCCESS, WILLIE! WE'VE DONE BETTER THAN I EVER DREAMED USING THAT HIDE, HIT AND RUN TECH-NIQUE!
IT WAS YOU THAT DID IT, ELOUISE!
MARRY ME AN' SETTLE DOWN, ELOUISE. WE GOT A PILE. WE CAN BUY A HOUSE AN' HAVE A GARDEN AN'...
YOU SILLY BOY! WE'VE JUST STARTED!
I HAVE PLANS! BIG PLANS! I'M GOING TO GET A MOB—GO IN FOR CRIME IN A BIG WAY. IT'LL PAY OFF FOR US, WILLIE. I'M TOO SMART AND YOU'RE TOO STRONG... FOR US EVER TO GET CAUGHT!
GANGSTERS SOON FOUND IT PAID TO TEAM UP WITH THE NEW AND SUCCESSFUL WELLER DUO...
COUNT US IN ON THE NEXT ONE, BABY!
THAT'S SMART, COOKIE! I'M EXPECTING BIG THINGS FROM YOU! WITH YOUR BOYS WITH ME I CAN ENLARGE THE ORGANIZATION!
THE WELLER MOB PULLED BIG-TIME JOBS. THERE WAS THE BANK ROBBERY IN PEORIA...
BAMMMM!
BLOW, ROCKY! THE COPPERS'LL BE COMIN' 'ROUND THE CORNER IN A FEW MINUTES!
HOP IN! THE MOTOR'S WARMED UP AND READY!
AND THEN THERE WAS THE ARMORED CAR STICKUP A FEW MILES OUT OF RACINE...
4

AND ALWAYS WHENEVER THERE WAS ANY TROUBLE ABOUT THE SPLIT...
YA CAN'T GET AWAY WITH IT, ELOUISE! WE DIDN'T GET A FAIR SLICE FROM THAT DAVENPORT JOB!
I AIN'T KIDDIN'! ME AN' THE BOYS WANTS ANOTHER FIFTEEN GRAND, OR YOU'RE GONNA KNOW WHAT A BULLET FEELS LIKE CHURNIN' AWAY INSIDE YOUR SKULL!
YOU CHEAP LITTLE PUNK!
SPLATT!
YIIII!
I'LL TEACH YOU TO THREATEN MISS WELLER! YOU AND YOUR GANGLAND ROUGH STUFF!
MY WRIST...YOU'LL BREAK IT...AAAAGGGHH!
CRAAACK!!
I OUGHT TO PULL YOU LIMB FROM LIMB!
OOOOOWW!
WILLIE! WILLIE! TAKE IT EASY! GET YOURSELF UNDER CONTROL. YOU SCARE ME WHEN YOU GO WILD LIKE THAT. YOU GET KIND OF... SAVAGE...
I CAN'T HELP IT, HONEY! WHEN ANYBODY BUT ME IS NEAR YOU, I SEE RED! THAT PUNK! I OUGHT TO—
THERE, THERE, WILLIE. IT'S OVER NOW. FORGET HIM! BESIDES, YOU AND I HAVE ANOTHER JOB TO DO!
5

THE CASE OF THE SAVAGE STRONGBOY

DAMES! ALWAYS WORRYIN'! WHAT COULD POSSIBLY HAPPEN TO ME?
YOU SHOULD HAVE SENT MISS WELLER THAT TWENTY GRAND, MISTER. SHE TOLD YOU THAT I'D HAVE TO COME AN' BREAK YOUR NECK IF YOU DIDN'T...
NNNNNGG!
TWENTY MINUTES LATER...
AAAAAAGHHHH!
BUT FOR EVERYONE WHO DID NOT PAY, THERE WERE FIVE WHO DID....
YOU'RE THE TOPS, ELOUISE. ALL THE BOYS ARE DYIN' TO CUT IN WITH YOUR CROWD! YOU'RE AS MUCH THE KING AS AL EVER WAS, HERE IN CHI.
ONLY THE BEGINNING, COOKIE!
I GO FOR YOU, BABY. YOU KNOW THAT. WHAT'S ABOUT YOU AN' ME GETTIN' SPLICED?
I-I DON'T DARE, COOKIE! THERE'S WILLIE... HE'S SO SAVAGE, HE SCARES ME...
HA! HA! HA! HE AIN'T SO SAVAGE HE WON'T STOP A .32 BULLET! I'LL TAKE CARE OF WILLIE...THEN I'LL COME BACK—FOR YOU, BABY!
I'LL BE WAITING, COOKIE!
NEXT NIGHT, IN FRONT OF A WATERFRONT WAREHOUSE...
SO LONG, FALL GUY! ELOUISE DOESN'T NEED YOU ANY MORE!
BAMMM! BAMMM! BAMMM!
7

SHE NEVER WENT FOR YOU AT ALL...YOU WERE JUST A BIG, DUMB, STRONG OX THAT SHE USED TO GET TO THE TOP. IT'S ME SHE GOES FOR! SO LONG—DEAD GUY!
BUT WILLIE BLAKE, THE SAVAGE STRONGBOY, WAS NOT DEAD. FOR A LONG TIME HE LAY THERE IN THE DAMP WET NIGHT UNTIL SOME OF HIS STRENGTH CAME BACK... AND THEN...
ELOUISE WOULDN'T DO THIS...NOT TO ME...COOKIE WAS LYING...
A WEIRD, GRIM FIGURE, THE STRONGBOY STUMBLED THROUGH THE NIGHT...ON AND ON...HALF-DEAD, BUT WITH ENOUGH LIFE LEFT TO GO WHERE HE WANTED...
I'LL ASK HER...FIND HER SOME-PLACE...ASK HER...
EEEEEEEEAAAGH!
LET HIM GO, YOU BEAST. TURN HIM LOOSE... YOU—YOU FRANKENSTEIN!
AAAAAGGGHHH!
THEN WILLIE WHIRLED AND TOOK ELOUISE IN HIS ARMS AND KEPT ON GOING...RIGHT OUT THE WINDOW OF THE FORTIETH-STORY APARTMENT. THE FRANKENSTEIN MONSTER ELOUISE WELLER HAD CREATED WAS HER GREAT SUCCESS—AND HER DOOM!
AIIIIEEEEEEEEEEEEEEEEE...
8

DOUBLE-CROSSED

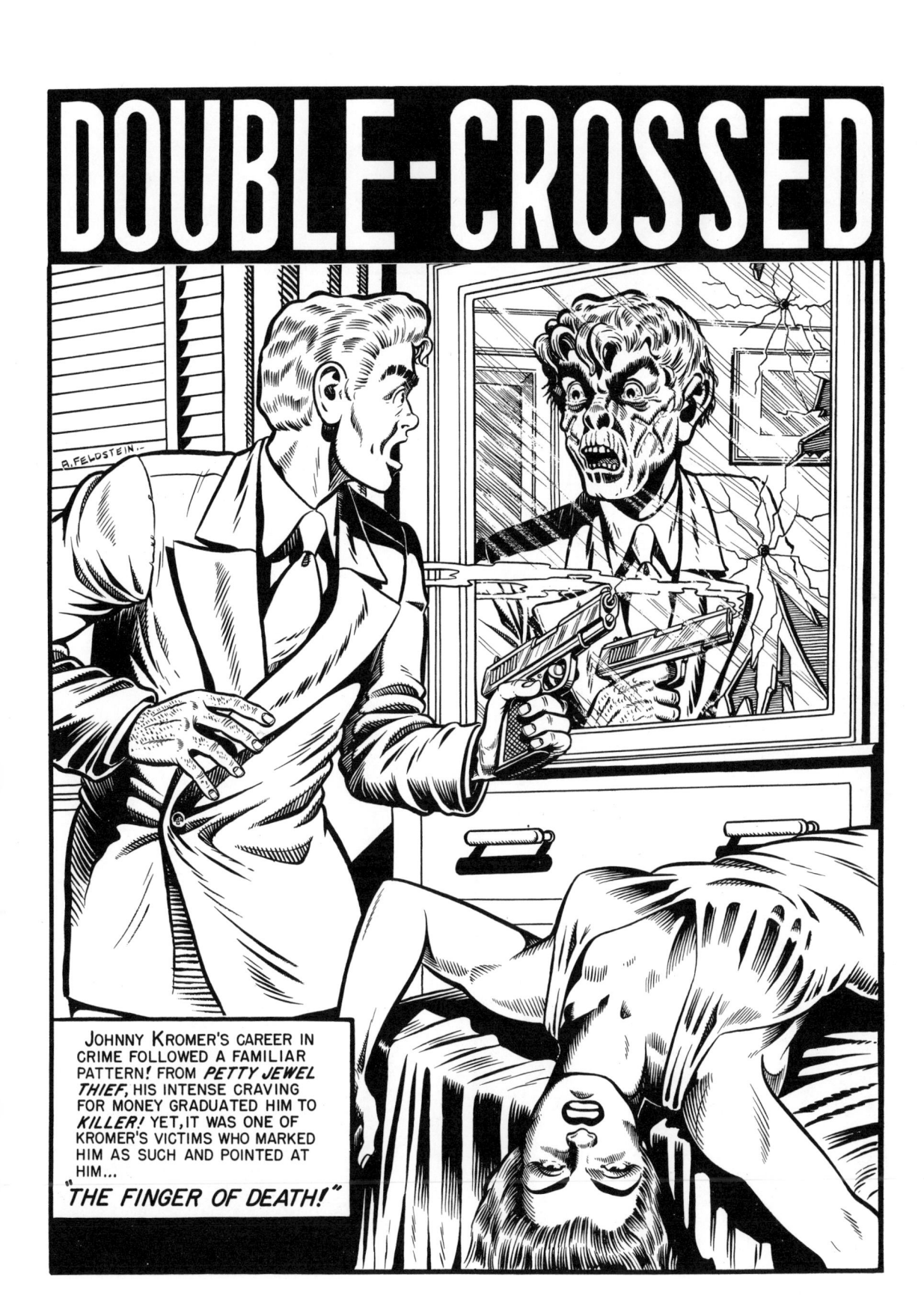

JOHNNY KROMER'S CAREER IN CRIME FOLLOWED A FAMILIAR PATTERN! FROM *PETTY JEWEL THIEF*, HIS INTENSE CRAVING FOR MONEY GRADUATED HIM TO *KILLER!* YET, IT WAS ONE OF KROMER'S VICTIMS WHO MARKED HIM AS SUCH AND POINTED AT HIM...

"THE FINGER OF DEATH!"

DOUBLE-CROSSED

DOUBLE-CROSSED

...THIS IS MRS. MUNN... 132 ELM DRIVE... ROBBER HERE....
AIEEEE!
CRAA-ASH!
N-NO... P-PLEASE..
TRY TO TURN ME OVER TO THE COPS, EH?
YIIII!
CRUNCH!
S-SHE'S AWFUL STILL.... I WONDER.... IF SHE'S....
SH-SHE'S...*DEAD!* I BETTER GET OUT OF HERE....
.... BEFORE THE FLATFEET GET HERE!
4

THE COPS ARE HERE... I GOTTA THINK FAST!
EEEE-EEEE
HOLD ON THERE, MISTER!
S-SURE, OFFICER!
AND WHEN I RANG THE OUTSIDE BELL... I HEARD SOMEONE SCREAM...
THANKS, BUD! WAIT THERE A MINUTE!
WHATEVER YOU SAY, OFFICER...
WHEW! SO FAR, SO GOOD! GOTTA CLEAR OUT OF HERE!
THEY'RE LOOKING FOR ME... IF I ONLY HAD A CAR....
5

..TH-THERE'S ONE! HOPE THE OLD CHARM WORKS.....
C-CAN YOU GIVE ME A HITCH TO THE DOCTOR'S, MISTER? M-MY... W-WIFE...
SURE, OLD MAN... GLAD TO HELP!
ANOTHER SUCKER! I'LL HITCH OUT OF TOWN.....
WHAT SEEMS TO BE THE TROUBLE...SAY, AREN'T THOSE POLICE SIRENS?
PROB'LY GOING TO RESCUE A CAT IN A TREE...YOU KNOW HOW THEY ARE!
I DON'T KNOW...THEY SEEM TO BE FOLLOWING *US*....
MAYBE YOU'RE RIGHT...
CLUNK!
AGHHH!
THE...C-COPS! GOTTA MAKE 'EM STOP...
6

DOUBLE-CROSSED

QUICK! LET'S SEE WHAT THEY SAY!
NIGHT EXTRA
THE EVENING GLOBE
DANGEROUS KILLER BEING HUNTED BY POLICE
THEY'VE EVEN GOT A DESCRIPTION OF YOU
HERE'S THE WAY OUT... THIS STORY ABOUT THE *PLASTIC SURGEON*
THIS IS THE PLACE! HE'S GONNA DO A QUICK CHANGE ON MY MAP...
MATHEWS M.D.
YOU'VE GOT TO HELP ME, DOC,.. THERE'S A GANG AFTER ME...
W-WHAT?
.... AND BESIDES, YOU DON'T HAVE ANY CHOICE, SEE?
Y- YES ....I'LL DO IT....
JUST A FEW MORE MINUTES....
REMEMBER, SAWBONES... ONE PHONEY MOVE AND I'LL BLOW YOUR HEAD OFF!
8

NOW THEY'LL NEVER RECOGNIZE ME....
I FEEL A LITTLE DIZZY... GOING TO GET A GLASS OF WATER!
...AND THEY ARE ARMED, SO BE CARE-FUL....
PULLING A CUTE TRICK, EH?
YOU SERVED YOUR PURPOSE, DOCTOR....PLEASANT DREAMS
AGHHH!
BLAMM!
AND SO HAVE YOU, CHUM...NOW NO ONE KNOWS WHAT I LOOK LIKE!
EEEEE!
BA-A-A-ANG!
GOTTA GET RID OF THIS FOLIAGE, BEFORE I GO OUT! THE COPS WILL NEVER SPOT ME, NOW!
TH-THEY'VE SPOTTED ME...BUT HOW? I GOT OUT WITHOUT BEING SEEN....
BILL'S BAR AN
---AND DOC MATHEWS POINTED THE FINGER AT YOU WHEN HE OPERATED! HE RECOGNIZED YOU.... AND WHEN HE CALLED HE TOLD US ABOUT X MARKING THE SPOT..... RIGHT ON YOUR KISSER!
9

THE MACHINE-GUN MAD MOBSTERS

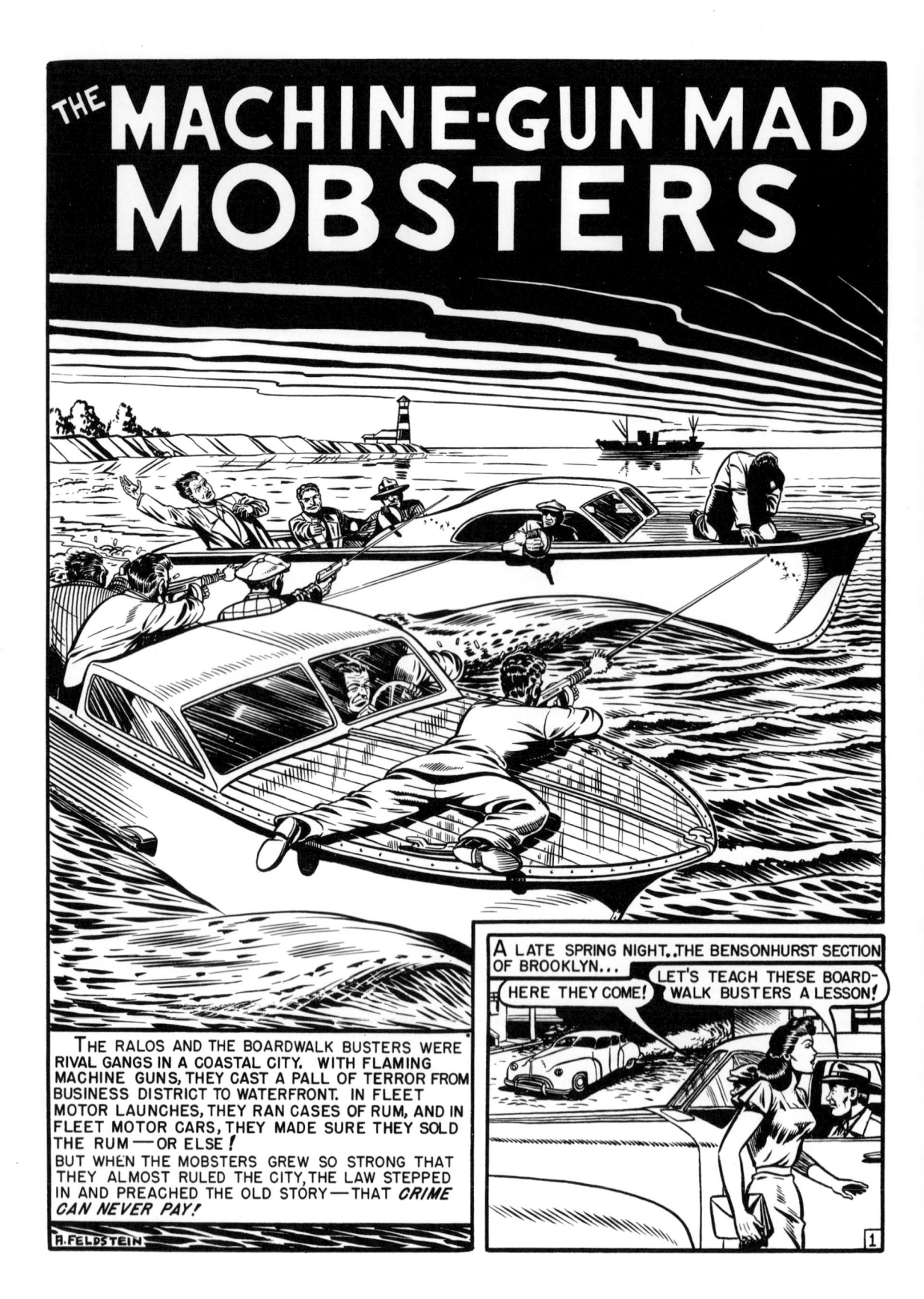

THE RALOS AND THE BOARDWALK BUSTERS WERE RIVAL GANGS IN A COASTAL CITY. WITH FLAMING MACHINE GUNS, THEY CAST A PALL OF TERROR FROM BUSINESS DISTRICT TO WATERFRONT. IN FLEET MOTOR LAUNCHES, THEY RAN CASES OF RUM, AND IN FLEET MOTOR CARS, THEY MADE SURE THEY SOLD THE RUM—OR ELSE!
BUT WHEN THE MOBSTERS GREW SO STRONG THAT THEY ALMOST RULED THE CITY, THE LAW STEPPED IN AND PREACHED THE OLD STORY—THAT *CRIME CAN NEVER PAY!*

A. FELDSTEIN

A LATE SPRING NIGHT...THE BENSONHURST SECTION OF BROOKLYN...

"HERE THEY COME!"

"LET'S TEACH THESE BOARDWALK BUSTERS A LESSON!"

RAT-A-TAT
TAT-TAT
RAT-A-TAT-TAT!
RAT-TAT-TAT-A-TAT!
EEEEEGGH!
BULLETS SHATTER GLASS AND METAL AS THEY SHOWER INTO THE ONCOMING CAR...
AAAAGGH!
YIIII!
C-CRAAASHH!
IF ANY OF 'EM IS STILL ALIVE, WE'LL FINISH 'EM OFF!
MAYBE THIS WILL TEACH THEIR GANG WE MEAN BUSINESS!
I CAN'T LOOK... I CAN'T LOOK! IT'S TOO AWFUL...
TWO HOURS LATER, IN A SMALL 'BUSINESS' OFFICE NEAR THE WATERFRONT...
ROCKS! WE JUST GOT WORD THE RALOS GUNNED DOWN CHICK AND ED AND BILLY!
WHAT?
INK
2

SO THE RALOS ARE PLAYING IT TOUGH, ARE THEY? THEY'VE GONE AND HIRED SOME GUNMEN, EH? OKAY, IF THAT'S THE WAY THEY WANT IT, WE'LL FOLLOW THEIR LEAD!
UNKNOWN TO ROCKS BALTERS AND THE BOARDWALK BUSTERS, THE RALO BROTHERS WERE DOWN AT THE WATERFRONT...
WE'LL KEEP THE BUSTERS OFF BALANCE. WE'LL TAKE THE CHICAGO BOYS WE HIRED OUT TO THE THREE-MILE LIMIT!
YEAH! THEN WHEN THE BUSTERS BRING IN THEIR RUM— WE'LL SPOIL IT FOR THEM!
THEY'RE GONNA GET THE SURPRISE OF THEIR LIVES!
THE BOARDWALK BUSTERS TOOK THE CASES OF RUM FROM A BIG OCEAN TRAMP...
THAT'S THE LAST LOAD! LET'S GET MOVIN'!
HEY! THAT LAUNCH IS MOVIN' CLOSER TO US!
THEY BETTER NOT GET TOO CLOSE!
SUDDENLY A BURST OF MACHINE-GUN FIRE RIPPED FROM THE RALO BOAT!
RAT-TAT-TAT-TAT-TAT-TAT!
GNNYYAAA!
AAAAGH!
DRAT-A-TAT-TAT---RAT-A-TAT---
3

WE'LL TAKE OVER DAT RUM!
YEAH! AN' TAKE YOUSE BUMS OVER AT DA SAME TIME!
DON'T MAKE A MOVE, YA CRUMBBUNS! WE'RE BORROWIN' DAT RUM YA SHIPPED OFF DA STEAMER!
YOU'LL NEVER GET AWAY WID IT!
THE STOLEN RUM WAS HIJACKED OFF THE LAUNCH--
THAT'S THE LAST OF 'EM!
AND A MOBSTER PUMPED BULLETS INTO THE RUDDER OF THE BUSTERS' LAUNCH--
DAT TAKES CARE OF DAT!
RAT-A-TAT-A-TAT!
RI-I-IPP!
SO LONG, SUCKERS!
HAW HAW HAW!
T'ANKS FER DA RUM!
LATER THAT SAME DAY--
THE RALOS? TWICE IN THE SAME DAY! THEY WON'T GET AWAY WITH THIS!
SQUINT! COME IN HERE A MINUTE-AND BRING YOUR ROD WITH YOU!
SURE THING, ROCKS!
4

WE AIN'T GONNA WASTE NO TIME! WE'RE STRIKIN' RIGHT AT THE HEAD OF THE RALO MOB... THE TWO RALO BROTHERS!
I SEE 'EM! LEAVE THOSE BABIES TO ME!
TWO DAYS LATER, AT A SEASHORE PICNIC GROUNDS.-
THAT'S ONE OF THE RALO BOYS AHEAD!
I'LL MAKE THIS A SURE THING...
GNNNYAAA!
BLAMMM! BLAMMM! BLAMMM!
AAAAAGHH!
WHAT HAPPENED?
THAT MAN WAS SHOT!
LET'S BLOW, CHICK! WE'LL GET AWAY EASY IN THE CONFUSION!
TWO WEEKS LATER, THE RALO GANG RETALIATED. ROCKS BALTER WAS GOING INTO A RESTAURANT WHEN TWO MEN WALKED SWIFTLY TOWARD HIM...
WATCH YOURSELF, HONEY, THOSE TWO TRIGGER BOYS—
5

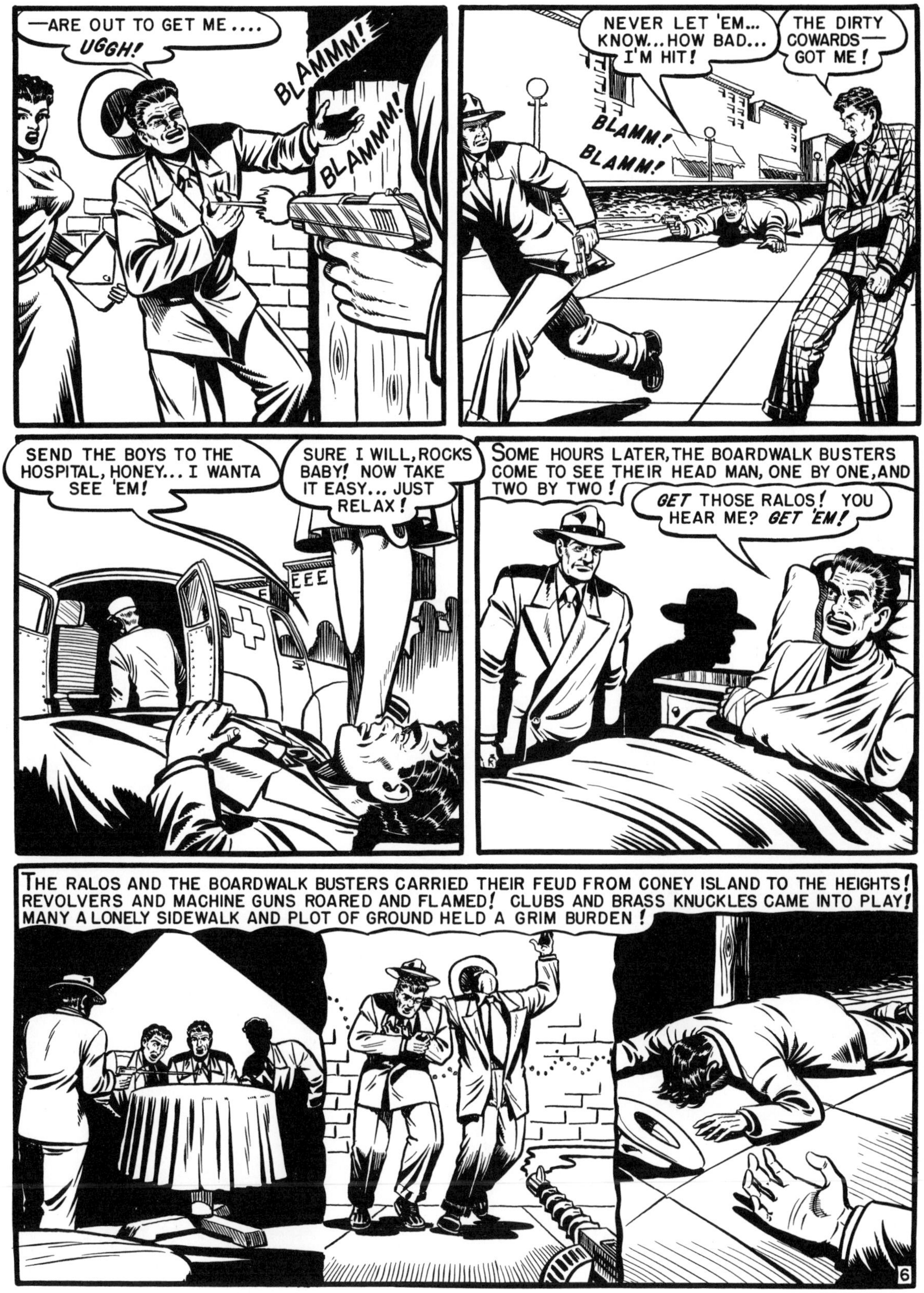
—ARE OUT TO GET ME.... UGGH!
BLAMMM!
BLAMMM!
NEVER LET 'EM... KNOW... HOW BAD... I'M HIT!
THE DIRTY COWARDS— GOT ME!
BLAMM!
BLAMM!
SEND THE BOYS TO THE HOSPITAL, HONEY... I WANTA SEE 'EM!
SURE I WILL, ROCKS BABY! NOW TAKE IT EASY... JUST RELAX!
SOME HOURS LATER, THE BOARDWALK BUSTERS COME TO SEE THEIR HEAD MAN, ONE BY ONE, AND TWO BY TWO!
GET THOSE RALOS! YOU HEAR ME? GET 'EM!
THE RALOS AND THE BOARDWALK BUSTERS CARRIED THEIR FEUD FROM CONEY ISLAND TO THE HEIGHTS! REVOLVERS AND MACHINE GUNS ROARED AND FLAMED! CLUBS AND BRASS KNUCKLES CAME INTO PLAY! MANY A LONELY SIDEWALK AND PLOT OF GROUND HELD A GRIM BURDEN!
6

AND THEN, ONE AFTERNOON, ONE OF THE BOARDWALK BUSTERS MADE A MISTAKE...
HEY, YOU! JUST A MINUTE!
CAN'T LET THAT COPPER FIND OUT WHAT'S IN HERE!
HERE Y'ARE, COPPER!
WHY YOU-!
I'LL PUMP YA SO FULL OF HOLES--
BIG TALK!
THUDD!
NNYYAAA!
YOU HOODLUMS HAVE BEEN GETTING AWAY WITH MURDER! IT'S ABOUT TIME SOMEBODY TAUGHT YOU A LITTLE RESPECT FOR THE LAW!
I THOUGHT SO! RUM! THE D.A. HAS BEEN WAITING FOR A BREAK LIKE THIS!
LESS THAN HALF AN HOUR LATER, THE OFFICER MADE HIS REPORT DIRECTLY TO THE DISTRICT ATTORNEY--
GREAT WORK, JIM! NOW THAT WE'VE CAUGHT ONE OF THESE PEDDLING WITH THE CROOKED BOOZE, WE'VE MADE A GOOD START!
IT WON'T GET YA NOTHIN', I AIN'T SPILLIN'!
I DON'T NEED YOUR TESTIMONY! I HAVE OTHER PEOPLE WILLING TO TALK OUT AGAINST YOU AND YOUR KIND! I'LL BRING THEM IN!
7

IN ORDER, THE GIRL WHO SAW THREE BUSTERS SLAIN, A FISHERMAN WHO SAW THE GANGSTER LAUNCHES BATTLE, A BYSTANDER WHO CAUGHT A SLUG, ALL FACE THE STARING MOBSTER...
I REMEMBER HIM! HE WAS IN THE CAR!
AN' HE WAS IN ONE O' THEM MOTOR LAUNCHES, TOO!
(GULP)
BOYS! WE HAVE THE PROOF WE NEEDED! THROW A CORDON OF MEN AROUND THE WATERFRONT! HAVE A UNIFORMED DETAIL SHADOW ALL THE NIGHT SPOTS!
IN THE DAYS THAT FOLLOWED, THE BLUECOATS WERE ACTIVE...
PLAY IT SMART, LET THE GUNS ALONE!
STRETCH FOR THE CEILING!
THE PLAINCLOTHESMEN RAIDED THE MOTOR LAUNCHES...
IF ANYBODY MAKES A MOVE TO RESIST, WE'LL LET YOU HAVE IT!
TOUGH-FACED MOBSTERS FACED THE LINE UP...
I DON'T KNOW A T'ING!
WE AIN'T TALKIN'!
BUT ONE DAY A MAN CRACKED...
LEMME OUT! LEMME OUT! I'LL SPILL WHAT I KNOW. I CAN'T STAND IT IN HERE...
IT'S DA RALOS AND DA BOARD-WALK BUSTERS! GANG WAR... AN' THE BUSTERS ARE GONNA MAKE A BIG RAID...TOMORROW NIGHT...
8

THE NEXT NIGHT, THE DISTRICT ATTORNEY HAD HIS MEN OUT IN FORCE...
THE BUSTERS ARE RAIDING THE RALOS IN THEIR WATERFRONT HIDEOUT. WE'LL LET THEM GET INSIDE— THEN RAID!
WE KNOW WHAT TO DO!
THOSE HUMAN RATS THINK THEY CAN RUN ROUGHSHOD OVER OTHER PEOPLE. THEY USE BULLETS AND MACHINE GUNS TO IMPOSE THEIR WILL ON THE HELPLESS! IT'S TIME WE STOPPED THEM! NOW, LET'S GO....
THERE THEY GO, SIR!
I'LL SIGNAL THE MEN. WE'LL GO IN THROUGH THE SKYLIGHT!
A FLASHLIGHT BLINKED TWICE. POUNDING FEET SHOOK THE CITY STREETS AS BLUECOATED OFFICERS LEAPED FORWARD WITH READY GUNS!
THIS IS IT!
THE WAREHOUSE DOOR WENT DOWN—
CRASH!
DA COPPERS!
NEVER MIND THE RALOS! GET THE BLUESHIRTS!
DROP YOUR GUNS OR WE FIRE!
EEEEEH!
OOOOWFF!
BAAMM!
BAMMMM!
9

YOU'LL NEVER TAKE ME ALIVE, COPPER!
THEN MAYBE I'LL TAKE YOU—
—DEAD!
GO BACK, BOYS! WE HAVE A BETTER WAY OF SMOKING OUT THESE RATS!
TEAR GAS!
I AIN'T STAYIN' HERE!
TEAR GAS
COME AN' TAKE US!
WE'RE QUITTIN'!
WE CAN'T SHOOT WHEN WE CAN'T SEE!
GOT THE WHOLE KIT AND KABOODLE OF THEM! A NICE HAUL! THEY'LL GO TO THE ELECTRIC CHAIR OR THE PENITENTIARY — ACCORDING TO THEIR CRIMES!
WHEN WILL THEY EVER LEARN THAT CRIME DOESN'T PAY?
MAYBE THEY'LL CATCH WISE SOMEDAY, SIR! THAT'S WHAT WE ALL KEEP HOPING!
10

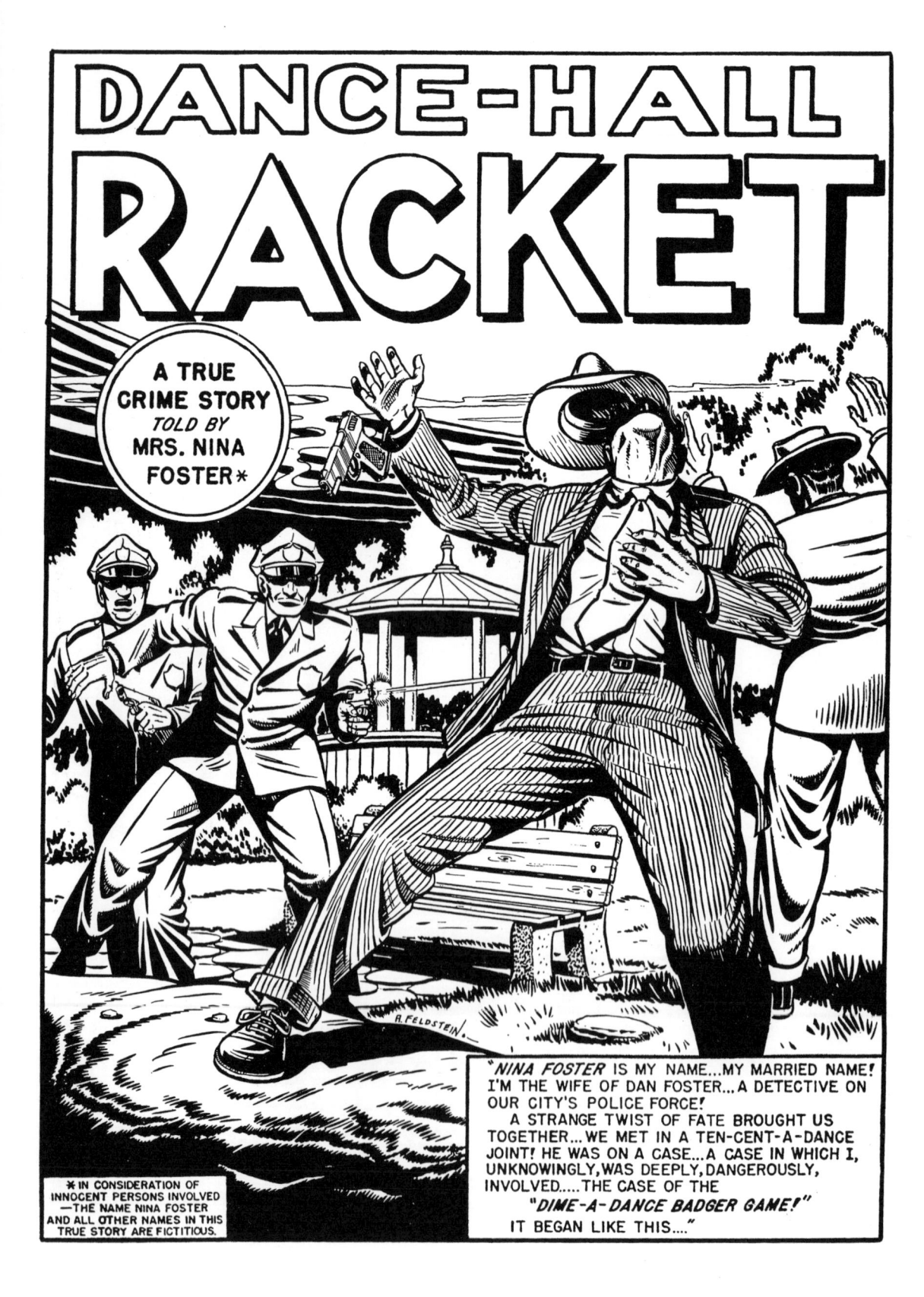

DANCE-HALL RACKET

A TRUE CRIME STORY TOLD BY MRS. NINA FOSTER*

"NINA FOSTER IS MY NAME...MY MARRIED NAME! I'M THE WIFE OF DAN FOSTER...A DETECTIVE ON OUR CITY'S POLICE FORCE!

A STRANGE TWIST OF FATE BROUGHT US TOGETHER...WE MET IN A TEN-CENT-A-DANCE JOINT! HE WAS ON A CASE...A CASE IN WHICH I, UNKNOWINGLY, WAS DEEPLY, DANGEROUSLY, INVOLVED.....THE CASE OF THE

"DIME-A-DANCE BADGER GAME!"

IT BEGAN LIKE THIS...."

*IN CONSIDERATION OF INNOCENT PERSONS INVOLVED —THE NAME NINA FOSTER AND ALL OTHER NAMES IN THIS TRUE STORY ARE FICTITIOUS.

"MY FATHER DIED WHEN I WAS TEN YEARS OLD, AND MOTHER SUPPORTED US WHILE I WENT TO SCHOOL. SHE HAD PLANS TO PUT ME THROUGH COLLEGE, SO THAT I COULD HAVE A CAREER, BUT THOSE PLANS WERE SHATTERED WHEN..."
HOW IS SHE, DOCTOR?
YOUR MOTHER IS A VERY SICK WOMAN, NINA! SHE MUST HAVE PLENTY OF REST...NO MORE WORK FOR HER! HER HEART COULDN'T STAND IT!
"MOTHER... SICK... HER HEART! THE YEARS OF STRUGGLE TO KEEP ME IN SCHOOL, WELL CLOTHED, AND A FINE HOME TO LIVE IN, HAD FINALLY TOLD ON HER... THERE WAS ONLY ONE THING I COULD DO..."
BUT, NINA! ALL THOSE YEARS OF STUDY AND WORK THROWN OUT! DON'T DO IT, DEAR! DON'T LEAVE SCHOOL! WE'LL MANAGE SOMEHOW!
NO, MOTHER! I'M ALL FINISHED WITH SCHOOL! I'VE GOT TO GET A JOB! WE'VE GOT TO EAT!
"MOTHER DIDN'T KNOW IT, BUT WHAT LITTLE SAVINGS SHE HAD MANAGED TO SCRAPE UP THROUGH THE YEARS HAD GONE TO PAY THE DOCTOR BILLS...WE WERE BROKE! THAT'S WHY IT WAS SO IMPORTANT THAT I START WORKING IMMEDIATELY..."
ACME EMPLOYMENT AGENCY
THIS IS AS GOOD A PLACE AS ANY TO START LOOKING!
722 750
701 721
YES? WHAT CAN I DO FOR YOU, YOUNG LADY?
GOOD MORNING! I'D LIKE TO APPLY FOR ONE OF THE JOB OPENINGS YOU ADVERTISED ABOUT IN THE PAPER!
OF COURSE! WHAT EXPERIENCE HAVE YOU HAD?
EXPERIENCE? WHY... NONE, YET! THIS IS MY FIRST ATTEMPT TO GET A JOB!
NO EXPERIENCE? OH, I'M AWFULLY SORRY! YOU SEE, WE ONLY PLACE EXPERIENCED WORKERS...WE CAN'T HELP YOU!
OH, I SEE! THANK YOU, ANYWAY!
2

DANCE-HALL RACKET

"NO EXPERIENCE! IT WAS LIKE THAT EVERY PLACE I WENT..."

SORRY, MISS! WE NEED SOMEONE WITH MORE EXPERIENCE!

COME BACK WHEN YOU'VE HAD MORE EXPERIENCE!

NOT ENOUGH EXPERIENCE!

NO EXPERIENCE!

"IT WAS LATE IN THE AFTERNOON...I WAS TIRED AND HUNGRY! I STOPPED IN AT A CAFETERIA AND SAT DOWN TO REST! I WAS FRIGHTENED...FRIGHTENED AND DESPERATE! WHILE I WAS SIPPING A CUP OF COFFEE, I LOOKED OUT ACROSS THE CROWDED, TRAFFIC-JAMMED STREETS!"

WHAT CAN I DO NOW? I'VE TRIED EVERYWHERE! WHAT CAN I DO?

"MUSIC FLOATED ON THE HOT AFTERNOON AIR. IT CAME FROM A DANCE HALL ACROSS THE STREET...IT DRIFTED LAZILY INTO THE CAFETERIA WHERE I SAT! I LOOKED UP AT WHERE IT CAME FROM AND SAW..."

"A STRANGE FASCINATION LURED ME ACROSS TO THE DANCE-HALL ENTRANCE...I KNEW THAT IT WASN'T A JOB FOR ME, YET I WAS CURIOUS. THERE WERE SOME PICTURES OUTSIDE AND I LOOKED AT THEM..."

SOME OF THE GIRLS LOOK NICE....

"SUDDENLY...AS I STOOD THERE...A FEELING OF UNEASINESS CAME OVER ME...SOMEONE WAS BEHIND ME...WATCHING ME...AND I SENSED IT..."

LOOKIN' FOR A JOB, SISTER? YOU *SEEM* INTERESTED!

OH...!! I BEG YOUR PARDON!

"I TURNED! HE WAS A DARK, RATHER HANDSOME MAN, BUT HIS EYES HAD A SINISTER, EVEN EVIL LOOK!"

I ASKED YOU IF YOU WERE LOOKING FOR A JOB! MY NAME IS BENNETT, STEVE BENNETT! I OWN THIS PLACE AND I COULD USE A GIRL LIKE YOU!

ER...WHAT KIND OF A JOB, MR. BENNETT? WHAT WOULD I DO?

DANCE-HALL RACKET

DANCE-HALL RACKET

"THE NEXT DAY, STEVE TOOK ME TO A BEAUTY PARLOR WHERE THEY FIXED MY HAIR AND SHOWED ME HOW TO PUT ON MAKE-UP! WHEN THEY FINISHED AND I SAW MYSELF IN THE MIRROR, I COULDN'T BELIEVE IT..."

YOU SEE, NINA! THAT'S THE WAY YOU SHOULD LOOK ALL THE TIME! YOU'RE BEAUTIFUL...

OH, STEVE!

"STEVE WAS VERY NICE TO ME...AND THE TIME PASSED SWIFTLY! THE JOB WASN'T TOO BAD...EXCEPT WHEN SOMEONE WOULD GET FAMILIAR WITH ME..."

C'MON, BABY! HOW'S ABOUT TELLIN' ME WHERE YA LIVE?

PLEASE, MISTER! YOU'RE HURTING MY ARM!

"BUT WHEN SOMETHING LIKE THAT HAPPENED, STEVE'S BOYS WERE ALWAYS AROUND TO TAKE CARE OF IT."

...AND DON'T EVER COME BACK, BUDDY, IF YOU KNOW WHAT'S GOOD FOR YOU!

"AND SO THE TIME PASSED. I EARNED A GOOD SALARY, AND KEPT MOTHER UNDER THE BEST CARE POSSIBLE. SHE NEVER FOUND OUT WHAT I WAS DOING, ALTHOUGH SHE QUESTIONED ME ON OCCASION. I DID NOTICE, HOWEVER, THAT STEVE MADE SURE THAT NO CUSTOMERS GOT TOO INTERESTED IN ME. MY SOCIAL LIFE WAS NIL SINCE I WORKED NIGHTS, AND THE ONLY MEN I MET WERE AT THE PLACE...BUT UNDER STEVE'S WATCHFUL EYE, I WAS KEPT FROM BECOMING FRIENDLY WITH ANY OF THEM. THIS HOLD HE HAD ON ME BECAME ANNOYING! I WAS *LONELY!*"

"ONE NIGHT..."

ER...A...MAY I HAVE THIS DANCE WITH YOU?

"I TOOK HIS TICKET, AND WE BEGAN TO DANCE. HE WAS RATHER GOOD LOOKING, DRESSED WELL...BUT WHAT STRUCK ME MOST WAS THAT HE JUST DIDN'T *BELONG* IN A PLACE LIKE THIS. HE WAS TOO FINE...TOO MUCH OF A GENTLEMAN. I WANTED TO ASK HIM ABOUT IT...BUT I COULDN'T. THEN HE SPOKE THE WORDS I WAS THINKING!"

WHAT'S A NICE GIRL LIKE YOU DOING IN A PLACE LIKE THIS?

YOU KNOW, I WAS GOING TO ASK *YOU* THAT SAME QUESTION!

WELL, LET'S JUST SAY I WAS LONELY!

...AND LET'S JUST SAY *I* NEED THE MONEY!

DANCE-HALL RACKET

"LATER THAT EVENING, DURING AN INTERMISSION, I WENT BACK TO THE DRESSING ROOM TO FRESHEN MY MAKE-UP! I WAS PASSING MR. BENNETT'S OFFICE WHEN I OVERHEARD!"
...THAT GUY THAT'S ALWAYS HANGIN' AROUND NINA! I WANT YOU TO FOLLOW HIM TONIGHT AND DUMP HIM IN SOME ALLEY! GIVE 'IM A GOOD GOIN' OVER!
MR. BENNETT PRIVATE
FRANK! YOU'VE GOT TO LEAVE IMMEDIATELY! DON'T ASK ANY QUESTIONS! JUST GO, QUICKLY!
WHY, NINA? WHAT'S WRONG?
I HEARD SOME TALK! THE BOYS ARE GOING TO BEAT YOU UP, TONIGHT! PLEASE, FRANK, I DON'T WANT YOU TO GET HURT!
BEAT ME UP? WHY? WHAT DID I DO?
YOU'VE BEEN PAYING TOO MUCH ATTENTION TO ME! THE BOSS IS JEALOUS, I GUESS! I REALLY DON'T KNOW WHAT THE REASON IS! BUT WHATEVER IT IS, DON'T QUESTION IT! GO, NOW, BEFORE IT'S TOO LATE!
ARE YOU SURE YOU'RE NOT TRYING TO GET RID OF ME, NINA?
OF COURSE NOT, FRANK! WHY SHOULD I WANT TO GET RID OF YOU! I'M ONLY TRYING TO SAVE YOU FROM TROUBLE!
THANKS, NINA, BUT I THINK YOU'RE MISTAKEN! THEY WOULDN'T TRY ANYTHING LIKE THAT! I'LL STICK AROUND!
"BUT I WASN'T MISTAKEN! FRANK WAS! THAT NIGHT THEY CAUGHT HIM IN AN ALLEY NEAR THE DANCE HALL!"
7

"I FELT TERRIBLE ABOUT WHAT HAD HAPPENED TO FRANK! HE HAD BEEN SWEET TO ME AND I HAD ENJOYED HIS COMPANY. ALTHOUGH I WAS NOT IN LOVE WITH HIM, I MISSED HIM WHEN HE NO LONGER CAME TO THE DANCE HALL. I RESOLVED THAT I WOULD NOT ALLOW WHAT HAD HAPPENED TO FRANK TO HAPPEN TO ANYONE ELSE! BUT STEVE BENNETT AND HIS HENCHMEN HAD OTHER PLANS!"
THE GUY HAD ALMOST A HUNDRED BUCKS ON HIM, STEVE! PRETTY GOOD, HUH?
HMMM! THAT GIVES ME AN IDEA!
"ALTHOUGH I WAS NOT AWARE OF IT AT THE TIME, I BECAME AN INNOCENT PARTICIPANT IN HIS DIABOLICAL SCHEME..."
HOW'S ABOUT TELLING ME WHERE YOU LIVE, SISTER? YOU AN' ME COULD GET BETTER ACQUAINTED!
I'M SORRY, SIR! I'M NOT ALLOWED TO GIVE MY ADDRESS TO CUSTOMERS!
SAY, BUDDY! THAT GAL YOU WERE JUST DANCING WITH...SHE TOLD ME TO TELL YOU TO MEET HER IN AN HOUR AT THE BANDSTAND IN THE PARK!
YEAH? HOT DOG! TELL HER I'LL BE THERE WITH BELLS ON!
"BUT WHEN HE GOT TO THE BANDSTAND, HE HAD AN UNEXPECTED SURPRISE! THEY WERE WAITING FOR HIM!"
WHAT'S THE MEANING OF THIS??
YOUR GIRL FRIEND COULDN'T MAKE IT...SO WE CAME INSTEAD! HAND OVER YOUR WALLET...AND BE QUICK ABOUT IT!
...AND WHEN YOU GET OUT OF THAT, BUDDY, DON'T GO TO THE COPS...OR YOU'LL REGRET IT FOR THE REST OF YOUR LIFE!
LET'S GO, BOSS!
GUL-- LUB ... UB!
"THEIR TERROR TACTICS WORKED! NONE OF THEIR VICTIMS WENT TO THE POLICE. AT LEAST THERE WERE NO INVESTIGATIONS! AS I SAID, ALL THIS TIME I KNEW NOTHING ABOUT WHAT STEVE WAS DOING...I DIDN'T LEARN ABOUT IT UNTIL...ONE EVENING...."
HELLO, BABY! LET'S DANCE A BIT!
SURE, MISTER! YOUR TICKET, PLEASE!
8

DANCE-HALL RACKET

"WE GOT UP AND DANCED AGAIN. I DIDN'T WANT TO ATTRACT ANY ATTENTION WHILE I TOLD DAN MY STORY!"
... AND FRANK CANE NEVER CAME BACK AFTER THAT! THEY MUST HAVE BEATEN HIM TERRIBLY! THEN, OTHERS, WHO WOULD DANCE WITH ME REGULARLY WOULD SUDDENLY STOP COMING AROUND... I DON'T KNOW WHAT HAPPENED TO THEM, BUT I'M AFRAID THAT WHATEVER IT WAS MIGHT HAPPEN TO YOU!
I WANT IT TO, NINA!
YOU WHAT?
I WANT IT TO! I'M CONVINCED, NOW, THAT YOU ARE INNOCENT OF WHAT IS GOING ON, AND THAT YOU ARE UNKNOWINGLY BEING USED IN THIS LITTLE RACKET, SO I'LL TELL YOU EVERYTHING! I'LL NEED YOUR HELP, THOUGH!
I... I DON'T UNDERSTAND!
I'M A DETECTIVE, NINA! I'M INVESTIGATING A SERIES OF MUGGINGS THAT LEAD DIRECTLY TO THIS DANCE HALL! YOU WERE MENTIONED IN EACH OF THEM... BUT ONLY AS A LURE! I THOUGHT AT FIRST THAT YOU WERE IN ON IT, BUT NOW I SEE YOU'RE NOT... AND I'M GLAD!
WHAT DO YOU WANT ME TO DO, DAN?
I WANT YOU TO TREAT ME AS YOU DID THE OTHERS WHO SUDDENLY DISAPPEARED! WE HAVE NO PROOF, SO WE HAVE TO CATCH THEM AT THEIR LITTLE GAME! WILL YOU HELP, NINA?
"EACH NIGHT, AFTER THAT, DAN CAME TO THE DANCE HALL. EACH NIGHT WE DANCED... AND AS I FELL MORE AND MORE IN LOVE WITH HIM... I BECAME MORE AND MORE AFRAID THAT HIS LITTLE PLAN MIGHT NOT WORK, THAT HE MIGHT GET HURT, EVEN KILLED... I DARED NOT THINK ABOUT IT! THEN... ONE NIGHT--"
SAY, BUDDY! THAT GIRL YOU WERE JUST DANCING WITH WANTS YOU TO MEET HER IN THE BANDSTAND IN THE PARK IN AN HOUR!
WELL, IT'S ABOUT TIME SHE GAVE ME A BREAK!
HELLO, CHIEF? FOSTER! OUR BREAK'S COME! BE AT THE BANDSTAND IN THE PARK, IN AN HOUR! BUST IN WHEN YOU GET THE SIGNAL! WE'LL CATCH THEM WITH THE GOODS!
GREAT WORK, DANNY! SEE YOU!
10

"LATER.... IN THE PARK..."
WHA... WHAT'S THE MEANING OF THIS? WHERE'S THE ... THE DAME?
SHE FORGOT THE DATE, CHUM, SO WE KEPT IT FOR HER! HAND OVER THAT LOADED WALLET, AND MAKE IT SNAPPY!
SURE, FELLOWS! HERE! I DON'T WANT NO TROUBLE!
THAT'S USING YOUR HEAD, CHUM!
NOW! YOU HAVE THE TROUBLE!
OKAY, CHIEF!
WHA...?? COPS!
LET'S GET OUTTA HERE!
NO YOU DON'T, MUGS! STAY WHERE YOU ARE!
NOT ME, COPPERS! I AIN'T GONNA LET YOU STICK ME IN NO JAIL!
BLAMMM!
BLAMM!
THEN, I'M AFRAID YOU'LL END UP IN THE GRAVE, BENNETT!
EEEEOWW!
BAMMMM!
WELL, DAN! I GUESS WE CAN MARK THIS CASE CLOSED!
NOT EXACTLY, CHIEF! I HAVE SOME UNFINISHED BUSINESS BACK AT THE DANCE HALL!
11

YES, CHARLES HANLEY, THIS IS IT!.. YOUR LAST MILE! I'VE BEEN WAITING FOR YOU A LONG TIME, HANLEY... A LITTLE LONGER THAN I HAVE TO WAIT FOR MOST CHUMPS... BUT IN A MINUTE, YOU'RE GOING TO SIT DOWN HERE, HANLEY, AND MY WAITING WILL BE OVER... MY WAITING AND YOURS! YES, HANLEY, IN A MINUTE YOU'RE GOING TO FEEL:
THE LAW'S REVENGE!
THE CASE OF CHARLES HANLEY * A TRUE CRIME STORY FROM POLICE FILES
DANGER HIGH VOLTAGE
* IN CONSIDERATION OF INNOCENT LIVING RELATIVES AND OTHER PERSONS INVOLVED IN THIS TRUE CRIME CASE, THE NAME CHARLES HANLEY AND ALL OTHER NAMES ARE FICTICIOUS!
A. FELDSTEIN

YOU THOUGHT YOU HAD IT ALL PLANNED, HANLEY, DIDN'T YOU? YOU WERE GOING TO ROB THE FIRM'S PAYROLL AND LEAVE TOWN-A SIMPLE PLAN—YET...
HERE HE COMES, NOW! RIGHT ON TIME, TOO! I'VE PLANNED THIS FOR A LONG TIME AND NOW....MY PLANS'LL PAY OFF!
OKAY, BINDER! STICK 'EM UP AND STEP INTO THIS ALLEY!
HANLEY! WE THOUGHT YOU WERE SICK WHEN YOU DIDN'T COME IN TODAY! YOU...YOU CAN'T BE SERIOUS....PUT AWAY THAT GUN!
SHUT UP AN' HAND OVER THAT SATCHEL, BINDER, AND MAKE IT SNAPPY!
NO! NO! I WON'T LET YOU DO IT!
BINDER! LEGGO!
NO....I WON'T LET YOU STEAL THIS MONEY! I ......
YOU FOOL, BINDER!
AAAAAHH!
BAMMM!
YET PLANS DON'T ALWAYS WORK OUT THE WAY THEY SHOULD, DO THEY, HANLEY? YOU DIDN'T PLAN ON THIS, DID YOU? YOU DIDN'T PLAN ON...MURDER!
HE'S DEAD...THE FOOL! DYING TO PROTECT SOMEONE ELSE'S DOUGH! I GOTTA SCRAM OUTTA HERE!
THAT NIGHT, YOU WERE HUNDREDS OF MILES AWAY, HANLEY, ON YOUR WAY OUT OF THE COUNTRY.... IN A FURNISHED ROOM, YOU LISTENED TO THE NEWS REPORTS....
....THE POLICE OF FOUR STATES ARE LOOKING FOR CHARLES HANLEY FOR THE HOLD-UP MURDER OF FRANK BINDER, CASHIER FOR THE FIRM OF....
THEY KNOW I DONE IT ALREADY!
2

...THE VICTIM IN A LAST BREATH WHISPERED HANLEY'S NAME TO WITNESSES JUST BEFORE HE DIED....A DESCRIPTION FOLLOWS...
WHO'S THERE?
KNOCK! KNOCK!
HAIR, DARK! EYES, DARK! HEIGHT, 5 FEET 10 INCHES! COMPLEXION, DARK! SCAR ON RIGHT CHEEK....
IT'S ME, MR. SMITH! YOUR LANDLADY! THE OTHER TENANTS HAVE BEEN COMPLAINING ABOUT YOUR RADIO BEIN' ON TOO LOUD–
...THIS MAN IS DANGEROUS... APPROACH WITH CAUTION.....
OKAY, OKAY! I'LL TURN IT DOWN....
WHY...WHY...YOU! YOU'RE THE MAN THEY'RE LOOKING FOR! YOU'RE CHARLES HANLEY!
I'M SORRY I GOTTA DO THIS, LADY...BUT I CAN'T LET YOU GO BLABBIN' TO THE COPS....
AGGH.... STOP...YOU'RE... CHOKING..... ME....
.....ANOTHER VICTIM, HANLEY? ANOTHER VICTIM IN YOUR FUTILE FLIGHT FROM THE LAW? IT'S NO USE, HANLEY! YOU CAN'T WIN!
...A GAS STATION! MAYBE I CAN BUY A CAR FROM 'EM!
HOWDY, MISTER! SOMETHIN' I KIN DO FER YUH?
YEAH! YOU GOT A CAR I CAN BUY?
NOPE! THE ONLY CAR WE GOT IS OUR OWN, AND THAT AIN'T FER SALE.... WHA? A GUN!
THEN I'M TAKIN' IT, CHUM! HAND OVER THE KEYS!
3

YES...A BLUE COUPE, LICENSE NUMBER A-7171! IT WAS HIM! THAT HANLEY FELLER! I HEARD HIS DESCRIPTION ON THE RADIO!
GAS
...BE ON THE LOOKOUT FOR A BLUE COUPE, LICENSE NUMBER A-7171... BELIEVED TO BE DRIVEN BY CHARLES HANLEY! ...CAREFUL....THIS MAN IS ARMED AND DANGEROUS....
HANLEY! HE'S THAT KILLER!
P.D.
SAY! THERE GOES A BLUE COUPE NOW... DOIN' 65 AT LEAST...
C'MON IT'S HIM! I SAW THE LICENSE PLATE!
P.D.
EEEEEEEEEEEEEEEEEE!
WHA...COPS! I GOTTA LOSE 'EM....
HE'S PICKING UP SPEED!
WE'LL GET HIM AT THE GRADE CROSSING! HE CAN'T PASS THAT TRAIN!
I'VE GOT TO BEAT THAT TRAIN TO THE CROSSING!
4

WHY...THE FOOL! HE'S TRYING TO BEAT IT...
HE'LL BE KILLED, FOR SURE
P.D.
P.D.
HE...HE MADE IT, THE LUCKY IDIOT!
WE'LL NEVER CATCH HIM NOW! THIS FREIGHT'LL TAKE TEN MINUTES TO PASS!
FULL STOP
STOP LISTEN CAUTION LOOK
THAT WAS CLOSE, HANLEY, BUT YOU WON THAT ROUND...NOW WHAT'S YOUR NEXT MOVE...WHAT CAN YOU DO NOW....??
I'VE GOT TO GET RID OF THE CAR! I'LL DRIVE IT OFF THIS BRIDGE!
SO LONG! THANKS FOR THE RIDE!
WHEW! LUCKY I'M NOT INSIDE! I'D BE A DEAD DUCK FER SURE! H...MMM! SAY.... WHY NOT! IF THEY FOUND ME AN' THAT CAR LIKE THAT, THEY'D STOP LOOKIN' FER ME...
5

AH! HERE COMES A CAR NOW! I'LL FLAG IT DOWN!
I'M IN LUCK! THE GUY'S JUST ABOUT MY SIZE!
WHAT'S WRONG, STRANGER? ANYTHING I CAN DO?
I...I HAD A LITTLE ACCIDENT! MY CAR SKIDDED OFF THE BRIDGE! I WONDER IF YOU COULD GIVE ME A LIFT TO TOWN?
WHAT? SKIDDED OFF? LET'S SEE!
HOLY SMOKES! HOW COULD YOU LIVE THROUGH THAT?
I COULDN'T! AND NEITHER COULD YOU!
CLUNK!
NOW TO CHANGE MY IDENTIFICATION WITH HIS...AND...THEN...
...HEAVE HIM OVER....OOOOF!
6

YES, HANLEY! YOUR FIENDISH PLAN WORKED! THE NEWSPAPERS TOLD THE STORY...
EXTRA DAILY GAZETT
VOL.35 NO.273 THURSDAY-
CHARLES HANLEY KILLED IN AUTO ACCIDENT...SEARCH ENDS
MURDERER KILLED WHILE ELUDING POLICE DRAGNET
INCOME TAX BILL GAINES SUPPORT IN HOUSE
SYEKOONS IS WORKING!
ARTIST CHASES FOX FOR PAY
HA-HA! THE FOOLS! THEY FELL FOR IT, HOOK, LINE AND SINKER! HA-HA!
...BUT WAIT, HANLEY! WAIT! THE LAW ISN'T THROUGH WITH YOU YET.. YOU HAVEN'T BEATEN THEM YET...
CHIEF, MAY I HAVE A WORD WITH YOU?
SURE, WALKER! C'MON IN!
DETECT LIEUTE JAME REILL
IT'S ABOUT THIS HANLEY CASE! I'VE BEEN STUDYING THESE PHOTOS OF THE ACCIDENT SCENE AND THERE'S SOMETHING FISHY... LOOK!
WHAT ARE YOU TALKING ABOUT, WALKER?
HERE! THE BODY WAS FOUND HERE! AND YET THE DOORS OF THE CAR ARE BOTH CLOSED...THE WINDOWS ONLY CRACKED, NOT SHATTERED...HOW DID HANLEY GET OUT OF THE CAR? AND...
WAIT A MINUTE, WALKER! THE DOOR COULD HAVE SWUNG OPEN AND SLAMMED SHUT AGAIN...
WHAT ABOUT *THIS! NO SKID MARKS* ON THE BRIDGE! I DON'T LIKE IT!
HMMM! LOOK HERE, WALKER! OFFICIALLY, THIS CASE IS CLOSED..BUT I'LL LET YOU WORK ON IT FOR A WHILE. UNOFFICIALLY, OF COURSE!
YOU SEE, HANLEY? YOU *HAVEN'T* BEATEN THEM! BUT *YOU* DON'T KNOW THAT! YOU'RE SURE OF YOURSELF... YOU *THINK* YOU'VE BEATEN THE LAW.. NOW, YOU'RE GOING TO BE SMART!
I'LL OPERATE MORE CAREFULLY NOW...PULL LITTLE JOBS... MASKED STICK-UPS...NIGHT JOBS ON SAFES, STORES...KEEP MOVIN'... THEY WON'T KNOW WHO TO LOOK FOR...I'M DEAD!
7

ONE NIGHT IN LITTLE ROCK...
OKAY, BUDDY! STICK 'EM UP AND HAND OVER THEM BOX-OFFICE RECEIPTS!
WHA...WHY! YOU CAN'T GET AWAY WITH THIS!
AND ANOTHER NIGHT IN HOT SPRINGS...
YOU MADE A NICE HAUL AT THAT GIN RUMMY GAME! NOW FORK IT OVER... QUICK!
S-SURE! HERE...
YES, HANLEY! WHILE YOU MOVED ABOUT DOING YOUR WORK... THE LAW WAS WORKING, TOO...
WELL, WALKER! WHAT DID YOU FIND OUT?
PLENTY, CHIEF! A MAN NAMED RALPH DUNCAN WAS REPORTED MISSING TWO DAYS AFTER HANLEY'S DEATH!
THIS GUY DUNCAN HAD A SUIT ON SIMILAR TO THE ONE HANLEY WAS KILLED IN... SAME HEIGHT AND BUILD... AND HIS CAR WAS FOUND ABANDONED OUTSIDE OF FORT LEE WHERE TWO HOLD-UPS WERE REPORTED LAST WEEK... I HAVE HIS WIFE COMING IN TO TAKE A LOOK AT HANLEY'S BODY... JUST IN CASE...
IT'S A STAB IN THE DARK, WALKER... BUT IT'S WORTH TAKING.
THE STRING IS RUNNING OUT, HANLEY! THE TIME IS SHORT... SOON THEY WILL KNOW... VERY SOON!
NOW, MRS. DUNCAN! ALL WE WANT YOU TO DO IS TELL US WHETHER YOU KNOW THIS PERSON... OKAY, BARKLEY, LIFT THE SHEET!
BUT I DON'T UNDER-STAND!
EEEEEEEEK! IT'S RALPH! IT'S MY HUSBAND!
WALKER, YOU WERE RIGHT!
I'LL SEND OUT AN ALARM, CHIEF! NOTIFY ALL STATES...
8

SO NOW THEY KNOW, HANLEY! YOUR LITTLE SECRET IS OUT...YOU MAKE ONE MISTAKE AND YOU'RE THROUGH...ONE MISTAKE, AND I GET YOU...
THIS ONE'S TOUGH! I'LL HAVE TO BLOW IT...I CAN'T SEEM TO OPEN IT!
AREN'T YOU FORGETTING SOMETHING, HANLEY? THERE'S A WATCHMAN IN THIS BUILDING! THIS MAY BE YOUR BIG MISTAKE....THIS MAY DO IT....
BOOM!
WHAT WAS THAT! SOUNDED LIKE IT CAME FROM THE OFFICE...... THE SAFE!
WHA...? THE ALARM! I'D BETTER SCRAM BEFORE EVERY COP IN TOWN GETS HERE...
R-I-I-N-N-G
NO NO, HANLEY! YOU CAN'T GO THAT WAY...THE LAW IS THERE! NOT THE OTHER WAY, EITHER...THE LAW'S THERE TOO! THE LAW IS EVERYWHERE...YOU CAN'T ESCAPE....
I'VE GOT TO RUN FOR IT!
ALRIGHT, BUDDY! STOP OR WE SHOOT!
BAAMMM!
BAMMMM!
9

THE LAW'S REVENGE!

SO NOW YOU'RE IN THE PRISON HOSPITAL, HANLEY! YOU'VE GOT PLANS...BIG PLANS...BUT...YOU'RE IN FOR A SURPRISE...

THEY DON'T KNOW WHO I AM! THEY CAN *ONLY* PIN THIS *ROBBERY* ON ME...HANLEY IS DEAD! THEY CAN'T PIN HIS KILLIN'S ON ME...I'LL GET A FEW YEARS...BUT I WON'T FRY...HEH...HEH!

HELLO, CHARLES HANLEY!

HUH? WHO? YOU GOT THE WRONG GUY!

NO WE HAVEN'T, HANLEY! WE'VE FINALLY CAUGHT UP WITH YOU...

HANLEY'S *DEAD!* HE WAS KILLED IN AN AUTO ACCIDENT! *HE'S DEAD...!!*

NO, HANLEY! THAT WAS RALPH DUNCAN YOU THREW OFF THAT BRIDGE! THE JIG'S UP, HANLEY! WE'VE GOT ALL THE PROOF WE NEED!

NO! NO! I'M *DEAD*, I TELL YOU... DEAD!

RAVE ON, CHARLES HANLEY, FOR SOON YOU *WILL* DIE...SOON YOU WILL PAY FOR YOUR CRIMES... AND LEARN THAT *CRIME DOESN'T PAY!*

CHARLES HANLEY! YOU HAVE BEEN FOUND GUILTY OF MURDER AND I HEREBY SENTENCE YOU TO DIE IN THE ELECTRIC CHAIR ON TUESDAY, NOV. 25 AT 12:01 A.M... MAY THE LORD HAVE MERCY ON YOUR SOUL!

NO! NO! NO! I DON'T WANT TO DIE...I DON'T WANT TO DIE!

PULL THE SWITCH, GUARD!

ZZZZZZZZZZT!

VICTOR WOLF & SAM BART
KIDNAPPERS

THEY TRIED TO PULL A SMART KIDNAPPING, BUT FOUND THAT THE F.B.I. WAS MUCH SMARTER! *

A TRUE CRIME STORY

TAKEN FROM THE FILES OF THE F.B.I.

DON'T! THEY'LL PAY THE RANSOM! WAIT A LITTLE LONGER... *PLEASE!*

THEY'D *BETTER* PAY *SOON*... IT'D BE A *SHAME* TO *SLIT* THAT LOVELY THROAT!

A. FELDSTEIN

*THE NAMES IN THIS TRUE CRIME STORY HAVE BEEN FICTIONIZED TO PROTECT INNOCENT PEOPLE INVOLVED!

VICTOR WOLF & SAM BART: KIDNAPPERS

ONE NIGHT IN APRIL 1947, ON A DARK STREET IN A MIDWESTERN TOWN...

HE'S LOCKING UP, NOW! HE'LL BE ALONG ANY MINUTE!

I HOPE HE'S GOT A PILE! WE'RE ALMOST BUSTED!

SHHH! HE'S CROSSING OVER! READY, NOW!

YEAH! I'M READY!

GOT A MATCH, BUDDY?

WHY... I...

DON'T MOVE, MISTER! THIS IS A STICK-UP!

NOW, JUST A MINUTE, FELLOWS...

AH, SHADDUP...!

CLUNK!

GO THROUGH HIS POCKETS, VIC! I'LL WATCH THE STREET!

YEAH, SAM!

QUICK! SOMEONE'S COMING!

I GOT HIS WALLET, LET'S SCRAM!

2

LATER... IN A DINGY FURNISHED ROOM...
THIRTY BUCKS!! THAT'S ALL THE BUM HAD ON HIM! A MEASLY THIRTY BUCKS!!
SHUT UP, SAM! DO YOU WANT SOMEONE TO HEAR YOU?
LISTEN, VIC! I'M SICK OF THIS PENNY-ANTE STUFF...LIVIN' IN FURNISHED ROOMS...EATIN' IN DIRTY LITTLE DIVES... I WANNA GO OUT AN' HAVE A GOOD TIME... LIVE IN A SWELL HOTEL... GO TO NIGHT CLUBS...GET SOME REAL DOUGH!
TAKE IT EASY, SAM! THIS LITTLE STUFF AIN'T MUCH BUT IT KEEPS THE COPS OFF OUR TAIL!
IF WE PULLED A BIG JOB LIKE A BANK OR SOMETHIN', EVERY COP IN THE COUNTRY WOULD BE LOOKIN' FOR US...
WHAT'S THE MATTER, HUH? YELLOW??
NOBODY CALLS ME "YELLOW"!! SEE?
CRACK!
OKAY, OKAY, VIC! I DIDN'T MEAN IT! LET'S FORGET IT!
AN' DON'T EVER CALL ME YELLOW AGAIN!
LATER...
HEY, BART! HERE Y'ARE! HERE'S TH' CHANCE TO MAKE SOME OF THAT BIG DOUGH YOU WANT!
WHERE, VIC, WHERE?
WHA...WHY THIS IS THE SOCIETY PAGE!
THAT'S RIGHT, AND THAT STORY ABOUT THAT DEBUTANTE GAVE ME THE IDEA!
3

WHAT'S THE IDEA, VIC?
THIS! IF WE COULD "SNATCH" HER... AND HOLD HER 'TILL HER FAMILY PAYS US...OH...SAY FIFTY GRAND...WITH A THREAT THAT IF THEY GO TO THE COPS...WE KILL HER...WHY THEY'D PAY OFF QUICK!
YEAH, AN' THEN WE COULD BEAT IT OUT OF THE COUNTRY, BEFORE THEY EVEN GET STARTED ON THE CASE! SOUNDS GREAT!
EXACTLY! NOW... HERE'S THE PLAN!
THE NEXT DAY AT THE VAN KOONES' ESTATE...
WHEN THAT CHAUFFEUR ROUNDS THIS CORNER...HE'S GONNA GET A SURPRISE!
CLUNK!
MEANWHILE...IN A PHONE BOOTH...
HELLO...MISS VAN KOONES? THIS IS YOUR DRESSMAKER, MISS VAN KOONES! CAN YOU COME DOWN TO THE SHOP FOR A SPECIAL FITTING? IT'S THE DRESS FOR YOUR DEBUT!
AND BACK AT THE VAN KOONES RESIDENCE...
WHO WAS IT, DEAR!
MY DRESSMAKER, MOTHER, I HAVE TO GO IN FOR A SPECIAL FITTING....
HENRY, WILL YOU HAVE WILLIAM BRING THE CAR AROUND?
YES, MODDOM!
4

VICTOR WOLF & SAM BART: KIDNAPPERS

YOUR FOLKS BETTER *PAY* THAT RANSOM, TOO, GIRLIE—OR IT'LL BE TOO BAD FOR YOU!
THEY'LL GET YOU TWO BEFORE THAT TIME COMES!
Y'KNOW, IT'D BE A SHAME TO SLIT YOUR LOVELY THROAT IF THEY DON'T!
WHY, YOU WOULDN'T DARE!
OH, NO?
CLICK!
EEEEEE...MMPH!
SHUT UP, YOU LITTLE FOOL! DO YOU WANT EVERY COP IN THE NEIGHBORHOOD HERE?
OOOOOWWW!
WHY YOU LITTLE *@*?X!
WHAM!
SOB... SOB...
THAT'LL TEACH YA TO GET SMART WITH SAM BART!
6

MEANWHILE...
AN' DON'T GO TO THE COPS OR YOU'LL NEVER SEE HER AGAIN... WRAP UP THE MONEY IN SMALL BILLS AND DROP IT FROM A CAR ON ROUTE 17 AT THE OLD SAWMILL!
WHAT ARE WE GOING TO DO, PAUL?
THERE'S ONLY ONE THING WE CAN DO, DEAR! CALL IN THE F.B.I.
BUT THEY SAID THEY'D KILL HER IF WE DID!
AND HOW DO WE KNOW THEY WON'T KILL JEAN AFTER WE PAY THE MONEY SO SHE CAN'T IDENTIFY THEM?
YOU WERE RIGHT, MR. VAN KOONES! THIS IS THE RIGHT THING TO DO! OUR MEN WORK FAST AND EFFICIENTLY! THERE WILL BE NO PUBLICITY ABOUT OUR BEING ON THE CASE!!! NOW! HERE'S WHAT YOU DO...
FOLLOWING THE INSTRUCTIONS OF THE F.B.I... MR. VAN KOONES DROPS A PACKAGE AT THE DESIGNATED SPOT AT THE DESIGNATED TIME!
WHEN THE KIDNAPPER PICKS UP THE PACKAGE, WE'LL TAIL HIM TO HIS HIDEOUT!
HERE COMES SOMEONE NOW, CHIEF!
HAH! LOOKS LIKE HE DONE WHAT HE WAS TOLD! HERE'S THE DOUGH! I'D BETTER SCRAM OUT OF HERE AN'... HMMM! MAYBE I'D BETTER COUNT IT FIRST!
7

WHAT TH..?? PAPER! A BUNDLE OF NEWSPAPER... THE DIRTY DOUBLE-CROSSING...
OKAY, MEN! HE'S ON TO IT! TAKE HIM!
UP WITH YOUR HANDS, YOU!
WHA...?? COPPERS! IT'S A FRAME-UP! YOU WON'T GET ME, COPPERS! NOBODY TAKES VICTOR WOLF!
RAT-A-TAT-A-TAT-A-TAT!
AAAAAAAAH!
IS HE DEAD?
YES, CHIEF! HE'S DONE FOR!
THIS IS A BAD BREAK, MEN! HIS CATCHING ONTO OUR TRICK RUINED EVERYTHING! WE'RE GOING TO HAVE TO WORK FAST NOW, IF WE'RE GOING TO SAVE THAT GIRL!
LATER, AT THE SHACK, SAM BART PACES THE FLOOR.
VIC SHOULD HAVE BEEN BACK BY NOW WITH THE DOUGH....
MAYBE HE GOT THE MONEY AND RAN OUT ON YOU....
AAH, HE WOULDN'T DO THAT TO ME! WHAT'S THAT? SOUNDS LIKE A CAR...
8

NAW! IT'S JUST A PLANE FLYIN' LOW...
MAYBE THEY CAUGHT HIM, AND NOW HE'S TELLING THEM WHERE THEY CAN FIND YOU!!
LISTEN, SISTER! IF THEY TRY TO TAKE ME, I'LL KILL YOU FIRST!
TWENTY MINUTES LATER...
HE SHOULD'A BEEN BACK BY NOW!!! MAYBE YOU WERE RIGHT! MAYBE THEY DID GET HIM! I GOTTA SCRAM OUT OF HERE...
BUT I AIN'T GONNA LEAVE YOU HERE TO TELL 'EM WHAT I LOOK LIKE... SO...
NO, DON'T..
ALL RIGHT IN THERE... THE HOUSE IS SURROUNDED!
COME OUT WITH YOUR HANDS UP... THIS IS THE F.B.I.
G-MEN! THEY WON'T GET ME... C'MON SISTER...
LISTEN, YOU COPPERS! I'M GETTIN' T' THAT CAR OVER THERE... OR THIS GIRL GETS IT IN THE BACK... TAKE YOUR CHOICE!
HOLD YOUR FIRE, MEN!
S'LONG, GIRLIE... THANKS FOR HELPIN' ME GET AWAY! I WON'T NEED YOU ANYMORE...
9

HELLO! HELLO! STATION ONE TO STATION TWO... HELLO! MIKE? FRED! STOP THE ROLLS-ROYCE HEADED YOUR WAY! ONE OF THE KIDNAPPERS IS TRYING TO GET AWAY IN IT...
HAW! HAW! PRETTY SLICK, SAM, EVEN IF I DO SAY SO MYSELF...
WHAT THE...?
RAT-TAT-TAT-TAT-TAT
RAT-A-TAT-A-TAT!
CRASH
AAAAAAAAH!
YEAH, MIKE, I HEARD IT! OKAY, BOYS! WRAP IT UP...THIS CASE IS FINISHED!
I DON'T KNOW HOW TO THANK YOU! TELL ME, HOW DID YOU FIND THE PLACE? DID THE OTHER HOODLUM TELL YOU?
NO! HE DIED BEFORE HE COULD TALK! IT WAS THE PILOT OF OUR OBSERVATION-SEARCH PLANE WHO SPOTTED THE ROLLS-ROYCE IN BACK OF THE SHACK! IT WAS HIDDEN FROM THE ROAD BUT NOT FROM THE AIR! HE THOUGHT IT WAS STRANGE THAT SUCH AN EXPENSIVE-TYPE CAR WAS PARKED NEXT TO SUCH A RUN-DOWN SHACK SO HE FLEW LOW AND INVESTIGATED! HE RECOGNIZED IT AS THE SAME ONE YOU WERE KIDNAPPED IN! THE REST WAS EASY...
OH, THEN THAT WAS THE LOW-FLYING PLANE WE HEARD!
10

MONEY-HUNGRY
NANCY BURTON'S* wild craving for money drove STEVE FAGIN into a career of CRIME!
A TRUE STORY FROM POLICE FILES
*THE NAMES AND PLACES IN THIS TRUE STORY ARE FICTIONAL IN ORDER TO PROTECT INNOCENT RELATIVES!
A. FELDSTEIN

MONEY-HUNGRY

HELLO, NANCY! READY TO GO?...WHA'SA MATTER? WHY AIN'T YOU DRESSED?

I'M NOT DRESSED BECAUSE I'M NOT GOING, STEVE!

YOU'RE NOT *GOING*? BUT...OUR DATE...I...I DON'T UNDERSTAND!

***YOU* DON'T UNDERSTAND? WELL, LISTEN CLOSELY, STEVE FAGIN, AND I'LL TRY TO MAKE IT CLEAR!**

...I'M SICK AND TIRED OF OUR "DATES"! CHEAP RESTAURANTS...TWO-BIT MOVIES...RIDING AROUND IN THAT TIN CAN YOU CALL A CAR...I'M *SICK* AND *TIRED* OF IT...

WHY CAN'T YOU TAKE ME OUT *SWELL*? GO TO NIGHT CLUBS...BUY ME JEWELS...A FUR COAT...GET A FLASHY CAR...*LOOK* LIKE SOMETHING...*TREAT ME RIGHT!!*

BUT, NANCY! YOU *KNOW* I CAN'T AFFORD THOSE THINGS!

THAT'S TOO BAD! WHY DON'T YOU *GET* YOURSELF SOME DOUGH?

BUT, NANCY! YOU KNOW I'M WORKING HARD AT MY JOB! MAYBE SOON I'LL GET A RAISE...AND SOMEDAY...WHO KNOWS...I MAY BE A MANAGER...IT TAKES TIME...

AND WHAT AM *I* SUPPOSED TO DO...THE MEANTIME...GROW OLD AND GREY...

BUT...I...

NO "BUTS", STEVE! YOU'D BETTER NOT BOTHER COMING *AROUND* ANYMORE...NOT UNTIL YOU'VE DONE SOMETHING ABOUT THIS! *GOODNIGHT!*

LATER... AT A NEARBY BAR...
WASHA MADDER...BUD? YOU LOOK SHO UNHAPPY!
AW, MY GIRL AND I HAD A LITTLE MISUNDERSTANDING!
OH, ISH THAT ALL? HAH! SHINK NUSHING OF IT, MY FREN'! HERE! LEMME BUY YOU A DRINK!
OH, NO THANK YOU! I WAS JUST LEAVING, ANYWAY!
PRIVATE
BUT I INSHISHT! BARTENDER. GIVE THISH MAN A DRINK!
WOW! LOOK AT THE PILE THAT GUY'S GOT! MUST BE PLENTY IN THAT ROLL!
IF I HAD THAT ROLL, I BET NANCY'S ATTITUDE WOULD BE A LOT DIFFERENT...
WHY NOT? I COULD FOLLOW THIS GUY AND...IT'D BE A CINCH!
WELL, SHO LONG FELLER! I GOTTA GO HOME, NOW!
OUTSIDE, STEVE FAGIN FOLLOWS THE DRUNK WITH THE BANKROLL UP NARROW DARK STREETS...
HE'S TURNING INTO THAT ALLEY! THIS PIECE OF PIPE WILL DO THE JOB NICELY!
CLUNK!
3

WHAT A CINCH! LE'ME SEE! TWENTY...FIFTY...ONE HUNDRED ...ONE HUNDRED AND FIFTY BUCKS! WOW! WHAT A HAUL!
HELLO...NANCY?...STEVE!! GET DRESSED...WE'RE GONNA PAINT THE TOWN...I'LL BE THERE IN TEN MINUTES!
LATER THAT NIGHT.
WELL, STEVE! THIS IS MORE LIKE IT!
HAVING A GOOD TIME, NANCY?
I'M HAVING A WONDERFUL TIME! BUT...WHERE DID YOU GET THE DOUGH?
DON'T ASK QUESTIONS...JUST ENJOY YOURSELF! LET ME WORRY ABOUT THAT!
WELL, G'NIGHT, STEVE! WHEN CAN YOU TAKE ME OUT AGAIN?
JUST AS SOON AS I CAN, NANCY! JUST AS SOON AS I CAN!
STEVE FAGIN'S CAREER IN CRIME HAD BEGUN! AFTER THAT IT WAS EASY! ON LONELY STREETS AND IN DARK ALLEYS HE WOULD DO HIS WORK...MUGGING...SNATCHING A PURSE...FAKING A HOLD-UP...
4

THIS FAKING HOLD-UPS WITHOUT A GUN IS NO GOOD! ONE OF THESE DAYS SOMEONE WON'T FALL FOR IT... I'VE GOT TO *GET* ONE!
THIS LOOKS LIKE AS GOOD A PLACE AS ANY...
GOOD AFTERNOON, SIR! WHAT CAN I DO FOR YOU!
I...WANT TO BUY A GUN! AN AUTOMATIC!
CERTAINLY! NOW HERE'S A SURPLUS ARMY "45" THAT I CAN LET YOU HAVE CHEAP!
Y' GOT ANY AMMUNITION TO GO WITH IT?
OH, OF COURSE! HERE, A CLIP FULL... AND A BOX OF 500 TO GO WITH THE SALE!
LE'SEE THE GUN!
HERE YOU ARE!
OKAY, NOW STICK 'EM UP AN' EMPTY THAT CASH REGISTER FOR ME... AN' BE QUICK ABOUT IT...!!
YES! YES! ONLY PLEASE BE CAREFUL! THAT GUN IS LOADED!
THEN DON'T TRY NO FUNNY BUSINESS AN' IT WON'T GO OFF!!!
5

BUT INSIDE THE CASH REGISTER DRAWER, THE CLERK REACHES FOR...
NOW! YOU DROP THAT...
NO, YOU DON'T!!
AAAAAAAAH!
BLAMM!
HE...HE'S DEAD! I'VE KILLED HIM! I...I...IT WAS AN ACCIDENT...I DIDN'T MEAN TO KILL HIM...I DIDN'T MEAN IT... I'VE GOT TO GET OUT OF HERE!
THE DOUGH! FIRST I'VE GOT TO TAKE THE DOUGH! THERE! NOW, I CAN BEAT IT!
HEY YOU! WHAT WAS THAT SHOT?
A COP!
PAWNBROKER
LOANS
BOUGHT
SOLD
EXCHANGED
BAAMMMMM!
6

NANCY, YOU'VE GOT TO HELP ME! I'M IN TROUBLE!
STEVE! WHAT'S THE MATTER?
I KILLED A GUY! IT WAS AN ACCIDENT! AN' THEN THE COP CAME AND... I SHOT... I HADDA GET AWAY...
KILLED A GUY...AND SHOT A COP..WHY? WHY?
IT WAS FOR YOU, NANCY! FOR YOU! I WAS DOIN' IT FOR YOU!
FOR ME? WHY, YOU CRAZY IDIOT!
BUT YOU WANTED MONEY, FURS, JEWELS...I WAS STEALIN' DOUGH FOR...
BUT NOBODY TOLD YOU TO KILL ANYBODY! NOW YOU'VE GOT TO GET OUT OF HERE....
BUT... LE'ME HIDE HERE...THEY'LL BE LOOKIN' FOR ME..!
NOBODY SAW YOU, DID THEY? YOU'LL BE SAFER AT YOUR OWN PLACE...SOMEONE MAY SEE YOU HERE AND GET SUSPICIOUS.. GO HOME AND LAY LOW 'TILL THIS BLOWS OVER...
OKAY, I GUESS YOU'RE RIGHT, NANCY! CALL ME AN' LEMME KNOW HOW YOU ARE...HUH? KEEP IN TOUCH WITH ME!
OH, STEVE! YOU'RE FORGETTING SOMETHING!
WHAT, NANCY? WHAT'D I FORGET?
THE MONEY! YOU DON'T WANT TO HAVE IT ON YOU IF THEY SHOULD STOP YOU...AND ASK QUESTIONS! BETTER LEAVE IT HERE...WITH ME!
7

MONEY-HUNGRY

LATER...
POLICE ARE STILL LOOKING FOR THE MAN WHO SHOT AND KILLED A PAWNBROKER WHILE ATTEMPTING A ROBBERY.... THEN KILLED A POLICEMAN WHILE ESCAPING...

THE PAWNBROKERS' ASSOCIATION HAS OFFERED A $5000 REWARD FOR INFORMATION LEADING TO THIS MAN'S ARREST...

5000 BUCKS! HOLY CHRISTMAS!

HELLO...POLICE DEPARTMENT...? THIS IS NANCY BURTON OF 225 LAFAYETTE STREET! IF YOU'LL GO TO 16 COLONIAL ROAD, YOU'LL FIND THE KILLER YOU ARE LOOKING FOR!!! YES! DID YOU GET *MY* NAME AND ADDRESS?

LATER...AT STEVE'S FLAT ON THE GROUND FLOOR 16 COLONIAL ROAD...

WHAT'S HAPPENED TO NANCY—WHY HASN'T SHE CALLED ME? OH, THAT MUST BE HER NOW!

KNOCK!!
KNOCK!!

NANCY, IT'S ABOUT TIME... *WHA*...? *COPS*!!!

DON'T TRY ANYTHING, FAGIN, AND YOU WON'T GET HURT.

HERE'S A GUN LIEUTENANT... A 45, TOO!

THERE'S BLOOD ON THIS GUY'S SUIT, LIEUTENANT!

LOOKS LIKE THAT TIP WAS OKAY! I GUESS SHE'LL GET THE REWARD!

REWARD? SHE? WHO'S GONNA GET A REWARD?

SOME GAL NAMED NANCY BURTON TIPPED US OFF WHERE TO FIND YOU! SHE'LL COLLECT A $5000 REWARD!

8

74

STOP HIM! HE JUMPED THROUGH THE WINDOW!
CRASH!
BLAMM! BLAMM!
I WINGED HIM, BUT HE GOT AWAY!
C'MON, BOYS!
AND... AT NANCY'S APARTMENT...
OH, BOY! 5000 BUCKS! WHAT I CAN'T DO WITH 5000 BUCKS! MINK COAT! YELLOW CONVERTIBLE!
STEVE!
NANCY...WHY DID YOU DO THIS TO ME? I THOUGHT YOU LOVED ME!
DON'T BE A FOOL... I NEVER LOVED YOU!
NANCY...WHAT ARE YOU SAYING?
ALL I WAS INTERESTED IN WAS MONEY AND A GOOD TIME... AND YOU WERE MY TICKET!
THERE HE IS, BOYS!
GRAB HIM!
OKAY, COPPERS! I'M READY NOW! I DON'T HAVE ANYTHING MORE TO LIVE FOR, ANYWAY!
9

NELL BAKER

SHE* KEPT ONE JUMP AHEAD OF THE LAW UNTIL IT CAME TO *MURDER!*

A TRUE CRIME STORY TAKEN FROM POLICE FILES

*IN CONSIDERATION OF INNOCENT PEOPLE INVOLVED IN THIS TRUE CRIME STORY, THE NAME NELL BAKER AND OTHER NAMES HAVE BEEN FICTIONIZED...

OUTSIDE OF CENTRALIA, ILLINOIS, ON A SPRING NIGHT IN 1946...

THIS IS THE PLACE, FRANK! THE TAVERN KEEPER CLOSES UP IN A FEW MINUTES!

I DUNNO, NELL! I NEVER DONE NOTHIN' LIKE THIS BEFORE!

LISTEN, FRANK! I'M TIRED OF TWO-BIT FURNISHED ROOMS AND CHEAP HONKY-TONKS! YOU AN' ME ARE GOING TO HIT THE BIG TIME! HERE, TAKE THIS!

WHA....?? A GUN!!

WHAT DID YOU *EXPECT* TO USE? A PEA-SHOOTER? NOW, HERE'S THE PLAN...
SORRY, FOLKS! THE BAR'S CLOSED FOR THE NIGHT! YOU'LL HAVE TO LEAVE...
'AT'S ALL RIGHT MR.! JUST PUT UP YOUR HANDS!
NOW EMPTY THE CASH REGISTER AN' MAKE IT SNAPPY!!
SURE! SURE! I DON'T WANT NO TROUBLE! HERE.!! *NOW YOU DROP THAT GUN!*
WHAT THE??
JUST STAND RIGHT THERE 'TILL I CALL THE POLICE...
SORRY, MR! BUT *I DON'T LIKE COPS!*
CLUNK!
NICE WORK, NELL!
GRAB THE DOUGH, FRANK...
I GOT IT, NELL! WHAT ABOUT HIM? MAYBE YOU *KILLED* HIM!
2

NAW, HE'S STILL BREATHIN'! LET'S SCRAM!
SURE THING, NELL!
IN A FURNISHED ROOM, AN HOUR LATER...
WHAT'LL WE DO NOW, NELL? THAT GUY KNOWS WHAT WE LOOK LIKE... HE'LL HAVE ALL THE COPS AROUN' LOOKIN' FOR US!
WE'RE LEAVIN' TOWN TONIGHT! WE GOT PLENTY OF DOUGH!
BUT IN A WEEK OF HIGH LIVING, THE MONEY WAS GONE! ONE NIGHT JUST SOUTH OF EFFING-HAM, ILLINOIS!
I CASED THE PLACE LAST NIGHT! HE DOES PLENTY OF BUSINESS... BUT IT GETS DEAD ABOUT NOW!
LET'S GO, THEN!
DINER
HOWDY, FOLKS! WHAT'LL IT BE??
REACH, BUDDY! THIS IS A STICK-UP!
I'LL KEEP A LOOKOUT, FRANK!
KRISP KRUNCH
NOBODY GETS MY DOUGH, SCUM!
FRANK! HE'S GOT A CLEAVER! LOOK OUT!! SHOOT FRANK! SHOOT!
AAAAAH!
THUD!
BLAMM!
EE-E-O-OW!
THE DOUGH! I GOT TO GET THE DOUGH!
NELL! GASP-- DON'T--LEAVE-- ME---
3

GET ME...TO A... DOC...I'M...BLEEDIN' BAD... GASP!
SURE FRANK... SURE!!
WHAT'S THAT? A CAR COMIN' THIS WAY! IT'S...IT'S TURNIN' INTO THE PARKIN' LOT! I GOTTA SCRAM!
BOY, LOOK AT THAT CAR TEAR OUT OF HERE! THAT GAL'S IN A HURRY!
JOE! LOOK! THERE'S A GUY LAYIN' OVER THERE! HE'S BLEEDIN'!
I'LL GO IN AND CALL AN AMBU-LANCE!
HEY, MIKE! THE COUNTERMAN'S BEEN SHOT! HE'S DEAD!
NEVER MIND THE AMBU-LANCE, JOE! THIS GUY'S DEAD TOO!
IN MATTOON, ILLINOIS, NELL...WORRIED THAT FRANK MAY TELL THE POLICE EVERY-THING...IS RELIEVED TO LEARN OF HIS DEATH! SHE BEGINS TO OPERATE ALONE! IN A NIGHT CLUB NEAR MATTOON....
THIS GUY MUST BE LOADED! HE'S WELL DRESSED...AND THAT SOLITAIRE HE'S WEARIN' MUST BE TWO CARATS, AT LEAST!
YOU SEE, JANE, MY WIFE DOESN'T UNDERSTAND ME....
(LISTEN TO THE OLD OIL!) ER...I'M TIRED! WOULD YOU LIKE TO DRIVE ME HOME...?
GULP...WOULD I!! OH, WAITER! CHECK, PLEASE!
4

LOVELY NIGHT, ISN'T IT, JANE?
YES, GEORGE! MAYBE YOU'D LIKE TO PARK FOR A WHILE AND WE COULD--- LOOK AT THE MOON.
HEH--HEH! WELL, HERE WE ARE!
BUT NOT FOR LONG, BUSTER! HAND OVER YOUR WALLET AND THAT DIAMOND RING AND GET OUT!
B-BUT I--I-- YOU CAN'T GET AWAY WITH THIS!
OH, CAN'T I--- YOU'RE GOING TO HAVE A TOUGH TIME EXPLAINING THIS TO THE POLICE!
54-412
BE SMART, BUSTER! FORGET IT! YOU'LL FIND YOUR CAR BACK AT THE CLUB! HAVE A NICE WALK!
I'LL LEAVE HIS CAR, PICK UP MINE AT THE CLUB, AND KEEP GOING UNTIL I'VE LEFT THIS BURG BEHIND!
NELL BAKER WOULD STRIKE SWIFTLY-- THEN MOVE ON.. ALWAYS TRAVELING...
ONE NIGHT IN DECATUR—
LET'S HAVE THE BAG, LADY! I SAW YOU DRAW THE DOUGH OUT OF THE BANK!
THE NEXT NIGHT IN CHAMPAIGN...
OKAY, MR.! HAND IT OVER!
IN KANKAKEE, NELL WAS THE LAST CUSTOMER TO LEAVE A BEAUTY SHOP...
I CAN'T LET THIS OPPORTUNITY GO BY...THIS GUY MUST HAVE A REGISTER FULL...HE'S CLOSED TO MORE CUSTOMERS! THE SHADES ARE DRAWN...IT'S A CINCH!
5

OKAY, MR! FORK OVER THE MOOLA AND MAKE IT TOOT-SWEET!
OH, BUT YOU ARE JOKING WEETH FRANCOIS!
$1
KEEP AWAY, BUDDY! I MEAN BUSINESS! THE DOUGH! QUICK!
BUT, NO, YOU CANNOT BE SERIOUS...THEES EES A PRANK! ZE GUN! PUT IT DOWN! YOU WEEL HURT SOMEONE....
LEGGO OF THE ROD— CHUMP!
GEEV EET TO ME!
SURE, FELLOW! I'LL GIVE IT TO YOU! TAKE IT!
BAAMM!! BAMMM!!
AND SO...NELL BAKER ADDED ANOTHER CRIME TO HER BOOK— MURDER....!!
CHUMP!
BUT, NELL BAKER WAS SOON TO LEARN WHO WAS THE CHUMP! WITHIN AN HOUR, THE WHEELS OF JUSTICE WERE TURNING, FASTER AND FASTER
LITTLE PIECES OF A GIANT PICTURE PUZZLE BEGAN TO FIT INTO PLACE... THE NOOSE WAS TIGHTENING!
THE WAY I SEE IT, CHIEF, THE CRIME WAS COMMITTED BY SOMEONE WHO HAD BEEN INSIDE THE STORE! THE DOOR WAS LATCHED FROM THE INSIDE! THE SHADES DRAWN!
PERHAPS A CUSTOMER! THERE WAS CUT HAIR ALL AROUND THE CHAIR...IF HE HAD BEEN THROUGH FOR THE DAY, HE WOULD HAVE SWEPT IT UP...
YES! THE GIRL WHO ROBBED MY TAVERN HAD THAT COLOR HAIR! THERE WAS A MAN WITH HER, TOO! THAT'S HIS PICTURE.
THAT'S THE MAN WE FOUND OUTSIDE THE DINER...THE GIRL WHO GOT AWAY HAD THAT COLOR HAIR!

SHE ROBBED ME OF MY DIAMOND RING AND WALLET! OF COURSE I CAN DESCRIBE HER...
SHE HAD FUNNY-SHAPED EYES.. TOOK MY POCKETBOOK WITH ALL MY SAVIN'S!
STEVE! GET ME AN ARTIST! I HAVE AN IDEA!
SURE THING, CHIEF!
LADIES AND GENTLEMEN! THIS IS WILLIAM SENIAG, A NEWSPAPER ARTIST! I WANT YOU EACH TO DESCRIBE THE GIRL AS BEST AS YOU CAN... MR. SENIAG WILL ATTEMPT TO DRAW HER PORTRAIT!
WHILE SENIAG IS IN THERE WITH THOSE WITNESSES, STEVE, I WANT YOU TO LOOK AT THIS MAP!
SURE CHIEF, WHAT ABOUT IT?
I'VE MARKED OFF THE CITIES IN WHICH THESE CRIMES TOOK PLACE AND NUMBERED THEM CHRONOLOGICALLY... SEE HOW THEY PROGRESS NORTHWARD THROUGH THE STATE! THIS GAL IS HEADED FOR CHICAGO.
CHICAGO
JOLIET
KANKAKEE 6
SPRINGFIELD
5 CHAMPAIGN
4 DECATUR
3 MATTOON
2 EFFINGHAM
1. CENTRALIA
NOW, KANKAKEE IS HERE, AND CHICAGO, THERE! BETWEEN THEM IS JOLIET! UNLESS I MISS MY GUESS, THIS GIRL WILL STOP IN JOLIET NEXT! WHEN SENIAG FINISHES THAT PORTRAIT, SEND IT TO THE POLICE IN JOLIET, TO BE DISTRIBUTED TO RESTAURANTS, GAS STATIONS, BEAUTY PARLORS — EVERY PLACE SHE MAY STOP!
CHICAGO
JOLIET
KANKAKEE 6
5
7

THE NEXT DAY...IN JOLIET, ILLINOIS...
I GOTTA CHANGE THE WAY I LOOK BEFORE THEY GET TOO HOT ON MY TRAIL! THIS BEAUTY SHOP OUGHT TO DO!
BEAUTY SHOP
HAIRDRESSER
GOOD AFTER-NOON, MADAM... ER...WHAT CAN I DO FOR YOU?
I D LIKE TO HAVE MY HAIR DYED! BLACK!
OF COURSE! WON'T YOU SIT DOWN IN THE FIRST BOOTH? I'LL BE WITH YOU SHORTLY!
OKAY, BUT I'M IN A HURRY!
CHECKING THE PICTURE GIVEN TO HIM BY THE JOLIET POLICE, THE BEAUTY PARLOR OPERATOR MAKES A HURRIED CALL...
IT'S HER! SHE'S HERE IN MY SHOP... HURRY!
WE'LL BE RIGHT OVER, CHARLES-THANKS!
OKAY SISTER! PUT UP YOUR HANDS!
YOU'RE UNDER ARREST!!
COPS!!
FACED WITH THE WITNESSES AND EVIDENCE GATHERED BY THE ILLINOIS POLICE, IN COOPERATION WITH LOCAL POLICE AUTHOR-ITIES...NELL BAKER CONFESSED TO HER LONG RECORD OF ROBBERIES AND MURDER!
OKAY! OKAY! I DID IT! I DID IT! I KILLED HIM! NOW...LEAVE...ME...ALONE!
8
ON SEPT. 2, 1946 NELL BAKER WAS SENTENCED!
NELL BAKER! YOU, BY YOUR OWN CONFESSION, ARE GUILTY OF MURDER! YOU SHALL BE PUT TO DEATH 12:01 A.M. DEC. 1, 1946 IN THE MANNER PRESCRIBED BY THE LAW OF THE STATE, AND MAY THE LORD HAVE MERCY ON YOUR SOUL...
NO! NO!
NELL BAKER'S CAREER IN CRIME WAS OVER! BY BRILLIANT POLICE WORK AND WITH THE COOPERATION OF THE WITNESSES, ANOTHER CRIMINAL HAD BEEN BROUGHT TO JUSTICE.

YOUR NEWSDEALER
HE IS YOUR FRIEND!

Panel 1:
- AW, HE CAN'T COMPARE WITH PEE-WEE REESE.
- WHAD'YA MEAN CAN'T COMPARE... HE'S *BETTER!?*
- TALK ABOUT BASEBALL, LOOK WHO'S COMIN'! HANK CARTER, THE STAR OF THE HIGHSCHOOL BASEBALL TEAM!

Panel 2:
- HY, HANK!
- WHAT SAY, HANK?
- HOW'S A-BOY, HANK?
- HY FELLERS! LET A GUY THROUGH, HUH?

Panel 3:
- MAKE WAY, GUYS! LET 'IM THROUGH!
- SAY, FELLERS! AREN'T YOU MAKING IT KINDA ROUGH ON MR. NEWSDEALER?

Panel 4:
- WHY, HANK? WE AIN'T BOTHERING HIM!
- NO, BUT YOU'RE HANGING AROUND BLOCKING THE ENTRANCE TO THE STORE! *YOU* MAY BE HAVING FUN BUT YOU'RE DISTURBING *HIS* CUSTOMERS...I'LL BET YOU EVEN SCARE SOME AWAY...

Panel 5:
- AFTER ALL, GUYS, MR. NEWSDEALER HAS TO MAKE A LIVING JUST LIKE YOUR DAD AND MINE! YOU GUYS BUY YOUR SODAS AND CANDY AND MAGAZINES FROM HIM, SURE... BUT HE DOESN'T ONLY DEPEND UPON YOUR BUSINESS... HE HAS TO SELL THINGS TO LOTS OF OTHER PEOPLE! AN' YOU GUYS HANGING AROUND MAKE IT HARD TO DO THAT...! AN' IF HE CAN'T MAKE HIS BUSINESS PAY, HE'LL CLOSE... AN' *THEN* WHERE WILL YOU GET YOUR SODAS AND CANDY AND COMICS!

Panel 6:
- THANKS, HANK! I LIKE THE BOYS FINE, BUT IF THEY'D JUST BUY WHAT THEY WANTED AND THEN GO DOWN TO THE PLAYGROUND OR "Y", IT'D BE BETTER ALL AROUND...
- WELL, MR. NEWSDEALER! I THINK THEY REALIZE IT NOW...THEY WON'T TROUBLE YOU AGAIN!

THE CRAIG GANG

A TRAIL OF ROBBERY AND MURDER FOLLOWED THEM THROUGH THE SOUTH...BUT A WOMAN SPELLED THEIR DESTRUCTION!

A TRUE CRIME STORY TAKEN FROM FBI FILES

*IN CONSIDERATION OF INNOCENT PEOPLE INVOLVED IN THIS TRUE CRIME STORY---ALL NAMES HAVE BEEN FICTIONIZED!

A. FELDSTEIN

THE CRAIG GANG

THAT NIGHT, JACK CRAIG AND BLANCHE CARTER BEGAN AN ASSOCIATION THAT WAS DESTINED TO END TRAGICALLY FOR BOTH...
LET'S GET MARRIED, BLANCHE! I GOTTA LEAVE TOWN AN' I DON'T WANT TO GO WITHOUT YOU!
I HARDLY KNOW YOU, JACK! BUT I'LL TAKE A CHANCE...
...SO THEY WERE MARRIED! THEIR HONEYMOON COTTAGE WAS A TOURIST CABIN JUST OUTSIDE OF MEMPHIS! ONE MORNING THEY HAD VISITORS!
HI'YA, JACK, OL' BOY!
SAY! WHO'S THE DAME?
WATCH DAT KINDA TALK, AL!
...THIS IS MY WIFE, BLANCHE!
YOUR WIFE!
JACK! YOU GONE CRAZY!
ER--BLANCHE, TAKE A WALK, HONEY! MY FRIENDS AND I GOT SOME BUSINESS TO DISCUSS!
SURE, JACK!
HOW WE GONNA OPERATE WITH A WOMAN ON OUR TAILS, JACK?
DITCH HER, JACK! SHE'S TROUBLE!
SHADDUP!
I'M THE BOSS HERE, AN' WHAT I SAYS GOES! SHE STAYS! AND DATS FINAL!
I DON'T LIKE IT, JACK! I DON'T...
CRACK!
OOOOOF!
3

NOBODY ASKED YOU! IF YOU DON'T LIKE IT, *GET OUT!*
OKAY, JACK! OKAY! YOU WIN! YOU'RE THE BOSS!
NOW, HERE'S THE PLAN! WE GET OURSELVES A PLACE AROUND HERE... PULL OUR JOBS IN NEIGHBORING TOWNS AND SCRAM BACK, DITCHING THE GETAWAY CAR ALONG THE WAY! WE LAY LOW 'TILL THE HEAT'S OFF, THEN STRIKE AGAIN! HOW'S IT SOUND?
OKAY, WIT ME, JACK!
WHAT ABOUT *YOU,* AL?
SOUNDS ALL RIGHT! I'M GAME!
BLANCHE! I WANTYA TO MEET MY BROTHERS, AL AN' MARC!
YOUR BROTHERS?
YEAH! THEY'RE GONNA LIVE WITH US FER A WHILE!
OH! I... SEE!
THE CRAIG GANG HOLED UP IN A LITTLE CABIN ABOUT FORTY MILES FROM MEMPHIS! THEY SEEMED LIKE A RESPECTABLE FAMILY! BUT EVERY ONCE IN A WHILE THEY WENT ON A "BUSINESS TRIP!"
SO LONG, HONEY! BE BACK THE DAY AFTER T'MORROW!
GOOD LUCK, JACK!
IN JACKSON, TENNESSEE, THEY HIT THE NATIONAL BANK...
THE *GUARD!* HE'S GOT A *GUN!*
TAKE *THAT, SUCKER!*
BLAMM!
4

OKAY, BOYS! LET'S GO!
C'MON BOYS! THE ALARM'S GONE OFF!
IN BLYTHEVILLE, ARKANSAS...
KEEP 'ER RUNNIN' MARC! WE'LL BE RIGHT BACK!
MAKE IT SNAPPY, JACK!
BANK
EVERYBODY AGAINST THE WALL!
A HOLD-UP!
IT AIN'T NO CLAMBAKE, LADY! LET'S HAVE THE DOUGH, YOU GUYS!
AN' KEEP YOUR HANDS AWAY FROM THOSE ALARMS!
TELLER
THE CRAIG GANG APPEARED IN LITTLE ROCK... NASHVILLE...EVEN MEMPHIS ITSELF...THEN THEY DISAPPEARED AS QUICKLY AS THEY CAME...
LINE UP!
THIS IS A STICK-UP!
DON'T ANY-BODY MOVE!
THE POLICE WERE BAFFLED...THE FBI WAS CALLED IN...
WE CAN'T TELL WHERE THEY WILL STRIKE NEXT! THEIR GETAWAY CAR IS ALWAYS FOUND...BUT WE CAN'T TRACE THEM AT ALL! THEY DISAPPEAR FOR WEEKS AT A TIME... THEN TURN UP OUT OF NOWHERE!
I SEE! GIVE ME ALL THE FACTS AND FIGURES! MY DISTRICT OFFICE WILL GET TO WORK!
MEANWHILE...BLANCHE CRAIG HAS BECOME SULLEN...
JACK! LET'S GET OUT OF HERE! I DON'T LIKE IT! YOU LEAVE ME ALL ALONE FOR DAYS AT A TIME! WHERE DO YOU GO? WHAT DO YOU DO?
BUSINESS, I TELL YUH! WE GO ON BUSINESS TRIPS!
5

WHAT KIND OF BUSINESS, JACK? YOU NEVER TOLD ME ANYTHING ABOUT IT.
THERE'S NUTHIN' T' TELL BLANCHE!
WELL, WHY CAN'T WE LIVE *IN* MEMPHIS, INSTEAD OF THIS WILDERNESS?
WE CAN'T, THAT'S ALL...WE *CAN'T*!
YOU DON'T LOVE ME ANYMORE! YOU DON'T... *YOU DON'T*...
BLANCHE!! *COME BACK HERE*!
MAYBE SHE'LL SQUEAL T' THE COPS, JACK!
FERGET IT! SHE DOESN'T KNOW ANYTHING! SHE'LL COME BACK!
DIS PLACE IS GETTIN' ON MY NERVES JACK! LET'S SPLIT THE LOOT AN' SPLIT UP!
WE GOT ONE MORE JOB... THE *BIG* ONE! THEN WE'RE THROUGH! WE'LL EACH HAVE 75 GRAND, THEN!
THE FEDERAL RESERVE BANK IN MEMPHIS IS GETTING A SHIPMENT OF OLD MONEY... TO BE SHIPPED BACK TO THE MINT... WE'RE GONNA GET IT!
FEDERAL RESERVE BANK! SOUNDS FISHY T' ME! I DON'T LIKE IT!
YOU'LL DO WHAT I SAY, MARC! I'M THE BOSS HERE AN' DON'T YOU FORGET IT!
OKAY, JACK OKAY! WHAT'S THE PLAN!
6

MEANWHILE...AT THE FBI DISTRICT OFFICE IN MEMPHIS...
NOW HERE'S A MAP WE'VE WORKED UP, MEN! NOTICE HOW THE GET-AWAY CARS WERE ALL ABANDONED EAST OF MEMPHIS IN THIS GENERAL AREA...
BUT THAT DOESN'T MEAN TOO MUCH, CHIEF!
---NOT BY ITSELF! BUT IF YOU TAKE INTO CONSIDERATION THE PLACES OF THE VARIOUS HOLDUPS... IT SEEMS THAT, FROM OUR REPORTS, THE GETAWAY ALWAYS HEADED BACK IN THIS GENERAL DIRECTION!
THEN... YOU MEAN, THEY'RE HIDING OUT SOME-WHERE IN THAT AREA?
I DO! PUT SOME MEN ON IT AND REPORT IN DAILY!
THE NEXT MORNING...AT THE CRAIG HIDEOUT!
THIS IS THE LAST "BUSINESS TRIP" HONEY! I PROMISE IT!
C'MON, JACK! LET'S GET GOING!
LAST ONE! HMMPH! THAT HAS A FAMILIAR RING! IF I DIDN'T LOVE HIM SO MUCH I'D LEAVE HIM, TODAY!
A LITTLE LATER...AN FBI MAN, DRESSED AS A HUNTER APPEARED AT THE CRAIG HIDEOUT...
YES, WHAT CAN I DO FOR YOU?
I WONDER IF I COULD USE YOUR TELEPHONE, LADY! MY CAR'S STUCK ABOUT A MILE BACK!
I'M SORRY, BUT I HAVEN'T A PHONE! CAN I GIVE YOU A CUP OF COFFEE?
WHY, THAT'D SURE HIT THE SPOT MA'AM!
7

LONELINESS HAS AFFECTED BLANCHE...FOR THE FIRST TIME SHE HAS SOMEONE TO TALK TO...SLOWLY SHE TELLS THE FBI MAN HER TROUBLES?
I GUESS A GIRL CAN GET PRETTY LONESOME OUT HERE! THOSE "BUSINESS TRIPS" TAKE HIM AWAY FOR DAYS AT A TIME!
YOU LIVE ALONE?
OH, NO! MY HUSBAND'S TWO BROTHERS LIVE WITH US...BUT THEY GO WITH HIM! THEY MUST BE IN BUSINESS TOGETHER!
OH, DO THEY? I SUPPOSE THEY HAVE A CAR?
FUNNY THING! EVERY TIME THEY COME BACK FROM A TRIP...THEY BUY A NEW ONE! NEVER COME BACK WITH THE OLD ONE! THEY CELEBRATE, I GUESS!
THAT'S THE STORY, CHIEF! IT'S THEM ALRIGHT! AND THEY'RE ON ANOTHER JOB....SO YOU'D BETTER NOTIFY ALL LOCAL POLICE DEPARTMENTS TO BE ON THE ALERT!
GOOD WORK, THOMPSON! WE'LL SEND SOME MEN UP THERE IMMEDIATELY!
AND WHEN THE CRAIG GANG APPEARED IN MEMPHIS, THE LOCAL POLICE AND FBI WERE WAITING...
JACK! LOOK! COPS!
IT'S A TRAP!
LET'S SCRAM!
THEY'RE AFTER US.....
STEP ON IT!
EEEEEEEEEEEEE!
RAT-TAT-TAT-TAT-TAT!
YOU GOT 'EM! THEY'RE SWERVING!
8

CRASH!
LOOK! ONE OF THEM'S GETTIN' AWAY INTO THE WOODS!
AFTER HIM, MEN! DON'T LET HIM GET AWAY!
THESE TWO IN THE CAR ARE DEAD!
LATER...AT THE CRAIG HIDEOUT..
JACK! WHAT'S HAPPENED? YOU'RE HURT!
SO...YOU SNITCHED! YOU TOLD 'EM WE WERE COMING!
TOLD WHO? I DON'T KNOW WHAT YOU'RE TALKING ABOUT!
WHY YOU...
JACK CRAIG!! THIS IS THE FBI! COME OUT WITH YOUR HANDS UP!
LISTEN, YOU MUGS! LEMME GET TO THAT CAR WITH THIS DAME OR SHE GETS IT IN THE BACK!
JACK! YOU'RE- YOU'RE NOTHING BUT A CHEAP CROOK!
BLANCHE! COME BACK OR I'LL KILL YOU!
SHE BROKE AWAY FROM HIM! LET HIM HAVE IT, MEN!
9
RAT-TAT-TAT-TAT-TAT!
A-A-A-AAAH!
FBI BULLETS MARKED THE END OF JACK CRAIG...A VIOLENT END TO A VIOLENT CAREER! BLANCHE CRAIG WAS CLEARED OF DIRECT PARTICIPATION IN THEIR CRIMES AND IS NOW LIVING IN A LARGE WESTERN CITY.... SO CONTINUES THE WAR AGAINST CRIME!

REVENGE CAME TO BIG-JIM DILLON* IN...

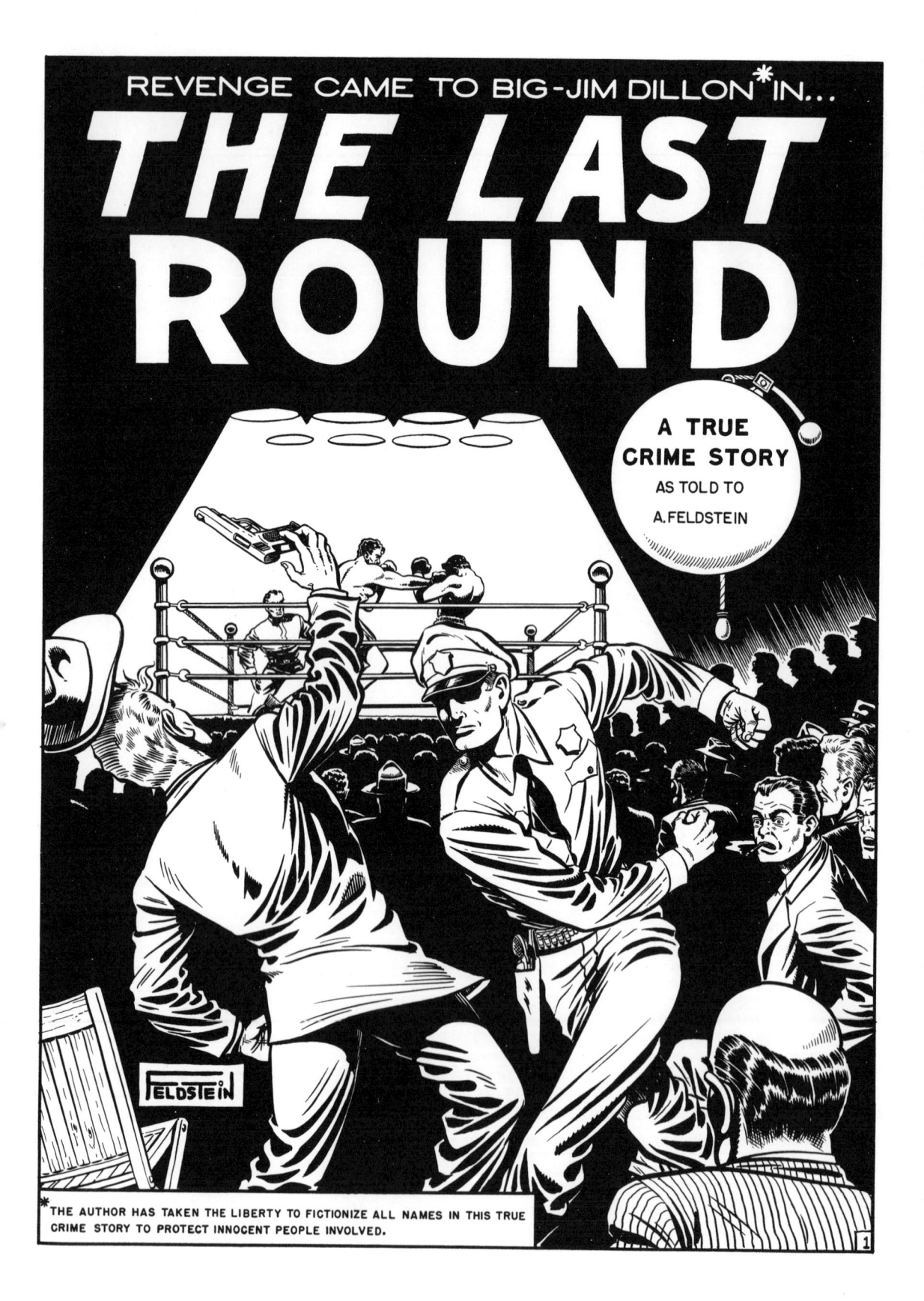

THE LAST ROUND

A TRUE CRIME STORY
AS TOLD TO A. FELDSTEIN

*THE AUTHOR HAS TAKEN THE LIBERTY TO FICTIONIZE ALL NAMES IN THIS TRUE CRIME STORY TO PROTECT INNOCENT PEOPLE INVOLVED.

IN THE SPACE OF SIX SHORT MONTHS SINCE I HAD JOINED BIG JIM DILLON'S ORGANIZATION, I HAD WORKED MYSELF UP TO BECOMING HIS RIGHT-HAND MAN. BIG JIM LIKED ME... I SAW TO THAT... AND HE TOOK ME WITH HIM WHEREVER HE WENT!
COME ON, FREDDY! THERE'S A SPOT ON THE EAST SIDE THAT'S REFUSING TO COOPERATE!
OKAY, DILLON! LET'S GO!
BIG JIM DILLON WAS THE MOST FEARED RACKETEER IN THE MID-WEST. HE HEADED A FABULOUS SYNDICATE OF PUGS AND GANGSTERS, EX-BOOTLEGGERS, NIGHT-CLUB OPERATORS, AND INNOCENT CITIZENS FORCED INTO JOINING!
I'LL TEACH THEM THAT NOBODY SAYS "NO" TO BIG JIM DILLON!
WANT MY ROD, DILLON?
DO YOU THINK I'M A SAP, FREDDY? I WOULDN'T LET THE COPS GET ANYTHING ON ME... LIKE THAT! NO! THESE KNUCKLES WILL DO THE JOB WELL ENOUGH!
THE EAST SIDE SPOT WAS A NIGHT CLUB THAT HAD REFUSED TO JOIN DILLON'S "PROTECTIVE SOCIETY". WHEN WE ARRIVED, THE SHOW WAS GOING ON...
YES, SIR... HOW MANY... OOOOFF!
OUT OF MY WAY! I WANT TO SEE YOUR BOSS!
DILLON FLUNG OPEN A DOOR MARKED "PRIVATE." A MAN BEHIND THE DESK JUMPED TO HIS FEET...
WHAT IS THE MEANING OF THIS..?
SIT DOWN, CHUMP! I HAVE SOMETHING I WANT TO SAY!
MY BOYS TELL ME THAT YOU DON'T WANT TO BRING YOUR JOINT INTO OUR ORGANIZATION! THAT ISN'T A HEALTHY ATTITUDE TO TAKE, MISTER! I CAN MAKE IT DIFFICULT FOR YOU...
BUT, I CAN'T MAKE ANY DEALS, NOW! I DON'T OWN THE PLACE ANYMORE!
WELL, GET ME THE NEW OWNER... I WANT TO TALK TO HIM!
I... HE'S OUT FRONT, BEING INTRODUCED TO THE CROWD...! ER... WHY DON'T YOU TAKE A TABLE AND WATCH?
2

THE LAST ROUND

WE SAT DOWN AT A TABLE AS THE LAST ACT FINISHED UP! BIG JIM PUFFED ON HIS CIGAR, AND I COULD SEE THAT HE WAS FUMING! HE WASN'T THE TYPE TO BE KEPT WAITING...SUDDENLY THERE WAS A FANFARE AND...

LADIES AND GENTLEMEN! "CLUB 27" TAKES GREAT PLEASURE IN PRESENTING ITS NEW OWNER...THE *FORMER HEAVYWEIGHT CHAMPION OF THE WORLD*... *WILLIAM "BILLY" JORDON*...

THERE WAS A ROUSING OVATION FOR JORDON! TWENTY YEARS BEFORE, HE HAD BEEN THE NATION'S IDOL....THE WORLD'S HEAVYWEIGHT CHAMPION! THEN HE HAD SLIPPED INTO OBSCURITY WITH HIS DEFEAT...I GLANCED AT BIG JIM...HE HAD PALED!

WE SINCERELY HOPE THAT YOU WILL CONTINUE TO PATRONIZE "CLUB 27" WHERE YOU...

DILLON! WHAT'S *WRONG?* YOU LOOK *SICK!*

LET'S GET OUT OF HERE, FREDDY, QUICKLY.

BUT, DILLON! WHAT ABOUT TALKING TO THIS GUY JORDON?

NEVER MIND...FORGET IT! LET'S GO!

BUT JORDON WAS WAITING AT THE EXIT...

WELL, WELL! BIG JIM DILLON! SO AT LAST WE MEET AGAIN! *YOU REMEMBER* OUR LAST MEETING, DILLON! DO YOU REMEMBER *WHAT I PROMISED?* I'M BACK TO CARRY IT OUT, DILLON! I'M *BACK!*

I...YOU... C'MON, FREDDY! LET'S GO!

BIG JIM WAS VISIBLY SHAKEN! WE RETURNED TO HIS LUXURIOUS APARTMENT...

P...POUR ME A DRINK, FREDDY!

SURE, CHIEF! SURE!

HERE Y'ARE! NOW, WHAT'S UP, DILLON? I NEVER SAW YOU LIKE THIS BEFORE!

IT WAS JORDON. HE WAS THE *LAST* MAN I *EVER* WANTED TO *SEE*...

WHAT DID HE MEAN ABOUT THE *PROMISE*, DILLON?

HE...HE'S GOING TO... *KILL ME!*

3

BUT... WHY?
IT'S A LONG STORY...GOES BACK TWENTY YEARS...BACK WHEN I WAS A FIGHTER...AND MY ORGANIZATION WAS SMALL... SMALL AND STUPID! I FINALLY WORKED UP TO A STAB AT THE CHAMPIONSHIP...IT MEANT EVERYTHING TO ME...MONEY... FAME...
"THIS GUY JORDON WAS CHAMP AT THE TIME! HE WAS HEAVILY FAVORED... I SCRAPED TOGETHER ALL THE MONEY I COULD....ALMOST TEN GRAND..."
NOW, IF WE CAN GET JORDON TO THROW THE FIGHT, WE'LL MAKE OVER A HUNDRED "G"'S, AND I'LL ALSO BE THE CHAMP!
YEAH, BUT HOW YOU GONNA GET HIM TO DO IT...? HE'S HONEST AS THE DAY IS LONG...
SIMPLE! YOU AND BURT GRAB HIS WIFE AN' KID, AND HOLD 'EM TILL AFTER THE FIGHT...HE'LL HAVE TO COME ACROSS!!
BUT, DILLON! THAT'S KIDNAPPING!
"THAT NIGHT, BURT AND MARTY VISITED MRS. JORDON IN HER SUBURBAN HOME..."
GET THE KID, MRS. JORDON! BILLY WANTS US TO TAKE YOU OUT TO THE TRAINING CAMP!
I...BUT...WHAT FOR?
HE'S WORRIED ABOUT LEAVING YOU ALONE HERE WHILE HE'S TRAINING FOR THE FIGHT!
IT'S FOR YOUR OWN PROTECTION!
"THEY DROVE HER TO A SECLUDED SHACK OUTSIDE OF TOWN...SHE AND HER FOUR YEAR OLD SON..."
THIS ISN'T BILL'S TRAINING CAMP! WHAT'S THE MEANING OF THIS?
SHADDUP, AN' GET INSIDE!
"...AFTER MRS. JORDON WAS SAFELY HIDDEN AWAY, WE GOT IN TOUCH WITH THE CHAMP..."
...AND IF YOU EVER WANT TO SEE YOUR WIFE AND KID ALIVE AGAIN, JORDON...YOU'LL TAKE A FALL IN THAT FIGHT TONIGHT!
WHY...!! YOU DIRTY...
4

THE LAST ROUND

JORDON KNEW WE HAD HIM...HE CAME INTO THE RING A BEATEN MAN! FOR NINE ROUNDS I POUNDED HIM...AND FINALLY, HE FELL TO THE CANVAS...BROKEN! HE HADN'T LIFTED A HAND IN SELF DEFENSE.

8...9...10...
YOU'RE OUT!

THE CROWD WENT WILD...AND I WAS THE NEW HEAVYWEIGHT CHAMPION OF THE WORLD...

AFTER THE FIGHT, WE HAD A LITTLE PARTY IN MY APARTMENT! AT THE HEIGHT OF FESTIVITIES, BURT CAME IN...HIS FACE SCRATCHED...TERROR IN HIS EYES...

BURT!! WHAT ARE YOU DOING HERE? WHY AREN'T YOU WITH MRS. JORDON?

JIM!! SOMETHIN' WENT WRONG.

WHAT HAPPENED?

IT'S THE JORDON DAME! SHE TRIED TO GET AWAY BEFORE THE FIGHT...I TRIED TO STOP HER...AN' THEN...MARTY SLUGGED HER WITH HIS GUN!

SO...SO...
C'MON!
WHAT'S WRONG?

SHE...SHE'S BEEN UNCONSCIOUS FOR FOUR HOURS NOW...I...I THINK SHE'S GOT A FRACTURE OR SOMETHING!!

YOU STUPID IDIOTS!
THAT NIGHT WE DUMPED HER AND HER KID ON HER FRONT LAWN...SHE DIED THE NEXT MORNING...BILLY JORDON CAME TO SEE ME THAT DAY...
DILLON! I CAN'T PROVE ANYTHING, BUT SOMEDAY I'LL SQUARE THINGS...SOMEDAY I'LL GET EVEN WITH YOU...IF I HAVE TO *KILL* YOU!
AND NOW HE *HAS* COME BACK, FREDDY! HE'S COME BACK TO GET ME!
WHAT ARE YOU WORRIED ABOUT, DILLON? WHY DON'T YOU HAVE THE BOYS RUB HIM OUT...
YEAH...YEAH...THAT'S IT...I'LL HAVE THEM TAKE HIM FOR A RIDE...YEAH...GET LOUIE, CHUCK, JACK...AN' CURLY!
SURE, CHIEF! I'LL CALL 'EM RIGHT NOW!
TWO DAYS LATER...
BIG JIM!! LOOK AT THIS!!
WHA...?? THEY GOT MY BOYS!! THE COPS GOT MY BOYS!! IT'S THAT JORDON!! *HE'S OUT TO GET ME!!*
DAILY HERALD
FOUR SEIZED IN ATTEMPTED MURDER
POLICE FOIL GANG ATTEMPT TO TAKE JORDAN FOR 'RIDE'
AFTER THAT, MANY OF BIG JIM'S OPERATIONS BEGAN TO FAIL...HIS HENCHMEN WERE ARRESTED RIGHT AND LEFT...THE SYNDICATE WAS BREAKING UP...
IT'S *JORDON!* HE KNOWS ALL MY PLANS... HE TELLS THE COPS AN' THEY GET MY BOYS...HE'S AFTER *ME!!*
MAYBE ONE OF THE BOYS WILL TALK, DILLON... AND IMPLICATE YOU...
6

NO! NOBODY'S GOT ANYTHING ON BIG JIM DILLON! ANYTHING THAT WILL IMPLICATE ME IS IN MY SECRET WALL SAFE...
MAYBE YOU'D BETTER DESTROY, IT, DILLON!
...AND GIVE UP ALL I WORKED FOR! NEVER! NEVER! I'LL GET JORDON FIRST!!
LOOK, DILLON! THERE'S A NOTE... SLIPPED UNDER THE DOOR...
BIG JIM... REVENGE IS SWEET! SOON YOU WILL BE ALONE...YOUR GUNMEN GONE...AND YOUR POWER GONE TOO... THEN I WILL TAKE MY REVENGE! Jordon
IT WAS TOUGH ON BIG JIM AFTER THAT...HE WAS NERVOUS AND FRIGHTENED! HIS MEN EITHER WERE ARRESTED OR LEFT HIM...HIS SYNDICATE WAS COMPLETELY DESTROYED...
FREDDY...YOU'RE THE ONLY ONE I HAVE LEFT...YOU'VE GOT TO HELP ME, FREDDY! YOU'VE GOT TO PROTECT ME FROM JORDON!
SURE DILLON! SURE! IF YOU NEED ME YOU KNOW WHERE I'LL BE!
FEAR STRUCK AT THE HEART OF BIG JIM DILLON...EVERYWHERE HE WENT HE WAS HAUNTED BY THE SPECTRE OF "BILLY" JORDON... FOLLOWING HIM...
NO!
NO!
NO! NO! FREDDY! FREDDY!!!
7

THE LAST ROUND

YOU BET I'M MAD, BIG JIM! FIGHTING MAD...
ENOUGH...JORDON...I... I'VE...HAD...ENOUGH!
NOT YET...DILLON! NOT YET...YOU HAVEN'T!
9

THE LAST ROUND

ALL RIGHT... YOU'D BETTER STOP BEFORE YOU KILL HIM!

Y...YES! I'D BETTER...

MY WIFE'S DEATH IS AVENGED...

YOU...!! YOU...!!

HELLO... BIG JIM!

FREDDY! YOU! A COPPER!!

YES, DILLON... AND THANKS FOR THE CONTENTS OF THE SAFE! THAT WILL PUT YOU AWAY FOR A LONG TIME! WHEN I BECAME A POLICEMAN, I REQUESTED THIS ASSIGNMENT... TO JOIN YOUR GANG... AND BRING YOU TO JUSTICE! IT WAS ONLY RIGHT THAT *I* DO IT...

YOU SEE, DILLON, THE WOMAN WHOSE DEATH YOU WERE RESPONSIBLE FOR... MRS. JORDON... WAS... *MY MOTHER!*

YOUR NEWSDEALER--HE IS YOUR FRIEND!

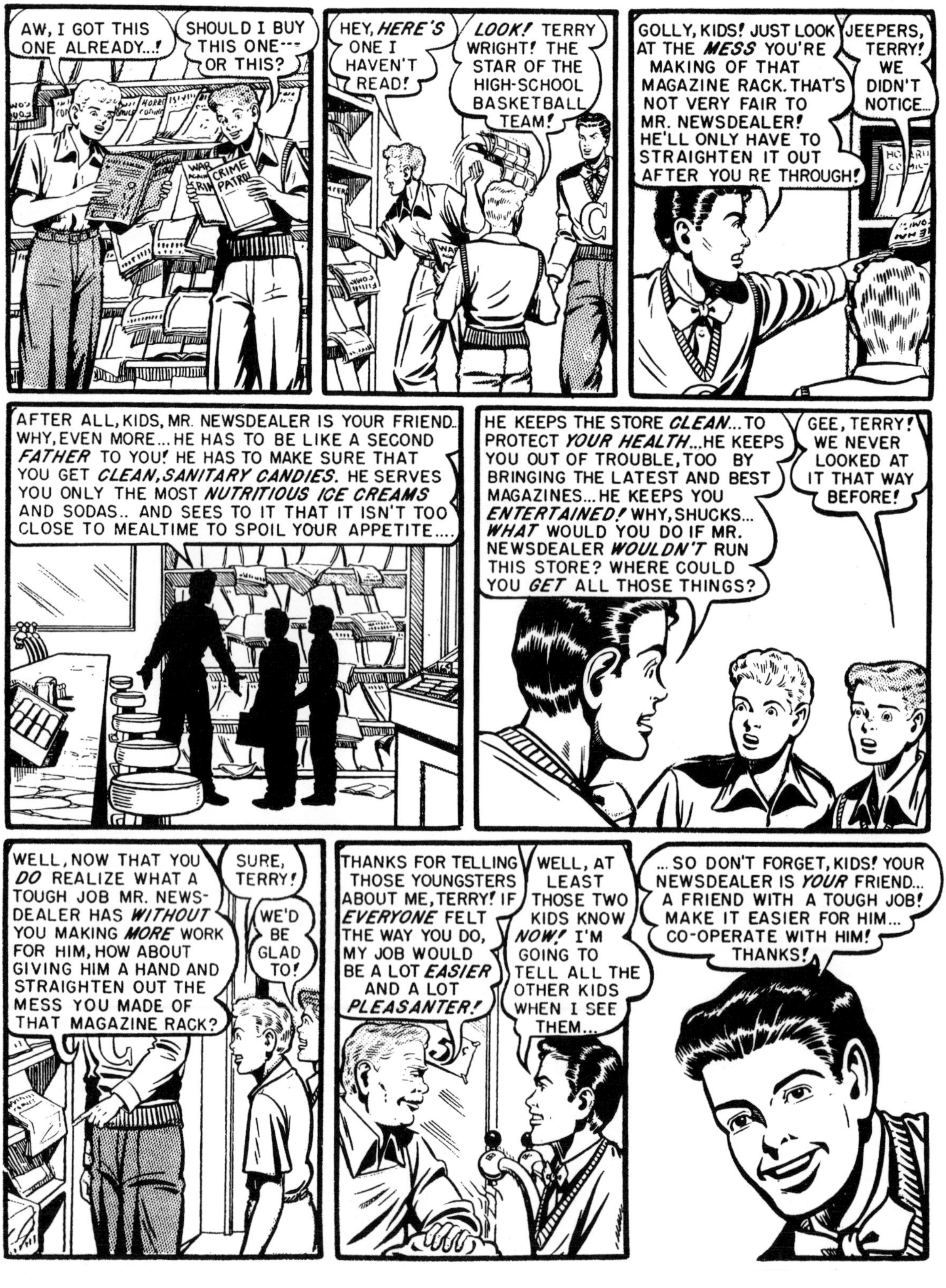

THE CASE OF THE FLOATING CORPSE!

A TRUE POLICE DETECTIVE FEATURE

WORK *WITH ME*, DETECTIVE-LIEUTENANT CRAIG DIXON* OF THE NEW YORK CITY HOMICIDE SQUAD, AS I UNRAVEL THIS BAFFLING CRIME AND TRACK DOWN

"THE GUILTY!"

*ALL NAMES IN THIS TRUE POLICE DETECTION STORY HAVE BEEN FICTIONIZED TO PROTECT INNOCENT PEOPLE EITHER DIRECTLY OR INDIRECTLY INVOLVED.

LATE ONE DARK NIGHT IN THE SUMMER OF 1947, A BLACK CAR STOPPED ON A WHARF OVER THE EAST RIVER. . . A SHADOWY FIGURE PULLED A LIMP FORM FROM THE CAR...
...AND DROPPED IT INTO THE MURKY, OIL-SLICKED WATER BELOW...
SEVERAL DAYS LATER... AS A TUG MADE ITS WAY UP RIVER...
LOOK, CAP'N! IT'S A DEAD MAN!
PULL ALONGSIDE... WE'LL HAUL 'IM ABOARD!
THE POLICE WERE NOTIFIED AND THE BODY WAS BROUGHT TO THE CITY MORGUE...
WHAT'S THE STORY, CORONER?
THIS MAN'S BEEN SHOT! YOU'D BETTER NOTIFY HOMICIDE!
I RECEIVED THE CALL AT MY APARTMENT...
DEAD ABOUT FOUR DAYS, EH? OKAY, FRED! I'LL BE RIGHT DOWN!
THERE IT WAS... A CORPSE... DEAD FOUR DAYS... NO WALLET OR OTHER VISIBLE MEANS OF IDENTIFICATION. . . JUST A MAN... OUT OF A TEEMING CITY! AND OUT IN THAT CITY... SOMEWHERE... WAS HIS MURDERER!
POLICE WORK... ESPECIALLY ON A CASE LIKE THIS... IS MOSTLY ROUTINE... IT FOLLOWS A REGULAR PLAN ...UNGLAMOROUS...TIRESOME...MONOTONOUS...NOT LIKE YOU SEE IN MOVIES OR READ ABOUT IN DIME NOVELS...BUT IT USUALLY GETS RESULTS...
CLANCY...THIS SUIT IS A CUSTOM-TAILORED JOB.. SEE IF YOU CAN FIND OUT WHO MADE IT...THE LABEL'S BEEN TORN OUT...
2

YES... MONOTONOUS ROUTINE... ENDLESS QUESTIONS... AND THEN ...A BREAK...
YES... THAT'S MY WORK... I CAN TELL! I'LL LOOK UP MY RECORDS AND TELL YOU WHO I MADE IT FOR!
HELLO, CHIEF! CLANCY! I GOT THE INFORMATION! THE SUIT WAS MADE FOR CARL BLAKE, 1701 EAST 92ND STREET...
GOOD WORK, CLANCY! I'LL GET RIGHT OVER THERE...
HERE WAS ANOTHER DISTASTEFUL JOB... I HAD TO BREAK THE NEWS TO BLAKE'S WIDOW.
SOB... SOB...
I... I'M SORRY... MRS. BLAKE! BUT IF YOU CAN COMPOSE YOURSELF FOR A MINUTE, I'D LIKE TO ASK A FEW QUESTIONS!
...GO AHEAD... I'D... LIKE TO HELP YOU... IF I CAN!
DO YOU KNOW WHO MIGHT HAVE DONE THIS, MRS. BLAKE?
NO... I CAN'T SAY OFFHAND! CARL HAD BEEN WORKING FOR ABOUT FOUR MONTHS FOR A GEORGE GRANGER... HE OWNS A NIGHT CLUB... THE GREEN SWAN. HE NEVER TOLD ME MUCH ABOUT HIS BUSINESS!
WAS THERE ANYTHING STRANGE ABOUT HIS ACTIONS, LATELY?
HE DID SEEM NERVOUS AND IRRITABLE RECENTLY... BUT HE NEVER TOLD ME WHAT WAS WRONG...
I SEE! WELL, THANK YOU VERY MUCH, MRS. BLAKE! I'LL SPEAK TO YOU AGAIN!
3

THE GREEN SWAN WAS A HOT SPOT IN GREENWICH VILLAGE. WHEN I ARRIVED...IT WAS EMPTY...EXCEPT FOR A GIRL REHEARSING FOR THE EVENING PERFORMANCES...
EXCUSE ME! I'M FROM HOMICIDE! I'M LOOKING FOR MR. GRANGER!
HOMICIDE!! I... HE'S IN HIS PRIVATE OFFICE!
GRANGER WAS A TOUGH-LOOKING LARGE MAN... HE CHEWED AN EXPENSIVE CIGAR AND DRESSED WELL... TOO WELL FOR A MAN WHO OWNED SUCH A SMALL CLUB.
WELL, DETECTIVE! WHAT CAN I DO FOR YOU?
DO YOU KNOW A CARL BLAKE, MR. GRANGER?
SURE...HE WORKED FOR ME TILL ABOUT TWO WEEKS AGO! I FIRED HIM! ANYTHING WRONG?
HE'S DEAD, GRANGER! ...BEEN SHOT!
OH? THAT'S TOO BAD! I...I'M SORRY I CAN'T HELP YOU, DETECTIVE!
I AM TOO... GRANGER! I'LL BE SEEING YOU AGAIN, THOUGH!
AS I MADE MY WAY TOWARDS THE EXIT...THE GIRL WHO WAS REHEARSING HER NUMBERS STOPPED ME...
I'VE GOT TO SEE YOU...I OVERHEARD ABOUT CARL...
MEET ME AFTER THE SHOW TONIGHT IN THE SIDE ALLEY!
THAT NIGHT...AFTER HER SONG...TONI THOMAS MET ME IN THE APPOINTED PLACE...
WHAT IS IT YOU WANT TO TELL ME...?
I KNOW WHO KILLED CARL BLAKE!
SUDDENLY I FELT A SHARP BLOW ON MY HEAD--- AND THEN THE WHOLE WORLD CAME DOWN ON ME ...AS I SLIPPED INTO A POOL OF BLACKNESS!
4

THE CASE OF THE FLOATING CORPSE!

WHEN THE COBWEBS CLEARED, AND THINGS CAME BACK INTO FOCUS...TONI WAS GONE... I LOOKED AROUND...

CLOSE TO MY FOOT WAS A PACK OF MATCHES. I PICKED IT UP... IT WAS FROM A MOTOR COURT OUTSIDE OF TOWN...

ONLY ONE MATCH HAD BEEN DISTURBED... IT WAS BENT IN HALF... BUT NOT TORN OUT! I HOPED THAT THIS WAS A CLUE THAT TONI HAD DROPPED FOR ME TO FIND! I HAD TO CHANCE IT! I HAD REACHED A STONE WALL, ANYWAY!

IT WAS AN HOUR'S DRIVE TO THE MOTOR COURT. I PARKED JUST DOWN THE ROAD AND WALKED OVER SO AS NOT TO AROUSE SUSPICION...

INSIDE ONE OF THE CABINS, TONI WAS BOUND AND GAGGED... A THUG GUARDING HER... I COULD SEE THEM THROUGH A TEAR IN THE SHADE...

...GOT TO SURPRISE HIM!... GET HER AWAY FROM HERE!

I EDGED AROUND TO THE PORCH... A LOOSE BOARD CREAKED...

WHAT WAS THAT? SOUNDED LIKE SOMEBODY OUTSIDE ON THE STEPS... THINK I'LL TAKE A LOOK...

THE DOOR OPENED... I PRESSED BACK AGAINST THE WALL... DEEP IN SHADOW...

...DON'T SEE ANYONE!

C'MON, BUDDY! STEP OUT HERE!

THE THUG REMAINED IN THE DOORWAY... THE SECONDS SEEMED LIKE HOURS...HE HAD TO STEP OUTSIDE FOR ME TO SURPRISE HIM... BUT HE DIDN'T MAKE A MOVE... I FELT AROUND IN MY POCKET.
MY BADGE!...
I TOSSED MY BADGE ACROSS THE DARK SHADOWS TO THE SIDEWALK... IT SHATTERED THE SILENCE! THE THUG STARTED...THEN STEPPED FORWARD...
WHAT WAS THAT? ALL RIGHT, YOU! C'MON OUTTA THERE!
DROP IT! DROP THE GUN, BIG BOY!
WHA...?
NOW GET INSIDE...
SUDDENLY THE THUG GRABBED THE DOOR... AND SWUNG IT! IT CAUGHT MY WRIST...AND THE GUN WENT CLATTERING ACROSS THE FLOOR...
SURE... LEMME CLOSE THE... DOOR!
OOOOF!
GOTTA GET THE GUN!
NO, YOU DON'T!
WE WRESTLED FOR POSSESSION OF THE AUTOMATIC.
...NOT IF I HAVE ANYTHING TO SAY ABOUT IT...
...YOU AIN'T...GOT NOTHIN'...TO SAY...
6

HE'S OUT COLD! NOW TO GET TONI OUT OF HERE!
THANK GOODNESS YOU'VE COME... MR. DIXON...
CRAIG TO YOU...TONI! YOU'LL BE FREE IN A MINUTE!
THE CAR'S JUST DOWN THE ROAD! C'MON!
AS WE REACHED MY CAR...WE SUDDENLY WERE BATHED IN LIGHT...
ANOTHER CAR'S COMING!
QUICKLY! GET IN!
HEY, WILLIE! THAT WAS THE DAME...
TURN AROUND...THE BOSS'LL HAVE US WIPED OUT IF SHE GETS AWAY!
7

THE CASE OF THE FLOATING CORPSE!

CRAIG... THEY'RE FOLLOWING US!

HOLD ON, HONEY! THIS IS GOING TO TAKE SOME FANCY DRIVING!

THEY'RE GAINING ON US, CRAIG...

THERE'S A SHARP TURN UP AHEAD, TONI... IF WE CAN MAKE IT WITHOUT SLOWING DOWN WE MAY LOSE THEM!

WHEW! THAT WAS CLOSE!

LOOK OUT, WILLIE!!

BACK AT HEADQUARTERS...TONI TOLD ME ALL SHE KNEW! I LEFT IMMEDIATLY TO PICK UP BLAKE'S MURDERER...ON THE WAY I STOPPED AT A PHONE BOOTH ....I HAD A PLAN...

NOW TO GET DOWN TO THE GREEN SWAN!

DIXON...WHAT DO *YOU* WANT!

I'VE GOT TONI AT HEADQUARTERS, GRANGER! I'VE COME FOR YOU!

YOU WON'T GET ME, DIXON... I'LL...
NO, YOU WON'T, GRANGER...
YOU'LL COME QUIETLY!
OOOF...
TONI'S TOLD ME EVERYTHING! SHE WAS LEAVING HER DRESSING ROOM WHEN SHE SAW YOU CARRY BLAKE'S BODY TO YOUR CAR...
NO! NO!
I DUMPED HIM... YEAH, BUT I DIDN'T KILL HIM ...YOU CAN'T PIN A MURDER ON ME... IT WAS...
GEORGE!
WHAT'S HE DOING HERE? WHAT DID YOU WANT TO SEE ME ABOUT?
SHE DID IT! SHE KILLED HIM!
SHE MADE ME GET RID OF THE BODY! BUT... SHE KILLED HIM! WE WERE IN LOVE. CARL WOULDN'T GIVE HER A DIVORCE. WE HAD A SCENE... HERE AT THE OFFICE...SHE PULLED A GUN FROM HER BAG!
YOU FOOL!! HE TRICKED YOU! HE COULDN'T HAVE PROVEN ANYTHING! HE DIDN'T KNOW ABOUT ME!
TONI! HE'S GOT TONI... SAFE!
THEN, WHY DID YOU CALL ME TO COME HERE? WHY DIDN'T YOU WARN ME?
NO, MRS, BLAKE! I CALLED YOU! YOU SEE, I KNEW YOU WERE IN ON THE MURDER OF YOUR HUSBAND WHEN YOU PULLED THIS SUIT LABEL FROM YOUR BAG ALONG WITH YOUR HANDKERCHIEF WHEN I LAST SAW YOU! THE QUESTION WAS... WHICH ONE OF YOU DID THE KILLING? NOW I KNOW!
9

THE FATAL TURN

THIS IS HOW IT BEGAN... A TWISTED MASS OF METAL AND FABRIC... THE GRIM REMAINS OF ONE OF THE MOST DIABOLICAL AND FIENDISH PLOTS TO COLLECT INSURANCE THAT I HAVE EVER BEEN ASSIGNED TO PROBE...

A TRUE INVESTIGATION STORY

BY
LEE MAXWELL
SPECIAL INVESTIGATOR
FOR
THE CONSOLIDATED MUTUAL
INSURANCE COMPANY*

* IN ORDER TO CONCEAL THE IDENTITIES OF PEOPLE, PLACES, AND COMPANIES INVOLVED IN THIS TRUE CRIME STORY, ALL NAMES HAVE BEEN FICTIONIZED!

THE MORNING AFTER THIS TRAGIC ACCIDENT OCCURED, I WAS SITTING IN MY OFFICE AT CONSOLIDATED MUTUAL WHEN...
WELL, LEE! I LOOKED OVER THE SCENE OF THE ACCIDENT! LOOKS LIKE THIS GUY CONLON COLLECTS AGAIN...
AGAIN! WHY? HAS HE COLLECTED BEFORE?
YEAH! ABOUT TWO YEARS AGO, A SIMILAR ACCIDENT OCCURED TO HIS WIFE... SAME SPOT, TOO... AND HE COLLECTED $20,000 INCLUDING A DOUBLE INDEMNITY ON HER... FROM COSMOPOLITAN LIFE!
AND NOW HE GETS $30,000 FROM US FOR THE ACCIDENTAL DEATH OF HIS BROTHER-IN-LAW!
LOOK, LEE! THIS WHOLE THING'S A LITTLE FISHY! MIND IF I INVESTIGATE ON MY OWN TIME?
GO AHEAD, BAKER! THIRTY GRAND IS A LOT OF DOUGH TO SAVE THE COMPANY!
I'LL KEEP IN TOUCH WITH YOU, LEE! LET YOU KNOW IF I UNCOVER ANYTHING!
SURE, BAKER! BUT TAKE CARE OF YOURSELF!
I DIDN'T HEAR ANYTHING FROM BAKER ABOUT THE CONLON CASE FOR ABOUT TWO MONTHS AFTER THAT. THEN, ONE NIGHT, THE TELEPHONE WOKE ME FROM A SOUND SLEEP...
H...HELLO!
LEE..? THIS IS BAKER! I GOT SOMETHING ON THE CONLON CASE...SOMETHING HOT!
I CALLED HIM AND HE'S AT HIS PLACE! I'M DRIVING UP THERE NOW TO TALK TO HIM ABOUT IT...I THINK HE REALIZES I KNOW SOMETHING...
BAKER! DON'T BE A FOOL! YOU...
CLICK!
HE HUNG UP ON ME BEFORE I COULD STOP HIM...I GOT OUT OF BED! IT WAS USELESS TO TRY TO INTERCEPT HIM BEFORE HE GOT TO CONLON'S HOTEL... HE HAD A TWO-HOUR HEAD START! I CALLED CONLON AT HIS HOTEL...IT WAS A SUMMER RESORT AND THE SEASON WAS OVER! THERE WAS NO ANSWER!
SHALL I TRY AGAIN, LATER, SIR?
YES, OPERATOR! KEEP TRYING!
2

MEANWHILE BAKER'S CAR TURNED ONTO ROUTE 31, THE MOUNTAIN ROAD THAT LED TO THE CONLON HOTEL...
THE ROAD WOUND ITS WAY ALONG A MOUNTAINSIDE...THE STEEP FACE OF THE MOUNTAIN TO ONE SIDE... A CLIFF... A SHEER DROP OF 300 FEET...TO THE OTHER...
SUDDENLY, AS HE SPED ALONG, OUT OF THE INKY BLACKNESS AHEAD, TWO PINPOINTS OF LIGHT KNIFED THE DARKNESS...
THE ONCOMING LIGHTS GREW STEADILY LARGER...A CAR WAS RAPIDLY APPROACHING FROM THE OPPOSITE DIRECTION...
BAKER'S GRIP GREW TIGHTER ON THE WHEEL! THE HEADLIGHTS WERE BEARING DOWN THE CENTER OF THE ROAD... BLINDING HIM! SUDDENLY THEY WERE ALMOST UPON HIM! HE SWUNG HIS WHEEL TO AVOID A HEAD-ON COLLISION.
A-A-A-A-A-A-A-A-A-A-A-A-A-A-A-A-H-!
THE NEXT MORNING, I LEARNED OF HIS DEATH! I WAS HEARTSICK! BAKER HAD BEEN MY ABLEST ASSISTANT! I DROVE OUT TO THE SCENE OF THE ACCIDENT! CONLON WAS THERE ARGUING WITH A STATE TROOPER AS I DROVE UP!
...BUT, IF YOU CLOSE THE ROAD YOU'LL RUIN MY BUSINESS! YOU CAN'T DO THAT! WHY DON'T YOU INSTALL LAMPS ON THOSE POLES...
WELL, WE'LL HAVE TO DO SOMETHING! THREE DEATHS IN THE SAME SPOT...THAT'S TOO MUCH...
3

THE FATAL TURN

THE SCENE OF THESE HARROWING ACCIDENTS WAS A SHARP TURN IN THE ROAD! THERE WAS A WIRE-ROPE FENCE ALONG THE CLIFFSIDE THAT HAD BEEN TORN THROUGH BY THE CAR AS IT PLUNGED OFF! EVEN A SIGN STRATEGICALLY PLACED, ADVERTISING CONLON'S HOTEL THREE MILES AHEAD, WARNED OF THE TURN! I COULD NOT FIGURE HOW THREE DIFFERENT PEOPLE COULD MISS THE SAME TURN AND GO HURTLING TO THEIR DEATH... IT WAS A STRANGE COINCIDENCE! I BEGAN TO SNOOP AROUND, EXAMINING EVERY INCH OF THE AREA... THE SKID MARKS... THE BROKEN WIRE-ROPE FENCE... THE POWER-LINE POLES... THERE WAS NOTHING... NOT A CLUE INDICATING THERE HAD BEEN ANY FOUL PLAY...

3 MORE MILES TO THE CONLON HOTEL

I MADE MY WAY DOWN THE SIDE OF THE CLIFF TO WHERE BAKER'S CAR HAD COME TO A STOP! IT WAS TOTALLY DESTROYED! NO ONE COULD HAVE POSSIBLY LIVED THROUGH THAT PLUNGE...

ABOUT 300 YARDS FROM THE CAR WAS A FARMHOUSE! A MAN WAS WORKING IN THE FIELD ADJACENT TO IT! I DECIDED TO ASK HIM WHAT HE KNEW... HE STOPPED HIS WORK AS I APPROACHED!

HOWDY, STRANGER! TOO BAD ABOUT THAT INSURANCE FELLER!

YES! CAN YOU TELL ME ANYTHING THAT MIGHT HELP? I'M FROM THE CONSOLIDATED MUTUAL INSURANCE COMPANY!

SAME OUTFIT, EH?

WHY YES! DID YOU KNOW HIM?

YEP! CAME TO SEE ME AFTER THAT OTHER FELLER WAS KILLED A COUPLE OF MONTHS AGO! I TOLD HIM ALL I KNEW! ASKED ABOUT THAT WOMAN THAT WAS KILLED HERE TWO YEARS AGO, TOO... I REMEMBER *THAT* ONE ALSO!

WHAT DID HE ASK YOU?

HE ASKED ME WHAT I HAD HEARD... THE SCREECH OF THE BRAKES... THE FALLING CAR... I TOLD HIM I DIDN'T HEAR BUT *ONE* CAR... AND THAT THE CAR DIDN'T HIT *ANYTHING* 'TILL IT LANDED DOWN BELOW... HE GOT PRETTY EXCITED... I HEARD THE *SAME* THINGS LAST NIGHT...

4

THE FATAL TURN

THE FATAL TURN

THEN I CALLED CONLON! I WANTED TO SEE HIM... TO CONFRONT HIM WITH THE EVIDENCE I HAD DISCOVERED---

MR. CONLON? THIS IS LEE MAXWELL OF CONSOLIDATED! I'D LIKE TO SEE YOU ABOUT YOUR BROTHER-IN-LAW'S INSURANCE...

THIS IS A STRANGE TIME TO CALL ON BUSINESS, MR. MAXWELL!

IT'S ABOUT ARRANGEMENTS FOR PAYING THE $30,000! I'M SURE YOU'RE INTERESTED!

I'LL BE HERE IF YOU CARE TO DROP IN...

AGAIN I WAS ALERT AS I PASSED THE FATAL TURN IN THE ROAD AND MY LIGHTS FELL ON THE HOTEL SIGN... BUT MY CAR HUGGED THE ROAD AND I BREATHED A SIGH OF RELIEF AS I SWUNG BY...

3 MORE MILES TO THE CONLON HOTEL

CONLON MET ME AT THE DOOR...HE INVITED ME IN AND OFFERED ME A DRINK...

NO, THANK YOU, MR. CONLON! THIS IS NO SOCIAL VISIT! I HAVE SOME UNPLEASANT NEWS! MY COMPANY IS POSTPONING PAYMENT OF YOUR CLAIM PENDING FURTHER INVESTIGATION!

WHAT? FOR WHAT REASON? THE POLICE CALLED IT AN ACCIDENT!

NOT ON THE BASIS OF NEW EVIDENCE THAT I HAVE DISCOVERED!

W...WHAT EVIDENCE?

THE WIRE-ROPE FENCE THAT BAKER CRASHED THROUGH WAS *CUT*... BY A *HACKSAW!*

YOU'RE *CRAZY!*

THINK SO, CONLON? NOT AS CRAZY AS *YOU* WERE TO PULL THIS THREE TIMES! I'LL KEEP AFTER YOU TILL I GET THE GOODS ON YOU...DAY AND NIGHT...I'LL GET YOU, CONLON! *I'LL GET YOU!!*

GET OUT! GET OUT!

119

THE FATAL TURN

I GOT OUT!!! CONLON WAS FURIOUS! JUST WHAT I WANTED! AN ANGRY MAN MAKES MISTAKES! WHEN I PASSED THE TURN IN THE ROAD, THE HIGHWAY PATROL WAS REMOVING THE CUT WIRE ROPE!

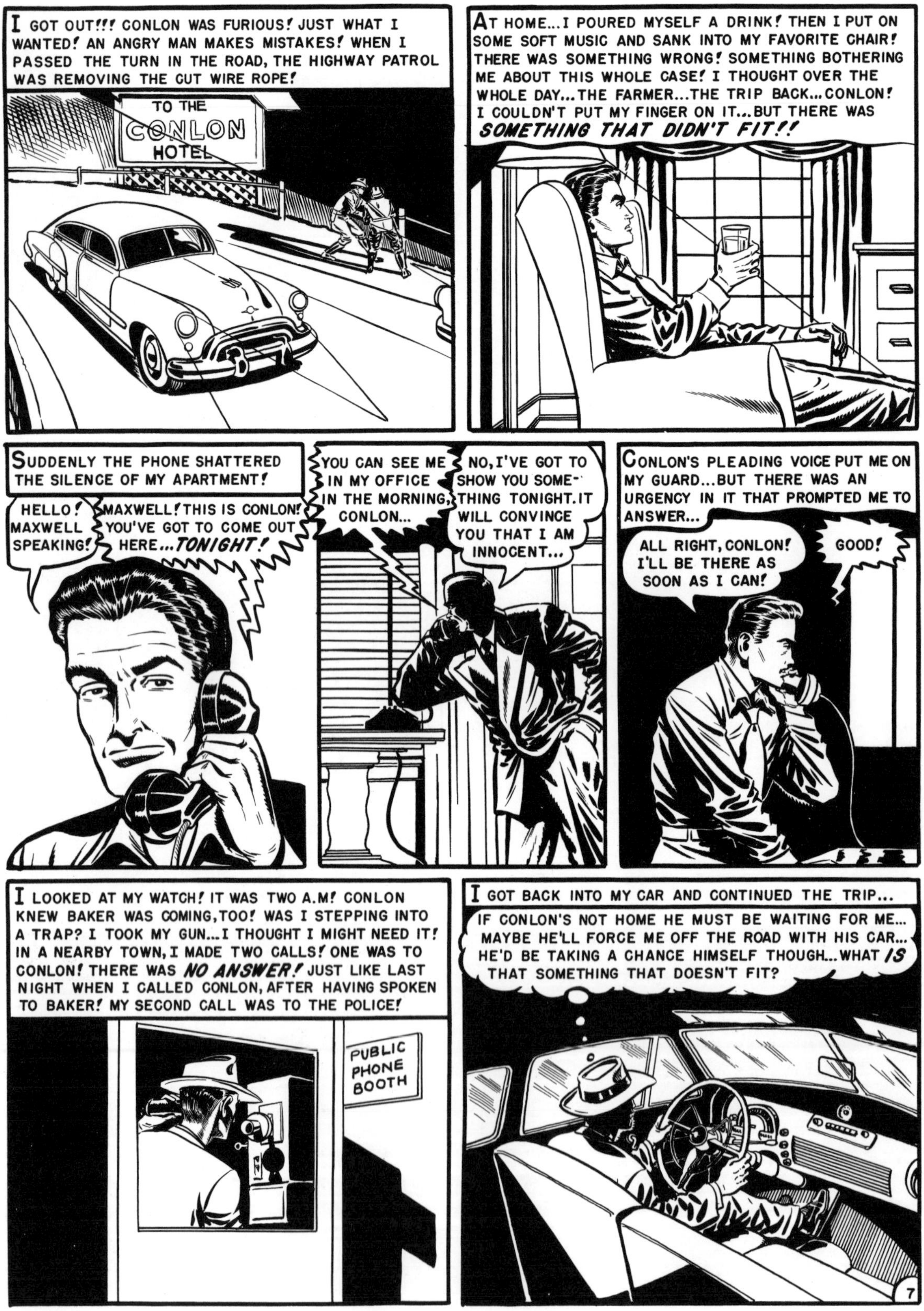

AT HOME... I POURED MYSELF A DRINK! THEN I PUT ON SOME SOFT MUSIC AND SANK INTO MY FAVORITE CHAIR! THERE WAS SOMETHING WRONG! SOMETHING BOTHERING ME ABOUT THIS WHOLE CASE! I THOUGHT OVER THE WHOLE DAY... THE FARMER... THE TRIP BACK... CONLON! I COULDN'T PUT MY FINGER ON IT... BUT THERE WAS *SOMETHING THAT DIDN'T FIT!!*

SUDDENLY THE PHONE SHATTERED THE SILENCE OF MY APARTMENT!

HELLO! MAXWELL SPEAKING!

MAXWELL! THIS IS CONLON! YOU'VE GOT TO COME OUT HERE... TONIGHT!

YOU CAN SEE ME IN MY OFFICE IN THE MORNING, CONLON...

NO, I'VE GOT TO SHOW YOU SOMETHING TONIGHT. IT WILL CONVINCE YOU THAT I AM INNOCENT...

CONLON'S PLEADING VOICE PUT ME ON MY GUARD... BUT THERE WAS AN URGENCY IN IT THAT PROMPTED ME TO ANSWER...

ALL RIGHT, CONLON! I'LL BE THERE AS SOON AS I CAN!

GOOD!

I LOOKED AT MY WATCH! IT WAS TWO A.M! CONLON KNEW BAKER WAS COMING, TOO! WAS I STEPPING INTO A TRAP? I TOOK MY GUN... I THOUGHT I MIGHT NEED IT! IN A NEARBY TOWN, I MADE TWO CALLS! ONE WAS TO CONLON! THERE WAS *NO ANSWER!* JUST LIKE LAST NIGHT WHEN I CALLED CONLON, AFTER HAVING SPOKEN TO BAKER! MY SECOND CALL WAS TO THE POLICE!

I GOT BACK INTO MY CAR AND CONTINUED THE TRIP...
IF CONLON'S NOT HOME HE MUST BE WAITING FOR ME... MAYBE HE'LL FORCE ME OFF THE ROAD WITH HIS CAR... HE'D BE TAKING A CHANCE HIMSELF THOUGH... WHAT *IS* THAT SOMETHING THAT DOESN'T FIT?

7

THE FATAL TURN

...AND THEN I WAS NEARING THE SPOT...

I KNOW THIS ROAD PERFECTLY NOW... BEEN OVER IT FOUR TIMES TODAY... PRETTY SOON MY LIGHTS WILL FALL ON THE SIGN AND THEN... WHAT *IS* THAT LITTLE THING THAT'S BOTHERING ME?

OH, OH... A CAR'S COMING! MUST BE CONLON! LET'S SEE! HOW FAR IS THAT TURN NOW... MUST BE PRETTY CLOSE... HERE'S THE POWER LINE AND THE FENCE STARTING... THAT CAR'S STILL COMING... WHERE'S THAT SIGN?

THE FARMER SAID ONLY ONE CAR... *ONE CAR* HE HEARD... THE SIGN?... WHY DOESN'T CONLON LIGHT THAT SIGN? ...HE HAS A POWER LINE RUNNING OVER IT!... BUT... BUT... YES! THAT'S IT!

THE *SOMETHING* THAT *DIDN'T FIT!* THAT WAS IT! THE SIGN *WAS* WIRED! I HAD NOTICED THE FEED LINE ...BUT THERE WEREN'T ANY LAMPS OR PROVISIONS FOR ILLUMINATION ANYWHERE... UNLESS... UNLESS... THE ONCOMING CAR WAS ALMOST UPON ME...

I STEPPED ON MY BRAKES! IF I WAS WRONG, THE ONCOMING CAR WOULD PLOW HEAD-ON INTO ME... BUT I DIDN'T SWERVE!... AS I CAME TO A STOP, THE HEADLIGHTS ON THE OTHER CAR STOPPED COMING TOO...

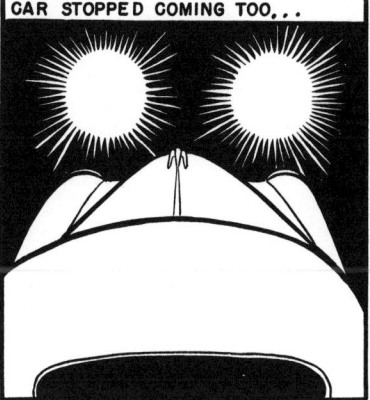

SUDDENLY THE HEADLIGHTS WENT OUT AND INSTEAD OF A CAR I SAW...

THE SIGN! THEN CONLON MUST BE AROUND HERE SOMEWHERE!

3 MORE MILES TO THE CONLON HOTEL

A SHOT RANG OUT AND SHATTERED THE WINDSHIELD... A BULLET WHISTLED BY MY EAR...

WOW... THAT WAS CLOSE! I'D BETTER DOUSE MY HEADLIGHTS!

8

121

WE WERE IN COMPLETE DARKNESS, NOW! THERE WAS NO MOON! I COULD HEAR CONLON MOVING IN THE BRUSH! I TOOK OUT THE GUN I HAD BROUGHT... AND REACHED FOR THE FLASHLIGHT I HAD USED EARLIER...
I FLICKED IT ON AND PLACED IT ON THE HOOD OF MY CAR... THEN I DOVE UNDERNEATH... CONLON EMPTIED HIS GUN TOWARDS THE GENERAL AREA OF THE LIGHT...
...THEN I FIRED AT THE FLASHES FROM CONLON'S GUN... AND I HEARD HIM SCREAM AS A BULLET STRUCK HIM... I GOT MY FLASHLIGHT...
GASP... I'M HIT! GET ME TO... A... DOCTOR...GASP..
YOU BET, CONLON! WE'VE GOT TO SAVE YOU...FOR THE ELECTRIC CHAIR..
THE POLICE I HAD CALLED ARRIVED, AND THEY TOOK CONLON INTO TOWN! THE INSPECTOR WANTED TO KNOW THE WHOLE STORY SO I TOLD HIM MY EXPERIENCES OF THE PREVIOUS TWO DAYS...
AMAZING! JUST HOW DID THIS THING WORK?
SIMPLE, INSPECTOR! THE "O'S" IN "CONLON" WERE THE HEADLIGHTS...
3 MORE MILES
TO THE
CONLON
HOTEL
I FUMBLED AROUND BEHIND THE SIGN AND FINALLY STARTED IT...
NOTICE HOW THE "O" STARTS TO OPEN LIKE A CAMERA-LENS APERTURE... FIRST SMALL... THEN LARGER AND LARGER... AS IF THE HEADLIGHTS ARE COMING CLOSER...
...AND THEN WHEN THE OPENING IS LARGE ENOUGH... THE HEADLIGHTS ZOOM OUT ON THESE EXPANDING GATE-LIKE ARMS... AND THE VICTIM SWERVES OFF THE CLIFF... WHERE THE WIRE-ROPE IS CONVENIENTLY CUT... TO AVOID THE ONCOMING CAR"!
HOTEL
AMAZING! CONLON WAS VERY CLEVER!
BUT NOT CLEVER ENOUGH, INSPECTOR! THESE GUYS'LL NEVER LEARN THAT THEY CAN'T DEFEAT THE FORCES OF LAW AND ORDER!
9

DEAN AND I WERE VERY MUCH IN LOVE! HIS FAMILY WERE FARMERS... MINE WERE MINERS! WE PLANNED TO BE MARRIED... AND THEN...

OUR FAMILIES CLASHED!

AS TOLD TO THE EDITORS OF *MODERN LOVE* BY CAROL LANE*

CAN TWO PEOPLE AS MUCH IN LOVE AS DEAN AND I ARE PLAN MARRIAGE WHEN OUR RESPECTIVE FAMILIES DO NOT CONSIDER US SUITED FOR EACH OTHER?

* * * *

CAN THEIR INTERFERENCE CAUSE OUR MARRIAGE TO FAIL... CAUSE OUR LOVE TO FADE AND DIE?

* * * *

READ MY STORY AND LEARN HOW A SHOCKING NEAR-TRAGEDY BROUGHT OUR PROBLEM TO AN EXPLOSIVE CLIMAX!

FELDSTEIN

a true MODERN *Love Story*

*IN THIS TRUE LOVE STORY, ALL NAMES AND PLACES HAVE BEEN FICTIONIZED TO PROTECT THE IDENTITIES OF THOSE INVOLVED!

THANK GOODNESS THE SUMMER VACATION WAS OVER AND I WAS GOING BACK TO COLLEGE! NOT THAT I HATED THE SMALL MINING TOWN THAT I CAME FROM... IT WAS PART OF MY LIFE! IT WAS *DEAN!* I'D BE SEEING HIM AGAIN!
GOOD-BYE, DADDY! MOTHER! JOE!
GOOD-BYE, CAROL! TAKE CARE!
S'LONG, SIS!
AS THE WHEELS OF THE SPEEDING TRAIN ROARED OVER THE RAILS, BRINGING ME CLOSER AND CLOSER TO DEAN... I THOUGHT ABOUT THE FIRST TIME WE MET! IT WAS LAST WINTER... AND SNOW BLANKETED THE CAMPUS! I WAS ON MY WAY TO BIO LAB WHEN I HIT A STRETCH OF ICE.
LOOK OUT!
ARE YOU HURT? HERE! LET ME HELP YOU!
IT... IT'S MY ANKLE! I'M AFRAID I'VE TWISTED IT... BADLY!
NO... DON'T GET UP! HERE! LET ME CARRY YOU!
OH... I...
HE LIFTED ME IN HIS STRONG ARMS AND STARTED TO CARRY ME INTO THE STUDENT LOUNGE! HE WAS TALL AND DARK... HIS EYES WERE KIND AND HIS SMILE WAS DIVINE... WHY HE WAS HAND-SOME!
HE PUT ME DOWN ON A SOFA IN THE STUDENT LOUNGE... AND KNELT TO REMOVE MY BOOT...
THERE WE ARE... H-MMM! THERE'S NO SWELLING!
THANK GOODNESS! I WAS AFRAID I HAD BROKEN IT!
HE STARTED TO MASSAGE MY ANKLE AND HIS TOUCH WAS GENTLE AND TENDER...
MY NAME'S DEAN DRAKE! WHAT'S YOURS?
CAROL LANE!
2

THAT'S THE WAY WE MET!...DEAN ASKED ME OUT FOR THE FOLLOWING SATURDAY NIGHT AND I ACCEPTED! IT WAS A BASKETBALL GAME-DANCE! WE HAD A GRAND TIME!
SAY! LET'S DO THIS AGAIN...REAL SOON!
OH, DEAN! I'D LOVE TO...
THE EVENING FLEW BY AND BEFORE I KNEW IT, DEAN AND I WERE ON MY DOORSTEP SAYING GOOD-NIGHT...
I HAD A WONDERFUL TIME TONIGHT, DEAN!
I...I'D LIKE TO KISS YOU GOOD-NIGHT, CAROL!
DEAN GATHERED ME INTO HIS ARMS AND KISSED ME FOR THE FIRST TIME... MY HEART SKIPPED A BEAT!
THE SNOWS MELTED AND SPRING CAME TO THE CAMPUS! DEAN AND I HAD BEEN DATING STEADY SINCE THAT FIRST NIGHT... WE WERE SURE THAT IT WAS REAL LOVE...
CAROL, DEAREST! I GRADUATE IN JANUARY! I...I WANT TO MARRY YOU, THEN!
WE'LL SEE, DEAN DARLING! JANUARY IS SO FAR AWAY!
IN JUNE, AFTER FINAL EXAMS, DEAN AND I HAD TO PART FOR THE SUMMER VACATION! IT WAS HARD, VERY HARD! WE HAD BEEN SEEING EACH OTHER SO OFTEN THAT TWO AND A HALF MONTHS APART WOULD SEEM AN ETERNITY.
WRITE TO ME, DARLING!
EVERY DAY, DEAN!
ONE WARM JULY NIGHT, AT HOME...
CAROL! HOW COME YOU DON'T GO OUT WITH ANY OF THE NICE YOUNG MEN AROUND TOWN...
I...I REALLY DON'T CARE TO, DADDY, DEAR!
WHAT IS IT? SOME FELLOW YOU MET AT COLLEGE!
T...THAT'S RIGHT! I'M IN LOVE WITH HIM AND I DON'T THINK IT WOULD BE RIGHT TO DATE BEHIND HIS BACK...
3

WHAT'S HE LIKE? WHERE DOES HE COME FROM?
HE LIVES UPSTATE, NEAR CARTERVILLE! HE'S VERY NICE... TALL, DARK... GOOD-LOOKING... AND HE LOVES ME TOO...
WHAT ABOUT HIS FAMILY? WHAT ARE THEY LIKE?
WHY... I NEVER THOUGHT TO ASK ABOUT HIS FAMILY!
HMMPH... DON'T YOU THINK IT'S IMPORTANT ENOUGH?
WHY... I... HE LOVES ME... THAT'S ALL THAT MATTERS TO ME!
BAH... THE IMPORTANT THING IS HIS FAMILY! WHY... THEY MIGHT BE... WELL ... *DIFFERENT* THAN WE ARE! HE MAY NOT BE *RIGHT* FOR YOU...
IF HE LOVES ME, AND I LOVE HIM... THAT'S *ENOUGH* TO MAKE US *RIGHT* FOR EACH OTHER, DADDY!
I CAN SEE THAT YOU DON'T UNDERSTAND!
AND I *COULDN'T* UNDERSTAND... NOR DID I REALIZE HOW SERIOUS FATHER'S ATTITUDE COULD BE! BUT NOW THE TRAIN WAS SPEEDING ME BACK TO COLLEGE... AND DEAN...
I WONDER IF DEAN HAS CHANGED MUCH OVER THE SUMMER?
DEAN CALLED ME JUST AFTER I UNPACKED! MY HEART THROBBED FASTER AS I REALIZED THAT IN A FEW MINUTES WE WOULD BE TOGETHER...
YES, DEAN, DARLING! AT OUR OLD SPOT... BY THE LAKE... YES, DEAR... IN TEN MINUTES... SEE YOU THEN...
THE WILLOWS HUNG HEAVY OVER THE STILL WATER AS I HURRIED ALONG THE LAKE PATH... AND THEN HE WAS THERE... AND I WAS IN HIS ARMS...
CAROL, DARLING!
DEAN... SWEET, DEAREST!
4

MY HEART POUNDED AS WE CLUNG TO EACH OTHER...
I MISSED YOU, CAROL DEAR...
AND I MISSED YOU, DEAN!
I TOLD MY FOLKS ABOUT YOU, DEAREST...AND THAT I PLAN TO MARRY YOU AFTER I GRADUATE! THEY...THEY WANT TO MEET YOU!
DO THEY, DEAN?
YES! IT'S...IT'S FUNNY, BUT, WELL, I COULDN'T TELL THEM TOO MUCH ABOUT YOU...YOUR FAMILY! YOU NEVER TOLD ME ABOUT THEM!
WHY, YOU NEVER ASKED, DEAN!
I DIDN'T THINK IT WAS IMPORTANT, CAROL! I'M NOT MARRYING YOUR FOLKS! I'M MARRYING YOU! BUT... MY PARENTS HAVE STRANGE NOTIONS...
MY FATHER ASKED ME ABOUT YOUR PARENTS TOO, DEAN! DO YOU THINK WE'RE GOING TO HAVE TROUBLE?
I DON'T KNOW, CAROL! ANYWAY, I HAVE THE CAR HERE. WE'LL DRIVE TO MY HOME THIS WEEKEND!
OF COURSE, DEAN! ANYTHING YOU SAY!
ON THE FOLLOWING SATURDAY MORNING, WE SET OUT FOR DEAN'S HOME. I HAD A STRANGE FEELING OF UNEASINESS AS WE NEARED THE END OF THE TRIP! I TRIED NOT TO SHOW IT, BUT DEAN SENSED MY ANXIETY!
DON'T WORRY, DEAR! EVERYTHING WILL BE ALL RIGHT!
I HOPE THEY LIKE ME, DEAN!
MRS. DRAKE WAS STANDING IN THE DOORWAY AS WE DROVE UP! IT WAS A MODEST FARM HOUSE SET AMONG TALL TREES! THE AIR WAS SWEET WITH THE SMELL OF NEW-MOWN HAY. OFF IN THE DISTANCE A BABY LAMB BLEATED FOR ITS MOTHER!
WELL, HERE WE ARE, DEAR! THERE'S MOM WAITING FOR US! CHIN UP!
5

MRS. DRAKE WAS A SMALL THIN WOMAN...PLAINLY DRESSED. AS WE APPROACHED, SHE SMILED AND STEPPED FORWARD, EXTENDING HER HANDS...
YOU MUST BE CAROL! DEAN HAS TOLD ME SO MUCH ABOUT YOU! COME IN!
I'M VERY GLAD TO MEET YOU, MRS. DRAKE!
MR. DRAKE CAME IN FROM THE FIELDS A FEW MINUTES LATER! HE WAS TALL AND WIRY! HIS HANDS AND FACE SHOWED THE SIGNS OF A LIFE-TIME OF FARMING...WEATHERBEATEN AND ROUGH...HE SMILED AT ME...
I CAME AROUND AS SOON AS I HEARD THE CAR! SO YOU'RE CAROL!
THAT'S RIGHT, MR. DRAKE!
YOU'LL EXCUSE MY APPEARANCE, BUT I DIDN'T KNOW WHEN YOU WOULD GET HERE! I 'SPECT I'M A MIGHT DIRTY!
OH, THAT'S QUITE ALL RIGHT, MR. DRAKE! YOU OUGHT TO SEE WHAT MY FATHER AND BROTHER LOOK LIKE AFTER A DAY IN THE MINES...
THE SILENCE WAS DEAFENING! THE SMILES ON THE FACES OF THE DRAKES VANISHED AS THEY STARED AT ME...THEN THEY BOTH TURNED TO DEAN!
COAL MINERS! DEAN! YOU DIDN'T TELL US...
WHY...WHAT'S THE DIFFERENCE WHAT HER FOLKS ARE?
IT MAKES A GREAT DEAL OF DIFFERENCE, DEAN! SHE'S NOT OUR KIND OF PEOPLE... SHE...
WHAT DO YOU MEAN...NOT OUR KIND.. I LOVE HER FOR WHAT SHE IS, NOT WHO SHE IS...
THEY ARGUED BACK AND FORTH... MR. DRAKE SAID THINGS ABOUT COAL MINERS...THINGS THAT WERE UNFAIR! I CHOKED BACK THE TEARS AND RAN OUT OF THE HOUSE...
CAROL...COME BACK!
LET HER GO, SON!
DEAN CAUGHT ME AND HELD ME IN HIS ARMS...I COULDN'T FIGHT THE TEARS ANY LONGER! I CLUNG TO HIM...CRYING LIKE A CHILD!
TAKE ME AWAY FROM HERE, DEAN! TAKE ME BACK TO SCHOOL!
I DON'T CARE WHAT HE SAYS, CAROL! I STILL LOVE YOU...
6

OUR FAMILIES CLASHED!

WE DROVE FOR A LONG TIME IN SILENCE! I STOPPED CRYING AFTER A WHILE! DEAN KEPT HIS EYES ON THE ROAD! FINALLY I SPOKE...

"DEAN...DON'T TAKE ME BACK TO SCHOOL...DRIVE ME HOME! I WANT YOU TO MEET MY FAMILY! TO SEE THAT WHAT YOUR FATHER SAYS ISN'T TRUE!"

"SURE, CAROL... SURE!!"

IT WAS EARLY EVENING WHEN WE PULLED UP IN FRONT OF MY HOUSE...THE WHISTLE AT THE SHAFTS TOOTED A WARNING THAT THE NIGHT SHIFT WOULD BE STARTING SOON! JOE, MY BROTHER, CAME OUT OF THE HOUSE...

"JOE! THIS IS DEAN!"

"HI, DEAN! SIS TOLD ME ALL ABOUT YOU! CONGRATULATIONS. I GOTTA RUN OR I'LL BE LATE FOR MY SHIFT! SEE YOU LATER..."

WE WENT IN. DADDY WAS SITTING IN HIS FAVORITE CHAIR... READING THE PAPER...AND MOTHER WAS DARNING! THEY BOTH LOOKED UP, SURPRISED!

"CAROL!" "WHAT'S WRONG?"

"NOTHING... DADDY, MOTHER! I BROUGHT A VISITOR!"

"THIS IS DEAN! DEAN...MY MOTHER AND FATHER..."

"WELL! SIT DOWN, BOY! I'VE BEEN ANXIOUS TO MEET YOU..."

"CAROL'S TOLD ME THAT YOU INTEND TO MARRY HER..."

"THAT'S RIGHT, SIR!"

"WELL, YOU LOOK LIKE A NICE HEALTHY YOUNG MAN! HOW...HOW DO YOU INTEND TO SUPPORT HER, DEAN?"

"WELL, I HAVE A LITTLE MONEY SAVED.. I INTEND TO BUY A FARM AND..."

"A FARM! JUST A MINUTE, SON... NO DAUGHTER OF MINE'S MARRYING A FARMER! YOUR FOLKS FARMERS TOO?"

"WHY, YES! WHAT'S WRONG WITH FARMERS?"

7

I DIDN'T SAY THERE WAS ANYTHING *WRONG* WITH THEM! I JUST THINK THAT MY DAUGHTER WOULDN'T BE HAPPY MARRIED TO ONE...
WHY DON'T YOU LET *HER* DECIDE THAT?
I'LL DECIDE *FOR* HER! I KNOW WHAT'S *BEST* FOR HER!
I THINK YOU'RE IN NO POSITION TO DO *ANY* DECIDING! SHE LOVES ME AND I LOVE HER AND WE'RE *GOING* TO GET MARRIED WHETHER YOU OR ANYONE..
SUDDENLY THE NIGHT WAS PIERCED BY THE SHRIEK OF THE MINE WHISTLE! ACCIDENT SIGNAL! THREE BLASTS! FATHER BOLTED FROM THE ROOM!
JOE! HE'S DOWN IN THE MINE... *NOW!*
WHAT? WAIT FOR ME!
IT WAS HORRIBLE! THERE HAD BEEN A CAVE-IN! JOE WAS TRAPPED UNDER A BEAM...THE OTHER MEN HAD GOTTEN OUT! SOMEONE HAD TO RISK ANOTHER CAVE-IN TO GET JOE OUT...DEAN DIDN'T WAIT! HE JUMPED ON THE ELEVATOR...
DEAN! STOP!
THE *FOOL!* WHAT DOES HE KNOW ABOUT MINES?
AND THEN IT HAPPENED! DEAN HAD GOTTEN TO JOE AND RELEASED HIM! HIS COLLAR-BONE WAS BROKEN! THEY HAD STARTED OUT WHEN ANOTHER CAVE-IN SEALED OFF THE ENTRANCE!
THEY WON'T LAST LONG. WE'VE GOT TO DIG FOR THEM!
CAROL! CALL DEAN'S PARENTS! THEY SHOULD KNOW WHAT'S HAPPENED!
THE WAITING WAS UNBEARABLE! DEAN'S PARENTS ARRIVED A LITTLE AFTER MIDNIGHT AND WE ALL STOOD AROUND WITHOUT SPEAKING AS THE TEAM DUG FAR INTO THE NIGHT. TOWARDS DAWN A MESSAGE CAME THROUGH THAT THEY HAD CONTACTED THE TRAPPED MEN AND THAT THEY WERE BOTH ALIVE...
THANK GOD! THANK GOD!
WE'LL HAVE 'EM OUT SOON, NOW!
SOB... SOB...
AFTER A FEW MORE WEARY HOURS, A HOLE LARGE ENOUGH FOR DEAN AND JOE WAS MADE...AND THEY BOTH CAME TO THE SURFACE...
JOE! MY BOY! MY BOY!
I'M OKAY, MOM, THANKS TO DEAN!
ARE YOU ALL RIGHT, SON?
I'M FINE, MOM!
8

JOE TOOK DEAN'S HAND AND MY HEART SWELLED WITH PRIDE...
I... I WANT YOU TO KNOW, DEAN, THAT I THINK YOU'RE A *GREAT* GUY FOR RISKING YOUR LIFE LIKE THAT... FOR ME!
I DIDN'T STOP TO THINK ABOUT IT, JOE! ALL I KNEW WAS THAT CAROL'S BROTHER WAS IN TROUBLE...
WE ALL WENT BACK TO THE HOUSE WHERE MOTHER MADE SOME COFFEE... DADDY AND MR. DRAKE WERE TALKING IN THE CORNER...
YOU HAVE A COURAGEOUS SON, MR. DRAKE! IT TOOK GUTS TO DO WHAT HE DID!
I... I'M PRETTY PROUD OF HIM MYSELF!
YOU KNOW... I NEVER REALLY REALIZED HOW DANGEROUS MINING WAS TILL TONIGHT! IT'S FUNNY HOW WRONG YOU CAN BE ABOUT SOME THINGS! WHY.. THIS MORNING I TOLD MY SON I WOULDN'T ALLOW HIM TO MARRY YOUR DAUGHTER, BECAUSE SHE CAME FROM A MINING FAMILY... AND NOW... WHY I'D BE RIGHT PROUD TO HAVE CAROL AS MY DAUGHTER-IN-LAW!
HMMM! MAKES ME FEEL ASHAMED OF MYSELF, TOO! YOUR SON CERTAINLY PROVED HIMSELF A MAN TONIGHT... AND IF THAT'S THE KIND OF MEN YOU FARMING FOLK TURN OUT... WHY I'D BE PLEASED TO HAVE HIM IN THE FAMILY... PLEASED AND HONORED!
A FEELING OF RELIEF SWEPT OVER ME! ALL THE UNHAPPINESS, ALL THE ANXIETY WAS GONE! DEAN AND I WERE GOING TO BE ABLE TO MARRY WITH EVERYONE'S BLESSINGS... AT LAST...
LOOK AT THEM, DEAN! THIS MORNING THEY WOULD HAVE BEEN AT EACH OTHER'S THROATS...
YES! BUT IT'S TOO BAD THAT IT HAD TO TAKE SUCH A SHOCK TO BRING THEM TO THEIR SENSES!
DEAN AND I STOOD ON THE PORCH AND WATCHED THE SUN COME UP OVER THE HILLS! BENEATH THESE HILLS, MEN LIKE DAD AND JOE BURROWED; AND OVER THEM, MEN LIKE DEAN AND HIS FATHER PLOWED! DEAN TOOK ME INTO HIS ARMS AND KISSED ME... FOREVER!
9

CASE NUMBER 318 MURDER

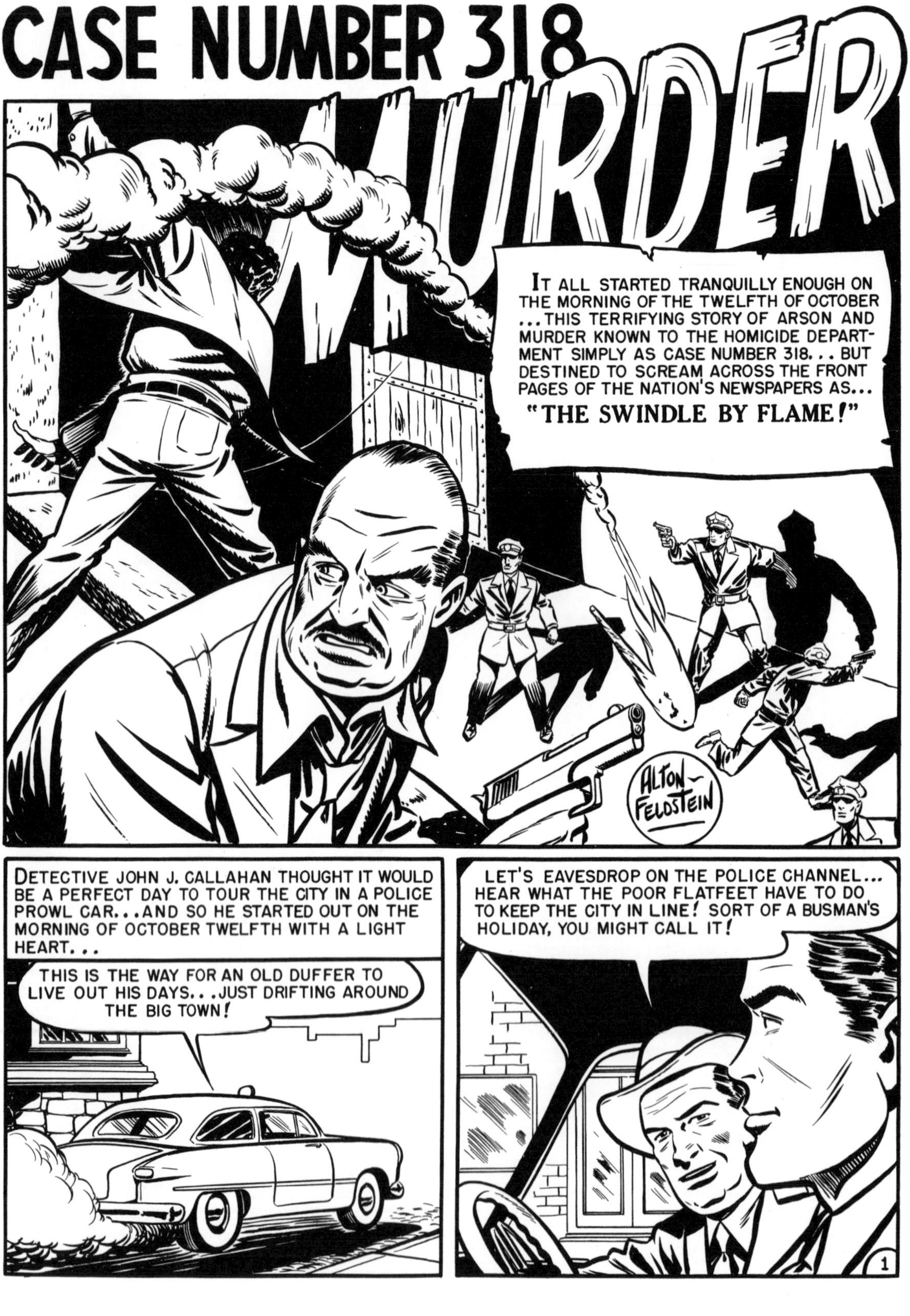

CASE NUMBER 318: MURDER

Panel 1:
CALLING CAR SEVEN-TWO...SEVENTY-TWO...HOMICIDE LIEUTENANT CALLAHAN REQUESTED TO PROCEED IMMEDIATELY TO CROWN STREET... ADDRESS ONE-ELEVEN! THREE ALARM FIRE... SUSPICIOUS CIRCUMSTANCES...

T-THAT'S *US!* OUR VACATION'S OVER ALREADY. GET GOING, SON!

Panel 2:
LOOKS AS IF THE WHOLE DANG FIRE DEPARTMENT IS OUT FIGHTING *THIS* ONE! BETTER PULL TO THE CURB JAMIE-BOY... WE'LL HAVE A LOOK AT THOSE *SUSPICIOUS CIRCUMSTANCES!*

Panel 3:
CLIMB INTO THAT DUMP, JAMIE...FIND OUT WHAT YOU CAN! PROBABLY ANOTHER CASE OF THE BOYS AT HEADQUARTERS GETTING ALL EXCITED OVER NOTHING!

GOTCHA, CHIEF! I'LL GET OUT MY MAGNIFYING GLASS AND SHERLOCK HOLMES HAT!

Panel 4:
LIEUTENANT...HERE'S A GUY WHO CLAIMS HE KNOWS SOMETHING ABOUT THIS BLAZE! GOT A STORY TO TELL... C'MON, MISTER, START TALKING!

Panel 5:
WALKING BY THE WAREHOUSE HERE A MINUTE OR SO BEFORE THE FIRE BROKE OUT! SEEN A BIG FAT GUY COME OUT...FOLLOWED BY A LITTLE SHIFTY RUNT! THEY RAN AROUND THE CORNER LIKE THEY WAS MIGHTY ANXIOUS TO SCRAM!

Panel 6:
HEY, CHIEF! FOUND SOMETHING UP HERE THAT'LL MAKE YOUR LITTLE HEART GO PITTY-PAT! A *BODY!* AS DEAD AS COOKED MACKEREL! AND I UNCOVERED SOMETHING ELSE...

H-HUH! BRING IT DOWN... HURRY UP!

Panel 7:
TAKE THIS GUY'S NAME SO WE CAN GET IN TOUCH WITH HIM IF WE NEED 'IM! THEN CALL HOMICIDE...TELL 'EM I WANT A MAN TO BRING THE OWNER OF THIS WAREHOUSE DOWN HERE PRONTO! NOT A SECOND TO LOSE!

CASE NUMBER 318: MURDER

"CHIEF! GOT SOMETHING IMPORTANT TO SHOW YOU..."

"BE RIGHT OVER, JAMIE BOY! SURE BEATS ME HOW THINGS KEEP COMING UP TO BEDEVIL A MAN! AND I THOUGHT THIS WOULD BE A NICE DAY FOR A DRIVE!"

"ALL RIGHT, SON, LET'S SEE WHAT YOU DUG UP!"

"NOT SO FAST, LIEUTENANT! YOU TOLD ME ALWAYS TO START A STORY AT THE BEGINNING... AND THAT'S WHAT I'M GOING TO DO!"

"I FOUND A MAN'S BODY UP IN ONE OF THE BACK ROOMS... BADGE ON HIS COAT IDENTIFIES HIM AS THE WATCHMAN FOR THE WAREHOUSE! BUT ONE THING'S MIGHTY FUNNY... HE WASN'T BURNT AT ALL! INSTEAD..."

"HE HAD POWDER BURNS ON HIM AS IF A GUN WERE FIRED VERY CLOSE TO HIM! AND THEN ACROSS THE ROOM... I FOUND THIS... WITH A SILENCER ATTACHED TO IT!"

"HMMM... NOW MY VACATION IS DEFINITELY OVER!"

"HI THERE, LIEUTENANT! GOT YOUR PHONE CALL AND RUSHED RIGHT OVER TO MISTER SWANN'S OFFICE... WE DROVE OVER IN HIS CAR! HE OWNS THIS PILE OF EMBERS!"

"THIS IS MISTER SWANN, LIEUTENANT... AND HIS ASSISTANT, MR. AXEL! HE OWNS A COUPLE OF WAREHOUSES LIKE THIS ONE... FIRST HE HEARD ABOUT THE FIRE WAS WHEN I BARGED IN!"

"IF I CAN DO ANYTHING TO HELP, LIEUTENANT..."

"I'M IN RATHER AN AWKWARD POSITION... MR. AXEL AND I JUST BOUGHT THIS WAREHOUSE AND THERE ARE SEVERAL PRICELESS OBJECTS STORED HERE... THINGS MONEY CANNOT REPLACE..."

"YEAH... I SYMPATHIZE WITH YOU, MR. SWANN..."

3

CASE NUMBER 318: MURDER

W-WHAT THE...? OH... MR. SWANN...
THOUGHT I SAW YOU COME THIS WAY, OFFICER! CAN WE GIVE YOU A LIFT?
NO THANKS, MR. SWANN... HOMICIDE HEADQUARTERS IS JUST A FEW BLOCKS FROM HERE...
I THINK MAYBE YOU'D BETTER COME WITH US!
YOU HEARD WHAT SWANN SAID, MISTER! BETTER GET INTO THE CAR...
H-HEY! WHAT IS THIS...?
JUMP 'IM, AXEL... NO ONE IN SIGHT!
WE KNOW HOW TO TAKE CARE OF SMART COPPERS WHO LIKE TO SNOOP!
YOU GUYS ARE CRAZY! TRYING TO BEAT THE LAW LIKE THIS...
HOLD 'EM JUST A MINUTE, JAMIE...
I-IT'S THAT OTHER COP, BOSS... THEY SPRUNG A TRAP FOR US!
H-HELP ME, AXEL!
AIN'T NO USE FOR BOTH OF US TO WIND UP IN THE CLINK, I'M SCRAMMING! TA TA!
OTHER ONE'S GETTING AWAY, JAMIE...
DOESN'T MATTER...WE'VE GOT THE BIG POTATO HERE! LET HIS LITTLE PAL DRIFT FOR A WHILE...GIVE US A CHANCE TO GRILL SWANN DOWN AT HEAD-QUARTERS!
5

AT EXACTLY ELEVEN-TWENTY ON THE MORNING OF THE TWELFTH OF OCTOBER...SOME FIFTEEN MINUTES AFTER SWANN'S CAPTURE...
GOT HERE AS FAST AS I COULD, BOYS! NICE WORK IN GRABBING THIS FAT CHISELER.
GOT HIM ALL READY TO BLUBBER, CHIEF!
AXEL AND I PULLED THAT ARSON JOB ON THE WAREHOUSE ...WE'VE BEEN MOVING THE VALUABLE STUFF OUT FOR WEEKS ...TRANSFERRING IT TO MY OTHER PLACE! WE REPLACED IT WITH CHEAP IMITATIONS...SETTING FIRE TO THE DUMP WOULD BRING IN A FORTUNE IN INSURANCE MONEY...
THE WATCHMAN INTERRUPTED US WHILE WE WERE SETTING THE STAGE FOR THE FIRE. AXEL SHOT HIM...AND GOT SCARED WHEN THE FLAMES LEAPED UP AROUND US! HE DROPPED THE GUN...AND WE SCRAMMED!
OKAY, MIKE, BOOK THIS BALL OF BLUBBER FOR ARSON AND HOMICIDE! JAMIE...GET SET FOR A LITTLE ACTION!
THAT DIRTY DOUBLE-CROSSER AXEL IS PROBABLY AT OUR OTHER WAREHOUSE... PLANNING TO RUN OUT ON ME... WITH ALL OF THAT VALUABLE STUFF WE MOVED THERE!
YOU HEAR THAT, JAMIE-BOY?
RIGHT, CHIEF!
THE MAIN WAREHOUSE OWNED BY SWANN AND AXEL WAS WITHIN TEN MINUTES OF HOMICIDE...AND AT THE END OF THAT SPAN OF TIME...
OKAY, BOYS...LET'S PUSH THIS BABY IN! HE'S HIDING INSIDE!
THERE SHE GOES!
ATTA BOY! C'MON OUT, AXEL...WITH YOUR HANDS UP! YOU HAVEN'T GOT A CHANCE IN THE WORLD... THE WHOLE STREET'S SURROUNDED!
TRY AND GET ME, WISE GUY!
TAKE COVER, BOYS... THIS GUY'S LOOKING FOR A FIREWORKS DISPLAY!
6

KEEP HIM BUSY FOR A COUPLE OF MINUTES, BOYS! I'M GOING TO TRY THAT STAIRWAY...SEE IF I CAN'T GET UP IN THE RAFTERS AND TAKE THIS MADMAN BY SURPRISE!
CLEAR OUT, WISE GUYS... THIS WHOLE PLACE IS GONNA GO UP IN FLAMES IN A MINUTE.
THIS GUY MAY BE BLUFFING... AND THEN AGAIN SWANN MAY HAVE PICKED A REAL PYROMANIAC TO WORK WITH HIM ON THAT OTHER WAREHOUSE!
OKAY, BOYS... YOU GOT A CHOICE! EITHER STAY WHERE YOU ARE AND GET ROASTED... OR ELSE SCATTER AND GIVE ME TARGET PRACTICE.
GOTTA STOP THIS IMBECILE BEFORE THE WHOLE PLACE GOES UP IN FLAMES!
DROP THAT GUN, AXEL... YOU'RE FINISHED!
H-HUH? OH... THE FRESH GUY, EH? SAY YOUR PRAYERS, MISTER...
YOU'RE ALL WASHED UP, SEE? HEH, HEH... WHATTA LAUGH... THE WHOLE POLICE FORCE SURROUNDED ...BY LITTLE ME!
I-I..H-HELP! S-SLIPPING... C-CAN'T SEEM TO .....
YIIIIII!
UP THERE! AXEL'S LOST HIS BALANCE... FALLING STRAIGHT TOWARD THE FIRE HE STARTED HIMSELF!
WITHIN HALF AN HOUR, THE FINISH HAD BEEN WRITTEN TO CASE NUMBER 318... AND THE FINISH TO SWANN'S FREEDOM... AS WELL AS AXEL'S WORTHLESS LIFE!
THAT WRAPS UP THE CASE, BOYS! SWANN'S TRIAL SHOULD BEGIN IN A COUPLA WEEKS... AND THERE'S NOTHING LEFT OF AXEL BUT A HANDFUL OF ASHES! KIND OF IRONIC... DESTROYED BY HIS OWN HAND AND... MIKE! WILL YOU PUT THAT MATCH AWAY? I'M... ER... KIND OF SENSITIVE ABOUT FIRE RIGHT NOW!
7

HERE IS A TALE TAKEN FROM
THE CRYPT OF TERROR

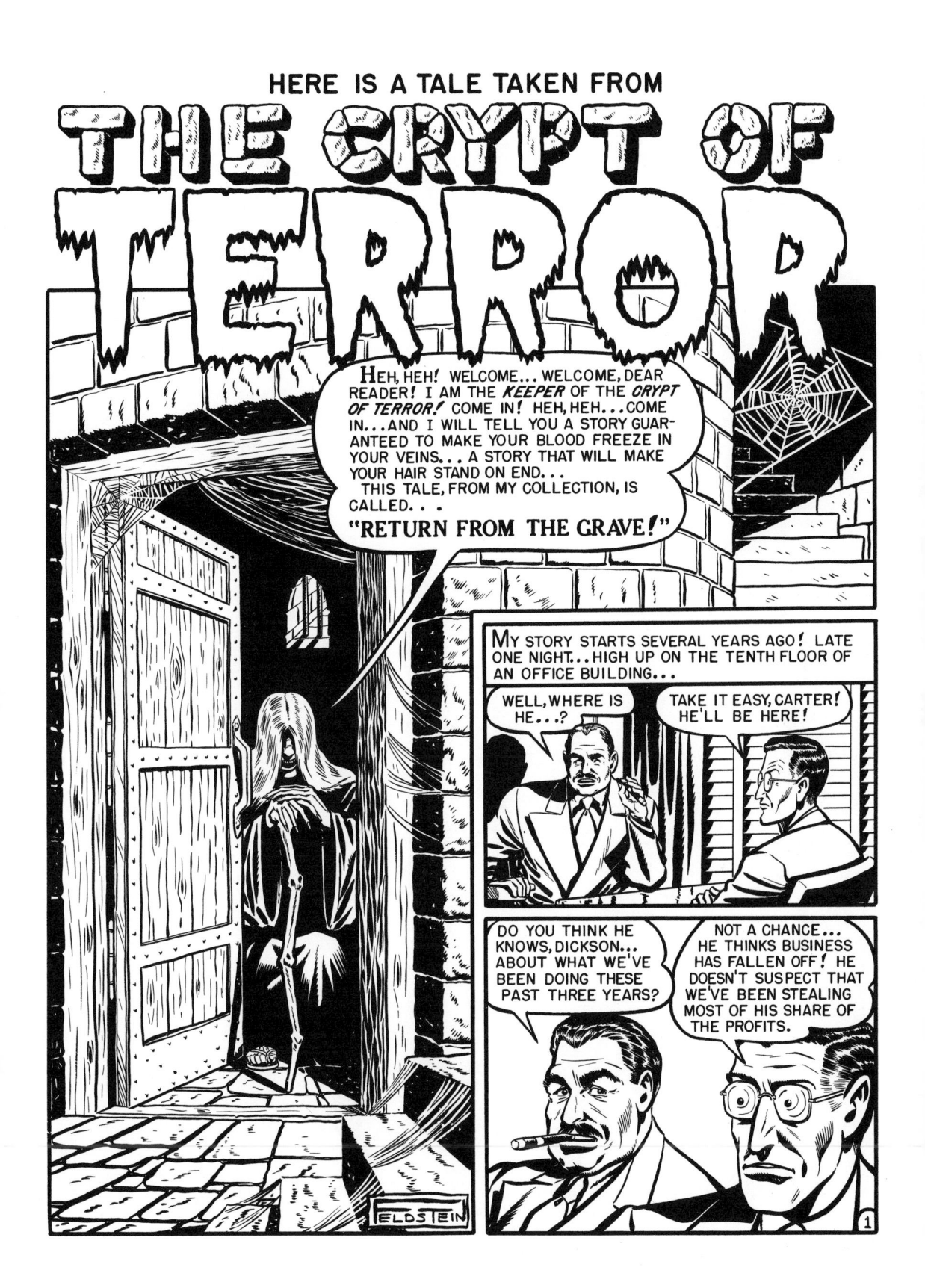

Heh, heh! Welcome... welcome, dear reader! I am the *Keeper* of the *Crypt of Terror!* Come in! Heh, heh... come in... and I will tell you a story guaranteed to make your blood freeze in your veins... a story that will make your hair stand on end...

This tale, from my collection, is called...

"RETURN FROM THE GRAVE!"

My story starts several years ago! Late one night... high up on the tenth floor of an office building...

"Well, where is he...?"

"Take it easy, Carter! He'll be here!"

"Do you think he knows, Dickson... about what we've been doing these past three years?"

"Not a chance... he thinks business has fallen off! He doesn't suspect that we've been stealing most of his share of the profits."

THEN WHAT IN THE WORLD DOES HE WANT WITH US, TONIGHT?
PROBABLY WANTS TO BORROW MORE MONEY! IF HE'D ONLY SELL OUT, LIKE WE WANT HIM TO...
HE'S STUBBORN! BUT IF...IF WE REFUSE TO LEND HIM ANY MORE... HE...MAY HAVE TO...
THEN YOU MEAN WE SHOULD REFUSE TO LEND HIM ANY MORE...OH... OH...HERE HE IS...
GLASS!
IT'S ABOUT TIME YOU SHOWED!
GOOD EVENING, GENTLEMEN.
WHAT'S IT ALL ABOUT, GLASS?
YES! WHAT DO YOU WANT WITH US?
IT... IT'S MY DAUGHTER. SHE...NEEDS ANOTHER OPERATION...I HAVEN'T THE MONEY...
AND YOU WANT TO BORROW FROM US AGAIN...?
HOW MUCH DO YOU THINK WE HAVE?
BUT YOU GENTLEMEN HAVE SAVED... YOU'RE NOT MARRIED...YOU HAVE OTHER INVESTMENTS...I HAVE ONLY THIS BUSINESS...
BUT...IF YOU BORROW MUCH MORE, GLASS, YOU WON'T EVEN HAVE THIS BUSINESS!
WHY DON'T YOU SELL OUT, GLASS? SELL OUT TO US AND YOU'LL HAVE YOUR MONEY!
NO! NO! NEVER! WHAT WOULD MY FAMILY HAVE IF I SHOULD DIE?
YOUR INSURANCE! THEY'D BE BETTER OFF, TOO... HAW, HAW!
YES, GLASS! WHY DON'T YOU KILL YOURSELF... AND MAKE IT LOOK LIKE AN ACCIDENT? THEN YOUR FAMILY WILL HAVE REAL SECURITY! HEH, HEH!
2

BUT YOU JEST, GENTLEMEN...
NO GLASS! WE'RE SERIOUS! WE'RE NOT LENDING YOU ANY MORE MONEY!
DICKSON! CARTER! WAIT!
GOOD NIGHT, MR. GLASS!
NICE PEOPLE...EH, DEAR READER? POOR MR. GLASS...HIS BUSINESS PARTNERS HAVE SUCH NICE SUGGESTIONS FOR HIM... WELL, AFTER THEY LEFT, GLASS SAT STARING OUT OF THE WINDOW...
HMMM! COMMIT SUICIDE... AN ACCIDENT...COLLECT INSURANCE...
IT'S FUNNY HOW AN IDEA CAN BEGIN TO WORK ON YOU...FOLLOW YOU WHEREVER YOU GO...WHEN YOU LIE IN BED AT NIGHT, TRYING TO SLIP OFF TO SLEEP... IN A CROWDED... BUS...POUNDING IN YOUR BRAIN...
SUICIDE! KILL YOURSELF! INSURANCE!
...AND THEN, ONE NIGHT...MR. DICKSON AND MR. CARTER RECEIVED A FRANTIC CALL FROM MRS. GLASS...
COME AT ONCE! SOMETHING TERRIBLE HAS HAPPENED TO MY HUSBAND!
WE'LL BE RIGHT OVER, MRS. GLASS!
WHAT'S HAPPENED?
YES, MRS. GLASS! WHAT'S WRONG?
IT'S JOHN! HE'S HAD A TERRIBLE ACCIDENT! FELL...SOB...IN FRONT OF A...TRUCK...KILLED!
THE FUNERAL WAS HELD ON A BLEAK DARK DAY, IN A HEAVY DOWNPOUR! THE COFFIN REMAINED CLOSED...AT THE UNDERTAKER'S INSISTENCE! MR. GLASS WAS TOO BADLY MANGLED...
SOB... SOB...
POOR JOHN!
WE WILL...MISS HIM!
3

DICKSON AND CARTER, ALTHOUGH OUTWARDLY HEARTBROKEN, WERE OVERJOYED AT THE TURN OF EVENTS! NOW THEY HAD THE BUSINESS TO THEMSELVES...
LOOK CARTER! IT CAME IN THIS MORNING'S MAIL... READ IT!
WHAT... AN ORDER FOR $50,000 WORTH OF OUR BEST PERFUME!
CALL THE LABORATORY AND HAVE THEM START WORK ON IT AT ONCE!
HELLO... IS THIS CARL, THE FOREMAN? WE HAVE A BIG ORDER FOR YOU TO GET OUT... 5,000 BOTTLES OF OUR BEST PERFUME...
WHAT?
WHAT IS IT, DICKSON? WHAT'S WRONG?
THE FORMULAS! WITHOUT THE FORMULAS THEY CAN'T POSSIBLY MAKE ANY!
ASK HIM WHERE THE FORMULAS ARE!
HE SAYS GLASS KEPT ALL THE FORMULAS...
WE'VE GOT TO FIND THEM!
THE SEARCH BEGAN! THEY WENT THROUGH EVERY DRAWER IN THE OFFICE..COVERED EVERY FOOT... BUT NO FORMULAS...
MRS. GLASS! MAYBE SHE HAS THEM!
C'MON!
CARTER AND DICKSON ARRIVED AT THE GLASS RESIDENCE BREATHLESS...
HAVE YOU ANY IDEA WHERE JOHN KEPT THE FORMULAS...
OF COURSE! HE KEPT THEM IN A BANK VAULT... BUT ONLY HE KNEW ITS NUMBER AND LOCATION!
4

B...B...BUT HE MUST HAVE KEPT A RECORD.. SOMEWHERE!
OH, YES! HE DID! HE HAD THE NUMBER AND LOCATION SEWN INTO THE LINING OF HIS BEST SUIT...
GET IT, QUICKLY!
I CAN'T! JOHN WAS... BURIED IN IT!
WELL, DEAR READER! THIS PRESENTED QUITE A PROBLEM... BUT NOT TO DICKSON AND CARTER! REMEMBER! THESE WERE TWO DESPERATE MEN... THEY HAD STOLEN FROM THEIR PARTNER AND DRIVEN HIM TO SUICIDE... A MERE SIX FEET OF EARTH AND A PINE BOX WOULD NOT STAND IN THEIR WAY NOW...
THIS IS THE SPOT!
HURRY, AND DON'T MAKE NOISE...
DON'T GIVE ORDERS! GRAB THE PICK AND HELP ME...
JOHN GLASS
FOR THREE HOURS, IN THE BLACK OF NIGHT, THEY DUG...STOPPING EVERY NOW AND THEN TO LISTEN FOR THE SOUND OF FOOTSTEPS...
THE COFFIN! YOU'VE STRUCK THE COFFIN!
GET DOWN HERE AND HELP ME!
HERE LIES
IT'S NAILED TIGHT! WE'LL HAVE TO PRY IT OPEN...
HERE... HERE'S A CROWBAR!
IT'S COMING...IT'S COMING... THERE!! SHINE A LIGHT DOWN HERE!
WHAT THE...?
5

IT'S EMPTY! THE COFFIN IS EMPTY!
B...B...BUT...WHERE'S GLASS? HE...HE... THERE'S A NOTE IN THE COFFIN!
THE NOTE READ...
MR. DICKSON:
MR. CARTER:
I HAVE DISCOVERED HO
YOU HAVE STOLEN MONEY FROM ME FOR THE LAST THREE YEARS,
DRIVING ME TO SUICIDE!
I HAVE RISEN FROM MY GRAVE... AND WILL NOT RETURN UNTIL I HAVE TAKEN MY REVENGE!
John Glass
LET'S GET OUT OF HERE,
Y...Y...YES! L...LET'S GO!
AH YES, DEAR READER... HERE WAS REAL TERROR... TWO MEN... HOUNDED BY A CORPSE...
ARE ALL THE WINDOWS LOCKED?
YES, AND THE DOOR IS BOLTED!
POUR M...ME A DRINK... I'M A LITTLE SH..SHAKY!
I COULD USE ONE MYSELF!
AAAAAH! THE GLASS! SOMETHING KNOCKED THE GLASS FROM MY HAND!
HE'S HERE! HERE... IN THIS ROOM...
OPEN THE WINDOW!!! CALL FOR HELP!
YES! YES!
6

RETURN FROM THE GRAVE!

SEE HOW TERRORIZED HUMAN BEINGS ACT, DEAR READER! LOOK... HOW FRANTICALLY DICKSON SCREAMS FROM THE WINDOW TEN STORIES ABOVE THE TRAFFIC BELOW! SEE... SEE HOW HE LEANS... TOO FAR...

CARTER! HELP! I'M SLIPPING...

AAAAAAAAHHH!

DICKSON! DON'T LEAVE ME ALONE WITH HIM...

THE GUN... CARTER! THE GUN YOU KEEP IN YOUR DESK DRAWER... GET IT! YOU'RE TERRIFIED NOW... YOU CAN'T BE LOGICAL... KILL YOURSELF!

YES! YES! YOU'LL NEVER GET ME, GLASS...

BUT WAIT, CARTER... LOOK WHO'S GETTING OUT OF THE ELEVATOR... IT'S GLASS... IN THE FLESH!

BAAAAAM!!

WHAT IN THE... A SHOT!

BUT GLASS WAS TOO LATE, DEAR READER! DICKSON AND CARTER WERE BOTH DEAD... ONE BY HIS OWN HANDS... ONE BY FALLING... BOTH BROUGHT ON BY TERROR!

YOU SEE, THE FUNERAL WAS STAGED AFTER GLASS FOUND OUT THAT HIS PARTNERS WERE SWINDLING HIM OUT OF HIS SHARE OF THE BUSINESS---HE WANTED TO IMPRESS THEM WITH HOW IMPORTANT HE WAS TO THE BUSINESS... HE KNEW THEY'D NEED THE FORMULAS TO MAKE THE PERFUME... SO HE SENT THAT BIG ORDER... HE WAS JUST COMING UP TO REVEAL HIS LITTLE PLOT...

NICE SENSE OF HUMOR, EH? HEH, HEH! WELL... I'LL SEE YOU NEXT ISSUE WITH ANOTHER TALE FROM THE **CRYPT OF TERROR...** BE SURE AND COME... WON'T YOU?

THE VAULT OF HORROR!

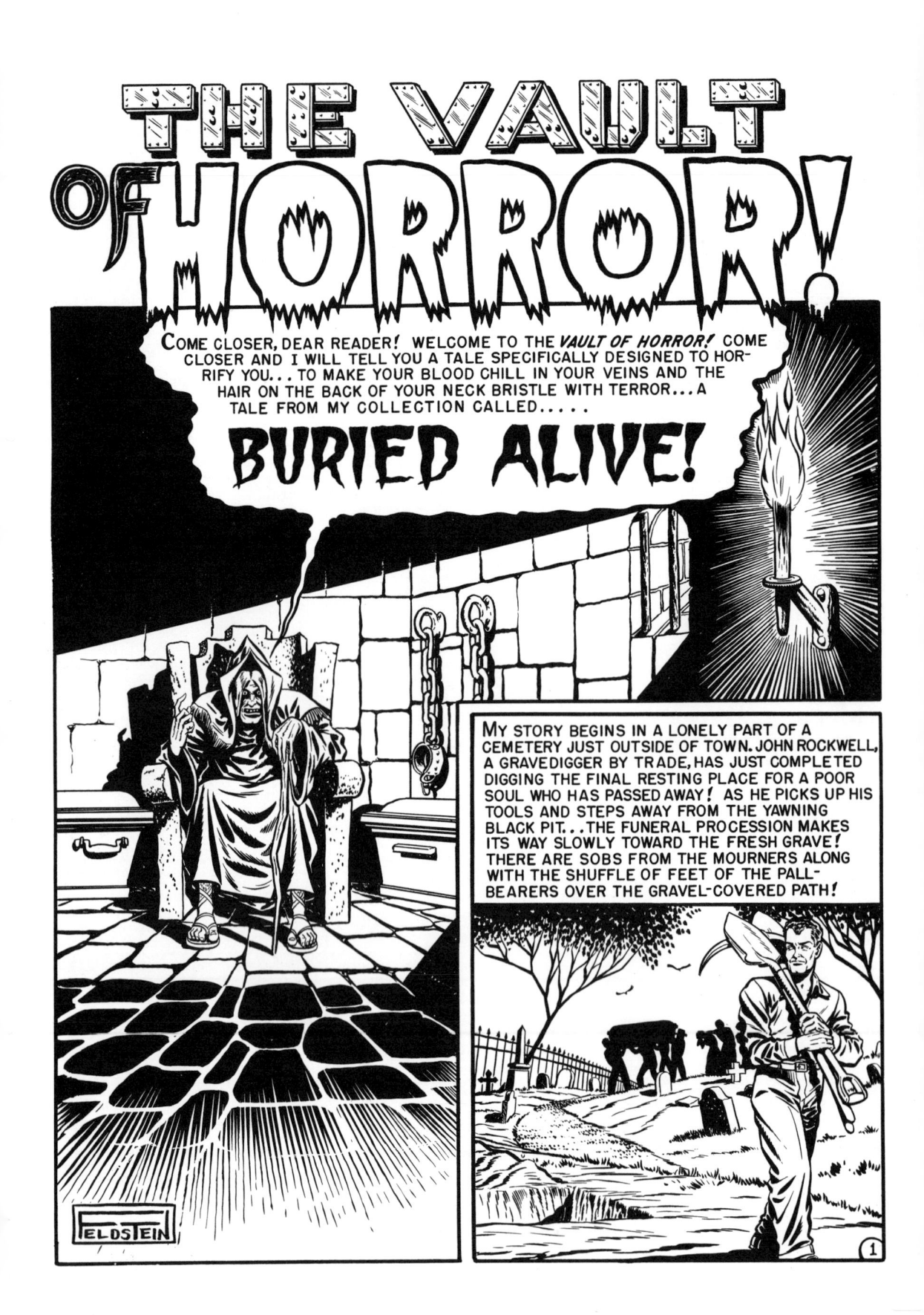

COME CLOSER, DEAR READER! WELCOME TO THE *VAULT OF HORROR!* COME CLOSER AND I WILL TELL YOU A TALE SPECIFICALLY DESIGNED TO HORRIFY YOU... TO MAKE YOUR BLOOD CHILL IN YOUR VEINS AND THE HAIR ON THE BACK OF YOUR NECK BRISTLE WITH TERROR... A TALE FROM MY COLLECTION CALLED.....

BURIED ALIVE!

MY STORY BEGINS IN A LONELY PART OF A CEMETERY JUST OUTSIDE OF TOWN. JOHN ROCKWELL, A GRAVEDIGGER BY TRADE, HAS JUST COMPLETED DIGGING THE FINAL RESTING PLACE FOR A POOR SOUL WHO HAS PASSED AWAY! AS HE PICKS UP HIS TOOLS AND STEPS AWAY FROM THE YAWNING BLACK PIT... THE FUNERAL PROCESSION MAKES ITS WAY SLOWLY TOWARD THE FRESH GRAVE! THERE ARE SOBS FROM THE MOURNERS ALONG WITH THE SHUFFLE OF FEET OF THE PALLBEARERS OVER THE GRAVEL-COVERED PATH!

BURIED ALIVE!

AS JOHN ROCKWELL WATCHES, THE SIMPLE CEREMONY IS COMPLETED...AND WITH A HOLLOW THUD, THE COFFIN IS LOWERED INTO THE GRAVE! JOHN SHUDDERS AT THE SOUND...SIGHTS LIKE THAT ALWAYS UNNERVE HIM!

AS THE SMALL GROUP OF MOURNERS TURN TO GO, HE STEPS FORWARD AND BEGINS TO FILL IN THE GRAVE. THE SOUNDS OF THE SOFT EARTH STRIKING THE HOLLOW COFFIN ECHO ACROSS THE NOW DESERTED CEMETERY!

HMMMPH! NEVER DID CARE FOR THIS WORK! GIVES ME A QUEER FEELING!

HIS WORK DONE, JOHN ROCKWELL NERVOUSLY MAKES HIS WAY OUT OF THE CEMETERY AND INTO A NEARBY BAR!

I NEED A DRINK! A FUNERAL ALWAYS GIVES ME *THE CREEPS!*

WELL! WELL!

OH, HELLO FRED! MOVE OVER! I NEED A PICK-ME-UP! JUST SAW ANOTHER BURYIN'!

OOOH! I DON'T ENVY *YOU*, JOHN! YOUR JOB CERTAINLY WOULD *BOTHER* ME...I'D ALWAYS BE *SCARED!*

SCARED OF *WHAT*, FRED?

OF BURYIN' SOMEONE WHO WAS *STILL ALIVE!*

I'VE HEARD OF CASES LIKE THAT! *CATALEPSY*, THEY CALL IT! A GUY LOOKS *DEAD*...BUT HE REALLY ISN'T! ONLY THEY CAN'T TELL VERY WELL...AND THEY BURY HIM...*ALIVE!!*

OH, YOU'RE BEING FOOLISH, FRED! THINGS LIKE THAT DON'T *HAPPEN!*

I GUESS NOT. ...STILL...

BUT THAT NIGHT...AS JOHN TOSSES AND TURNS IN RESTLESS SLEEP...HE HAS A STRANGE DREAM! HE DREAMS HE IS WATCHING THE FUNERAL AGAIN...THE SAME ONE HE HAD WATCHED WITH FASCINATION THAT VERY AFTERNOON! HE CAN SEE THE FACES OF THE MOURNERS AGAIN...EVERYTHING IS EXACTLY AS IT WAS EARLIER IN THE DAY!
THEN, AFTER THE PROCESSION LEAVES, JOHN TRIES TO SHOVEL EARTH INTO THE GRAVE...BUT HE CANNOT. SOMETHING IS STOPPING HIM...SOMETHING HE CANNOT UNDERSTAND! HE STANDS ROOTED ON THE EDGE OF THE GRAVE, AND THEN...HE HEARS...
MOOOOAAAAANN!
WHAT'S THAT?
NO NO NO! I'M ALIVE! ALIVE!
JOHN AWAKES WITH A START! HE IS COVERED WITH PERSPIRATION ...AND FRIGHTENED!
I'VE GOT TO FIND OUT! I'VE GOT TO SEE FOR MYSELF!
AND SO IN THE INKY BLACKNESS OF THE NIGHT, JOHN ROCKWELL GOES TO THE CEMETERY AND DIGS UP THE GRAVE...TO FIND OUT IF HIS DREAM HAD ANY MEANING!
HERE LIES
SOON HE REACHES THE COFFIN...AND OPENS IT! THE BODY INSIDE IS STIFF AND COLD! YES, JOHN! HE'S DEAD! STONE DEAD!
IT MUST BE...MY NERVES! I'LL FILL IN THE GRAVE AND GET OUT OF HERE BEFORE I'M SEEN...
THE NEXT MORNING, JOHN AWAKES FEELING FOOLISH OVER HIS ACTIONS OF THE NIGHT BEFORE...
I THINK I NEED A VACATION! YES, THAT'S A GOOD IDEA! I'LL TRY TO GET AWAY NEXT WEEK!
3

BURIED ALIVE!

However, John's morning paper carries unexpected headlines...

GRAVE ROBBED AND DESECRATED IN TOWN CEMETERY...LEFT OPEN! CLOTHES AND VALUABLES REMOVED FROM DECEASED.

B...BUT, I...I DIDN'T TAKE ANYTHING! I...I'M SURE I COVERED THE GRAVE. IT SAYS HERE THAT IT WAS LEFT *OPEN*! I...I DON'T KNOW...I *DON'T* KNOW!

John stops in at the bar on the way to work to steady his nerves...

S'MATTER, JOHN! YOU LOOK ILL!

IT...IT'S NOTHING, FRED!

TAKE MY ADVICE, AS A LIFE-LONG FRIEND OF YOURS, JOHN! *QUIT* THAT ROTTEN JOB OF YOURS! IT'S RUINING YOUR HEALTH... AFFECTING YOUR NERVES!

I...I GOT A VACATION IN A WEEK OR SO... I *MIGHT* QUIT AFTER THAT!

Several nights later...after witnessing a funeral that same afternoon...John dozes in his chair! He dreams the same strange dream! He is watching the very funeral he watched that afternoon... He recognizes the faces of the mourners...

And after they leave, again he cannot lift his spade to fill the grave...and again he hears the same low moan...

NO... NO... NO... *I'M ALIVE!*

John awakes with a start! He cannot help it... but again he feels that he *must* go to the grave ....that he *must* see for *himself!*

THOSE DREAMS *MEAN* SOMETHING! I'VE GOT TO FIND OUT WHAT IT IS!

4

AND AGAIN HE FINDS THAT THE BODY IN THE CASKET IS QUITE DEAD.
I... I MUST BE... LOSING MY MIND TO BE DOING A THING LIKE THIS!
THIS TIME JOHN MAKES SURE THAT THE GRAVE IS LEFT EXACTLY AS HE FOUND IT...
I'LL BE SURE THIS TIME THAT IT ISN'T ME THAT THEY ARE ACCUSING OF GRAVE ROBBING!
BUT THE NEXT MORNING AS JOHN OPENS HIS MORNING PAPER...
DAILY
SECOND GRAVE IN A WEEK ROBBED AND LEFT OPEN!
GOLD WATCH AND RING STOLEN FROM DECEASED
PERHAPS I DO THINGS WITH-OUT REMEMBERING THEM THE NEXT MORNING? I...I
A FEW DAYS LATER, FRED BAKER... JOHN'S GOOD FRIEND KNOCKS ON JOHN'S DOOR...
HMMM! HE DOESN'T ANSWER...
FRED TRIES THE DOOR AND FINDS IT OPEN! HE STEPS INTO THE DINGY ROOM!
JOHN!
HE'S DEAD!
5

BURIED ALIVE!

Panel 1: POOR FELLOW! HE *LOOKED* PRETTY BAD THE LAST TIME I SAW HIM BUT I NEVER EXPECTED *THIS*...

Panel 2: FRED TAKES CARE OF ALL THE DETAILS OF THE FUNERAL...
YES...I WANT HIM TO HAVE THE BEST...HE HAS A LITTLE MONEY AND NO RELATIVES SO HE MIGHT AS WELL HAVE A NICE FUNERAL!

Panel 3: FRED MAKES ARRANGEMENTS, AS JOHN HAD NO FAMILY, THAT HIS WATCH AND RINGS AND VALUABLES BE BURIED WITH HIM TO AVOID CONFUSION...
YES, HE'D HAVE WANTED IT THAT WAY!

Panel 4: AND SO JOHN ROCKWELL IS BURIED IN THE CEMETERY IN WHICH HE HAD WORKED SO MANY YEARS! THERE ARE FEW MOURNERS FOR HIS FUNERAL...JUST FRED AND SOME SLIGHT ACQUAINTANCES...

Panel 5: AFTER A SIMPLE CEREMONY...THE MOURNERS LEAVE AND THE GRAVE IS FILLED! THEN, SILENCE DESCENDS UPON THE CEMETERY...*DEAD* SILENCE!

Panel 6: AS THE SHADOWS LENGTHEN ACROSS THE GROUND AND NIGHT CLOSES IN, THE ONLY SOUND THAT IS HEARD IS THE OCCASIONAL RUSTLING OF A FALLING LEAF...

Panel 7: SUDDENLY...
AAAAAAHHH!

YES, DEAR READER! I HEARD IT TOO...A SCREAM! A SPINE-TINGLING, BLOOD-CURDLING SCREAM! IT CAME FROM JOHN'S GRAVE! NOW THE MEANING OF HIS DREAMS ARE CLEAR! IT WAS HIMSELF THAT JOHN WAS DREAMING ABOUT...
LET ME OUT! HELP ME! I'M ALIVE!
JOHN HAD HAD AN ATTACK OF CATALEPSY! THE VERY THING THAT HE HAD FEARED HAD HAPPENED TO THE OTHERS! AND NOW...THEY HAD BURIED HIM ALIVE!
I'VE GOT TO FREE MYSELF... BEFORE THE AIR IN HERE GIVES OUT...
FRANTICALLY, JOHN PUSHES ON THE CASKET LID OVER HIM... BUT HE STRUGGLES IN VAIN...THE WEIGHT OF EARTH ABOVE HIM IS TOO MUCH...
I...CAN'T...BUDGE IT...!
I... I'M BURIED ALIVE! SO THAT'S WHY I HAD THOSE AWFUL DREAMS! IT WAS A PREMONITION... AND NOW...I'M GOING TO SUFFOCATE...
SUDDENLY THE EVENTS OF THE PAST WEEKS FLASH THROUGH JOHN'S MIND, AND HE REMEMBERS SOMETHING!
YES... PERHAPS... I'VE GOT TO LIE QUIET... CONSERVE THE AIR SUPPLY... UNTIL...
JOHN ROCKWELL
THE SECONDS DRAG BY INTO MINUTES AND THE MINUTES INTO HOURS ...JOHN IS GASPING FOR WHAT LITTLE OXYGEN IS LEFT...
CAN'T... GASP... LAST... MUCH LONGER... GASP...
AND THEN... HE HEARS IT...THE SOUND HE HAS BEEN WAITING FOR...
A SPADE STRIKES THE SOFT EARTH SIX FEET ABOVE HIM!
7

BURIED ALIVE!

CAN HE LAST UNTIL THE PERSON ABOVE CAN REACH HIM...
I'VE GOT TO...GASP... LAST...GASP... GOT TO...

SLOWLY THE HOLE ABOVE THE COFFIN WIDENS AND LENGTHENS AS THE GRAVE-ROBBER DIGS...
HURRY! HURRY!

AT LAST THE SPADE STRIKES THE HOLLOW BOX...
HE...HE'S STRUCK THE COFFIN...EVERYTHING... IS...GASP...GOING...BLACK...

AS THE LAST TRACES OF OXYGEN ARE DRAINED FROM THE COFFIN, JOHN SLIPS INTO UNCONSCIOUSNESS...THE LID IS PRIED OPEN AND A LIGHT IS FLASHED UPON HIM...
HEH...HEH...WHAT A HAUL *THIS* TIME.

BUT THE FRESH AIR REVIVES JOHN AND HE FILLS HIS LUNGS...OPENS HIS EYES AND SEES...
YOU!
NO! AAAAAAAAAH!

FRED!!! YOU! YOU'RE THE GRAVE ROBBER...
YOU...YOU...YOU'RE DEAD...I SAW...I SAW YOU... DEAD...AHAH! AHAH-HAH-HAH-HAH...NO... HAH-HAH! YOU'RE... DEAD!!

FRED WENT *COMPLETELY MAD* FROM THE SHOCK, DEAR READER! *YOU* CAN *UNDERSTAND!* GRAVE-ROBBING IS A NERVE-WRACKING BUSINESS! AND *THIS* WAS THE STRAW THAT BROKE THE CAMEL'S BACK! THEY HAVE HIM IN A PADDED CELL NOW...ONE THAT HE WON'T BE ABLE TO DIG HIS WAY OUT OF! AND JOHN! OH HE'S WORKING IN AN UNDERTAKING ESTABLISHMENT NOW...IT KEEPS HIS CONSCIENCE CLEAR...

DROP IN AGAIN *NEXT ISSUE* WHEN I'LL HAVE ANOTHER TALE FROM *THE VAULT OF HORROR!*

IF YOU LIKE THIS TYPE OF STORY, WON'T YOU WRITE TO: THE EDITOR, E-C COMICS, 225 LAFAYETTE ST. N.Y.C., 12, N.Y. AND TELL ME... *THANK YOU!*

8

I was a 'B'-GIRL!

IF YOU HAVE NEVER HEARD OF THE NOTORIOUS "B"-GIRLS THAT INHABIT MOST OF THE NIGHT CLUBS AND CAFES AROUND THE COUNTRY... READ THIS CONFESSION OF ALICE PATTON*AND FIND OUT HOW THEY OPERATE... WHAT MAKES THEM TICK... AND HOW ONE OF THEM FOUND LOVE!

*AT THE AUTHOR'S REQUEST, ALL NAMES AND PLACES IN THIS MODERN LOVE STORY HAVE BEEN ALTERED TO CONCEAL TRUE IDENTITIES!

"YOU LOOK LONESOME, BUDDY! C'MON! BUY ME A DRINK..."

"SURE, HONEY! SIT DOWN..."

I WAS FIFTEEN WHEN MOTHER DIED! WE LIVED ON A SMALL FARM NEAR ST. LOUIS, AND FOR FOUR LONG YEARS AFTER THAT, I WORKED HARD FOR MY FATHER... BEING BOTH "HIRED HAND" AND HOUSEKEEPER FOR HIM...

"AND AFTER THE MILKIN', SCRUB UP THE KITCHEN..."

"YES, FATHER!"

HE WAS CRUEL AND HEARTLESS AND I HATED HIM FOR THE WAY HE DROVE ME! MY ONLY HOPE FOR ESCAPING WAS HANK GREYSON... THE BOY WHO LIVED AT THE NEXT FARM...
HANK... YOU'VE ALWAYS SAID YOU WANTED TO MARRY ME SOMEDAY...
Y'MEAN... Y'MEAN... WILL YUH, ALICE? WILL YUH?
IF YOU WANT ME, HANK!
SHUCKS, DO I? THAR HAIN'T NO GAL IN THIS VALLEY KIN DO CHORES AN' KEEP HOUSE LIKE YOU KIN! WHY, SHUCKS! NOW I KIN LET MY HIRED HAND GO...
THAT NIGHT, I PACKED MY BAG, TOOK WHAT LITTLE MONEY I HAD SAVED, AND RAN AWAY...
IT'S NO USE! I'VE GOT TO GET AWAY BEFORE THEY WORK ME TO DEATH!
I BOUGHT A TICKET TO CHICAGO AND SAT AROUND THE STATION WAITING FOR THE TRAIN TO COME IN! I WAS NERVOUS AND FRIGHTENED... BUT AT LAST IT STEAMED INTO THE STATION...
...AND I WAS ON MY WAY! THERE WAS AN EMPTY SEAT NEXT TO A RATHER NICE-LOOKING MAN...
IS THIS SEAT TAKEN?
IT IS NOW! SIT DOWN! YOU LOOK ALL FLUSHED!
I... I'M A LITTLE EXCITED! I... I'M GOING TO CHICAGO TO LOOK FOR A JOB! I'VE JUST... ER... LEFT HOME...
A JOB, EH? I COULD USE A GOOD-LOOKER LIKE YOU!
Y... YOU MEAN YOU COULD GIVE ME A JOB...
SURE! I GOT A NIGHT CLUB IN CHI... YOU COULD BE ONE OF MY "B"-GIRLS!
2

I WAS A 'B'-GIRL!

Panel 1:
— A "B"-GIRL! WHAT'S THAT?
— BOY, YOU ARE A SMALL-TOWN GIRL...

Panel 2:
A "B"-GIRL'S A...A HOSTESS! SHE MAKES THE CUSTOMERS FEEL AT HOME...GETS THEM TO BUY HER DRINKS...ONLY THE DRINKS ARE COLORED WATER! SHE GETS A PERCENTAGE OF EVERY "DRINK" THEY BUY HER...

Panel 3:
— THAT'S WHERE THE NAME COMES FROM! SHE BUMS DRINKS...BUM-GIRL..."B"-GIRL! GET IT?
— Y...YES! I DON'T THINK THAT'S A JOB FOR ME!

Panel 4:
— SUIT YOURSELF, SISTER! ONLY IF YOU CHANGE YOUR MIND, LOOK ME UP! MY NAME'S SHOLE...MARTY SHOLE! I OWN THE *GOLD SWAN* ON THE LOOP!
— I...I WILL, MR. SHOLE! *IF* I CHANGE MY MIND!

Panel 5:
CHICAGO WAS WONDERFUL! TALL BUILDINGS...CROWDS OF PEOPLE...THE ELEVATED...THE LAKE...IT WAS EXCITING...BREATHTAKING! THEN I GOT DOWN TO BUSINESS! FINDING A JOB! I THOUGHT THE AGENCIES WERE MY BEST BET!
— NEED A JOB REAL BAD, EH? WHAT CAN YOU DO?
— WELL...YOU SEE...THAT'S IT! I CAN'T DO ANYTHING!

Panel 6:
— COME, COME! THERE MUST BE *SOMETHING* YOU CAN DO...
— MY ARM...YOU'RE HURTING ME!

Panel 7:
— IF YOU COOPERATE, I'M SURE I CAN FIND A POSITION FOR YOU...
— LET ME GO! LET ME GO!

3

WHY YOU... YOU...
OUCH!
YOU LITTLE TRAMP! YOU'LL NEVER FIND A JOB NOW! I'LL HAVE YOU BLACKLISTED WITH EVERY AGENCY IN TOWN...YOU'LL BE SORRY...YOU WAIT AND SEE!
HE WAS RIGHT, TOO! I TRIED SEVERAL OTHER PLACES BUT I GOT A QUICK BRUSH-OFF! HE MUST HAVE HAD PLENTY OF FRIENDS! I WAS DESPERATE! MY MONEY WAS RUNNING OUT...
THE... THE GOLD SWAN!
MR. SHOLE RECOGNIZED ME THE MINUTE I OPENED THE DOOR...
WELL, WELL! YOU CERTAINLY CHANGED YOUR MIND QUICKLY...
I HAD TO! MY MONEY'S ALMOST GONE!
DON'T WORRY ABOUT A THING, KID! HERE'S A TEN SPOT IN ADVANCE! YOU START TONIGHT! WARDROBE WILL FIX YOU UP WITH A GOWN...
TH-THANK YOU, MR. SHOLE!
AND SO I BECAME A "B"-GIRL! THERE WERE PLENTY OF "SUCKERS," AS THE OTHER GIRLS CALLED THEM, AND I MADE A GOOD LIVING! ONE NIGHT AT CLOSING TIME...
I'LL DRIVE YOU HOME, ALICE!
WHY, THAT'S VERY NICE OF YOU, MR. SHOLE!
BUT WHEN WE REACHED MY APARTMENT BUILDING...
HOW'S ABOUT ME COMING UP FOR A NIGHT-CAP?
SORRY, MR. SHOLE! IF YOU'LL LET ME OUT...
4

DON'T BE LIKE THAT, ALICE! DON'T FORGET, YOU'RE *WORKING* FOR ME!
AND THAT'S *ALL!* I DO MY WORK! IF YOU EXPECT ANY *MORE*, YOU'RE WRONG!
YOU'RE MAKING A MISTAKE, ALICE! I COULD MAKE IT TOUGH FOR YOU...
I'LL PICK UP MY THINGS IN THE MORNING...
OKAY, OKAY! LET'S FORGET IT! I WAS WRONG! I...I'M SORRY!
THANKS, MR. SHOLE! AND NOW, GOOD-NIGHT!
WHY WERE ALL MEN LIKE THAT? ALWAYS TAKING ADVANTAGE! THEY WERE SELFISH...EVIL! I HATED THEM! ALL OF THEM! MY FATHER...HANK...MR. SHOLE...THEY WERE ALL THE SAME! I WONDERED IF I WOULD EVER FIND A MAN I COULD TRULY LOVE! THAT NIGHT I CRIED MYSELF TO SLEEP! I WAS LONELY! TERRIBLY ALONE!
AND THEN I SAW *HIM!* ONE NIGHT, HE WAS SITTING AT THE BAR! MY HEART BEAT FASTER AS I SLIPPED ONTO THE STOOL BESIDE HIM!
H...HELLO!
WHY.., HELLO!
YOU LOOKED...*LONESOME* SO I THOUGHT I'D JOIN YOU!
I... I *AM!* THANKS! CAN I BUY YOU SOMETHING?
ER... NO, THANKS. WHAT'S YOUR NAME?
REX! REX PAUL! WHAT'S YOURS?
5

MY NAME'S ALICE PATTON! I WORK HERE AS A... HOSTESS!
THEN IF I COME HERE AGAIN, I'LL SEE YOU...?
SURE! ANYTIME!
I'D...LIKE THAT!
REX DID COME BACK! AGAIN AND AGAIN! WE DANCED! WE TALKED! WE LAUGHED TOGETHER! AND THERE WERE TIMES WE JUST SAT QUIETLY HOLDING HANDS!
REX, DARLING! I THINK I AM FALLING IN LOVE!
SAME HERE, ALICE DEAR!
I WAS DELIRIOUSLY HAPPY! REX WAS EVERYTHING I HAD ALWAYS SEARCHED FOR...GOOD, KIND, GENTLE! I WANTED SO MUCH TO HAVE HIM TAKE ME IN HIS ARMS AND KISS ME...AGAIN AND AGAIN...BUT THEN, ONE NIGHT...
REX! YOU NEVER TOLD ME ABOUT YOURSELF...WHAT YOU DO...
I..I'M A TRUCK DRIVER, ALICE! IT'S NOT A WONDERFUL JOB, BUT...
...THE PAY IS GOOD... AND...THE KIDS NEED CLOTHES...
KIDS? YOU HAVE CHILDREN??
I WANTED TO CRY BUT I WAS TOO SHOCKED! REX... JUST LIKE ALL THE OTHERS...MARRIED...AND I WAS BEING THE "SUCKER!"
ALICE...WAIT! COME BACK!
SOB...SOB
THAT NIGHT I QUIT THE CLUB AND LEFT CHICAGO! I HATED REX FOR MAKING ME FALL IN LOVE WITH HIM! HATED HIM...AND YET I KNEW I WOULD ALWAYS LOVE HIM, NO MATTER WHAT HE HAD DONE... MARRIED OR NOT! THAT'S WHY I LEFT! I FOUND A JOB AS A WAITRESS IN A DINER OUTSIDE OF THE CITY! ONE NIGHT...
WELL, WELL...
YOU!
6

LOOK, ALICE! I KNOW WHAT YOU THINK OF ME BUT THAT DOESN'T MATTER... IT'S THAT REX GUY I'M THINKING OF...
I'D RATHER NOT TALK ABOUT HIM...
HE'S BEEN HAUNTING THE PLACE EVER SINCE YOU LEFT...TOLD ME ALL ABOUT YOU TWO! HE SAID YOU WOULDN'T LET HIM EXPLAIN ABOUT HOW HIS WIFE DIED THREE YEARS AGO LEAVING HIM WITH TWO CHILDREN! HE LOVES YOU, ALICE!
OH, MR. SHOLE... SOB...SOB... I'VE BEEN A FOOL!
STAY HERE, ALICE! I'LL BE BACK SOON!
BUT MR. SHOLE NEVER DID COME BACK! AN HOUR LATER... A BIG TRUCK PULLED UP OUTSIDE THE DINER! IT WAS REX!
REX!
DARLING! I'VE LOOKED ALL OVER CHICAGO FOR YOU! YOU DIDN'T GIVE ME A CHANCE TO EXPLAIN!
DON'T, REX! I'VE BEEN A FOOL! I KNOW ALL ABOUT IT, NOW!
MARRY ME, ALICE, DEAR?
OH, DEAREST! I WANT TO... SO MUCH!
REX AND I HAVE FOUR CHILDREN TODAY... AND I LOVE THEM... EACH AND EVERY ONE... AS MUCH AS ANY MOTHER COULD LOVE HER CHILDREN! WE'RE A WONDERFUL HAPPY FAMILY... NOW!
7

HERE IS ANOTHER TALE TAKEN FROM
THE CRYPT OF TERROR

WELCOME, DEAR READER! WELCOME AGAIN TO THE **CRYPT OF TERROR**! I HAVE ANOTHER **CHILLING** TALE TO TELL YOU! A STORY GUARANTEED TO MAKE YOUR BLOOD *FREEZE* IN YOUR VEINS... AND THE HAIR ON YOUR NECK BRISTLE WITH *HORROR*... A TALE SPECIFICALLY DESIGNED TO *TERRORIZE* YOU! *THIS* STORY FROM MY COLLECTION IS CALLED...

THE SPECTRE IN THE CASTLE!

ANOTHER ILLUSTRATED SuspenStory

THE SPECTRE IN THE CASTLE!

MY STORY BEGINS AT THE OFFICE OF CARLTON DAVIS, LAWYER FOR THE LATE ENOS BALTER, MILLIONAIRE MANUFACTURER...

AH, MR. AND MRS. BALTER! DO BE SEATED!

LET'S GET THIS OVER WITH, MR. DAVIS! I KNOW MY UNCLE NEVER LIKED ME SO... I DON'T *EXPECT* ANYTHING!

OH, BUT YOU'RE *WRONG*, MR. BALTER! YOUR UNCLE ENOS HAS LEFT YOU THE *BULK* OF HIS ESTATE! HE...ER..LEFT *ME* A GOODLY SUM TOO, KIND SOUL....ABOUT $12,000! BUT THE ESTATE AND HIS HOLDINGS GO TO *YOU*...ABOUT $750,000, I WOULD ESTIMATE!

WHAT???

ON *ONE* CONDITION!

OH! THERE'RE STRINGS ATTACHED! OKAY! WHAT'S THE CATCH?

WELL, YOU REMEMBER THE TIME YOUR UNCLE HAD THE HOUSE-WARMING... TO CELEBRATE THE COMPLETION OF THE CASTLE HE HAD SHIPPED HERE, STONE BY STONE, FROM ENGLAND...?

"WE WERE SITTING AROUND THE MASSIVE DINING TABLE, AFTER A MOST DELICIOUS MEAL..."

...AND NOW, MY HONORED GUESTS! I SUPPOSE YOU ARE ALL WONDERING *WHY* I SPENT SUCH A TREMENDOUS FORTUNE TO BRING THIS GLOOMY OLD CASTLE HERE FROM ENGLAND!

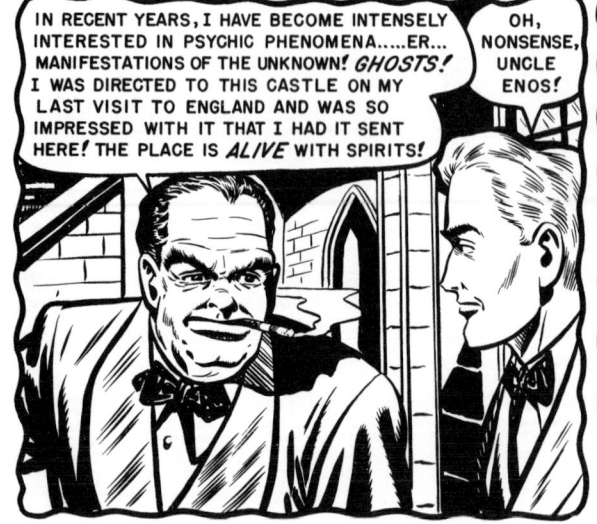

IN RECENT YEARS, I HAVE BECOME INTENSELY INTERESTED IN PSYCHIC PHENOMENA......ER... MANIFESTATIONS OF THE UNKNOWN! *GHOSTS!* I WAS DIRECTED TO THIS CASTLE ON MY LAST VISIT TO ENGLAND AND WAS SO IMPRESSED WITH IT THAT I HAD IT SENT HERE! THE PLACE IS *ALIVE* WITH SPIRITS!

OH, NONSENSE, UNCLE ENOS!

SO, MY DEAR NEPHEW! YOU DO NOT BELIEVE IT! WELL, YOU'LL SEE! ONE OF THE STORIES CONNECTED WITH THIS PLACE INVOLVES THE RETURN OF THE MASTER OF THE CASTLE TO MURDER ONE OF ITS LIVING INHABITANTS TEN DAYS AFTER THE MASTER'S DEATH! THIS HAS HAPPENED FIVE TIMES IN THE PAST THREE HUNDRED YEARS...AND NOW, *I* AM THE MASTER OF THIS CASTLE!

THE SPECTRE IN THE CASTLE!

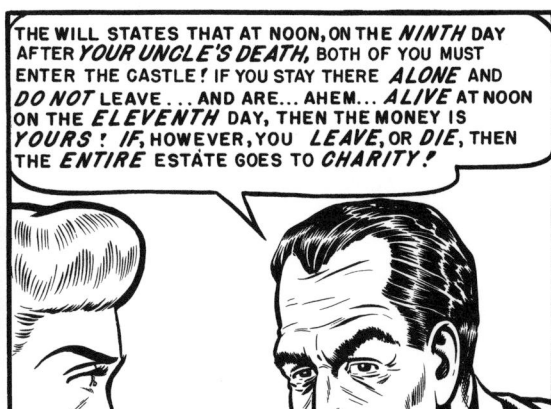

Tom: YES, I REMEMBER IT VERY WELL, MR. DAVIS! BUT WHAT DOES *THAT* HAVE TO DO WITH MY UNCLE'S WILL?

Davis: *EVERYTHING*, MR. BALTER!

Davis: THE WILL STATES THAT AT NOON, ON THE *NINTH* DAY AFTER *YOUR UNCLE'S DEATH*, BOTH OF YOU MUST ENTER THE CASTLE! IF YOU STAY THERE *ALONE* AND *DO NOT* LEAVE... AND ARE... AHEM... *ALIVE* AT NOON ON THE *ELEVENTH* DAY, THEN THE MONEY IS *YOURS*! IF, HOWEVER, YOU *LEAVE*, OR *DIE*, THEN THE *ENTIRE* ESTATE GOES TO *CHARITY*!

Tom: THIS IS *PREPOSTEROUS*! UNCLE ENOS MUST HAVE BEEN *MAD* WHEN HE WROTE THAT...

Mary: I AGREE THAT IT *IS* A BIT QUEER, BUT... THOSE ARE THE CONDITIONS!

Davis: AND SINCE I AM *EXECUTOR* OF THE WILL, I MUST INSIST THAT THE CONDITIONS BE FULFILLED OR ELSE THE MONEY WILL GO TO SOME WORTHY CHARITY!

Narrator: HEH... HEH! *WELL*, DEAR READER! UNCLE ENOS HAS PRESENTED QUITE A PROBLEM TO TOM AND MARY BALTER! WOULD *YOU* STAY IN A HAUNTED OLD CASTLE... AND FACE A *MURDERING GHOST*... FOR $750,000? THAT'S A *TIDY* SUM! I'LL BET *YOU* THINK THE LEGEND IS A *FAKE*! WOULD YOU... *BET YOUR LIFE*?

AT THE APPOINTED DAY, CARLTON DAVIS FERRIED TOM AND MARY BALTER ACROSS THE LAKE TO THE ISLAND ON WHICH OLD ENOS BALTER HAD BUILT HIS CASTLE! IT HAD BEEN OVERCAST ALL MORNING... AND NOW FLASHES OF LIGHTNING KNIFED THROUGH THE DARKENED SKY...

Mary: BRRR... WHAT A HORRIBLE DAY!

Tom: LOOKS LIKE A STORM'S BREWING!

AT THE LANDING DOCK, LAWYER DAVIS TOOK HIS LEAVE!

Tom: WELL, I HOPE EVERYTHING GOES WELL! DON'T WORRY! I THINK IT'S ALL NONSENSE, MYSELF! SEE YOU AT NOON, DAY AFTER TOMORROW!

Davis: YOU'D BETTER HURRY OR YOU'LL BE CAUGHT IN THE STORM, DAVIS!

THE SPECTRE IN THE CASTLE!

Tom and Mary watched as Davis disappeared into the gathering fog! Then they turned and gazed up at the grey cold towers of the castle...

"Doesn't look very inviting, does it?"

"Well, we might as well go inside! It's going to be our home for the next two days..."

"And nights! Oh, Tom! I'm afraid!"

"Nonsense! C'mon! It's starting to rain..."

A clap of thunder crashed across the castle as the door swung open!

"It's awfully dark in there, Tom!"

"These places weren't built for comfort!"

"Here's a candle! C'mon!"

"I'm right here WITH you! Don't worry!"

As the frightened couple stepped into the castle, the massive door swung shut... and the sound it made echoed through the empty corridors...

"Must have been the wind! These old castles are drafty..."

"Eerie, too! Listen to the echoes!"

"Mary! THE DOOR! It's LOCKED!"

"We're trapped! We couldn't get out NOW if we wanted to... sob... sob..."

"There, there, dear! There must be OTHER doors! Besides! We're not SUPPOSED to leave ANYWAY! Davis will let us out when the time comes!"

"I... I... I'd be lots happier if I could leave when I WANTED to..."

4

AS THE LIGHT FROM THE CANDLES THAT TOM LIT PIERCED THE GLOOM OF THE MASSIVE INTERIOR OF THE CASTLE, MARY'S EYES FELL UPON...
LOOK, TOM! A SUIT OF ARMOR! IT LOOKS GENUINE, TOO!
YES! UNCLE HAD THE ORIGINAL FURNISHINGS BROUGHT OVER WITH THE BUILDING!
AS DARKNESS FELL UPON THE ISLAND, THE STORM BROKE WITH ALL ITS FURY!
YOU'D THINK YOUR UNCLE WOULD HAVE BROUGHT ELECTRICITY INTO THE CASTLE!
HE WANTED TO KEEP EVERYTHING AS AUTHENTIC AS POSSIBLE!
SUDDENLY FROM THE ROOM UPSTAIRS, TOM AND MARY HEARD...
CLANK! CLANK!
WHAT'S THAT?
SOUNDS LIKE CHAINS OR... OR... ARMOR!
QUIETLY, THEY SLIPPED TO THE HEAD OF THE STAIRS AND LOOKED DOWN! EVERYTHING WAS DARK AND STILL...
EEEEEEEK! LOOK....! THE ARMOR! IT MOVED!
YOU'RE IMAGINING THINGS, MARY! HOW COULD IT?
I DON'T KNOW. I DON'T KNOW! IT WAS OVER ON THE OTHER SIDE OF THE ROOM!
ARE YOU SURE, MARY?
YES, I'M POSITIVE! IT WAS OVER NEXT TO THAT TAPESTRY!
WELL, LET'S SEE IF THERE'S ANYONE OR ANYTHING IN IT!
LOOK OUT, MARY!!
EEEEEEEEK!
CRASH!
5

THE SPECTRE IN THE CASTLE!

TOM...SOB...SOB...THERE'S SOMEONE *HERE*...TRYING TO *KILL* US! LET'S GO HOME...

BUT, MARY! IF WE LEAVE, WE LOSE THE INHERITANCE!

TOM! THE SUIT OF ARMOR IS *GONE!!*

WHAT THE...?

The terrorized couple rushed upstairs to their room...

WE'LL *LOCK* OURSELVES IN...

TOM...I'M *FRIGHTENED!*

Tom slipped the massive bolt into place...

THERE! ONLY A TRUCK COULD GET THROUGH THAT DOOR, NOW!

LET'S GET OFF THIS ISLAND FIRST THING IN THE MORNING, TOM! PERHAPS WE CAN FIND A BOAT...

WE'LL TRY! MAYBE THERE *IS* SOMETHING TO THE LEGENDS ABOUT THIS CASTLE!

Outside their room, lightning flashes knifed the inky blackness of the night, and the thunder lashed at the castle towers. Tom and Mary tossed in the immense bed as they tried to sleep...but their fears kept them from dozing off! The candle sputtered...then died out! Suddenly...from the darkness...

MO-O-O-OAN-N-N!

WHAT'S THAT?

OH, FORGET IT, HONEY! JUST THE ROOF CREAKING...

EEEEEEE---TOM!! LOOK!

NO! NO! NO!! IT'S UNCLE ENOS!!!
HE'S COME BACK! ...TO KILL US!
YIIIII!
DON'T COME ANY CLOSER, WHATEVER YOU ARE!!
TOM-M-MPH!
MARY!!
I'LL GET YOU... YOU...FIEND!
TOM SLIPPED INTO THE PASSAGEWAY, JUST AS THE PANEL SNAPPED SHUT BEHIND HIM...
THERE IT GOES! ...AND IT'S CARRYING MARY!
7

THE SPECTRE IN THE CASTLE!

THE STAIRCASE OPENED OUT INTO THE FURY OF THE STORM AT THE TOP OF ONE OF THE CASTLE TOWERS! AS TOM REACHED IT...

NO! *STOP!!* YOU *MONSTER!*

AAAAAAAH

OH, TOM,...SOB...IT WAS *HORRIBLE!*

YOU'RE SAFE *NOW,* MARY DARLING! IT'S ALL OVER!!

LOOK, TOM! DOWN THERE... AT THE BEACH! *A BOAT!*

YES! *DAVIS' BOAT!*

THEN...THEN THE BODY DOWN THERE... IS... *CARLTON DAVIS!*

YES, DEAR! SHALL WE... GO DOWN?

...AND THAT'S THE TALE, DEAR READER! CARLTON DAVIS, AS EXECUTOR OF THE ESTATE, WOULD HAVE CONTROLLED OLD ENOS' *ENTIRE* FORTUNE IF TOM LEFT THE CASTLE OR DIED! SO KNOWING THE CONTENTS OF ENOS' WILL, AND HAVING DISCOVERED, AMONG HIS EFFECTS, THE BLUEPRINTS OF THE CASTLE SHOWING THE MAZE OF SECRET PASSAGES AND PANELS HIDDEN THERE, DAVIS PROCEEDED WITH HIS DIABOLICAL SCHEME OF FRIGHTENING TOM AND MARY FROM THE CASTLE! AFTER HE LEFT THEM...HE DOUBLED BACK TO THE ISLAND! OLD ENOS' GHOST WAS NOTHING MORE THAN A PROJECTED PICTURE! DAVIS BECAME DESPERATE WHEN NIGHT FELL...AND HE DECIDED TO *KILL* THEM BOTH! HE...HEH,HEH... OVERPLAYED HIS HAND, THOUGH, DON'T YOU THINK? WELL, I'LL HAVE ANOTHER TALE FROM

THE CRYPT OF TERROR!

NEXT ISSUE! BE SURE AND COME, WON'T YOU?

IF YOU LIKE THIS TYPE OF STORY, WON'T YOU WRITE TO: THE EDITOR, E.C. COMICS, 225 LAFAYETTE ST., N.Y.C.—AND LET ME KNOW?

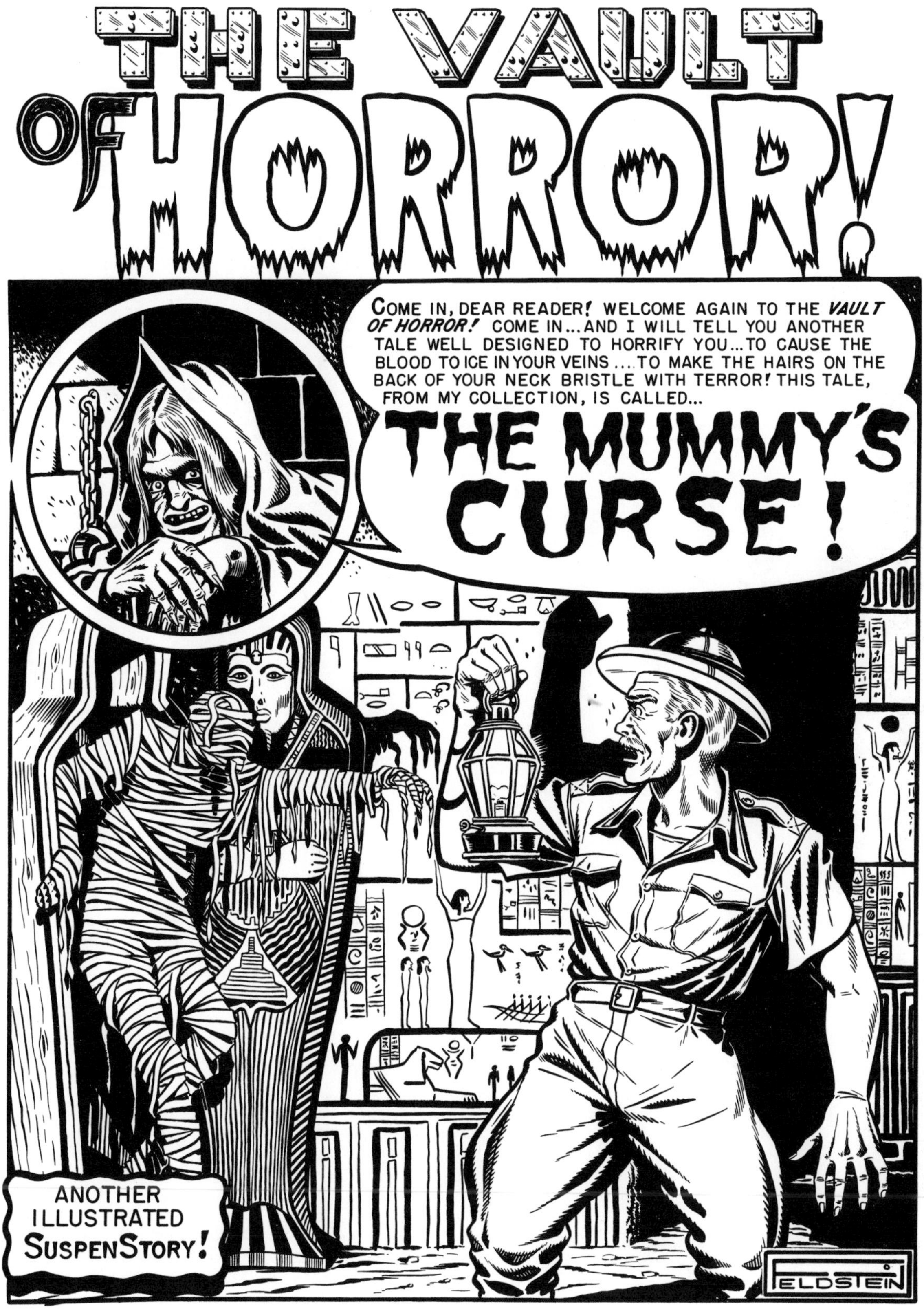
THE VAULT OF HORROR!
COME IN, DEAR READER! WELCOME AGAIN TO THE *VAULT OF HORROR!* COME IN... AND I WILL TELL YOU ANOTHER TALE WELL DESIGNED TO HORRIFY YOU... TO CAUSE THE BLOOD TO ICE IN YOUR VEINS.... TO MAKE THE HAIRS ON THE BACK OF YOUR NECK BRISTLE WITH TERROR! THIS TALE, FROM MY COLLECTION, IS CALLED...
THE MUMMY'S CURSE!
ANOTHER ILLUSTRATED SUSPENSTORY!
FELDSTEIN

THE MUMMY'S CURSE!

My story begins in the office of the curator of the Egyptological division of the British Museum...

THANK GOODNESS YOU'VE FINALLY ARRIVED IN ENGLAND, PROFESSOR GLADSTONE! PERHAPS *NOW* YOU CAN CLEAR UP THIS *NONSENSE* YOU WROTE ABOUT YOUR EXPEDITION!

IT'S *NOT NONSENSE*, MR. BLAKELY! EVERY WORD I WROTE WAS THE TRUTH!

I WAS SHOCKED TO HEAR OF PROFESSOR UPJOHN'S UNTIMELY DEATH! BUT... THIS GIBBERISH ABOUT A MUMMY *RISING* FROM HIS SARCOPHAGUS AND ATTACKING YOU... TRYING TO *KILL* YOU...

IT'S *TRUE*, EVERY WORD OF IT! I JUST BARELY ESCAPED WITH MY LIFE...

BUT, YOU *DID* FIND THE TOMB OF KING ANKH-MU-TAMEN!

YES... WE FOUND IT! THEN UPJOHN SLIPPED AND FELL DOWN THE CREVICE... AND THE MUMMY...

GLADSTONE! *ANOTHER* EXPEDITION IS BEING FORMED! WE WANT TO LEAVE IN A WEEK! *YOU'LL* ACCOMPANY US OF COURSE? IT'S IMPERATIVE THAT YOU SHOW US THE *LOCATION* OF THE TOMB!

NEVER! I'LL *NEVER* GO BACK TO THAT PLACE!

COME, COME, PROF. GLADSTONE! AREN'T YOU ACTING A BIT CHILDISH?

Reluctantly, Professor Gladstone agreed to return with the new expedition to the tomb of King Ankh-Mu-Tamen and the scene of the harrowing experience that still burned in his memory! Two weeks later, as a small riverboat moved slowly up the Nile toward the Valley of the Kings....

I HOPE THEY CAN'T FIND UPJOHN'S BODY IN THAT CREVICE WHERE I *PUSHED* HIM! I DON'T THINK I COULD STAND IT!

So... dear reader! Professor Upjohn didn't *FALL* into the crevice! He was *PUSHED*! Perhaps now we will find out what *REALLY* happened on that first expedition!

...TO THE RIGHT OF THAT LARGE BOULDER, UNDER THE OVERHANG...

AH, YES! I SEE IT! THE OPENING TO THE TOMB! WE'LL CAMP HERE!

THE MUMMY'S CURSE!

THAT NIGHT, AFTER CAMP WAS MADE, PROFESSOR GLADSTONE TOSSED UNEASILY ON HIS COT! HIS THOUGHTS WENT BACK TO THE FIRST EXPEDITION... THE DAY HE AND PROFESSOR HARVEY UPJOHN DISCOVERED THE ENTRANCE TO THE TOMB... ALMOST THREE MONTHS BEFORE...

HARVEY! HERE! LOOK!

I'M COMING, CARL! HOLD ON!

CAREFUL, HARVEY! A SLIP ON THESE ROCKS MEANS CERTAIN DEATH...

DON'T WORRY, CARL! I'M STILL PRETTY AGILE FOR AN OLD MAN...

YOU'RE RIGHT, CARL! THIS DOES LOOK LIKE AN OPENING!

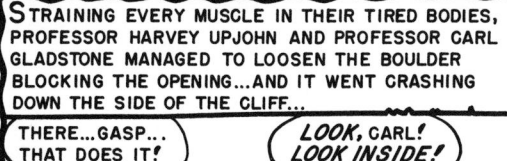

HELP ME PUSH THIS BOULDER ASIDE!

STRAINING EVERY MUSCLE IN THEIR TIRED BODIES, PROFESSOR HARVEY UPJOHN AND PROFESSOR CARL GLADSTONE MANAGED TO LOOSEN THE BOULDER BLOCKING THE OPENING... AND IT WENT CRASHING DOWN THE SIDE OF THE CLIFF...

THERE... GASP... THAT DOES IT!

LOOK, CARL! LOOK INSIDE!

GLADSTONE AND UPJOHN ENTERED THE DARK INTERIOR! THE MUSTY, FOUL SMELL OF THE LONG-SEALED TOMB FILLED THEIR LUNGS, BURNING THEIR NOSTRILS!

THIS MUST BE THE OUTER CHAMBER!

LIGHT YOUR LANTERN! THERE'S ANOTHER OPENING!

AS THE LIGHT FROM THE LANTERN THAT HARVEY UPJOHN CARRIED FLOODED THE DARKENED TOMB, THEY MOVED FORWARD...

THIS MUST BE THE INNER CHAMBER!

YES! LOOK! THE TREASURES OF KING ANKH-MU-TAMEN!

GOLD! PRECIOUS STONES!

A FABULOUS FORTUNE... UNTOUCHED BY HUMAN HANDS FOR 3000 YEARS!

THE MUMMY'S CURSE!

Frenzied by the sight of the magnitudinous wealth which surrounded him, wild thoughts flashed through the mind of Carl Gladstone!

"A fantastic *fortune*... I could be *rich*... have everything I always wanted... *retire!* But... what about *Upjohn*... and the *museum*?"

"I... could *kill* him... *hide* his body... remove *some* of the treasure... and return to England! I could say that we *never found* the tomb... that when Upjohn died... I *quit!* Then... I could return secretly and take the remaining treasure to America... yes... yes..."

Suddenly Harvey Upjohn's shout shocked Carl Gladstone from his diabolical thoughts...

"This *sarcophagus!* It's *not* the *king's!*"

"But... *whose* is it?"

"An attendant... or a bodyguard! Then this is *not* the sepulchral chamber! But it must be somewhere... *hidden*..."

"...and the mummy of King Ankh-Mu-Tamen... with even *greater* treasures... in it!"

Carl Gladstone was convinced! With even more wealth to be discovered... he *had* to get rid of Harvey Upjohn... *now!*

"Come, Carl! Let's look for the king's chamber!"

"Harvey! I... I'm *tired!* Let's return to camp! It's late... and we can get a fresh start tomorrow morning! All this excitement has sapped my strength!"

"Of course, Carl! As you wish!"

"Come along then! We have a long climb down to our camp!"

THE MUMMY'S CURSE!

SUDDENLY, AS THE TWO MEN CAME OUT OF THE TOMB INTO THE GATHERING TWILIGHT... CARL STEPPED BEHIND HARVEY! WITH ALL THE STRENGTH HE COULD MUSTER, HE LUNGED!

NO! NO! CARL!

THROUGH THE SILENCE OF THE DESERT EVENING, A BLOOD-CURDLING SCREAM ECHOED UP AND DOWN THE CLIFF FACE...

AAAAHH!

...THEN *SILENCE!* SLOWLY... CAUTIOUSLY... CARL GLADSTONE MADE HIS WAY DOWN THE CLIFFSIDE TO THE CAMP!

THAT TAKES CARE OF HARVEY UPJOHN! TOMORROW... I WILL SEAL THE TOMB AND RETURN TO ENGLAND... THE TREASURE AND ITS LOCATION, MINE ALONE!

BUT PROFESSOR GLADSTONE WAS *WRONG!* THE DESERT WINDS DO STRANGE THINGS... AS THEY SWEEP ACROSS THE VAST EXPANSE OF THE SAHARA! THERE, AT THE BOTTOM OF THE CREVICE INTO WHICH HARVEY UPJOHN HAD FALLEN, YEARS OF SHIFTING SANDS HAD PILED, ABSORBING THE SHOCK OF HIS FALL...

HORRIFIED AT GLADSTONE'S TREACHERY, AND THANKFUL FOR HIS OWN GOOD FORTUNE, HARVEY UPJOHN MADE HIS WAY UP THE SIDE OF THE CREVICE AND BACK INTO THE TOMB..

HE... GASP... TRIED TO MURDER ME... GASP! I'LL GET EVEN! I'LL GET EVEN!

CAREFULLY, UPJOHN FORMULATED A PLAN! IF HE COULD FRIGHTEN GLADSTONE... SCARE HIM INTO FLEEING, TERRIFIED, FROM THE CAVE... PERHAPS HE WOULD MEET THE FATE FROM WHICH UPJOHN HAD SO NARROWLY ESCAPED!

...OR IF HE DOESN'T FALL, PERHAPS HE'LL RUN OFF INTO THE DESERT... WHERE THIRST AND HEAT WILL CLAIM HIM...

UPJOHN'S PLOT WAS FIENDISH! FIRST... HE LIFTED THE MUMMY OF THE KING'S ATTENDENT FROM IT'S CASE! GENTLY HE REMOVED THE DECAYING WINDINGS FROM IT...

AFTER I REMOVE THESE WRAPPINGS, I'LL HAVE TO HIDE THE MUMMY'S REMAINS!

THE MUMMY'S CURSE!

The mummy unwrapped, Harvey Upjohn carried it to the brink of the cliff and flung it over...

It landed in the same crevice from which Upjohn had previously dragged himself!

That done, he returned to the tomb and began the tiring task of wrapping *HIMSELF* in the ancient and rotted windings of the mummy...

Towards morning, his work completed, Upjohn climbed into the sarcophagus!

Carefully, he replaced the lid... leaving an air space...

He did not have long to wait! Gladstone, eager to find the hidden king's chamber, climbed the cliff to the tomb opening as soon as it was light. When he reached the top, he looked down into the crevice...

I can just make out his body down there...

Frantically, Gladstone went to work... tapping... digging... searching... trying to discover the secret entrance to the fabulous sepulchral chamber!

THE ENTRANCE! IT... MUST BE HERE... SOMEWHERE!

SUDDENLY, A MOVEMENT BEHIND GLADSTONE CAUGHT HIS EYE...
WHAT THE...?
SLOWLY THE LID OF THE MUMMY CASE SLID OFF... AND...
NO...NO!! IT CAN'T BE!
CARL GLADSTONE STOOD PARALYZED WITH HORROR AS THE MUMMY AROSE IN THE SARCOPHAGUS...
I MUST BE LOSING MY MIND!
CRAZED WITH FEAR AND TERROR, GLADSTONE RUSHED AT THE MUMMY... PUSHING IT BACK INTO ITS CASE...
I WON'T BELIEVE IT...NO! NO! GET BACK WHERE YOU BELONG!
SUMMONING ALL HIS STRENGTH, GLADSTONE FORCED THE LID DOWN ON THE STRUGGLING UPJOHN...AS...
THE ROOF!! IT'S CAVING IN!!!
TONS OF ROCK AND EARTH CASCADED DOWN UPON THE CLOSED MUMMY CASE, SEALING PROFESSOR HARVEY UPJOHN IN! IRONICALLY, CARL GLADSTONE MANAGED TO ESCAPE FROM THE CAVE-IN! HE RAN, SCREAMING, FROM THE TOMB... CONVINCED THAT THE MUMMY WAS REAL...
I TOUCHED IT... I TOUCHED IT... IT WAS ALIVE!!
OUT ACROSS THE DESERT HE RAN, UNTIL HE WAS DISCOVERED, HALF-STARVED, BY A GROUP OF WANDERING ARABS WHO RETURNED HIM TO CIVILIZATION! AFTER A FEW WEEKS OF REST, PROFESSOR GLADSTONE WAS ABLE TO RETURN TO ENGLAND! BUT NOW, HE WAS BACK AT THE SCENE OF HIS HARROWING EXPERIENCE...
WAKE UP, CARL... WE'RE READY TO START UP THE CLIFF...
UH— OH, YES! BUT... LET ME WARN YOU! I SAW IT!!
7

CAUTIOUSLY...THE PARTY, LED BY BLAKELY AND THE RELUCTANT GLADSTONE, ASCENDED THE STEEP CLIFF TO THE TOMB ENTRANCE...
AT LAST...THE TOMB OF ANKH-MU-TAMEN BELONGS TO THE WORLD...
THERE! THERE!!
THERE'S WHERE THE MUMMY IS BURIED! UNDER THAT PILE OF RUBBLE...
JENSEN, GET BUSY! DIG UP THE MUMMY CASE! WE'LL CONVINCE GLADSTONE THAT IT'S JUST THAT... A LONG-DEAD CORPSE!
YES, MR. BLAKELY!
FOR AN HOUR THEY DUG, UNTIL FINALLY THEY HAD UNEARTHED THE MUMMY CASE... AND OPENED IT...
THERE, GLADSTONE...YOU SEE! IT'S JUST A MUMMY...
WAIT, JENSEN! LOOK! QUICKLY! UNWRAP THE MUMMY!!
SWIFTLY, THE CLOTH BINDINGS WERE REMOVED FROM THE MUMMY... AND THEN...
LOOK...IT'S A MODERN MAN!
HE'S IN KHAKI!
UPJOHN!! NO!! NO!!
NO! IT CAN'T BE YOU...YOU'RE DOWN THERE...IN THE CREVICE... WHERE I PUSHED YOU! I KILLED YOU!! THE MUMMY...WAS ALIVE!! NO...NO...SOB...SOB...
GRAB HIM, JENSEN! HE'S LOST HIS SENSES! HIS MIND HAS SNAPPED!
YES, DEAR READER, PROFESSOR CARL GLADSTONE'S MIND HAD SNAPPED! HE WAS RETURNED TO ENGLAND, A RAVING, RANTING, GIBBERING IDIOT! WHEN UPJOHN WAS BURIED ALIVE IN THE MUMMY CASE, HIS STRUGGLING TO FREE HIMSELF HAD LOOSENED THE WINDINGS, AND BLAKELY HAD NOTICED THE FLESH UNDERNEATH! OH...HEH, HEH...BY THE WAY! THE INNER KING'S CHAMBER WAS LATER DISCOVERED! STRANGELY, OVER THE SARCOPHAGUS OF KING ANKH-MU-TAMEN WAS INSCRIBED..."I SHALL PUNISH ALL WHO TRESPASS MY RESTING PLACE!" HE KEPT HIS WORD, DIDN'T HE? WELL....I'LL HAVE ANOTHER TALE FROM THE VAULT OF HORROR NEXT ISSUE! BE SURE AND COME, WON'T YOU? I'LL BE WAITING FOR YOU!
IF YOU LIKE THIS TYPE OF STORY, WON'T YOU LET ME KNOW? WRITE: THE EDITOR, E.C. COMICS, 225 LAFAYETTE ST. N.Y.C., 12, N.Y.
8

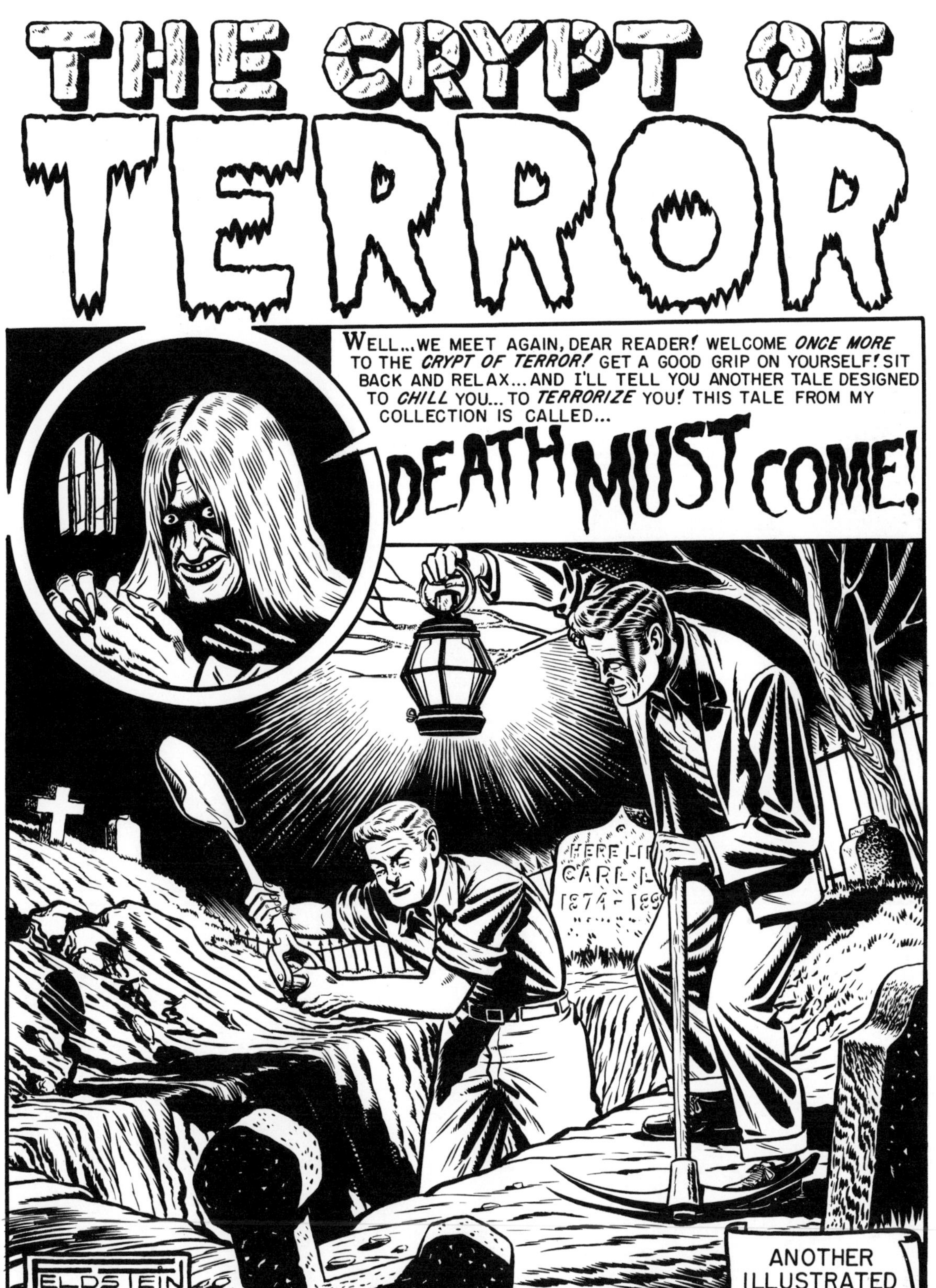

THE CRYPT OF TERROR
WELL...WE MEET AGAIN, DEAR READER! WELCOME *ONCE MORE* TO THE *CRYPT OF TERROR!* GET A GOOD GRIP ON YOURSELF! SIT BACK AND RELAX... AND I'LL TELL YOU ANOTHER TALE DESIGNED TO *CHILL* YOU... TO *TERRORIZE* YOU! THIS TALE FROM MY COLLECTION IS CALLED...
DEATH MUST COME!
FELDSTEIN
ANOTHER ILLUSTRATED SUSPENSTORY!

DEATH MUST COME!

DEATH MUST COME!

"AH, YES, FREDERICK... I REMEMBER WELL! THE PAPER TOLD OF A YOUNG COLLEGE STUDENT'S UNTIMELY DEATH! OUR EXPERIMENTS HAD PROVEN THAT THE GLAND REMAINED ACTIVE AFTER SUDDEN DEATH FOR 48 HOURS! THAT NIGHT, WE WENT TO THE CEMETERY AND EXHUMED THE STILL-WARM CORPSE...

QUIET! WE MUST NOT BE CAUGHT!

I DON'T LIKE THIS, FREDERICK! I DON'T LIKE THIS AT ALL!

"AND IN THE EARLY HOURS OF THAT MORNING, I REMOVED YOUR GLAND... AND SUBSTITUTED THAT OF AN EIGHTEEN YEAR OLD BOY IN ITS PLACE...

IT IS OVER, FREDERICK! THE OPERATION WAS A SUCCESS! HOW DO YOU FEEL?

A LITTLE SICK FROM THE ANESTHETIC ...BUT ALL RIGHT!

"THAT WAS *FIFTY YEARS* AGO! TWENTY YEARS LATER, I WAS OVER *FORTY-FIVE*... YOU SENT FOR ME! WHAT A SHOCK TO SEE YOU... STILL YOUNG... STILL FULL OF YOUTH!"

AMAZING, FREDERICK! AMAZING!

IT'S GOOD TO SEE YOU AGAIN, HENRY! SIT DOWN!

WHY DID YOU SEND FOR ME, FREDERICK?

IT...IT'S MY HANDS... LOOK! THEY'RE BEGINNING TO SHOW SIGNS OF WRINKLES...

BUT, OF COURSE! THAT GLAND WE REPLACED... IT IS GROWING WEAK... IT IS NO LONGER SECRETING THE FLUID THAT DISSOLVES THE BODY WAXES...

THEN... YOU MEAN I WILL BEGIN TO GROW OLD... NO! NO!

WE MUST REPLACE IT... WITH A YOUNG, STRONG GLAND! WE MUST CONTINUE WITH THE EXPERIMENT! WE MUST!

AND THE GLAND? YOU KNOW WHERE WE CAN GET ONE..?

YES... HERE! THE OBITUARY COLUMN! ANOTHER YOUTH... DEAD! WE STILL HAVE TIME... TONIGHT... TO REMOVE THE GLAND IN GOOD CONDITION!

THIS IS WRONG! ALL WRONG!

179

DEATH MUST COME!

Panel 1:
"WHAT HARM IS THERE? HE'S *DEAD*, ISN'T HE? COME! WE HAVEN'T A MOMENT TO LOSE!"
"YES, FREDERICK!"

Panel 2:
"AND SO AGAIN WE WENT TO A CEMETERY... JUST AS WE HAD THAT *FIRST* TIME...
"THE COFFIN! YOU'VE STRUCK THE COFFIN!"
"GIVE ME THE SHEET! I'LL WRAP THE BODY IN IT!"

Panel 3:
"AND AGAIN I PERFORMED THE OPERATION... SUCCESSFULLY! THE YOUTH WAS A GOOD SPECIMEN... NINETEEN! HE HAD BEEN HIT BY A TRUCK... BUT THE GLAND WAS UNINJURED...
"THERE! IT IS DONE!"

Panel 4:
"THEN YOU WENT TO AMERICA... AND SHORTLY AFTER, AN OPPORTUNITY PRESENTED ITSELF, AND I FOLLOWED! ABOUT FIFTEEN YEARS AFTER THE SECOND OPERATION... I RECEIVED A LETTER!
"HENRY! I MUST SEE YOU! COME AT ONCE! ANOTHER OPERATION IS IMPERATIVE! FREDERICK!"

Panel 5:
"AT FIRST, I DID NOT WANT TO GO! I WAS ALMOST *SIXTY*! WHAT WOULD I FIND? THE SAME YOUNG, HANDSOME BOY I HAD KNOWN THIRTY-FIVE YEARS BEFORE? BUT, MY SCIENTIFIC CURIOSITY GOT THE BETTER OF ME, AND I CAME!"
"FREDERICK! IT CAN'T BE! *NO*! IT *ISN'T* YOU!"
"YES, HENRY! IT *IS* ME! STILL YOUNG!. STILL FRESH!"

Panel 6:
"AREN'T YOU SORRY, *NOW*, THAT YOU DIDN'T CONSENT TO A *MUTUAL* EXPERIMENT..."
"PERHAPS! PERHAPS *NOT*! I DO NOT KNOW! ANYWAY... THAT IS OF NO MATTER! WHAT CONCERNS ME IS *YOU*! YOU SAY ANOTHER OPERATION IS NECESSARY?"

Panel 7:
"YES! THE WAXES ARE FORMING AGAIN! YOU KNOW THAT, ACCORDING TO OUR CALCULATIONS, IT IS THESE WAXES THAT STIFLE OTHER GLANDS FROM OPERATING CORRECTLY, THEREBY BRINGING ON A BREAKDOWN OF TISSUE, AND "OLD AGE"!"
"YES, AND THAT THE GLAND LOCATED ON THE SPLEEN SECRETES A FLUID WHICH IN YOUTH, DISSOLVES THESE WAXES! BUT AS THE GLAND WEAKENS WITH TIME, THE WAXES BEGIN TO FORM... AND SOON..."

EXACTLY! WELL, THE GLAND HAS WEAKENED...IT MUST BE REPLACED! HENRY, IT MUST BE REPLACED TONIGHT!
FREDERICK! HOW LONG DO YOU INTEND TO KEEP THIS UP?
UNTIL I AM SEVENTY...OR EIGHTY! THEN WE WILL TELL THE WORLD!
I MAY NOT BE HERE BY THEN, FREDERICK! WHY NOT TELL... NOW?
WE'LL SEE, HENRY! BUT NOW.. WE HAVE WORK TO DO...
"AND SO, FOR THE THIRD TIME, WE WENT TO A CEMETERY...REMOVED THE BODY...
"...AND I PERFORMED ANOTHER OPERATION! THIS TIME, IT WAS A TWENTY-TWO YEAR OLD MAN! HE HAD BEEN KILLED IN A BRAWL...
"AFTER YOUR RECOVERY, THE CONVERSATION ABOUT PUBLISHING A REPORT WAS FORGOTTEN...AND I WENT AWAY! BUT TEN YEARS LATER YOU SENT FOR ME AGAIN!"
SO SOON, FREDERICK? SO SOON?
THE GLAND MUST WORK MUCH HARDER NOW! IT CANNOT LAST AS LONG!
FREDERICK! I AM ALMOST SEVENTY!
YOU CAN DO IT, HENRY! YOU'VE DONE IT THREE TIMES BEFORE!
5

"AND SO, FOR THE FOURTH TIME IN FORTY-FIVE YEARS, WE WENT AGAIN TO A CEMETERY AND REMOVED A BODY NOT YET COLD IN DEATH...
I CANNOT HELP YOU, FREDERICK! I AM TOO OLD TO DO THIS KIND OF WORK!
JUST HOLD THE LIGHT, HENRY! I AM STRONG. I WILL MANAGE IT ALONE!
"AND THAT SAME NIGHT..."
USE A LOCAL ANESTHETIC, I WANT TO WATCH IN THAT MIRROR ON THE CEILING!
AS YOU WISH, FREDERICK!
AND AFTER YOUR RECOVERY, FIVE YEARS AGO...WE PARTED! AND NOW YOU SEND FOR ME AGAIN! CAN'T YOU SEE WHAT IS HAPPENING, FREDERICK?
YES, HENRY! THE TIME BETWEEN OPERATIONS IS GROWING SHORTER!
AND THIS WILL CONTINUE UNTIL YOU WILL NEED A NEW GLAND EVERY YEAR...EVERY MONTH...EVERY WEEK!
NO...IT WILL NEVER COME TO THAT! PERHAPS A YOUNGER GLAND! A CHILD'S!!
I CANNOT GO ON, FREDERICK! I REFUSE!
YOU MUST!! YOU MUST!
NO! I REFUSE! I WILL NOT PERFORM THE OPERATION AGAIN!
DODDERING OLD FOOL!
OOOOF!
6

DEATH MUST COME!

Panel 1:
YOU...YOU STRUCK...ME...GASP...YOU...FREDERICK! MY HEART!!
HENRY!

Panel 2:
HE...HE'S DEAD! WHAT WILL I DO? WHAT WILL I DO NOW?

Panel 3:
I'M GROWING OLDER RAPIDLY! THE PAINS...I...I COULDN'T DIG UP A GRAVE NOW! I...I HAVEN'T THE STRENGTH! I MUST THINK OF SOMETHING!

Panel 4:
WELL, DEAR READER! OLD...ER...THAT IS IN YEARS...FREDERICK IS IN A MESS, NOW! HE NEEDS A NICE YOUNG VIRILE SPECIMEN...BUT QUICKLY!
HELLO...POSTAL UNION! I WANT TO SEND A TELEGRAM...QUICKLY...TO FREDERICK CASTON...

Panel 5:
CLEVER, THESE SCIENTISTS! SENDING A TELEGRAM TO HIMSELF...THAT WILL BRING A YOUNG MESSENGER TO HIS HOME...
WHEN HE GETS HERE, THIS RAG SOAKED IN CHLOROFORM OVER HIS NOSE AND MOUTH WILL TAKE CARE OF HIM! HURRY! HURRY! I'M AGING FASTER NOW!

Panel 6:
...SHARP PAINS SHOOT THROUGH FREDERICK CASTON AS HE WAITS! WRINKLES BEGAN TO APPEAR IN HIS SKIN, IN HIS FACE, HIS HANDS...AND THEN...THE DOORBELL...
YES?
TELEGRAM FOR FREDERICK CASTON! I....

Panel 7:
MMMPH---!!
HEH...HEH...THIS WAS TOO EASY! NOW I'LL GIVE HIM A HYPO TO KILL HIM!

CAREFULLY, FREDERICK PREPARES FOR THE OPERATION! IT WILL BE TRICKY... THE LOCAL ANESTHETIC... THE REMOVING OF THE GLAND... AND THEN, OPERATING UPON HIMSELF!
...BUT... IT HAS TO BE DONE!
...AND THEN... AS THE SCALPEL LAYS BARE THE PLACE WHERE THE GLAND IS LOCATED...
NO! NO! NO!
AAAAAAH!
SHOCKED AND HORRIFIED, FREDERICK STAGGERS FROM THE LABORATORY! THERE IS NO HOPE NOW!
GASP... GASP...
SLOWLY... THE FLESH DRAWS TIGHT OVER HIS BONES... THE HAIR GRAYS... THE EYES REDDEN... THE FINGERS GNARL...
WEAKLY, HE SINKS TO THE STEPS... HIS BODY BENT AND OLD... HIS FEATURES CONTORTED... UGLY... WRINKLED... WITHERED...
A FINAL SCREAM... AND THEN SILENCE! THE DEEP SILENCE OF DEATH...
AND THAT'S THE STORY, DEAR READER! FREDERICK FINALLY DID DIE, AN OLD MAN! WHO KNOWS? HE MIGHT HAVE LIVED LONGER IF HE HADN'T CRAVED ETERNAL LIFE! OH... BY THE WAY... I SUPPOSE YOU'RE WONDERING WHAT FREDDY SAW WHEN HE... ER ... OPENED UP... THAT MESSENGER! WELL... HE FOUND NOTHING! IT SEEMS THAT PART OF THE BOY'S SPLEEN HAD BEEN REMOVED... THE PART WITH THE GLAND! SEEING THAT GAVE OLD FREDDY THE SHOCK OF HIS LIFE! WELL... I'LL SEE YOU NEXT ISSUE WITH ANOTHER TALE FROM
THE CRYPT OF TERROR!
BE SURE AND COME, WON'T YOU?
IF YOU LIKE THIS TYPE OF STORY... WILL YOU WRITE AND TELL ME? THE EDITOR; E.C. COMICS; 225 LAFAYETTE ST; N.Y.C., 12, N.Y.
8

HE WAS TRYING TO KILL ME! HE HATED ME! AND THEN, ONE NIGHT, HE ALMOST SUCCEEDED... THE NIGHT I RODE A...

TERROR TRAIN

Another SuspenStory *from* THE VAULT OF HORROR!

It all started the day I decided to run away from RALPH! He was going to *KILL* ME! I *KNEW* that! I had to get away! I packed a small bag and hailed a taxi...

"THE RAILROAD TERMINAL... AND PLEASE HURRY!"

"YES, MA'AM!"

As the taxi sped downtown, I huddled in the corner of the seat... afraid that he might see me! Ralph *HATED* me so! I don't remember how it started, but it had developed to a point where I feared for my life! I remember one day, Ralph came home with a package...

"WHAT DID YOU BUY, RALPH?"

"OH... NOTHING, GLORIA DEAR! SOMETHING FOR MY OWN PERSONAL USE!"

TERROR TRAIN

It was *POISON!* I had to be on my guard! I watched the bottle carefully and when I noticed some of the poison missing, I didn't eat... pretending some excuse! I was careful. He *FAILED* that time!

I said... here's the terminal, lady!

Oh... I beg your pardon!

I paid the fare and looked up and down the street! I didn't see Ralph! I rushed into the station!

I.. I'd like a ticket to... to... New York!

That'll be thirty-four ten, ma'am!

I stuffed the ticket into my purse and looked around! If Ralph ever caught me doing this... I drove the thought from my mind! *NO!* I *WOULD* get away! I *HAD* to! I would be *SAFE* then! I sat down on a bench in a corner of the waiting room and hid behind a newspaper...

My train wasn't due for twenty minutes! Suppose Ralph called at home? There would be no answer! He would *KNOW!* I thought of that night last month when I awoke to find Ralph standing over me... a kitchen knife in his hand...

RALPH!

I... I found this knife on your night table, Gloria! You... shouldn't leave things like this around!

He had stammered out a lame excuse! He was going to *MURDER* me, and I had discovered him in time! I didn't sleep the rest of that night... I just *LAY* there... *LISTENING*...

Pardon me, ma'am! That's your train! You'd better hurry or you'll miss it!

Oh... thank you!

I went out to the platform and boarded the train! I found my seat! Why didn't we start? I glanced out of the window! Someone was running down the platform! It... it looked like...

RALPH!

As the train began to move, the man swung himself up into the car behind mine! I wasn't sure! It *COULD* be Ralph! It... *LOOKED* like him... and yet... I was frightened! It was too *LATE* to get off! The train was on its way...

It's... it's just my nerves! I... I need a drink! I wonder if there's a club car on the train?

2

I MADE MY WAY TO THE CLUB CAR! IT WAS SMOKY AND CROWDED! I SLIPPED ONTO A STOOL AT THE BAR...
WHAT'LL IT BE, LADY?
I...I'LL HAVE A SCOTCH AND SODA, PLEASE!
THE DRINK BURNED GOING DOWN! I SHUDDERED! SUDDENLY, A REFLECTION IN THE MIRROR CAUGHT MY EYE!
...GASP... RALPH!
I WAS AFRAID TO TURN AROUND! IT WAS RALPH I HAD SEEN IN THE MIRROR! HAD HE SEEN ME? I STEPPED AWAY FROM THE BAR AND RAN FROM THE CAR!
OH...I BEG YOUR PARDON!
EXCUSE ME, LADY!
I HAD GONE OUT THE WRONG END OF THE CLUB CAR! I WAS IN A COACH... NOT A PULLMAN! IF I WANTED TO GET BACK TO MY CAR, I WOULD HAVE TO GO THROUGH THE CLUB CAR AGAIN...
ER...IS THIS SEAT TAKEN?
WHY, NOT THAT I KNOW OF!
RALPH WOULDN'T LOOK FOR ME HERE IN THE COACHES! HE KNEW I ALWAYS TRAVELED PULLMAN! I SAT DOWN! I WOULD WAIT TILL IT WAS SAFE AND THEN SNEAK BACK TO MY BERTH!
I THOUGHT ABOUT GETTING OFF THE TRAIN AT THE NEXT STOP...BUT ALL MY CLOTHES...MY MONEY...MY TICKET...WERE IN THE OTHER CAR! WHY DID HE WANT TO KILL ME? I REMEMBERED ONE NIGHT, ABOUT THE TIME THAT IT ALL STARTED...
GLORIA! I'VE TAKEN OUT SOME INSURANCE POLICIES! LIFE INSURANCE! IF...SOMETHING HAPPENS TO EITHER OF US... THE OTHER GETS $25,000!
OH? I... I SEE RALPH!
PERHAPS THAT WAS IT! THE MONEY! $25,000 IS A LOT OF MONEY! SUDDENLY, MY HEART STOPPED! I FELT A HAND ON MY SHOULDER...
YOUR TICKET, MISS?
OH! I...I LEFT IT IN THE OTHER CAR!
3

TERROR TRAIN

Panel 1:
THE CONDUCTOR LOOKED AT ME QUIZZICALLY! HE MUST HAVE THOUGHT I WAS TRYING TO RIDE FREE!
"NO, REALLY! I'VE A BERTH BACK IN THE PULLMANS!"
"YOU'D BETTER SHOW ME, MISS!"

Panel 2:
AS WE PASSED THROUGH THE CLUB CAR AGAIN, I SEARCHED THE FACES OF THE PEOPLE! RALPH WASN'T THERE! PERHAPS I HAD MADE A MISTAKE! THE DRINK! MAYBE IT HAD BEEN THE SCOTCH AND SODA!
"THIS IS MY BERTH! I'LL GET MY TICKET!"
"ALL RIGHT, MISS!"

Panel 3:
THE CONDUCTOR WAS SATISFIED! MY BERTH WAS MADE UP, AND SINCE I FELT A LITTLE DIZZY FROM THE DRINK, I DECIDED TO GET SOME SLEEP!
"IT MUST HAVE BEEN SOMEONE WHO *LOOKED* LIKE RALPH! I'LL FEEL BETTER IN THE MORNING..."

Panel 4:
...AND SAFER, TOO! THE TRAIN, HURTLING THROUGH THE NIGHT, WAS PUTTING MORE AND MORE MILES BETWEEN RALPH AND ME! I CLOSED MY EYES! THE TRAIN RUMBLED ON...AND ON...AND I FELT MYSELF DRIFTING INTO SLEEP...SLEEP...

Panel 5:
SUDDENLY I WAS AWAKENED BY AN EAR-SPLITTING, PIERCING SHRIEK! I LOOKED OUT OF MY BERTH! THE CURTAINS ON THE OTHER BERTHS WERE ALL CLOSED...AND THE CAR WAS DARK EXCEPT FOR A SMALL LIGHT AT THE REAR! WHAT *WAS* IT THAT I HAD HEARD?
"...A SCREAM?...OR WAS IT JUST THE TRAIN WHISTLE?"

Panel 6:
A BERTH AT THE FAR END OF THE CAR WAS MARKED "PORTER". I MADE MY WAY TOWARD IT! I'D ASK HIM IF *HE* HAD HEARD IT TOO. I PULLED ASIDE THE CURTAIN!
"...GASP... NO! NO! EEEEEEEK!"

Panel 7:
IT WAS GHASTLY! HE WAS *DEAD*! COLD AND STIFF! HIS EYES, WIDE WITH HORROR...THE BEDCLOTHES SMEARED WITH BLOOD! I CLOSED THE CURTAINS...
"HELP!"

TERROR TRAIN

Panel 1: THERE WAS NO ANSWER! NO ONE STIRRED! I CRIED OUT AGAIN! COULDN'T THEY HEAR ME? FRANTICALLY, I TORE ASIDE THE CURTAINS OF THE NEXT BERTH...

AAAAAAAAH!

Panel 2: IT WAS HORRIBLE! THE OCCUPANT OF *THAT* BERTH WAS DEAD, TOO! ICY FINGERS CLOSED ABOUT MY HEART! A WAVE OF NAUSEA SWEPT OVER ME AS I WENT FROM BERTH TO BERTH, FLINGING THE CURTAINS BACK! THEY WERE DEAD... ALL DEAD! I WAS ON A DEATH TRAIN! RALPH! IT *WAS* RALPH! HE WAS *MAD*!

"HE MUST BE ON THE TRAIN... LOOKING FOR ME..."

Panel 3: SUDDENLY, I HEARD THE SHRIEK AGAIN... AND I WAS THROWN TO THE FLOOR! THIS TIME IT *HAD* BEEN THE SHRIEK OF BRAKES... THE TRAIN HAD COME TO A STOP...

"THIS... THIS IS MY CHANCE!"

Panel 4: I RAN TO THE END OF THE CAR AND LEAPED FROM THE TRAIN...

"...MY CHANCE TO GET AWAY!"

Panel 5: AS I STOOD BEHIND A TREE... WATCHING, THE TRAIN BEGAN TO MOVE! SQUEAKING... STRAINING... SLOWLY... IT GAINED MOMENTUM! IT WAS PULLING AWAY... AND I HAD ESCAPED!

"NO ONE GOT OFF WITH ME... I... I'M SAFE!"

Panel 6: I LOOKED AROUND ME! A HOUSE! I SAW A HOUSE ON THE TOP OF THE HILL... AND THERE WAS A LIGHT ON! I MADE MY WAY THROUGH THE GRASS TOWARD IT!

"IF THEY HAVE A PHONE, I'LL CALL THE POLICE! THEY COULD STOP THE TRAIN AT THE NEXT STATION..."

Panel 7: NEAR THE HOUSE, I NOTICED SOMETHING STRANGE! SOMEONE HAD BEEN DIGGING... A YAWNING BLACK PIT... THE SHAPE... OF...

"A GRAVE!"

NOW I WAS LETTING MY IMAGINATION GET THE BETTER OF ME! I PUSHED THE THOUGHT OUT OF MY MIND! WHY DID I THINK IT WAS A GRAVE ? WHAT WAS SO STRANGE ABOUT AN EXCAVATION NEAR A FARMHOUSE ? THEY WERE PROBABLY MAKING A WATER TROUGH! I KNOCKED ON THE DOOR...
ANYONE IN THERE ? OPEN THE DOOR! PLEASE...
THERE WAS NO ANSWER. THEN, I HEARD THE LATCH CLICK AND THE DOOR SLOWLY SWUNG OPEN...THE RUSTY HINGES CREAKING...
H...HELLO ? ANYONE...HOME ?
I STEPPED INSIDE! I LOOKED AROUND! THE ROOM WAS BARE EXCEPT FOR...
...GASP... A COFFIN!
I SPUN AROUND! THE DOOR WAS CLOSED BEHIND ME...AND STANDING IN FRONT OF IT WAS...
RALPH!
I'VE BEEN WAITING FOR YOU, GLORIA!
HE CAUGHT ME IN A VISE-LIKE GRIP! I CRIED OUT! I STRUGGLED, BUT I COULD NOT FIGHT HIS OVERWHELMING STRENGTH!
NO NEED TO SCREAM, GLORIA. NO ONE WILL HEAR YOU.
LET ME GO! LET ME GO!
HE FORCED ME TO THE COFFIN!
WHAT ARE YOU GOING TO DO TO ME, RALPH?
DON'T YOU KNOW, GLORIA?
I COULD DO NOTHING! HE CLOSED THE LID OF THE COFFIN... DOWN UPON ME... AND I HEARD THE SHARP BLOWS OF A HAMMER! HE WAS NAILING ME IN...
RALPH! PLEASE... HAVE MERCY!
6

THEN I FELT THE COFFIN BEING DRAGGED ACROSS THE FLOOR! I HEARD THE SQUEAK OF THE RUSTY HINGES AS RALPH OPENED THE DOOR...
HE'S TAKING ME OUTSIDE... TO...TO THAT GRAVE!
I FELT THE JAR AND HEARD THE HOLLOW BOOM OF THE COFFIN AS RALPH PUSHED ME INTO THE GRAVE ... THEN HIS FIENDISH LAUGHTER ... HIS HYSTERICAL RAVING...
GOOD-BYE, GLORIA! SLEEP PEACEFULLY!
HE WAS FILLING IN THE GRAVE! THE SOFT EARTH THUDDED ON THE COFFIN LID! THEN... ALL WAS QUIET! I GUESS I BROKE DOWN AT THAT POINT...
HELP... SOB... HELP ME... SOMEBODY...PLEASE...PLEASE!
I WAS CRAZED WITH FEAR! I WAS GOING TO SUFFOCATE... BURIED ALIVE BY A MADMAN... MY HUSBAND... RALPH! I POUNDED ON THE COFFIN! I COULD FEEL THE FLESH OF MY FISTS TEAR AS I POUNDED! I LOST ALL CONTROL! I SCREAMED AND BEAT THE SIDES OF THE COFFIN...
SUDDENLY THERE WAS A BLINDING LIGHT! I SAT UP WITH A START AND LOOKED AROUND ME...
HERE SHE IS, GENTLEMEN!
YOU'D BETTER STOP THAT RACKET, LADY... AND COME QUIETLY!
I...I HAD BEEN DREAMING! I WAS STILL IN MY BERTH ON THE TRAIN! AND RALPH, WITH PITY IN HIS EYES, WAS COMFORTING ME... STROKING MY HAND!
NO! KEEP AWAY! TAKE HIM AWAY FROM ME! HE WANTS TO KILL ME!
SURE, LADY! SURE! YOU COME WITH US! WE'LL TAKE CARE OF YOU! HE WON'T HURT YOU! WE'LL SEE TO THAT!
THE MEN IN WHITE TOOK ME AWAY! THEY PUT ME IN A NICE HOUSE WITH NICE PEOPLE... A HOUSE THAT HAS BARS ON ALL THE WINDOWS SO RALPH CAN'T GET IN AND KILL ME! AND NOW I'M SAFE FROM HIM!
...AND THAT'S MY STORY! PERHAPS YOU'D LIKE TO COME AND...VISIT ME SOMETIME AGAIN?
THE END
7

PERHAPS YOU HAVE NEVER HEARD THE LEGENDS ABOUT THE OKEFENOKEE SWAMP. . . HOW MEN HAVE GONE INTO THAT 40-MILE STRETCH OF BOGS, QUICKSAND, WATER, AND OVERGROWTH AND NEVER COME OUT! HERE IS THE *REAL* STORY BEHIND THESE LEGENDS!

THE THING IN THE SWAMP!

LET'S GO OVER AND SEE WHAT HE'S RAVING ABOUT! HE LOOKS TERRIFIED!
OKAY, SAM!
PLEASE! DON'T GO PAST THIS SPOT... PLEASE! PLEASE!
WHAT'S THE TROUBLE, OLD MAN?
YOU MUSTN'T GO ON INTO THE SWAMP! YOU'LL NEVER COME OUT ALIVE IF YOU DO!
LOOK, STRANGER! WE'VE HEARD ALL ABOUT THIS SWAMP! ALL ABOUT PEOPLE WHO GO INTO IT AND ARE NEVER SEEN AGAIN!
...BUT WE THINK IT'S ALL NONSENSE! I'VE MAPPED OUR TRIP SO FAR! IT'LL BE A SIMPLE MATTER TO RETRACE OUR STEPS...
NONSENSE, EH? GENTLEMEN! I WARN YOU! THE LEGEND OF THE OKEFENOKEE IS REAL! I KNOW! YOU'LL NEVER COME OUT ALIVE...UNLESS YOU LET ME GUIDE YOU!
OH, I GET IT NOW! LOOKIN' FOR A FAST BUCK ... THAT'S ALL!
NO! NO! YOU'RE WRONG! I'LL DO IT FOR NOTHING!
JUST WHAT IS IT IN THIS SWAMP THAT PEOPLE ARE SO AFRAID OF?
ONLY I KNOW WHAT IT ACTUALLY IS...
TELL US, OLD MAN! WHAT IS IT?
COME INTO MY SHACK...AND I'LL RELATE THE WHOLE STORY...
2

THE THING IN THE SWAMP!

THE OLD MAN LEADS THE OTHER TWO INTO HIS CRUDE HUT! THEY SEAT THEMSELVES ON ROUGHLY HEWN CHAIRS! THEN THE OLD ONE BEGINS TO SPEAK...

"ABOUT TWENTY-FIVE YEARS AGO, THREE PEOPLE CAME TO THIS PART OF THE OKEFENOKEE... THREE SCIENTISTS! ONE WAS MIDDLE-AGED, ONE WAS A YOUNG WOMAN, HIS DAUGHTER, AND THE THIRD... A YOUNG MAN... THE GIRL'S FIANCEE..."

"THEY HAD A *DREAM*, THESE THREE! THEY WERE GOING TO SOLVE THE PROBLEM THAT HAD *BAFFLED* SCIENCE FOR *CENTURIES*! THEY WERE GOING TO SOLVE THE SECRET OF *LIFE*...!"

"BUT, WHY *THIS* GOD-FORSAKEN PLACE, FATHER?"

"HERE, WE CAN WORK UNDISTURBED BY OUTSIDERS, MARIE! NO PUBLICITY... NO REPORTERS... NO PRYING EYES!"

"YES, MARIE! AFTER ALL, WE WOULD RECEIVE A GREAT DEAL OF CRITICISM! TO *CREATE* LIVING MATTER... TO CREATE *LIFE*... IS SOMTHING THAT IS CONSIDERED *BEYOND* THE REALM OF SCIENCE..."

"SO YOU SEE, MARIE, WE MUST SEPARATE OURSELVES FROM SOCIETY... AT LEAST FOR A WHILE..."

"AND SO, PROFESSOR CARL WARD, MARIE WARD, AND ROBERT COLBY SET TO WORK, BUILDING A LABORATORY... HERE... HERE IN THE OKEFENOKEE..."

"AT LAST... WE ARE FINISHED!"

"NOW WE CAN UNPACK OUR EQUIPMENT... ALL OUR APPARATUS... AND BEGIN OUR WORK!"

"THEIR EXPERIMENTING BEGAN..."

"WE *KNOW* WHAT PROTOPLASM... LIVING TISSUE... CONTAINS! WE HAVE ANALYZED IT AND WE KNOW *EVERY* CHEMICAL... IN ITS *PROPER PROPORTION*! AND YET... WHEN WE PLACE THEM TOGETHER... COMBINE THEM... THEY DO NOT BEGIN TO... TO... *LIVE*! THERE IS ONE 'ELEMENT' MISSING..."

"THE SPARK OF LIFE, EH, PROFESSOR?"

"EXACTLY! WE ARE LACKING A CERTAIN 'CONDITION'! A CERTAIN STIMULUS!"

"PERHAPS... ELECTRICITY, FATHER? PERHAPS IF WE *SHOCKED* THIS COMBINATION OF COMPOUNDS AND ELEMENTS... THE LIVING PROCESS WOULD *BEGIN*..."

"WE WILL TRY IT, MARIE! WE WILL TRY EVERYTHING! THE CONDITION OR STIMULANT IS WHAT WE *MUST* DISCOVER..."

THE THING IN THE SWAMP!

"IN THE DAYS AND WEEKS THAT FOLLOWED...THEY TRIED *EVERYTHING*..."

THIS TIME WE'LL TRY .004 MICRO-VOLTS! IF IT DOESN'T WORK...ELECTRICITY AS WE KNOW IT IS NOT THE ANSWER! READY..?

READY!

WHAT DO YOU SEE, ROBERT?

NO SIGN OF LIFE, PROFESSOR!

EXPERIMENT 214! *FAILURE!*

"FOR FOUR LONG MONTHS, THE THREE SCIENTISTS WORKED...TRIED...FAILED..."

X-RAY, 10,000 VOLTS!

EXPERIMENT 702... *FAILURE!!*

RADIUM... EXPOSURE... 3 SECONDS AT 2 INCHES...

EXPERIMENT 1045... *FAILURE!*

INFRA-RED!

ULTRA-VIOLET!

HIGH-FREQUENCY SOUND-WAVES...

URANIUM!

FAILURE!

FAILURE!!

FAILURE!!

IT'S *USELESS!!* *USELESS!!*

NO! NO!! DON'T...PROFESSOR WARD!!

4

THE THING IN THE SWAMP!

"IN A FIT OF RAGE, PROFESSOR WARD HAD FLUNG THE BEAKER CONTAINING THEIR PRECIOUS COMBINATIONS OF CHEMICALS THROUGH THE WINDOW INTO THE STAGNANT, MURKY WATERS OF THE SWAMP...

"SLOWLY THE BEAKER SANK...AND THE MIXTURE SPREAD OVER THE SURFACE OF THE STILL WATER...

"LAZILY...IT DRIFTED ALONG...COMING TO REST NEAR A ROTTED LOG...

"AND THEN...IT *HAPPENED!* THERE, IN THE DANK, DARK WATERS OF THE SWAMP...IN THE HEAT...AND THE STENCH... AND THE DAMPNESS...IT *HAPPENED!* UNKNOWN...UNEXPLAINED...THE CONDITION THAT *THEY* HAD TRIED FOR FIVE LONG MONTHS TO CREATE...CAME ABOUT...

"IT *LIVED!* THE SMALL MIXTURE OF CHEMICALS AND BASIC ELEMENTS BEGAN TO *LIVE!* A SIMPLE FORM OF LIFE...WITH NO STRUCTURE! JUST A SHAPELESS, AMOEBA-LIKE MASS OF LIVING PROTOPLASM!

"AT FIRST, IT REMAINED SMALL, FEEDING ON MICROSCOPIC ORGANISMS! BUT THEN, AS IT GREW...LARGER AND LARGER...IT SOUGHT LARGER FOOD...SMALL FISH...INSECTS! IT ENVELOPED THEM... AS AN AMOEBA DOES...SECRETING DIGESTIVE JUICES THAT DISSOLVED THE VICTIMS INTO A FORM MORE EASILY *ABSORBED*...

"AND STILL IT GREW, UNCONTROLLED, BIGGER...BIGGER! IT MOVED ABOUT NOW... OUT OF THE WATER ONTO THE LAND...ENVELOPING AND ABSORBING EVERYTHING IN ITS PATH...

"MEAWHILE, PROFESSOR WARD AND HIS DAUGHTER HAD MET WITH A NEW PROBLEM! ROBERT COLBY!"
WHAT ARE YOU SAYING, COLBY?
EXACTLY WHAT I MEAN! I'M QUITTING! THIS...THIS THING WE'RE TRYING TO DO...! IT'S...IT'S... WRONG!
A SCIENTIST...TALKING LIKE THAT! WHAT'S COME OVER YOU, COLBY?
I...I DON'T KNOW! ONLY I'M GETTING OUT... BEFORE IT'S TOO LATE...
ARE YOU COMING WITH ME, MARIE?
BUT...BUT...BOB!
YOU SEE, MARIE! HE'S TURNED OUT TO BE A SNIVELING COWARD! GO ON...COLBY...GET OUT! A TRUE SCIENTIST IS NEVER AFRAID...OF ANYTHING!
ARE YOU COMING, MARIE?
MY PLACE IS HERE, ROBERT... WITH MY FATHER... AND OUR WORK! YOU'D BETTER GO...!
"COLBY TURNED AND LEFT! HE CROSSED THE RICKETY WALK FROM THE HOUSE OVER THE SWAMP TO THE BANK! SUDDENLY HE HEARD A TERRIFIED SCREAM...
EEEEEEEEEEEEEEEEEEEEEK!
WHAT THE...?
"WHAT HE SAW MADE HIS BLOOD FREEZE...HIS HAIR STAND ON END! THE LABORATORY WAS COLLAPSING INTO A MASS OF QUIVERING, WRITHING LIVING MATTER...
NO! NO! IT CAN'T BE...!!
6

THE THING IN THE SWAMP!

THE CRYPT OF TERROR

SO, WE MEET AGAIN, DEAR READER! WELCOME ONCE MORE TO THE *CRYPT OF TERROR!* THIS TIME, I HAVE DUG *DEEP* INTO MY COLLECTION OF BLOOD-CURDLING TALES TO FIND A STORY THAT I'M *SURE* WILL *TERRIFY* YOU! THIS *HAIR-RAISER* I CALL...

THE MAESTRO'S HAND!

THE MAESTRO'S HAND!

My story begins just outside of a deserted log cabin in a lonely stretch of woods! Doctor Emanuel Hellman approaches over an overgrown trail...

AH? AT LAST... I AM HERE! NOW I WILL BE ABLE TO *REST*, AND *FORGET* THE HORRORS OF THESE LAST FEW MONTHS!

As the doctor unlocks the long-sealed door, his eyes fall upon...

WHAT THE...? A *PACKAGE!* ADDRESSED TO *ME!* BUT... WHO... WHO *KNEW* I WAS COMING HERE?

I WONDER WHAT IT CAN BE? BR-R-R-R! IT'S COLD! I'LL START A FIRE FIRST!

As the glow of the fire pierces the dim interior of the cabin, Dr. Hellman sinks wearily into a chair...

I CAN'T GET VIRGINIA OUT OF MY MIND! OH... WHY... *WHY* DID SHE *KILL* HERSELF?

As the flames of the fire leap higher... and its warmth spreads through the cabin... Dr. Emanuel Hellman sits staring into its dancing light...

I REMEMBER IT AS IF IT WERE YESTERDAY... THE NIGHT IT ALL BEGAN...

Yes, Doctor Hellman! You remember it *WELL!* You had taken your fiancee, Virginia Caddy, to hear the great Vladimir Borrstein play... and as the piano music grew and swelled to its stirring crescendo...

OH, MANNY! HE... HE'S *WONDERFUL!*

HE PLAYS WELL, VIRGINIA!

You sat there and watched Virginia, as the concert went on! She listened, enthralled... and when it was over... she stood up to applaud...

WE MUST GO BACKSTAGE TO MEET HIM, MANNY DEAR! HE'S... *MAGNIFICENT!*

REALLY, VIRGINIA...

2

YOU OBJECTED, DR. HELLMAN... BUT IN THE END, YOU JOINED THE GROUP OF ADMIRERS CROWDED AROUND MAESTRO BORRSTEIN! VIRGINIA WORKED HER WAY FORWARD ... AND THEN... THEIR EYES MET...
BRAVO, MR. BORRSTEIN! YOU PLAYED... SUPERBLY!
WHY, THANK YOU SO MUCH, MISS... MISS...
CADDY! VIRGINIA CADDY! I WANT SO MUCH TO TALK TO YOU AGAIN... ABOUT YOUR MUSIC! WILL YOU CALL ME? I'M IN THE BOOK!
DELIGHTED... MISS CADDY! DELIGHTED!
...THAT'S HOW IT BEGAN! WHEN I SAW HER SMILE AT HIM LIKE THAT, I FELT MY FACE GROW HOT... AS NOW, FROM THE HEAT OF THE FIRE!
YES, DR. HELLMAN! THAT WAS THE BEGINNING... THE BEGINNING OF THE END! THEY SAW EACH OTHER MUCH AFTER THAT NIGHT...
WHY, VLADIMIR! I DIDN'T KNOW YOU PAINTED!
A LITTLE! DO YOU LIKE IT?
LIKED IT? SHE LOVED IT! SHE WAS MAD ABOUT ANYTHING HE DID! SHE HAD ALWAYS ADMIRED GENIUS... CREATIVE ABILITY! BORRSTEIN WAS THE ANSWER... THE TYPE OF MAN VIRGINA COULD...
YES, EMANUEL! I LOVE HIM! WE ARE GOING TO BE MARRIED!
BUT... VIRGINIA!
SHE GAVE YOU BACK HER RING! YOU... THE GREAT DOCTOR HELLMAN... THE RENOWNED SURGEON...
IT'S MERELY AN INFATUATION, VIRGINIA! YOU ARE NOT IN LOVE WITH HIM! YOU ARE IN LOVE WITH HIS TALENTS ... A DREAM!
THEN MAY I NEVER AWAKEN, EMANUEL!
SHE WILL COME BACK TO ME! SHE WILL COME BACK TO ME... SHE WILL ... SHE MUST! I'LL MAKE HER FORGET HIM IF I HAVE TO...
3.

THE MAESTRO'S HAND!

AH, DEAR READER! WHAT EVILS MEN WILL COMMIT FOR THE LOVE OF A BEAUTIFUL WOMAN! AND DR. HELLMAN WAS NO EXCEPTION! HIS CHANCE CAME ONE NIGHT WHEN...

AAAAAAAH-H-H!

VLADIMIR... WHAT IS IT? WHAT'S HAPPENED?

I... THE KNIFE... SLIPPED! I... I HAVE CUT... MYSELF... BADLY!

YOU MUST GO TO A DOCTOR... *EMANUEL!* I'LL CALL HIM AND TELL HIM WE ARE COMING...

JUST LIKE THE NURSERY RHYME ABOUT THE SPIDER AND THE FLY, EH, DOCTOR? THEY CAME TO *YOU*... THE *FOOLS!*

HURRY, MANNY! IT'S BLEEDING BADLY!

WAIT OUT HERE, VIRGINIA! COME IN, MR. BORRSTEIN!

HIS HAND... HIS WONDERFUL HAND FROM WHICH SUCH BEAUTIFUL MUSIC FLOWED! HOW YOU HATED IT! HOW YOU *HATED* WHAT IT HAD DONE TO YOU... AND YOUR LOVE!

SIT DOWN, MR. BORRSTEIN! LET'S TAKE A LOOK...

CAREFUL WITH THE BANDAGES, DOCTOR! IT IS VERY *PAINFUL!*

IT WAS A BAD SLASH! BUT... NOT NEARLY BAD ENOUGH TO WARRANT WHAT *YOU* HAD IN MIND...

SHE WOULD BE MINE ONCE MORE! HE WOULD NEVER PLAY... EVER AGAIN!

I AM GOING TO GIVE YOU A HYPO, MR. BORRSTEIN! IT WILL STOP THE PAIN AND MAKE YOU SLEEP!

GOOD! IT DOES *HURT* QUITE A BIT...

THEN... YOU SENT VIRGINIA HOME...

HE... HE SEVERED AN ARTERY! I'VE GIVEN HIM A SEDATIVE! I HAVE A TOURNIQUET ON, NOW! THERE'S NO NEED FOR YOU TO WAIT AROUND... IT WILL BE HOURS BEFORE HE AWAKENS!

ALL RIGHT! CALL ME AS SOON AS HE DOES, MANNY!

SHE LEFT, AND YOU WENT BACK INTO YOUR OFFICE... TO THE INSTRUMENT CABINET...
HE'LL NEVER PLAY AGAIN...
YES, DOCTOR HELLMAN! YOU REMEMBER IT WELL! IN FACT, YOU'LL NEVER FORGET IT... EVER! THE BLOOD... THE TEARING FLESH... THE SAWING OF THE BONE... AND THEN...
IT... GASP... IS DONE!
YOU DIDN'T SLEEP WELL AFTER THAT, DID YOU, DOCTOR? BORRSTEIN, DOWNSTAIRS... UNDER THE ANESTHETIC... AND YOU IN YOUR SWEATY BED...
A-A-H-H-H-H!
BORRSTEIN! HE'S AWAKE!
MY HAND! WHERE IS MY HAND?
EASY, BORRSTEIN! EASY! IT COULDN'T BE HELPED! THE BLEEDING... IT WOULDN'T STOP... NOT EVEN A TOURNIQUET... AND THE GANGRENE... I HAD TO DO IT... TO SAVE YOUR ARM!
I SHALL NEVER PLAY AGAIN! NEVER! NEVER! SOB... SOB...
HERE, TAKE THIS, BORRSTEIN! IT WILL MAKE YOU SLEEP!
YOU DID THIS TO ME! YOU CUT MY HAND OFF ON PURPOSE! YOU HATE ME BECAUSE I TOOK VIRGINIA FROM YOU... AND NOW YOU'VE TAKEN REVENGE! I CURSE YOU... I CURSE YOU... WITH THE HAND YOU CUT FROM ME...
BORRSTEIN... WAIT! YOU'RE IN NO CONDITION TO LEAVE...
IN THE MORNING, HE WAS DEAD! YOU READ IT IN THE PAPERS! VLADIMIR BORRSTEIN HAD JUMPED IN FRONT OF A SUBWAY TRAIN... MANGLED BEYOND RECOGNITION! THEN... SHE CAME...
VIRGINIA!
HE TOLD ME WHAT YOU DID TO HIM... HE CALLED ME BEFORE HE KILLED HIMSELF! I HATE YOU! YOU'RE EVIL... I HATE YOU HATE YOU... HATE YOU!
5

THE MAESTRO'S HAND!

AND THEN, *SHE KILLED HERSELF...* AND YOU CAME HERE, DOCTOR, TO THIS LONELY CABIN... TO FORGET!

FORGET! YES! TO *FORGET!* OH... THE *PACKAGE...*

SLOWLY, DOCTOR HELLMAN UNWRAPS THE PARCEL! INSIDE IS A SMALL BOX... AND AS HE OPENS IT...

A... HAND!

SWIFTLY, LIKE A CAT, THE HAND SPRINGS FROM THE BOX... TO HIS THROAT...

ULP... GASP... NO... GLUG-G-GH!

SUMMONING ALL HIS STRENGTH, DOCTOR HELLMAN TEARS AT THE HAND CLUTCHING HIS THROAT, AND WRENCHES IT FROM HIM!

T...TH...*THERE!* THE...THE *FIRE* WILL DESTROY IT!

BUT EVEN AS HE WATCHES, THE HAND, SINGED AND BLACK, JUMPS FROM THE FIRE AND SCURRIES UP THE CHIMNEY...

IT'S... *GETTING AWAY!*

I CAN *HEAR* IT... CLATTERING OVER THE ROOF! THE *DOORS!* THE *WINDOWS!* I'VE GOT TO LOCK IT OUT!

AND EVEN AS HE WATCHES FROM THE WINDOW, DOCTOR HELLMAN CAN SEE THE HAND MOVING ABOUT IN THE GRASS NEAR THE HOUSE...

6

THE MAESTRO'S HAND!

The minutes become hours... and Doctor Hellman sits, terrified, in a chair...

I cannot let the fire go out! The windows and doors are locked! But if the fire dies... the hand will come back down the chimney!

But as the hours drag on... Doctor Hellman's eyes, heavy with sleep... close! Suddenly... the room is filled with music... PIANO MUSIC!

NO! NO!

Cautiously, Doctor Hellman slips toward the piano... and then he sees it...

BORRSTEIN! It's BORRSTEIN'S right hand! The hand I CUT OFF!

If I could grab it as it plays... I could kill it by holding it in the flames...

Quietly, Hellman moves closer... and closer... and then he lunges...

GOT IT!

Quickly he stumbles across the room... and falling on his knees before the fire, he thrusts the squirming hand into it...

AAAAAAAAH!

As the hungry flames lick Doctor Hellman's fingers, and he becomes conscious of the pain... he relaxes his grip on the writhing hand...

NO... NO... it's GETTING AWAY again...

7

205

THE HAND DARTS ACROSS THE FLOOR...RUNNING ON ITS FINGERS...THE STUMP OF THE WRIST RAISED!
COME BACK...YOU UGLY, HORRIBLE MONSTER! I'LL GET YOU! I'LL OUTSMART YOU...YET!
BUT AS DOCTOR HELLMAN STAGGERS AFTER THE SCAMPERING HAND...
SUDDENLY THE HAND TURNS AND SPRINGS AT THE DOCTOR'S THROAT...
VAINLY, DOCTOR HELLMAN STRUGGLES, TRYING TO PULL THE HAND FROM ITS STRANGLEHOLD ON HIS THROAT...
BUT, AFTER A WHILE, HIS STRENGTH EBBS...AND THE DOCTOR'S GRIP RELAXES! HE IS DEAD FROM STRANGULATION!
A FEW DAYS LATER, WHEN THE CARETAKER DISCOVERS HIS BODY... AND CALLS THE POLICE...
QUEEREST THING I EVER SAW! THE GUY CHOKED HIMSELF TO DEATH! LOOK AT THE GRIP HE'S GOT ON HIS OWN NECK!
AND THAT'S THE STORY, DEAR READER! THE "HAND" WAS IN DOCTOR HELLMAN'S OWN MIND! THAT'S WHAT HE GOT FOR COMMITTING SUCH AN UNDERHANDED TRICK! GRIPPING TALE, WASN'T IT! WELL, IF YOU CAN STAND IT, THERE ARE MORE STORIES FROM MY COLLECTION FOLLOWING THIS ONE! TAKE A GOOD HOLD OF YOURSELF...HEH-HEH...AND READ ON!
IF YOU LIKE THIS STORY AND THE OTHER STORIES IN THIS BOOK, WON'T YOU WRITE ME? ADDRESS YOUR LETTERS TO: THE CRYPT-KEEPER, DEPT. 18 ROOM 706 225 LAFAYETTE STREET N.Y.C., 12, N.Y.
8

THE VAULT OF HORROR!
SO...WE MEET AGAIN, DEAR READER! WELCOME! WELCOME ONCE MORE TO THE VAULT OF HORROR! FOR THE BENEFIT OF ANY NEWCOMERS, I AM THE KEEPER OF THE VAULT OF HORROR! EACH ISSUE, I TELL YOU TALES FROM MY VAST COLLECTION OF CHILLING, HAIR-RAISING, SPINE-TINGLING STORIES...TALES THAT I GUARANTEE WILL MAKE YOUR BLOOD FREEZE IN YOUR VEINS, AND THE HAIR ON THE BACK OF YOUR NECK BRISTLE WITH TERROR! THIS TALE, I CALL...
THE DEAD WILL RETURN!
ALL RIGHT, FLO! THIS IS FAR ENOUGH! PUSH HIM OVERBOARD...
YES, BERT...
FELDSTEIN
1

THE BODY WENT OVER THE SIDE OF THE SMALL DINGHY, AND SANK OUT OF SIGHT...
IN A COUPLE OF DAYS, HE'LL WASH ASHORE DOWN THE COAST A WAYS...
LET'S GO BACK, BERT! I FEEL CHILLED!
THE MAN CALLED BERT TURNED THE BOAT AROUND AND MADE FOR THE BEACH BELOW THE TOWERING LIGHTHOUSE...
...AND WHEN THEY COME AND ASK YOU ABOUT HIM, YOU'LL TELL THEM HE'S AWAY ON A FISHING TRIP!
YES, BERT... I UNDERSTAND!
THE WOMAN, FLORENCE, STEPPED QUICKLY FROM THE DINGHY AS IT SCRAPED THE SAND OF THE SHORE...
AND... WHEN THEY FIND HIS BODY... THEY'LL THINK THAT HE DROWNED AT SEA... AND THEN... THEN YOU'LL BE FREE TO MARRY ME!
YES, BERT! AND HIS MONEY... WE'LL HAVE HIS MONEY... OVER $16,000! A FORTUNE!
THE TWO PEOPLE CLIMBED THE STEPS OF THE LIGHT-HOUSE AND ENTERED...
...TALKING ABOUT THAT MONEY, WHERE DID YOUR HUSBAND KEEP IT?
I DON'T KNOW FOR SURE... BUT IT'S AROUND HERE... SOMEWHERE...
I KNOW HE KEPT IT WELL HIDDEN!
WELL, WE MIGHT AS WELL START LOOKIN' FOR IT, SO AS WE CAN LAM OUTTA HERE JUS' AS SOON AS THEY FIND HIS BODY!
CAN'T IT WAIT TILL MORNING, BERT...?
WHY... SURE... HONEY!
DARLING! I'M RID OF HIM AT LAST...
IT'S GONNA BE SMOOTH SAILING FROM NOW ON, BABY!
2

BUT THE NEXT DAY, THINGS DID NOT GO AS SMOOTHLY AS THEY HAD PLANNED! BERT AND FLO COULD NOT FIND A TRACE OF THE MONEY...
YOU SAY HE KEPT IT HERE IN THE LIGHT-HOUSE!
YES! YES! HE KEPT IT SOMEWHERE IN THIS PLACE! KEEP LOOKING...
AND LOOK THEY DID! FOR ALMOST TWO WEEKS THEY SEARCHED! THEY COVERED THE LIGHTHOUSE WITH A FINE-TOOTHED COMB...EVERY INCH...BUT NO MONEY!
IT'S GOT TO BE HERE... IT'S GOT TO!
MAYBE...MAYBE IF HE DIDN'T KEEP IT HERE... MAYBE HE HID IT OUTSIDE... THE STOREHOUSE...OR THE BOAT SHED...
I'LL GO DOWN TO THE BEACH TO THE SHED, BERT! YOU TRY THE STORE-HOUSE! DON'T WORRY! WE'LL FIND IT!
CAUTIOUSLY, FLO MADE HER WAY DOWN THE STEPS TO THE BEACH...
I DON'T THINK HANK WOULD HAVE KEPT HIS MONEY DOWN HERE! IT WOULDN'T HAVE BEEN SAFE...
SLOWLY, SHE ROUNDED THE ROCKS NEAR THE SHED...
A HIGH SEA COULD TAKE THIS SHED... AND... AND... GASP...
E-E-E-A-A-A-A-H-H!
FLO! FLO... WHAT IS IT?
IT...IT'S HANK! MY HUSBAND! HE'S...HE'S COME BACK! HE'S COME BACK FROM THE SEA...
3

BERT RUSHED TO THE SIDE OF THE HORRIFIED FLORENCE...
OH, BERT! IT... IT'S HORRIBLE!
DON'T LOOK AT HIM, FLO! HE'S HARDLY RECOGNIZABLE... AFTER TWO WEEKS IN THE WATER...
WHAT WILL WE DO, BERT? WE CAN'T REPORT THAT HIS BODY WASHED ASHORE HERE! IT... IT'S TOO MUCH OF A COINCIDENCE!
WE'VE GOT TO PUT HIM BACK, FLO... BACK INTO THE SEA...
FIGHTING THE NAUSEA THAT SWEPT OVER THEM, THE TWO PEOPLE LIFTED THE CORPSE AND CARRIED IT TO THE CAR...
WE'LL DRIVE OVER TO MARINER'S POINT AND THROW IT OFF! THAT'S FAR ENOUGH AWAY! THE CURRENT'S BOUND TO CARRY HIM UP THE COAST FROM THERE...
YES... BERT...
IN THE BLACK OF THE NIGHT, THEY DROVE TO A SPOT HIGH OVER THE ROARING SEA... MARINER'S POINT... AND FLUNG THE REMAINS OF THE MURDERED HANK OFF THE CLIFF...
ONE... TWO... TH-R-R-EE! THERE! THAT'LL TAKE CARE OF HIM...
BERT... I... I FEEL SICK! LET'S GET OUT OF HERE!
IN THE DAYS THAT FOLLOWED, FLO LISTENED CAREFULLY TO EACH RADIO NEWS REPORT...
NOTHING! NOT A WORD ABOUT ANYONE FINDING A BODY...
DON'T WORRY, FLO! IT'LL TURN UP...
BUT HANK'S BODY DIDN'T TURN UP... AND THEN, ONE DAY...
I CAN'T STAND IT ANY LONGER! THIS WAITING IS DRIVING ME NUTS!
BERT! WHY DON'T YOU TAKE THE DINGHY OUT AND DO A LITTLE FISHING... IT'LL CALM YOUR NERVES!
BERT MADE HIS WAY DOWN THE STEPS FROM THE LIGHTHOUSE TO THE BEACH! FISHING SOUNDED LIKE A GOOD IDEA...
I'LL DIG ME SOME CLAMS FOR BAIT! I OUGHTA GET A MESS OF PORGIES THIS TIME OF... NO!
NO! NO!
4.

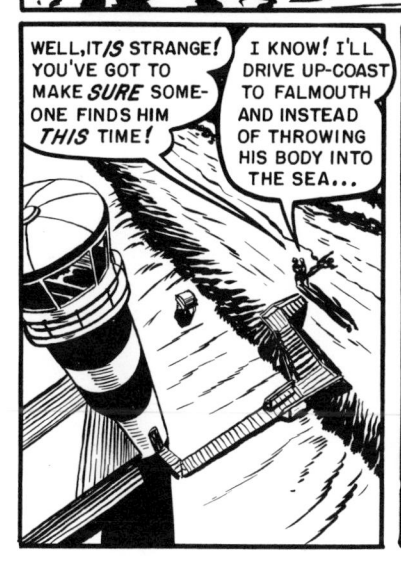

THE DEAD WILL RETURN!

FLO! COME QUICKLY!

WHAT IS IT, BERT? WHAT...WHA... OH...NO! IT CAN'T BE!

IT'S *HIM*, FLO! COME *BACK AGAIN!* WE CAN'T GET *RID* OF HIM!

IT'S *GHASTLY!* HE... HE'S ALL...*ROTTED!*

DON'T LOOK AT HIM, FLO! THE FISH AND CRABS HAVE MADE HIM *HORRIBLE!*

WHAT WILL WE DO WITH HIM *THIS* TIME, BERT? WHY DON'T WE PHONE THE POLICE AND...

NO...WE CAN'T! IF HE'S SUPPOSED TO BE OUT ON A FISHING TRIP, IT'D BE A STRANGE COINCIDENCE THAT HIS BODY WASHED UP *HERE*...BACK *HOME!*

WELL, IT *IS* STRANGE! YOU'VE GOT TO MAKE *SURE* SOMEONE FINDS HIM *THIS* TIME!

I KNOW! I'LL DRIVE UP-COAST TO FALMOUTH AND INSTEAD OF THROWING HIS BODY INTO THE SEA...

...I'LL LEAVE IT RIGHT *ON* THE BEACH...AS IF IT WAS WASHED UP THERE! THEN SOMEONE'S *SURE* TO FIND IT!

THAT'S A GOOD IDEA, BERT!

AND SO, THAT NIGHT, BERT DROVE TO FALMOUTH, TWENTY MILES NORTH OF THEIR DESERTED LIGHTHOUSE...AND LEFT THE BODY ON THE BEACH!

THERE! SOMEONE'LL FIND IT, COME MORNING!

BUT THE DAYS PASSED...AND NO WORD CAME! FLO LISTENED TO EVERY NEWS BROADCAST, BUT THERE WAS NO MENTION OF FINDING HANK'S BODY!
WHAT'S HAPPENED TO HIM, BERT? WHY HAVEN'T THEY FOUND HIM...YET?
I CAN'T UNDERSTAND IT, FLO! I LEFT HIM RIGHT ON THE FALMOUTH BEACH! FOLKS MUST PASS THERE...
THEY'LL FIND HIM, SOON! C'MON! LET'S LOOK FOR THE MONEY AGAIN!
THE MONEY! THE MONEY! THAT'S ALL YOU THINK OF! DOESN'T IT BOTHER YOU THAT HANK'S BODY KEPT COMIN' BACK FROM THE SEA? DOESN'T IT BOTHER YOU THAT THEY STILL HAVEN'T FOUND HIM?
SURE! SURE IT BOTHERS ME! WHAT CAN I DO ABOUT IT?
DRIVE UP TO FALMOUTH AGAIN! SEE IF HIS BODY'S STILL ON THAT BEACH!
OKAY! IF YOU WANT ME TO! I'LL GO NOW! I'LL MAKE IT BY MIDNIGHT, AND I CAN BE BACK BY TWO A.M.!
I'LL WAIT UP FOR YOU!
BERT LEFT THE FRIGHTENED FLORENCE AND STARTED OUT FOR FALMOUTH! THE MINUTES DRAGGED BY... AND THE CLOCK CHIMED ELEVEN! OUTSIDE, IN THE BLACK NIGHT, THE SOUND OF THE ROARING SEA POUNDING THE ROCKS SHATTERED THE DARKNESS!
I KNEW, WHEN BERT FIRST CAME TO THE LIGHT... TO WORK FOR HANK...
I KNEW, THEN, THAT NOTHIN' GOOD WOULD COME OF HIM AN' ME! AND YET...I COULD NOT HELP MYSELF! I WAS CRAZY WITH LONELINESS! HANK AN' ME, ALONE HERE FOR TWO YEARS! SEEIN' NO ONE! NEVER TAKIN' ME ANYWHERE! I COULDN'T HELP MYSELF! WHEN BERT CAME...I FELL IN LOVE WITH HIM...
...AND NOW WE'VE MURDERED HANK! AND WE THREW HIM TO THE SEA...BUT THE SEA KEEPS GIVIN' HIM BACK...TO... GASP...WHAT'S THAT? LOOKS LIKE SEAWATER...COMIN' IN FROM UNDER THE DOOR!
IT'S HANK! HE'S OUTSIDE THAT DOOR!... COME TO GET ME!
6.

THE DEAD WILL RETURN!

THE TERRIFIED FLORENCE BACKED AWAY FROM THE DOOR... BACK... BACK TO THE SPIRAL STAIRCASE THAT LED TO THE TOP OF THE LIGHTHOUSE!

HE'S RATTLIN' THE KNOB! HE'S GOING TO COME *IN* AND...

SLOWLY, SHE BACKS UP THE STAIRCASE...

THE DOOR...HE'S OPENED THE DOOR! I CAN HEAR HIM... COMIN' ACROSS THE SITTIN' ROOM! COMIN'... TO THE STAIRS...

HE'S ON THE STAIRS NOW! I CAN HEAR HIS FOOTSTEPS... COMIN' UP... COMIN' UP AFTER ME...

SUDDENLY, FLORENCE FOUND HERSELF AT THE TOP OF THE LIGHTHOUSE... NO PLACE TO GO... CAUGHT... LIKE A RAT IN A TRAP...

I'M CORNERED! I CAN'T... *GASP*... HIDE! THE LIGHT! I'LL... TURN IT OFF! MAYBE HE WON'T SEE ME!

HE'S COMIN' CLOSER! HE'S REACHIN' THE TOP OF THE STAIRS! HE'LL BE HERE... SOON... HE... HE'S... COMIN'... *COMIN'*... I...I...

A-A-A-H-H-H!

A FEW MINUTES LATER, A CAR DROVE UP! IT WAS BERT!

H-M-M-M! THAT'S STRANGE! THE LIGHT IS OUT...

213

THE DEAD WILL RETURN!

THE CRYPT OF TERROR

So... we meet again, dear reader! WELCOME! Welcome once more to the *CRYPT OF TERROR!* As you know, in each issue of my terror-ific magazine, I tell you chilling tales from my vast collection which I keep here in this crypt! This story is one of my VERY BEST... well designed to thrill you... to make your blood run cold... to make little shivers run up and down your spine! I call it:

GHOST SHIP!

GHOST SHIP!

MY STORY BEGINS HIGH OVER THE ATLANTIC OCEAN, A FEW HUNDRED MILES NORTH OF BERMUDA! A TINY PLANE IS WINGING ITS WAY THROUGH A CLOUDLESS SKY...

OH, DARLING! WHAT A *WONDERFUL* WAY TO BEGIN OUR HONEY-MOON... *FLYING* TO BERMUDA!

I THOUGHT YOU'D LIKE IT, DEAR!

LIKE IT! I LOVE IT! IT'S LIKE A FAIRYLAND... WITH THE BEAUTIFUL BLUE OF THE OCEAN FAR BELOW...

SAY! LOOKS LIKE A FOG BANK COMING IN OVER THE HORIZON...

SWIFTLY, THE SMALL PLANE SPEEDS THROUGH THE BLUE TOWARD THE MENACING FOG BANK...

I'LL TRY TO GO UP *OVER* IT, CAROL!

CAN'T WE AVOID IT... GO AROUND IT?

NO... IT WOULD TAKE US TOO FAR OFF OUR COURSE... AND MY GAS SUPPLY MIGHT NOT LAST! NO... I'LL TAKE HER UP OVER IT...

THE DRONE OF THE MOTOR GROWS LOUDER AS DON'S PLANE STRAINS TO CLIMB ABOVE THE BLANKET OF FOG BEFORE THEM...

I DON'T THINK WE'RE GOING TO MAKE IT, CAROL... IT... IT'S TOO MUCH FOR HER...

SPUT... SPUT...

THE MOTOR'S CONKED OUT... WE'RE GOING DOWN!

DON! WE'LL BE KILLED!

DOWN... DOWN THROUGH THE THICK PEA-SOUP FOG THE PLANE AND ITS TWO OCCUPANTS DROP... AND THEN...

THERE'S AN OPENING IN THE FOG! I'M GOING TO TRY TO PUT HER DOWN ON THE WATER! FASTEN YOUR SAFETY BELT, CAROL...!

2

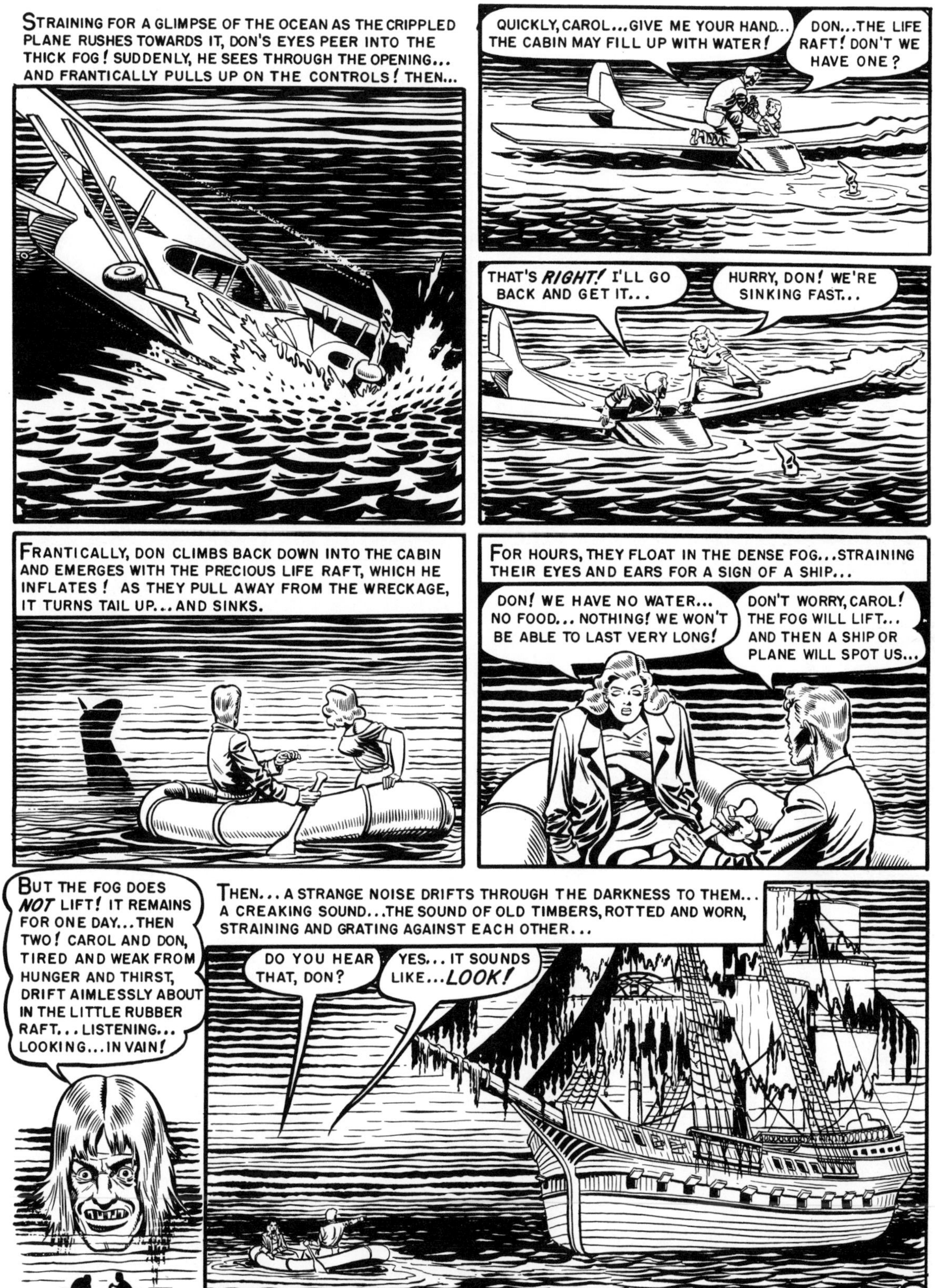
STRAINING FOR A GLIMPSE OF THE OCEAN AS THE CRIPPLED PLANE RUSHES TOWARDS IT, DON'S EYES PEER INTO THE THICK FOG! SUDDENLY, HE SEES THROUGH THE OPENING... AND FRANTICALLY PULLS UP ON THE CONTROLS! THEN...
QUICKLY, CAROL... GIVE ME YOUR HAND... THE CABIN MAY FILL UP WITH WATER!
DON...THE LIFE RAFT! DON'T WE HAVE ONE?
THAT'S RIGHT! I'LL GO BACK AND GET IT...
HURRY, DON! WE'RE SINKING FAST...
FRANTICALLY, DON CLIMBS BACK DOWN INTO THE CABIN AND EMERGES WITH THE PRECIOUS LIFE RAFT, WHICH HE INFLATES! AS THEY PULL AWAY FROM THE WRECKAGE, IT TURNS TAIL UP... AND SINKS.
FOR HOURS, THEY FLOAT IN THE DENSE FOG... STRAINING THEIR EYES AND EARS FOR A SIGN OF A SHIP...
DON! WE HAVE NO WATER... NO FOOD... NOTHING! WE WON'T BE ABLE TO LAST VERY LONG!
DON'T WORRY, CAROL! THE FOG WILL LIFT... AND THEN A SHIP OR PLANE WILL SPOT US...
BUT THE FOG DOES NOT LIFT! IT REMAINS FOR ONE DAY...THEN TWO! CAROL AND DON, TIRED AND WEAK FROM HUNGER AND THIRST, DRIFT AIMLESSLY ABOUT IN THE LITTLE RUBBER RAFT... LISTENING... LOOKING... IN VAIN!
THEN... A STRANGE NOISE DRIFTS THROUGH THE DARKNESS TO THEM... A CREAKING SOUND...THE SOUND OF OLD TIMBERS, ROTTED AND WORN, STRAINING AND GRATING AGAINST EACH OTHER...
DO YOU HEAR THAT, DON?
YES... IT SOUNDS LIKE...LOOK!
3.

GHOST SHIP!

"IT'S A *SHIP!* AN OLD *SAILING VESSEL!*"

"ALL DECAYED AND... IT'S A WONDER IT STAYS *AFLOAT!*"

"LET'S GO ABOARD, CAROL..."

"NO, DON! I'M *AFRAID!* THERE'S SOMETHING... *STRANGE*... ABOUT IT..."

"BUT CAROL! IF THIS FOG HANGS ON MUCH LONGER, WE'LL DIE OF THIRST... PERHAPS WE MIGHT FIND FOOD AND WATER ABOARD..."

"LOOK... DON! ISN'T THAT A LIGHT...?"

"SEE... THERE *IS* SOMEONE ON BOARD!"

"HELLO!! HELLO UP THERE!!!"

"THAT'S FUNNY! THERE'S NO ANSWER!"

"HERE'S A ROPE LADDER! COME ON, CAROL! WE'LL TIE THE RAFT UP AND SEE WHAT IT'S ALL ABOUT..."

DON REACHES THE TOP OF THE LADDER AND TURNS TO HELP CAROL UP ON TO THE DECK...

"THANKS DEAR... I... WHAT'S THAT?"

"WHAT? WHERE?"

"LOOK, DON! A *SKELETON*... LASHED TO THE HELM!"

"GOOD LORD!"

218

GHOST SHIP!

AND... GASP... ONE HANGING FROM THE YARDARM...

I... I DON'T UNDERSTAND!

LOOK... I WAS RIGHT! THERE *IS* A LIGHT IN THE CABIN...

C'MON! LET'S TAKE A LOOK!

THERE'S SOMEONE DOWN THERE...

HE'S READING A BOOK...

THE FRIGHTENED COUPLE MADE THEIR WAY DOWN THE DARK STAIRS TO THE CABIN AND KNOCKED ON THE DOOR! THERE WAS *NO ANSWER!* DON LIFTED THE LATCH AND THE DOOR SQUEAKED OPEN...

WHY... THERE'S NO ONE HERE, *NOW!*

DON! I'M AFRAID! LET'S GO BACK TO THE RAFT!

NONSENSE! WE PROBABLY SCARED WHOEVER IT WAS AWAY! *LOOK!* HERE'S THE *BOOK* HE WAS READING!

IT... IT LOOKS LIKE THE *SHIP'S LOG!*

GREAT SCOTT! THE LAST ENTRY IS DATED JANUARY 6TH, 1854!

GO BACK A BIT AND READ WHAT HAPPENED UP TO THAT DAY, DON!

"October 17th 1853: Today seized the British Frigate Golden Star, killing all hands aboard and capturing booty of jewels and gold coin. The men are dissatisfied with the split; I taking almost half for myself! Captain Henry Dragoon."

WHY, THEN THIS WAS A *PIRATE VESSEL*... AND DRAGOON WAS ITS CAPTAIN!

YES, BUT LISTEN TO *THIS!*

5.

219

GHOST SHIP!

"October 27th, 1853:
A mutiny is stirring, led by one of the men, Charles Groggins. I fear for the lives of myself and my mate, Captain Henry Dragoon."

...AND THEN THE WHOLE TREASURE WILL BE OURS... TO SHARE FAIRLY! ARE YOU WITH ME...?

LET'S STRING THEM UP.. THE CHEATS!

"October 29th, 1853:
They have killed the other officers and I myself remain, locked in this cabin! I can hear them outside, ready to break down the door! This will probably be my last entry in this log. The battering is already shattering the door panels and I..."

IT ENDS ABRUPTLY! THEY PROBABLY KILLED HIM!

LOOK! ON THE NEXT PAGE... ANOTHER ENTRY.. IN A DIFFERENT HANDWRITING!

"October 30th, 1853: Today, as the new captain of this vessel, I ordered Henry Dragoon to walk the plank. In his parting words, he cursed us and swore revenge and return..."

MARK MY WORDS! I WILL RETURN TO ONCE AGAIN COMMAND THIS VESSEL! DEATH TO ALL OF YOU WILL BE MY REVENGE...

GO ON... STOP YOUR CHATTERING AND TAKE YOUR FINAL STEP..

"The men laughed and he disappeared into the briny sea. I immediately set about to find the share of the treasure he had taken...but to no avail. It had vanished! The men will not like this bad news. Charles Groggins."

WHAT? HIS SHARE IS GONE? WHAT MEANS THIS, GROGGINS?

IT IS THE TRUTH, MEN...THE BOOTY IS NOWHERE IN THE CABIN!

BAH!

GRUMBLE

"November 13th, 1853: The men have begun to quarrel and bicker among themselves. They do not believe that there is no treasure. They do not trust me!"

I SAY, LET'S STRING 'IM UP! HE'S TRICKED US!

AYE! HE WANTS THE CAPTAIN'S SHARE FOR HIMSELF!

"November 15th, 1853:
The men have given me until today to produce the Captain's share of the booty! I cannot find it and all my pleading has been in vain. They are at the door now. I fear that my hours are numbered!
Charles Groggins."

AND THAT'S THE LAST ENTRY IN HIS WRITING!

WHO CONTINUES IT, DON?

"November 16th, 1853:
A thorough search of the cabin has not produced the treasure. Charles Groggins body swings from the highest yardarm, and I am taking it upon myself to continue this log. John Bates."

WHAT'S HAPPENED? THE SAILS ARE SLACK!

THE SHIP IS BECALMED! THERE'S NO WIND... NOT A DROP!

6

220

GHOST SHIP!

"December 5th 1853:
There has been a dead calm for three weeks now. The ship has slowly drifted into a great sea of seaweed and we are held fast by its millions of entwining plants."

WE'LL NEVER GET OUT OF THIS NOW... EVEN IF WE DID GET A BREEZE!

WE ARE DOOMED! I SAY TAKE TO THE SMALL BOATS...!

NO... WE WOULD DIE OF EXPOSURE AND STARVATION...!

WE'LL TAKE WHAT'S LEFT OF THE STORES AND WATER!

IT'S FOLLY! I SAY STAY ON THE SHIP! PERHAPS A STRONG ENOUGH WIND WILL TAKE US OFF...

I AGREE WITH THE OTHERS! LET'S TAKE TO THE SMALL BOATS!

"December 18th 1853:
Most of the men took their shares of the stores and left the ship in the small boats. There are but a few of us left."

LOOK! AN ALBATROSS!

IF WE KILL IT, WE COULD BE ASSURED OF FOOD FOR A LITTLE LONGER!

IT IS BAD LUCK TO KILL AN ALBATROSS! BAD LUCK!

"January 3rd 1854:
My hand can hardly hold the plume. I am weak with hunger. Our food and water ran out four days ago, and still the Albatross hovers over us, its screeching driving us out of our minds."

IT'S LAUGHING AT US... LAUGHING...

BY HEAVEN I'LL KILL IT...

WAIT... WAIT! FEEL THAT! A BREEZE! AND LOOK... STORM CLOUDS...

"January 4th 1854:
The storm hit last night at eight bells. Our sails are full-set but still this cursed sea of seaweed holds us fast. Already the ship, battered by the stormy sea, is beginning to crack and strain. Johnson has tied himself to the helm so that he may steer us out should we break loose."

THAT CURSED ALBATROSS IS GONE, ANYWAY! BUT... WE STILL DO NOT MOVE...

THE SHIP WILL NOT BE ABLE TO TAKE THIS MUCH LONGER!

"January 5th 1854:
Carter has strangled while tying a sail on the mizzen mast and he hangs like a banner in the wind. Johnson still remains tied to the helm and I here in the cabin. The water is beginning to fill the hold. We are sinking fast! I will finish this entry and take to the sea. It's my last hope! John Bates."

IS THAT ALL, DON?

NO! THERE'S THIS LAST ENTRY DATED JANUARY 6th 1854! IT SAYS, "THE SHIP IS MINE AGAIN! I WILL SAIL IT INTO ETERNITY! CAPTAIN HENRY DRAGOON!"

GHOST SHIP!

"THIS IS CRAZY, CAROL! THE LAST ENTRY IS IN DRAGOON'S HANDWRITING, TOO!"

"LISTEN... DID YOU HEAR THAT? A FOGHORN!"

THE COUPLE RUSHES TO THE DECK OF THE STRANGE VESSEL! THROUGH THE GLOOM OF THE FOG, THE LIGHTS OF A TANKER COME TOWARD THEM!

"A SHIP, DON! A SHIP! WE'RE SAVED!!"

"AHOY!! AHOY THERE!"

"THEY DON'T HEAR US! THEY'RE COMING RIGHT AT US!"

"THEY'RE GOING TO RAM US!"

"WHA...?"

"GOOD LORD!!"

"C'MON, CAROL! WE'VE GOT TO GET TO OUR LIFE RAFT!"

"I...I...I THINK I'M GOING TO FAINT!"

QUICKLY, DON AND CAROL CLIMB DOWN THE SIDE OF THE OLD ROTTED SHIP INTO THEIR RAFT! THEY PADDLE FURIOUSLY CALLING AFTER THE TANKER...

"HELP! AHOY! HELP!"

"LISTEN! MAN OVERBOARD!"

ONCE ON BOARD, THEY ARE FED AND MADE COMFORTABLE! THEN DON AND CAROL TELL THEIR FANTASTIC STORY...

"UTTER NONSENSE! AN ILLUSION CAUSED BY EXPOSURE AND STARVATION!"

"OUR SHIP PASSED RIGHT THROUGH IT, YOU SAY? I THINK YOU BOTH NEED REST... PLENTY OF REST!"

AND THAT'S THE STORY! STRANGE? WHAT DO YOU THINK HAPPENED? WAS IT ALL IN THEIR MINDS... OR DID DON AND CAROL ACTUALLY SAIL ON A GHOST SHIP? WELL.... IF YOU'RE NOT A LITTLE... ER... SEA-SICK... TURN THE PAGE AND READ ANOTHER OF MY TALES!

THIS TALE IS ONE OF MY FAVORITES! I CALL IT...
THE STRANGE COUPLE!
YOU HAVE BEEN DRIVING FOR TWO HOURS THROUGH THIS BLINDING DOWNPOUR! AT TIMES, YOU CAN HARDLY SEE THE ROAD AHEAD! HEADLIGHTS DON'T HELP! THEY ONLY REFLECT BACK FROM THE SHEETS OF DRIVING RAIN... GIVING THE EERIE EFFECT THAT YOU ARE FOLLOWING A SOLID WALL OF WATER! WAIT... THERE'S A LIGHT UP AHEAD! IT'S MOVING UP AND DOWN! IT... IT'S A MAN... STANDING IN THE ROAD... A STATE TROOPER... SIGNALING YOU TO STOP...
YOU'LL HAVE TO TURN BACK, MISTER! THE BRIDGE'S WASHED OUT UP AHEAD!
BUT... I'VE GOT TO GET THROUGH! ISN'T THERE ANOTHER WAY?
SCRIPT & ART BY FELDSTEIN
ROAD
YOU CAN TAKE THIS SIDE ROAD! IT CROSSES THE RIVER 'BOUT TWO MILES BELOW! BAD ROAD, THOUGH...
THANKS, OFFICER... I'LL CHANCE IT!
YOU BACK THE CAR UP AND SWING ONTO THE SIDE ROAD! THE CAR BUMPS AND ROCKS AS YOU GUIDE IT THROUGH THE BLACKNESS! THE OFFICER WAS RIGHT! THIS IS A BAD ROAD... FULL OF HOLES, NOW FILLED WITH WATER...
...HOPE NONE OF THESE RUTS ARE DEEP! IF THE ENGINE GOT WET, I'D BE STUCK GOOD!
1

THE STRANGE COUPLE!

YOU CONTINUE ON, SPLASHING AND ROLLING, FOR WHAT SEEMS LIKE HOURS! YOU'RE TIRED NOW! THE STRAIN OF DRIVING IN THIS DREADFUL DOWNPOUR IS BEGINNING TO HAVE ITS EFFECT! SUDDENLY...

BLAST!
SPUT-T

THE ENGINE HAS STALLED! THAT LAST DITCH YOU WENT THROUGH PROBABLY WET THE WIRES! YOU'RE STUCK NOW... STUCK OUT IN THIS GODFORSAKEN SPOT!

WELL, THERE'S NO USE TRYING TO WALK ANYWHERE! THE RAIN IS TOO HEAVY FOR THAT...!

MIGHT AS WELL MAKE MYSELF COMFORTABLE!... GOT TO WAIT FOR THIS BEASTLY STORM TO STOP... TIRED ANYWAY... HO-HUM... I'LL...

SUDDENLY, YOU SIT BOLT UPRIGHT! A LIGHT... SHINING THROUGH THE BLACK DOWNPOUR! FUNNY! YOU DIDN'T NOTICE IT BEFORE! MAYBE IT'S A HOUSE! MAYBE...

PERHAPS THEY HAVE A *PHONE*... NEED A MECHANIC TO FIX THE CAR!

YOU PULL YOUR COLLAR UP AROUND YOUR NECK, PULL YOUR HAT DOWN, AND MAKE A BREAK FOR THE HOUSE...

I HOPE THEY CAN PUT ME UP FOR THE... PANT... NIGHT! I'M... PANT... *HUNGRY*, TOO!

THE HOUSE IS OLD AND RUN-DOWN! THE SHUTTERS ARE BROKEN AND ARE CLATTERING AGAINST THE WINDOWS! ICY FINGERS GRIP YOUR SPINE AS YOU STAND BEFORE THE BATTERED DOOR! THERE IS SOMETHING STRANGE ABOUT THIS HOUSE... SOMETHING FOREBODING...

OUGH... SHUDDER... THIS PLACE GIVES ME THE CREEPS....

YOU KNOCK! THE HOLLOW BOOM ECHOES THROUGH THE INTERIOR.... AND HEAVY SLOW FOOTSTEPS APPROACH THE DOOR! THE RUSTY HINGES SQUEAK AND STRAIN AS THE DOOR SWINGS OPEN...

GO AWAY... GO AWAY FROM HERE!

BUT THE STORM ...I...I...

YOU'RE FRIGHTENED! THE WOMAN HAS A WILD, ALMOST MANIACAL LOOK IN HER GLEAMING EYES! HER HOARSE WHISPER BURNS YOUR EARDRUMS...
YOU'RE NOT WANTED! IT'S DANGEROUS FOR YOU HERE! GO AWAY!
BUT MY CAR... IT'S STUCK DOWN THERE... I THOUGHT...
LET THE GENTLEMAN COME IN, HEPSIBAH! LET HIM COME IN! I WOULDN'T TURN AWAY A DOG ON A NIGHT LIKE THIS!
WHY... THANK YOU, SIR! I WAS WONDERING IF YOU COULD PUT ME UP...
GO, WHILE THERE'S STILL TIME...
YOU MUSTN'T MIND MY WIFE, SIR! SHE'S ... NOT WELL!
OH... I SEE!
THAT'S WHY WE LIVE OUT IN THIS DESERTED PLACE! I CAN KEEP MY EYE ON HER... TAKE CARE OF HER!
I... UNDERSTAND! DO YOU THINK I COULD ... GET SOMETHING TO EAT?
OF COURSE! WAIT HERE! I'LL GO DOWN INTO THE WINE CELLAR... AND BRING UP A BOTTLE OF MY BEST VINTAGE!
YOU SIT DOWN! YOU LOOK AROUND! THE WOMAN IS COWERING IN THE CORNER! HER BEADY EYES FOLLOW THE MAN AS HE DISAPPEARS INTO THE CELLAR! THEN SHE RUSHES TO YOU... CLAWING AT YOUR ARM...
PLEASE! I BEG OF YOU! GO! YOU ARE IN GREAT DANGER HERE! MY HUSBAND! HE IS INHUMAN!
INHUMAN?
MY HUSBAND... IS A VAMPIRE! THAT IS WHY YOU MUST LEAVE! TRUST ME! THAT BOTTLE HE'S GETTING... IT'S ALMOST EMPTY! IT'S NOT WINE! IT'S BLOOD!
GOOD LORD! THE WOMAN IS MAD!
3

THE STRANGE COUPLE!

THE FOOTSTEPS ON THE CELLAR STAIRS WARN THE OLD WOMAN OF HER HUSBAND'S RETURN... AND SHE SLIPS INTO THE SHADOWS BEYOND THE FIREPLACE...

AH... HERE WE ARE!

THE MAN PUTS THE BOTTLE ON THE TABLE... AND YOU STARE AT IT! IT IS ALMOST EMPTY, AND THE CONTENTS ARE A DEEP RED... *BLOOD RED...*

YOU'LL JOIN ME, SIR?

I... I'D RATHER NOT!

HE JUMPS UP IN A FIT OF RAGE! HE RUSHES TO THE WOMAN WHO SITS HUDDLED IN THE DARKNESS...

YOU'VE BEEN *TALKING!* GO UPSTAIRS TO YOUR ROOM! *GO AHEAD!*

YES, FEDOR!

YOU CAN SEE THAT HE'S IRRITATED! HE RETURNS TO THE TABLE AND POURS A GLASS OF THE RED LIQUID FOR HIMSELF! HE DRINKS IT DOWN AND LICKS HIS LIPS! THEN HE LEANS TOWARD YOU...

I SEE THAT I MUST TELL YOU ABOUT MY WIFE! SHE IS *INSANE!* HOPELESSLY INSANE! BUT HER AFFLICTION IS WORSE THAN ANY FIEND COULD IMAGINE! MY WIFE... IS A *GHOUL!*

ICY FINGERS AGAIN CLOSE AROUND YOUR HEART AS THE MAN RELATES A STRANGE TALE!

WE HAD A DOG! ONE DAY, IT DIED! I TOOK THE POOR THING AND BURIED IT IN THE GARDEN BEHIND THE HOUSE! THAT NIGHT, I WAS AWAKENED BY THE SOUND OF A SPADE IN THE SOFT EARTH! I LOOKED OUT OF MY WINDOW...

...IT WAS *MY WIFE!* SHE WAS DIGGING AT THE DOG'S *GRAVE!* I PUT ON MY ROBE! I WENT DOWNSTAIRS! SHE WAS GONE WHEN I GOT TO THE GARDEN, BUT THE DOG'S *CORPSE* WAS STILL THERE... AND IT WAS *PARTIALLY DEVOURED!*

YOU SHUDDER! A FEELING OF NAUSEA SWEEPS OVER YOU! YOUR THROAT IS TIGHT AND DRY! THE MAN RISES... TAKES THE BOTTLE AND GOES DOWN INTO THE CELLAR ONCE MORE! SUDDENLY YOU HEAR FOOTSTEPS BEHIND YOU! YOU TURN...

HE KILLED THE DOG! HE DRAINED ITS BLOOD! LOCK THE DOOR TO YOUR ROOM TONIGHT! I BEG YOU! LOCK THE DOOR... PROTECT YOURSELF... I WARN YOU!

I... I WILL!

226

SHE SCURRIES UP THE STAIRS AS THE MAN RETURNS! HE HANDS YOU A KEY!
THIS IS A KEY TO THE CLOSET IN YOUR ROOM! LOCK IT TONIGHT! SHE CAN GET IN THAT WAY IF YOU DON'T! COME... I WILL SHOW YOU YOUR ROOM!
YES! I... I'M COMING!
HE OPENS THE DOOR TO A SMALL ROOM! THERE IS NO WINDOW... ONLY ONE OTHER DOOR! THE CLOSET!
GOOD NIGHT, SIR! REMEMBER WHAT I TOLD YOU... LOCK THE CLOSET WITH THAT KEY!
YES... I WILL! I'LL REMEMBER!
HE IS GONE... AND YOU ARE TERRIFIED! LORD, HOW YOU WISH YOU COULD RUN FROM THIS CURSED HOUSE... BUT THE RAIN... YOU CAN HEAR IT PAT-TERING ON THE ROOF ABOVE... WHERE CAN YOU GO...
I'LL BARRICADE MYSELF IN!
FIRST YOU LOCK THE CLOSET WITH THE KEY THE MAN GAVE YOU! THEN, YOU LOCK THE DOOR TO THE ROOM...
THAT BUREAU LOOKS HEAVY ENOUGH!
YOU PUSH THE HEAVY BUREAU UP AGAINST THE DOOR TO THE ROOM...
THAT OUGHT TO DO IT! HE CAN'T MOVE *THAT*!
...AND SHOVE THE BED UP AGAINST THE CLOSET DOOR...
IF I LIE ON THE BED... SHE WON'T BE ABLE TO PUSH IT OPEN!
NERVOUSLY, YOU LIE DOWN ON THE BED! YOU ARE TIRED... BUT YOU *DARE* NOT SLEEP! WHOM CAN YOU BELIEVE? WHICH ONE IS TELL-ING THE TRUTH?
MAYBE... MAYBE THIS IS ALL A HORRIBLE JOKE THEY ARE PLAYING...
5

THE STRANGE COUPLE!

Suddenly your blood freezes in your veins! You sit up! A noise... footsteps outside your room!

THE DOOR? IS IT THE MAN?

You try to peer into the gloom! The noise... again...

THE CLOSET? IS IT THE WOMAN?

Then... a thin pencil stripe of light falls across the room...

THE WALL... A PANEL IS OPENING...

Sheer horror clutches at your pounding heart... The panel opens wider... wider... and then...

NO! NO! IT'S BOTH OF THEM!

You back up... but there's no place to go! The room is small... the doors barricaded... and the two of them, that HORRIBLE COUPLE, are coming at at you...

MY BOTTLE IS ALMOST EMPTY...

HURRY, FEDOR! FINISH QUICKLY... SO THAT I MAY FEAST...

You scream... loudly... with all the strength you can muster! You claw against the wall behind you and SCREAM...

A-A-A-A-H!

6

THE STRANGE COUPLE!

Suddenly there is a blinding flash of light and you open your eyes...

GOOD LORD!

You are in your car... the rain pounding on the metal top... echoing in your brain! You're wet with perspiration... and sick...

I... I must have been dreaming!

You press your foot on the starter of your car! There is no sound!

...DEAD! The water must have shorted the battery!

You look around! A light... shining through the downpour! A house...

Maybe they have a phone! I could get a mechanic...

You pull your collar up around your neck, pull your hat down over your eyes, and break for the house...

If they have no phone, at least they could put me up until morning!

The house seems strangely familiar! Run-down... clattering shutters, battered door! Almost like the house in that horrible nightmare you just had...

BAH! It was only a dream!

Footsteps, slow and heavy, approach in answer to your frantic hammering! The door squeaks open...

GO AWAY! GO AWAY FROM HERE... BEFORE IT'S TOO LATE!

LET THE GENTLEMAN COME IN, HEPSIBAH! I WOULDN'T TURN AWAY A DOG ON A NIGHT LIKE THIS...

Only a dream? WELL! Then what are you frightened of? Go on! GO ON IN!

THE OFFICE BOY OF THE T. TOT COMIC MAGAZINE PUBLISHING COMPANY PROUDLY PRESENTS:

THE LOVE STORY TO END ALL LOVE STORIES!

FROM THE COMPLETELY FICTITIOUS EXPERIENCES OF T. TOT*

SWEET ANGEL! EVERY MINUTE THAT I AM WITH YOU IS SHEER TORTURE! KNOWING YOU HAS BEEN THE MOST OBNOXIOUS EXPERIENCE OF MY LIFE, DEAR HEART!

AND I, MY DARLING, HAVE KNOWN NO GREATER REPULSION THAN THE REVOLTING NAUSEA I FEEL WHEN I GAZE INTO YOUR GIMLET EYES! WON'T YOU BE MY...MY HELPMATE? MY LITTLE WOMAN? MY...WIFE?

*THE NAME T. TOT, AND NO OTHER NAMES IN THIS RIDICULOUSLY FALSE, UNTRUE-TO-LIFE LOVE STORY ARE REAL, ABSOLUTELY... POSITIVELY!

BLAME THIS ON FELDSTEIN

ONE WARM SPRING MORNING, WHEN BIRDS ARE TWITTERING AND BUDS ARE BURSTING FORTH ON GREEN BOUGHS, AT THE OFFICE OF T. TOT... COMIC BOOK PUBLISHER...

GOOD MORNING, GENTLEMEN! THERE WILL BE A MEETING OF THE EDITORIAL STAFF IN MY OFFICE IN EXACTLY TWO MINUTES AND TWENTY-ONE SECONDS!

YES, MR. TOT!

YES, T.T.!

SH! GENIUS AT WORK!

AND SO... YOU'RE LATE, GENTLEMEN! TEN SECONDS LATE! BUT NO MATTER! I AM IN A GOOD MOOD THIS MORNING! GENTLEMEN! I...T. TOT... PUBLISHER OF COMIC BOOKS...AM...IN LOVE!

YES, MR. TOT!

YES, T.T.!

THE LOVE STORY TO END ALL LOVE STORIES!

"LET ME TELL YOU ABOUT IT!"

"YES, MR. TOT!"

"YES, T.T.!"

"IT ALL BEGAN THE NIGHT I VISITED THE 102ND FLOOR OF THE EMPIRE STATE BUILDING! I HAD GONE THERE BECAUSE I WAS FEELING LOW..."

"HO...HO... MR. TOT!"

"HA...HA... T.T.!"

"HMMPH!"

"SUDDENLY, MY HEART BEGAN TO POUND WILDLY...AND MY BLOOD, HOT AND BUBBLING, COURSED MADLY THROUGH MY VARICOSE VEINS! COULD IT BE? WAS MY FOOLISH IMAGINATION PLAYING TRICKS ON ME? WAS SHE REAL?"

"OH, BE STILL, MY THROBBING HEART! SHE IS BUT AN ILLUSION!"

"THERE, FLYING THROUGH THE NIGHT ON A BROOM, WAS THE LOVELIEST CREATURE THESE BLOODSHOT EYES HAVE EVER FEASTED PASSIONATELY UPON..."

"ON A BROOM, EH, MR. TOT? WITCH BROOM? HAW, HAW!"

"OH, SHUT UP OR I'LL CRONE YOU!"

"HMMPH! ARE YOU QUITE THROUGH, GENTLEMEN?"

"SHE WAS GORGEOUS...SENSATIONALLY BEAUTIFUL! SHE BECKONED TO ME, BUT I COULD NOT GO TO HER! THE WINDOWS WERE ALL LOCKED! I MOTIONED TO HER THAT I WOULD MEET HER DOWNSTAIRS, AND SHE DROPPED OUT OF SIGHT!"

"WANTED TO GET DOWN TO EARTH, EH, MR. TOT?"

"SHE REALLY FELL FOR YOU, EH, T.T.?"

"HMPH!"

"WE MET IN THE LOBBY, AND I TOOK HER TO DINNER! OH, GLORIOUS NIGHT! HOW WELL I REMEMBER THE SWEETNESS OF HER PERFUME MIXED WITH THE AROMA OF THE MUSHROOMS...HER GLOWING HAIR, FALLING LOOSELY ABOUT HER SHOULDERS AND INTO HER SOUP...THE TOUCH OF HER LOVELY HAND AS SHE PASSED ME THE CHECK! AS WE SAID GOODNIGHT, IN HER DOORWAY..."

"I MUST SEE YOU AGAIN, COBINA! MY LIFE WILL BE EMPTY UNTIL THEN..."

"OH, KISS ME GOODNIGHT AND CUT THE GAB!"

"I TOOK HER IN MY PUNY ARMS, AND THE WARMTH OF HER NEARNESS PENETRATED TO MY RHEUMATIC BONES! MY JOY KNEW NO BOUNDS! SHE WAS MINE! I BENT TO PLACE MY LIPS UPON HERS... THE FULL REDNESS OF THEM...INVITING..."

"BOY! AM I HUNGRY!"

"GOODNIGHT, SWEET COBINA! PARTING IS SUCH SWEET... AH...SWEET...OH DEAR...AH... I FORGOT THE LINE! I'LL CALL YOU!"

THE LOVE STORY TO END ALL LOVE STORIES!

GET ME EDGAR ALLEN POE, H.G. WELLS, RUDYARD KIPLING, MARGARET MEEDE... GET ME... KINZEY! I WANT THE BEST LOVE STORIES MONEY CAN BUY!
I WANT VINCERNT VON GOH, PEBBLO PICADO, MIKE ELANGELO, REM BRANDT AND CHESTER GOLD! ONLY THE BEST ARTWORK WILL BE USED!
AND SO, ON THAT WARM SPRING MORNING, A NEW AND REVOLUTIONARY IDEA IS BORN... THE LOVE COMIC BOOK! AFTER WEEKS OF HARD WORK, THE BOOK IS FINISHED!
SOB... SOB... GENTLEMEN! THIS BOOK IS GREAT! SUCH PATHOS ... SUCH POIGNANT DRAMA...
SNIFF, MR. TOT!
SOB, T.T.!
MODERN LOVE
AROUND THE COUNTRY, HYSTERICAL WOMEN STRUGGLE TO OBTAIN A COPY OF MODERN LOVE!
EEEEK!
LEGGO OF MY HAIR!
MY NYLONS... RUINED!
HALP!
AND A FEW MONTHS LATER...
GENTLEMEN! MODERN LOVE IS A COMPLETE SELL-OUT! CHANGE ALL THE TITLES! T. TOT PUBLISHING COMPANY IS DROPPING ITS CRIME!
NO MORE "CRIME MIGHT PAY"? NO MORE "CRIME COULD PAY"? NO MORE "CRIME OUGHT TO PAY"? NO MORE "CRIME SHOULD PAY"? NO MORE "CRIME USED TO PAY"? NO MORE "CRIME DOES SO PAY"? NO MORE CRIME, T.T.?
NO! I WANT... "LOVE MIGHT PAY," "LOVE COULD PAY," "LOVE OUGHT TO PAY," "LOVE SHOULD PAY," "LOVE USED TO PAY," AND "LOVE DOES SO PAY"! IT WILL PAY!
YES, MR. TOT!
YES, T.T.!
MEANWHILE, AT A RIVAL COMIC BOOK PUBLISHING COMPANY...
T. TOT HAS MADE A KILLING! CHANGE OUR COMIC BOOK LINE! FROM NOW ON... IT'S LOVE... LOVE...LOVE!!
YES, MR. WOLF!
YES, V.W.!
WOLF COMICS MAKE 'EM HOWL!
CRIMES BY DOGS
CRIMES BY CATS
CRIMES BY CRIMINALS
4

AND SO, THE COUNTRY IS FLOODED WITH LOVE COMICS! EVERY PUBLISHER SWITCHES TO LOVE... AND THE PUBLIC EATS IT UP...
CHOMP... CHOMP...
YUMMM! YUMMM!
THAT'LL BE TWO DOLLARS AND THIRTY CENTS FOR THOSE TWENTY-THREE LOVE BOOKS, MISS!
OH, GOODY, I HAVE ENOUGH LEFT FOR TWO MORE!
THE COMIC BOOK INDUSTRY GOES BERSERK! HERE IS THE GREATEST MONEYMAKER SINCE "SOUP-OR-MAN."
BOOST THE PRINT ORDERS OF MY SEVENTY-NINE LOVE TITLES TO 1,000,000 EACH! FROM NOW ON, CALL ME LOVE GREASIN!
YES, "LOVE"!
YES, L.G.!
TIPS
THE MAGAZINE FOR HORSES
TAPS
THE MAGAZINE FOR PLUMBERS
THE NUMBER OF LOVE COMICS ON THE STANDS REACHES STAGGERING PROPORTIONS...
HALP!!
SOON... THE SUPPLY IS GREATER THAN THE DEMAND... AND RETURNS (UNSOLD COPIES) BEGIN TO POUR IN...
YE GADS! I'M RUINED... AGAIN!
RUINED, MR. WOLF!
ABSOLUTELY, V. W.!
MY GOO
MY FOO
AND AT THE OFFICES OF T. TOT, PUBLISHER...
MODERN LOVE SOLD TWENTY NINE COPIES, T.T! YOU LOST NINETY-SEVEN THOUSAND DOLLARS THIS MONTH...
HMMPH!
AND STILL THE RETURNS POUR IN... BULGING THE PUBLISHING HOUSES TO A DANGER POINT...
LOVE COMICS... BAH!
AT THE OFFICES OF ARNOLD HARVEY HERMANN...
STOP ALL PUBLICATION! LOVE IS FINISHED! CHANGE THE FORMATS! CHANGE THE TITLES! CHANGE THE STORIES! PUT OUT ANYTHING... EVEN... HORROR!
HORROR, A. H.?
HORRORS, A. H.!
5

MEANWHILE, T. TOT...MY BOSS...RUSHES TO COBINA'S SIDE, FOR SOLACE AND COMFORTING AFFECTION...
SWEET DEAREST! IN MY HOUR OF SADNESS, I COME TO YOU...MY CRYING HEART AWAITING YOUR WORDS OF LOVE! LIKE JEWELS TO A BEGGAR, THEY WILL BRING ME WHAT I LONG FOR... PEACE FOR MY TROUBLED ACHING SOUL...
LET'S EAT!
SAY THE WORDS, MY DEAREST...THE WORDS THAT WILL FILL MY EMPTY HEART TO THE BRIM...AND CAUSE IT TO RUNNETH OVER WITH JOY AND LOVE FOR YOU! WORDS THAT WILL TAKE ME FROM THE DEEP DARK DEPTHS OF UTTER DESPAIR AND LIFT ME HEAVEN-BOUND TO A CONTENTMENT FAR, FAR GREATER THAN I HAVE EVER KNOWN...
I KNOW A LITTLE CHOP-SUEY JOINT AROUND THE CORNER... MMMMM... PICKLED PIGS' KNUCKLES...
RELEASE ME, BELOVED, FROM THIS TORMENT... THIS PAIN THAT I FEEL... THIS SADNESS THAT I'M ENDURING OVER LOSING SO MUCH MONEY...
...AND WON-TON SOUP WITH EGG DROPS... I... *I*... *WHA?*
WHAT WHAT?
DID YOU SAY YOU *LOST* ALL YOUR *MONEY?*
OH, NO! I'M *LOSING* IT! I'LL KNOW HOW I STAND NEXT MONTH WHEN THE REPORTS ON MY *OTHER SIX* LOVE BOOKS COME IN...
OH...
WELL...CALL ME *THEN*...
SWEET HEAVEN! SHE'S TAKEN ME IN HER ARMS...
I'M *HUNGRY!*
6

THE LOVE STORY TO END ALL LOVE STORIES!

SPURNED BY HIS HEART'S BURNING FLAME, T. TOT MAKES HIS WAY SADLY TO HIS MODEST PENTHOUSE APARTMENT HIGH OVER PARK AVENUE...

OH, LOVE, THY TASTE IS LIKE THE TASTE OF HONEY! AND YET... HUNGER FOR LOVE...FOR THY DELICIOUSNESS... CAN BE BITTER, BITTER PAIN! COBINA, MY COBINA... *HUH?*

WELL, WELL! JACK LYMAN AND JOE CURRY! WHAT ARE YOU DOING HERE?

WAITING FOR *YOU*, T. TOT!

YES, T. TOT! WE'VE BEEN WAITING FOR YOU TO COME HOME! ORIGINALLY WE HAD PLANNED TO *SHOOT* YOU...

YES...WE FOLLOWED YOU INTO THE "LOVE FIELD," AND NOW WE'RE RUINED... *RUINED!* BUT WE'RE *NOT* GOING TO KILL YOU...WE'RE GOING TO LET YOU *SUFFER!*

WE'RE GOING TO KILL *OURSELVES!* GOODBYE, T. TOT! *SUFFER WELL!*

GOODBYE T. TOT!

OH, MY POOR TORMENTED SOUL! *BLOOD* UPON MY HANDS... HONEST... KIND... EDITORS' BLOOD! RIVAL EDITORS' BLOOD! I DROVE THEM TO IT... *I DID IT!*

IF I HAD PUSHED THEM OFF THAT BALCONY, I WOULDN'T HAVE BEEN MORE GUILTY THAN I AM! *I DID IT! I AND LOVE!*

I HATE LOVE!

7

THE NEXT MORNING, WHEN MR. TOT COMES INTO THE OFFICE...
GOOD MORNING, GENTLEMEN! THERE WILL BE A MEETING OF THE EDITORIAL STAFF IN MY OFFICE IN EXACTLY TWO MINUTES AND TWENTY SECONDS!
YES, MR. TOT!
YES, T. T.!
AND SO...
GENTLEMEN! I HAVE DECIDED TO DROP OUT OF LOVE! I HATE LOVE! HATE IT, DO YOU HEAR! HATE IT!!
HATE, MR. TOT?
LOVE, T. T.?
UR SALES
I'M GOING TO PUT OUT... AH...ER...
YOU'RE NOT GOING TO PUT OUT ANYTHING, T.T.! YOU'RE BANKRUPT! YOUR SEVEN LOVE MAGAZINES.. THEY ALL SOLD A TOTAL OF 249 COPIES... YOU LOST $2,475,322.48! YOU'RE FLAT BROKE, T.T.!
FINANCIAL STATEMENT OF T. TOT PUBLISH CO.
SUICIDE! I'LL COMMIT SUICIDE... IF I HAD A GUN!
I'VE TAKEN THE LIBERTY, MR. TOT! HERE YOU ARE!
LOADED TOO... T.T.!
AT THAT MOMENT...
GOOD MORNING, TOTTY BOY! I'M HUNGRY! LET'S EAT!
YOU... YOU DID IT! YOU RUINED ME...
BLAMM!
BLAMM!
BLAMM!
BLAMM!
T. TOT PRIVATE
GULP... WHAT WAS THAT?
P.K. L.L.B.
THEY WERE DEAD! ALL FOUR OF THEM! AND I, THE OFFICE BOY OF T. TOT PUBLICATIONS, AM THE ONLY ONE LEFT! SO IF YOU LIKE THIS TYPE OF STORY, AND WANT TO SEE MORE LIKE IT IN FUTURE ISSUES. . . WHICH I SHALL PUBLISH... WRITE ME! ADDRESS YOUR LETTERS TO: THE OFFICE BOY MODERN LOVE ROOM 706-DEPT 8 225 LAFAYETTE ST. N.Y.C. 12, N.Y.
8

THE WITCH'S CAULDRON!

HEH-HEH! WELL... WE MEET AGAIN! COME IN! COME IN! I AM *THE OLD WITCH... MISTRESS* OF *THE HAUNT OF FEAR!* IN EACH ISSUE OF THIS, MY *VERY OWN* MAGAZINE, I LIGHT THE FIRE BENEATH MY CAULDRON... AND AS THE EMBERS GLOW, I BREW FOR YOU ANOTHER TALE ABOUT THE INHABITANTS OF MY HORRIBLE ABODE... THE VAMPIRES... THE WEREWOLVES... THE SHAPELESS GHOSTS...

THIS TIME, DUE TO THE MANY REQUESTS I HAVE RECEIVED, I AM GOING TO TELL YOU A STRANGE TALE ABOUT TWO MEN... TWO MEN WHO ARE THE EDITORS OF THE E.C. COMIC MAGAZINE PUBLISHING COMPANY... AND HOW THEY ENCOUNTERED...

HORROR BENEATH THE STREETS!

MY STORY BEGINS ON A DANK, DISMAL NIGHT! THE CITY IS ASLEEP! THE BUILDINGS STAND, COLD AND BARE LIKE TOMBSTONES IN A CROWDED CEMETERY! ALL IS SILENT... ALL IS DARKNESS... EXCEPT FOR A SINGLE LIGHTED WINDOW, HIGH UP IN ONE BUILDING... THE OFFICES OF THE E.C. COMIC MAGAZINE PUBLISHING COMPANY! INSIDE... TWO MEN BREATHE A SIGH OF RELIEF...

WELL, AL! THAT DOES IT!

YEP, BILL! "MODERN LOVE" IS FINALLY FINISHED! AND... RIGHT ON THE DEADLINE, TOO...

C'MON, AL! LET'S GET ON HOME!

I'LL PUT OUT THE LIGHTS, BILL! BE RIGHT WITH YOU!

HORROR BENEATH THE STREETS!

THE LIGHTS ARE PUT OUT, AND ALL THE DOORS ARE LOCKED! THE TWO MEN TURN AND MAKE THEIR WAY SLOWLY DOWN A LONG DARK CORRIDOR... THEIR FOOTSTEPS ECHOING THROUGH THE BLACKNESS...

PRETTY EERIE AROUND HERE AT NIGHT, EH, BILL?

H-M-MM! THAT GIVES ME AN IDEA!

THE HUM OF THE ELEVATOR APPROACHING BREAKS THE THICK SILENCE...

WHAT KIND OF AN IDEA, BILL?

EERIE...TERROR...HORROR! BOY! THAT WOULD BE *TERRIFIC*! *HORROR* IN COMICS!

THE ELEVATOR BEGINS TO DESCEND... CARRYING THE TWO MEN DOWN TOWARD THE DARK STREETS BELOW...

YOU MEAN *CREEPY* STORIES...LIKE GHOSTS AND STUFF?

SURE! I BET THAT'D GO OVER BIG!

THE SILENCE IN THE STREET IS SHATTERED AS THE DOOR TO THE BUILDING SLAMS SHUT...AND THE TWO MEN START TO WALK...

NAH! OUR READERS WOULDN'T GO FOR *HORROR STORIES!*

I DON'T KNOW ABOUT THAT! *EVERYBODY* LIKES A GOOD *GHOST STORY!*

THEY TURN THE CORNER AND CROSS OVER TO THE OTHER SIDE...

A-A-AH! NOBODY BELIEVES THAT KIND OF TRASH!

MAYBE THEY DON'T *BELIEVE* 'EM...BUT... I'LL BET THEY'D *LIKE* THEM...

HEY, BILL! DON'T TURN AROUND...BUT I THINK WE'RE BEING FOLLOWED!

HUH?

THE CLACKETY-CLACK OF QUICK FOOTSTEPS ECHOES UP AND DOWN THE SILENT FACES OF THE COLD BUILDINGS, AS THE TWO MEN INCREASE THEIR SPEED...

IT...HE...IT'S *STILL BEHIND* US! WHERE IN THE BLAZES DID YOU PARK YOUR CAR?

DOWN THIS STREET! C'MON!

239

BILL! HE'S STILL FOLLOWING US! HURRY! HURRY!
C'MON! I THINK IT'S AROUND THIS CORNER...
GOOD LORD!
TRAPPED! IT'S A DEAD END!
MAYBE... MAYBE IT'S ONLY A COINCIDENCE, BILL! MAYBE HE ISN'T REALLY FOLLOWING US!
WE'LL... SEE! IF HE TURNS THAT CORNER...
GULP!
IT ISN'T ANY COINCIDENCE! C'MON!
WHERE YUH GOING? YOU CAN'T CLIMB BRICK WALLS!
LOOK! AN OPEN MANHOLE!
THE TWO TERRORIZED MEN SCAMPER DOWN THE YAWNING BLACK HOLE... AS THE CLACK-CLACK OF THE FOOTSTEPS BEHIND THEM GROWS LOUDER...LOUDER...
HURRY... HURRY!
I'M NO ATHLETE! TAKE IT EASY! I'M RUSHIN' ALL I CAN!
SWIFTLY, THEY PULL THE LADDER DOWN WITH THEM... THEREBY FOILING ANY ATTEMPT AT BEING FOLLOWED! THEN...
BILL! HE'S CLOSING THE LID!
LISTEN! LISTEN TO HIS HORRIBLE LAUGH!
3

A-A-H-HA HA HA HA HA HA HA HA HA HA
WE'RE TRAPPED, BILL! TRAPPED!
MAYBE... MAYBE HE'LL GO AWAY!
SUDDENLY... THE HYSTERICAL RANTING OF THE PERSON ABOVE THEM STOPS... AND QUICK FOOTSTEPS SCURRY AWAY IN THE STREET...
HE... HE'S GONE!
PUT UP THE LADDER! LET'S TAKE A LOOK!
IT... UGH... IT'S STUCK! I... OOOF... I CAN'T BUDGE THIS LID!
WHAT'LL WE DO, AL? WHAT'LL WE DO?
MAYBE WE CAN FIND ANOTHER EXIT... GET OUT THAT WAY?
LET'S GIVE IT A TRY!
SLOWLY... CAUTIOUSLY... THE TWO MEN MOVE FORWARD IN THE GLOOM OF THE MUSTY SEWER...
I'M SCARED, BILL!
I THOUGHT YOU DIDN'T BELIEVE IN... CREEPY... HORROR STUFF!
I... I... DON'T! ONLY... WELL ...THIS PLACE IS DIFFERENT! I'VE NEVER BEEN IN A SEWER BEFORE!
OH... AND HAUNTED HOUSES... OLD CASTLES... GRAVEYARDS... TOMBS... YOU'VE BEEN IN THOSE?
OH, SHUT UP! I...I... A-A-A-G-H-H!
WHAT'S THE MATTER, AL?
4

HORROR BENEATH THE STREETS!

L...L...LIGHT A M...M...MATCH, BILL! I...I'M STEPPING ON S...S...SOMETHING! S... S...SOMETHING *SOFT!*

IT'S N...NOTHING... AL! P...PROBABLY JUST A PILE OF G...GARBAGE... S--SEE?

Y-I-I-I-I-I!

A BODY!

Blindly, the two men rush from the harrowing sight of the decayed corpse...slushing through the stench...falling...crawling! Fear... *FEAR* in their hearts... *FEAR* in their minds... *FEAR*... and *HORROR* pursuing them...

Exhausted... they stop...leaning on the dripping walls for support...

GASP...I... GASP...CAN'T.. GO...ON...MUCH...FURTHER!

LOOK, BILL! A LIGHT...UP AHEAD!

C'MON! MAYBE IT'S A WAY OUT OF THIS GODFORSAKEN HOLE?

YOU...TAKE A LOOK...WHILE ...I...REST UP...

OKAY! I'LL BE RIGHT BACK! WAIT HERE! I'LL SEE WHAT IT'S ALL ABOUT! I...

BILL! WHERE ARE YOU?

242

GONE! DISAPPEARED INTO THIN AIR!
I'M GETTING OUT OF HERE!
SUDDENLY, AS AL ... TERRIFIED... TURNS A CORNER IN THE TUNNELS...
GULP...OH!
COME IN! I'VE BEEN WAITING FOR YOU!
MEANWHILE, THE OTHER ONE, BILL, FINDS HIMSELF IN A STRANGE DIMLY LIT ROOM... FACING HIS CAPTOR...
WHO... WHO ARE YOU?
I? I AM THE KEEPER OF THE CRYPT OF TERROR!
THE CRYPT OF WHAT?
TERROR! DON'T YOU KNOW WHAT TERROR IS?
YOU... YOU'RE DARN TOOTIN' I DO... AND ..YOU .. YOU AREN'T H...H.. HELPING ME FORGET IT!
GOOD! I'VE BEEN LOOKING FORWARD TO MEETING YOU! I HAVE A PROPOSITION
WHILE AL... UP AHEAD IN THE STENCH-FILLED SEWER...
WHAT...DO YOU...WANT WITH ME?
COME IN AND WE'LL TALK IT OVER! I... AM THE KEEPER OF THE VAULT OF HORROR!
6

ALL IS STILL NOW IN THE MUSTY TUNNELS BENEATH THE STREETS! ALL, THAT IS, EXCEPT FOR THE OCCASIONAL SHRIEKING OF A RAT! THEN... A SPLASH...AND ANOTHER! SOMEONE IS COMING!
AL? WHERE ARE YOU?
DOWN AT THE OTHER END OF THE TUNNEL, ANOTHER SPLASH IS HEARD!
BILL? IS THAT YOU?
BOY, I WAS NEVER HAPPIER TO SEE ANYONE IN MY LIFE! LISTEN TO WHAT HAPPENED TO ME!
YOU HAVEN'T HEARD ANYTHING!
... AND SO THIS CREEP WHO CALLS HIMSELF THE KEEPER OF THE CRYPT OF TERROR STICKS A CONTRACT UNDER MY NOSE! WHAT COULD I DO? I SIGNED IT!
GULP! YOU TOO? LOOK! I SIGNED ONE WITH SOME FIEND CALLED THE KEEPER OF THE VAULT OF HORROR!
WELL, AL! THEY GOT US! I GUESS WE'LL HAVE TO PUBLISH THEIR STUFF!
COME ON, BILL, LET'S GET OUT OF HERE!
AND THAT'S THE STORY, DEAR READER! WELL...ALMOST! PERHAPS YOU'RE WONDERING WHO IT WAS THAT FOLLOWED THE TWO EDITORS AND FORCED THEM TO ENTER THAT HORRID SEWER! WELL... THAT WAS ME... THE OLD WITCH! AND WHEN I LET THEM OUT AGAIN, THEY HAD TO PAY MY FEE... AND THAT'S HOW THE HAUNT OF FEAR WAS BORN! THAT'S HOW I GOT MY CONTRACT! AND NOW YOU KNOW THE WHOLE STORY BEHIND THE VAULT OF HORROR, THE CRYPT OF TERROR, AND THE HAUNT OF FEAR! I'LL SEE YOU NEXT ISSUE! 'BYE, NOW!
THE TERRIFIED EDITORS OF THE HAUNT OF FEAR WOULD LIKE TO KNOW WHICH STORY IN THIS MAGAZINE YOU LIKED BEST! VOTE FOR YOUR FAVORITE!
1. NIGHTMARE! A PSYCHOLOGICAL STUDY!
2. MONSTER MAKER! A SCIENTIFIC SUSPENSTORY!
3. TELEVISION TERROR! A JOURNEY INTO THE SUPERNATURAL!
4. THE WITCH'S CAULDRON: HORROR BENEATH THE STREETS! AN ADVENTURE IN TERROR!
ADDRESS YOUR LETTERS TO:
THE OLD WITCH, THE HAUNT OF FEAR
ROOM 706, DEP'T. 17
225 LAFAYETTE STREET
N.Y.C. 12, N.Y.
7.

THE CRYPT-KEEPER'S TALE
WELL...HEH, HEH... I SEE IT'S TIME FOR ME TO TELL YOU ANOTHER SPINE-TINGLING TALE...ONE OF MY VAST COLLECTION OF CHILLERS WHICH I KEEP HERE IN THE CRYPT! THIS STORY IS A FAVORITE OF MINE...ONE THAT I GUARANTEE WILL MAKE YOUR BLOOD RUN COLD AND YOUR HAIR STAND ON END! I CALL IT...
THE THING FROM THE SEA!
13
YOU ARE ABOUT TO BEGIN A FRIGHTFUL ADVENTURE...CONCERNING A LUXURIOUS OCEAN LINER AND THE STRANGE AND UNEXPLAINED EVENTS THAT WILL OCCUR IN...
STATEROOM 13!
FELDSTEIN

THE THING FROM THE SEA!

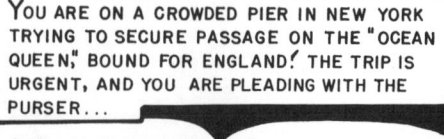

YOU ARE ON A CROWDED PIER IN NEW YORK TRYING TO SECURE PASSAGE ON THE "OCEAN QUEEN," BOUND FOR ENGLAND! THE TRIP IS URGENT, AND YOU ARE PLEADING WITH THE PURSER...

"BUT YOU MUST HAVE *ONE* BERTH OPEN... I'LL TAKE *ANY* CLASS!"

"WELL, AS A MATTER OF FACT, SIR... THAT IS... IF YOU'RE NOT *SUPERSTITIOUS*..."

WHAT WONDERFUL LUCK! ONLY *ONE* OF THE TWO BERTHS IN STATEROOM 13 HAS BEEN TAKEN! YOU PAY THE PURSER AND BOARD THE SHIP! AND NOT A MOMENT TOO SOON... FOR AS YOU REACH THE TOP OF THE GANGPLANK...

"CAST OFF THE FORWARD LINES..."

"MAKE READY FOR DEPARTURE..."

"LAST CALL... ALL ASHORE THAT'S GOING ASHORE..."

YOU WATCH AS THE DOCK SLIPS AWAY... THE LITTLE TUGS STRAINING AND PUSHING THE GIANT LINER OUT INTO MIDSTREAM! THEN...

"MAY I TAKE YOUR BAGS AND SHOW YOU TO YOUR CABIN, SIR?"

"WHY... THANK YOU, STEWARD!"

"AH... WHAT NUMBER STATEROOM DO YOU HAVE, SIR?"

"WHY... 13!"

THE COLOR DRAINS FROM THE STEWARD'S CHEEKS... HIS EYES FILL WITH HORROR AS HE STARES AT YOU...

"WHY... WHAT SEEMS TO BE THE TROUBLE, STEWARD?"

"OH... ER... NOTHING, SIR... NOTHING!"

THE STEWARD SETS YOUR BAGS DOWN IN YOUR STATEROOM, CHECKS THE PORTHOLE TO SEE THAT IT IS SECURELY BOLTED, AND THEN EDGES TOWARD THE DOOR! THERE IS A LOOK OF FEAR ON HIS FACE...

"WHAT IS IT, OLD MAN? WHAT IS THERE ABOUT THIS CABIN THAT FRIGHTENS YOU?"

"I... I... DON'T KNOW, ONLY... ONLY..."

NO ONE WHO HAS EVER BEEN ASSIGNED *THIS* CABIN HAS *COMPLETED* HIS CROSSING IN IT! SOMETHING... SOMEONE... *FRIGHTENS THEM* INTO *LEAVING IT!* WHY ONE PASSENGER EVEN WENT *MAD* FROM WHAT HE SAW HERE...

"WHA...? WHAT *DID* THEY SEE? *TELL ME!*"

THE THING FROM THE SEA!

THE STEWARD MUMBLES SOMETHING ABOUT GHOSTS AND SLIPS FROM YOUR GRASP! YOU WATCH AS HE HURRIES DOWN THE CORRIDOR, AND THEN YOU CLOSE THE DOOR...

GHOSTS... BAH! HE'S PROBABLY PLAYING A TRICK ON ME... SUGGESTION AND STUFF...

YOU STOW YOUR BELONGINGS IN YOUR ASSIGNED BERTH AND SURVEY THE CABIN! IT IS SMALL, WITH ONE PORTHOLE... AND THE TWO BERTHS...

HMMM! I WONDER WHO HAS THE *UPPER*? HIS BAGGAGE IS HERE! HE'S PROBABLY UP ON DECK SAYING GOODBYE TO THE GOOD OLD U.S.A.!

AFTER DINNER, YOU DECIDE TO TURN IN! YOU ARE TIRED, AND THE FRESH SEA AIR HAS MADE YOU SLEEPY...

OH... HELLO! I GUESS YOU MUST BE MY ROOMMATE! GLAD TO MEET YOU!

SAME HERE! RATHER SMALL STATEROOM, ISN'T IT? HAD TO TAKE IT... ONLY ONE LEFT!

YES... THAT'S WHAT THEY TOLD *ME*! WELL... GUESS I'LL TURN IN! I'M PRETTY TIRED!

ME, TOO! GLAD YOU'RE HERE, THOUGH! THE STEWARD TOLD ME SOME AWFUL YARN ABOUT THIS ROOM...

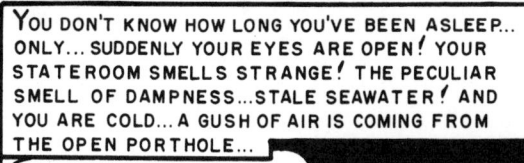

OH, I WOULDN'T TAKE IT SERIOUSLY! HE'S PROBABLY PULLING YOUR LEG!

YES... WELL... GOOD-NIGHT!

YOU DON'T KNOW HOW LONG YOU'VE BEEN ASLEEP... ONLY... SUDDENLY YOUR EYES ARE OPEN! YOUR STATEROOM SMELLS STRANGE! THE PECULIAR SMELL OF DAMPNESS... STALE SEAWATER! AND YOU ARE COLD... A GUSH OF AIR IS COMING FROM THE OPEN PORTHOLE...

BLAST! THE PORTHOLE IS OPEN! I'D BETTER CLOSE IT... OR RISK A NASTY COLD!

YOU GET UP AND STUMBLE TO THE PORTHOLE IN THE DARKNESS! THE BOLTS HAVE BEEN LOOSENED AND THE FINE SPRAY FROM THE SEA WETS YOUR FACE! YOU SLAM IT SHUT, BOLTING IT TIGHTLY... AND THEN, FROM THE BERTH ABOVE YOURS, COMES A BLOOD-CURDLING CRY...

A-A-H-H!

WHAT THE...?

247

WITH A SINGLE LEAP, YOUR ROOMMATE SPRINGS FROM HIS BERTH TO THE FLOOR AND DASHES MADLY TOWARD THE STATEROOM DOOR...
WHAT *IS* IT? *WHAT'S WRONG!*
NO! NO! NO!
YOU LISTEN TO HIS FOOTSTEPS RUNNING FULL SPEED DOWN THE CORRIDOR! POOR OLD BOY! PROBABLY SEA-SICK! YOU SHUT THE DOOR AND GROPE YOUR WAY BACK TO YOUR BERTH! YOUR EYES CLOSE, AND YOU SLEEP AGAIN! THEN, DURING THE EARLY MORNING HOURS, YOU ARE AWAKENED BY A GROAN...
O-O-O-O-O-OH!
HMMMM! NOT A VERY GOOD SAILOR... POOR CHAP! LISTEN TO HIM MOAN...
THE NEXT MORNING, THE SUN STREAMING THROUGH THE PORT-HOLE AWAKENS YOU AND YOU DRESS QUICKLY! THE CURTAINS OF THE UPPER BERTH ARE DRAWN... YOU LEAVE WITHOUT DISTURBING YOUR ROOMMATE...
...PROBABLY ISN'T IN THE MOOD FOR BREAKFAST ANY WAY!
ON DECK, THE SHIP'S DOCTOR STOPS YOU...
I...I WONDER IF YOU CAN TELL ME WHAT HAPPENED LAST NIGHT? WE FOUND YOUR ROOMMATE COWERING IN A PASSAGE... BABBLING LIKE AN IDIOT!
WHA...? YOU MEAN... HE DIDN'T COME BACK TO THE STATEROOM?
NO! WE HAVE HIM IN THE SHIP'S HOSPITAL! HE'S SUFFERING FROM SHOCK! CAN YOU TELL ME WHAT HE SAW THAT MIGHT HAVE CAUSED IT?
I...I HAVE NO IDEA!
LOOK! I HAVE A LARGE CABIN! WHY DON'T YOU BRING YOUR THINGS OVER THERE AND SPEND THE REST OF YOUR TRIP WITH ME?
OH, REALLY, DOCTOR? ARE YOU IMPLYING THAT THE RUMORS ABOUT STATEROOM 13 ARE *TRUE?*
YOU LAUGH, REFUSING THE DOCTOR'S INVITATION! YOU SPEND THE DAY RELAXING IN YOUR DECK CHAIR... SWIMMING IN THE SHIP'S POOL... AND PLAYING CANASTA IN THE GAME ROOM AFTER DINNER! IT IS VERY LATE WHEN YOU RETURN TO YOUR ROOM...
HO-HUM! GAD, I'M TIRED! THAT BERTH CERTAINLY LOOKS INVITING!
4

YOU CHECK THE PORTHOLE TO SEE THAT IT IS SECURELY BOLTED AND THEN YOU STRETCH OUT ON YOUR BERTH! YOU LAY AWAKE THINKING ABOUT THE AGONIZING SCREAM OF YOUR ROOMMATE THE NIGHT BEFORE, WHEN...
WHAT THE...? THE PORTHOLE IS OPEN AGAIN...AND...PHEW...THAT SMELL OF SEAWATER AND DECAY...
YOU GET UP AND CLOSE IT! YOU ARE FRIGHTENED! YOU DISTINCTLY REMEMBER CHECKING IT BEFORE YOU WENT TO BED! YOU TIGHTEN THE BOLTS WITH ALL OF YOUR STRENGTH AND STAND THERE FOR A WHILE...STARING OUT TO SEA! SUDDENLY...
WHAT'S THAT? A MOAN... COMING FROM THE UPPER BERTH...
O-O-O-O-O-O-H!
YOU SPRING TO THE BERTH AND TEAR THE CURTAINS APART...THRUSTING YOUR HAND IN, TO DISCOVER IF THERE IS ANYONE THERE...
THAT SMELL...THAT NAUSEATING SMELL OF STAGNANT SALTWATER! AND... AND... AAAAAAGH!
YOU TAKE HOLD OF SOMETHING...SOMETHING COLD AND WET...ICY COLD...SOMETHING LIKE A MAN'S ARM! AND AS YOU PULL, THE CREATURE HURLS ITSELF FROM THE BERTH...A CLAMMY, OOZY MASS!
KEEP AWAY! KEEP AWAY!
IN AN INSTANT, THE HORRIBLE MONSTROSITY HAS DARTED OUT OF THE STATEROOM DOOR!
GOOD LORD! SO THAT'S WHAT IT IS! I...I'LL ...FOLLOW IT!
YOU CHASE THE DARK SHADOW THROUGH THE DIMLY LIT PASSAGE, AND UP TO THE COMPANIONWAY!
BLASTED THING! IT'S GETTING AWAY!
YOU WATCH AS IT SEEMS TO GO OVER THE RAIL AND INTO THE SEA...
I...MUST BE DREAMING! THAT CURSED MEAL TONIGHT...IT... IT DIDN'T AGREE WITH ME!
5

THE THING FROM THE SEA!

YOU CANNOT RETURN TO THAT HORRIBLE ROOM SO YOU WALK THE DECK, FINALLY CURLING UP IN A DECK CHAIR UNDER A STEAMER BLANKET TO SLEEP A DREAMLESS SLEEP! THE MORNING SUN BLINDS YOU AS YOU ARE SHAKEN AWAKE...

OH... IT... IT IS YOU, CAPTAIN!

I WENT TO YOUR STATEROOM! YOU WEREN'T THERE! IS ANYTHING WRONG?

WELL FRANKLY, CAPTAIN, THERE *IS!* SOMETHING VERY HORRIBLE HAPPENED IN MY STATEROOM LAST NIGHT! IT MIGHT HAVE BEEN MY IMAGINATION BUT...

WHY DON'T YOU LET ME FIX YOU UP IN THE OFFICERS' QUARTERS FOR THE REMAINDER OF THE TRIP?

LOOK HERE, CAPTAIN! CAN'T WE GET TO THE BOTTOM OF THIS? THERE *MUST* BE A LOGICAL EXPLANATION!

YOU ARE RIGHT, SIR! ONLY, WHAT CAN *I* DO? I'M INCLINED TO *BOARD UP* THE ROOM!

THAT WILL SOLVE NOTHING! PERHAPS IT IS ONLY A STOWAWAY... TRYING TO FRIGHTEN PEOPLE OUT OF THAT STATEROOM SO THAT HE CAN SPEND THE REMAINDER OF THE TRIP IN COMFORT! A MANIAC PERHAPS!

HMMM! THAT THOUGHT HAS NEVER OCCURED TO ME! YOU MAY BE RIGHT! I TELL YOU WHAT!

TONIGHT, I WILL STAND WATCH WITH YOU! IF HE SHOWS HIS FACE, WE'LL BE ABLE TO OVERPOWER HIM... TOGETHER!

GOOD, CAPTAIN! I'M GLAD *YOU* ARE TAKING A MORE REALISTIC ATTITUDE THAN YOUR SUPERSTITIOUS CREW!

YOU ARE RELIEVED THAT YOU WILL NOT HAVE TO SPEND ANOTHER NIGHT *ALONE* IN THAT ACCURSED STATEROOM! TOGETHER WITH THE CAPTAIN, TONIGHT YOU MAY SOLVE THIS BAFFLING PROBLEM!

SEE YOU THEN, AT ABOUT TEN!

YES... STATEROOM 13!

YOUR DAY IS SPENT ANXIOUSLY... AND TOWARDS EVENING, YOU FIND YOURSELF BECOMING NERVOUS! FINALLY, IT IS TEN O'CLOCK... AND YOU MAKE YOUR WAY DOWN TO THE STATEROOM!

AH, CAPTAIN! RIGHT ON TIME I SEE!

LET'S GO IN!

6

IF YOU LIKE MY TALES AND HAVE *TIME TO KILL*... DROP ME A FEW LINES! WRITE TO: THE CRYPT-KEEPER, RM. 706, DEPT. 20, 225 LAFAYETTE ST., N.Y.C. 12, N.Y.

HONG KONG INTRIGUE!
I STOOD ON THE TERRACE OUTSIDE MY HOTEL ROOM, PUFFING AN AMERICAN CIGARETTE...
SO THIS IS HONG KONG! FROM UP HERE, IT DOESN'T LOOK HALF BAD!
SUDDENLY A FLASH OF LIGHT ON THE NEXT BALCONY CAUGHT MY EYE...
H-M-M-M! SOMEONE'S HIDING IN THE SHADOWS...WITH A KNIFE!
FELDSTEIN
1

HE WAS CHINESE! HE HADN'T NOTICED ME COME OUT ON MY TERRACE! HIS EVIL SLANTING EYES WERE GLUED ON THE OCCUPANT OF THE NEXT HOTEL ROOM...
HE'S OPENING THE DOOR...
THE STILLNESS OF THE ORIENTAL NIGHT WAS SHATTERED BY A PIERCING SCREAM! THAT WAS ENOUGH FOR ME! I VAULTED THE SEPARATING WALL...
THAT'S A GIRL HE'S AFTER...
A PRETTY BLONDE...HER EYES WIDE WITH TERROR...WAS CRINGING AGAINST A WALL! I LUNGED...
KNIVES ARE DANGEROUS TOYS...BUSTER!
I CAUGHT HIM COMPLETELY BY SURPRISE! THE KNIFE CLATTERED ACROSS THE FLOOR AS WE WENT DOWN...
...AND I DON'T LIKE GUYS WHO BULLY WOMEN...
I DROVE MY FIST INTO HIS PUDGY FACE, AGAIN AND AGAIN...
THIS OUGHT TO LEAVE AN IMPRESSION ON YOU!
THE FORCE OF MY BLOW SENT THE BEGGAR CRASHING THROUGH THE GLASS BALCONY DOORS...
HE MELTED INTO THE SHADOWS AND WAS GONE! I WENT BACK INSIDE! THE GIRL WAS SOBBING ON THE BED...
LUCKY THING I SPOTTED THE WRETCH... OR ELSE YOU'D BE A GONER BY NOW, HONEY!
OH, THANK YOU, MR... MR...
2

KING! GREGG KING! CALL ME GREGG! MAYBE YOU'D BETTER TELL ME WHAT THIS IS ALL ABOUT!
YES! SIT DOWN! PERHAPS YOU CAN HELP ME! I HAVE NO ONE TO TURN TO! MY NAME IS CAROL STANTON...
SLOWLY CAROL'S STORY UNFOLDED...
AND WHEN MY FATHER OBTAINED THE PROOF... HE CAME TO HONG KONG... TO BRING THE INFORMATION TO THE AUTHORITIES!
WHERE IS YOUR FATHER?
THEY KIDNAPPED HIM! I DON'T KNOW WHETHER HE'S STILL ALIVE OR NOT! AND NOW THEY WANT TO SILENCE ME! WHAT CAN I DO...WHERE CAN I GO? THEY FOLLOW ME EVERYWHERE!
YOU SAY YOUR FATHER CAN PROVE BEYOND A SHADOW OF A DOUBT THAT THE NORTHERN REBELS ARE TAKING ORDERS DIRECTLY FROM A FOREIGN POWER?
YES! BUT ONLY HE KNOWS WHERE THE EVIDENCE IS HIDDEN!
THEN LET'S GO! WE'VE GOT TO RESCUE HIM! THE FATE OF ALL OF EAST ASIA DEPENDS UPON IT!
I KNOW WHERE WE CAN BEGIN! THE BLUE DRAGON CAFÉ! THAT'S WHERE FATHER WENT THE NIGHT HE DISAPPEARED!
WE TOOK A RICKSHAW TO THE BLUE DRAGON CAFÉ! IT WAS AN EVIL-LOOKING PLACE...SMOKE-FILLED AND DIMLY LIT! WE SAT AT A TABLE IN THE REAR...
KEEP YOUR EYES OPEN, CAROL!
LOOK, GREGG!
I FOLLOWED HER GLANCE! IT WAS THE SLANT-EYED DEVIL THAT HAD ATTACKED HER WITH A KNIFE! HE WAS SLIPPING THROUGH A CURTAINED DOOR AT THE REAR OF THE CAFÉ...
LET'S GO, CAROL! WE'LL FOLLOW HIM!
I'M RIGHT BEHIND YOU, GREGG!
3

WE STEPPED THROUGH THE CURTAINED DOORWAY AND FOUND OURSELVES IN A DARK ALLEY IN THE REAR OF THE CAFÉ...
THERE HE GOES... INTO THAT BUILDING!
C'MON, CAROL!
IT WAS A GLOOMY DESERTED WAREHOUSE! THE CHINAMAN WE WERE FOLLOWING WAS NOWHERE AROUND!
LOOK, GREGG! A LIGHT COMING FROM UNDER THAT DOOR!
QUIET, NOW! LET'S SEE IF WE CAN HEAR WHAT'S GOING ON!
WE CREPT SILENTLY TOWARD THE DOOR! A FEELING OF UNEASINESS CAME OVER ME! SUDDENLY...
GREGG! LOOK OUT!
I DON'T KNOW HOW MANY OF THEM THERE WERE! I STARTED SWINGING! I FELT MY FISTS CRUNCHING BONES AND TEARING FLESH...
ONE OF THEM HAD A KNIFE! I FELT A SEARING PAIN AS IT TORE INTO MY SLEEVE...THEN THE CEILING SEEMED TO FALL IN ON ME...
WHEN I CAME TO, I FOUND MYSELF ON THE FLOOR OF A DINGY ROOM! CAROL WAS BENDING OVER THE HUDDLED FORM OF AN OLD MAN...
IT'S FATHER! LOOK WHAT THEY'VE DONE TO HIM!
I...GASP...DIDN'T TELL THEM...GASP...
HE HAD TAKEN A LOT OF PUNISHMENT! HIS FACE AND BODY WERE BRUISED AND CUT! HE MOTIONED TO US TO BEND CLOSER...
I...I CAN'T HOLD ON...MUCH LONGER! THE PAPERS... ARE IN...KEROSENE LAMP... BLUE DRAGON CAFÉ... HID THEM... BEFORE...THEY... GASP...
HE'S... HE'S DEAD, CAROL!
4

SHE THREW HERSELF ACROSS HIS LIMP FORM AND WEPT! I LOOKED AROUND FOR A MEANS OF ESCAPE...
NO WINDOWS! ONLY THAT ONE DOOR!
JUST THEN, THE DOOR OPENED AND AN OBSCENELY FAT ORIENTAL ENTERED... FOLLOWED BY TWO ARMED GUARDS...
HE IS DEAD? TOO BAD! THEN WE WILL HAVE TO GET THE INFORMATION FROM YOU, MISS STANTON!
YOU DIRTY BEASTS! I WON'T TELL... ANYTHING!
THE FAT ONE GARBLED SOME ORDERS IN CHINESE TO THE GUARDS, AND THEY MOVED IN...
STAY WHERE YOU ARE, MISTER! YOU WILL SEE HOW WE EXTRACT INFORMATION FROM PRETTY, FRAIL WOMEN...
THE TWO GUARDS GRABBED CAROL! I HAD SEEN ENOUGH!
SHE SAID... SHE ISN'T GOING TO... TELL!
CRAACK!
THE FAT ONE WAS PULLING A GUN FROM HIS KIMONO... BUT A WELL-PLANTED KICK CHANGED HIS MIND...
I PICKED UP THE GUN THAT FATBOY HAD SO KINDLY DROPPED AND TOOK CAROL'S HAND...
C'MON, CAROL! IT'S GETTING HOT IN HERE!
5

WE DARTED OUT OF THE DOOR! A HALLWAY LED TO A FLIGHT OF STAIRS...
THIS WAY OUT!
GREGG! LOOK OUT!
AT THE TOP OF THE STAIRS, A FIGURE STOOD... A HATCHET IN HIS RAISED HAND...
I HATE TO SPOIL YOUR FUN, GEORGIE...
THE BULLET STOPPED HIM RIGHT BETWEEN HIS EYES! HE TOPPLED PAST US DOWN THE STAIRS...
HOPE YOU LIKE YOUR TRIP!
ANOTHER APPEARED! HE FLUNG HIMSELF AT US...BRANDISHING A KNIFE! THE GUN BLAST CAUGHT HIM FULL IN THE FACE...
FATBOY AND THE TWO GUARDS WERE AFTER US AS WE CAME OUT INTO THE ALLEY!
GO GET THOSE PAPERS FROM THE LAMP IN THE CAFÉ, CAROL! I'LL TAKE CARE OF THESE PUNKS!
YES, GREGG!
I SLIPPED INTO THE SHADOWS OF A DOORWAY AND WAITED! THEY CAME ON THE RUN...
AS THEY NEARED THE SPOT, I STUCK OUT MY FOOT...
HOW CLUMSY OF ME...
6

THE THREE OF THEM WENT DOWN IN A HEAP... AND MY GUN BUTT QUIETED THEIR OBJECTIONS!
CAROL CAME UP AS I WAS GOING THROUGH FATBOY'S WALLET!
I HAVE THE PAPERS, GREGG! THEY WERE THERE, WHERE FATHER SAID HE HID THEM!
LOOK AT THIS, CAROL! FATBOY'S A REAL PRIZE!
THE OBESE ORIENTAL WAS A FOREIGN SPY! I GRABBED HIM BY HIS COLLAR AND DRAGGED HIM TO THE STREET!
HY SAY! WOT'S GOIN' ON 'ERE!
YOU'LL FIND A FEW BOYS BACK THERE IN THE ALLEY AND IN THAT WAREHOUSE, OFFICER! I'M TAKING THIS ONE TO THE CONSULATE PERSONALLY!
AND AT THE CONSULATE...
THESE PAPERS ARE OF EXTREME IMPORTANCE, MISS STANTON! I'M SENDING THEM ON TO THE PROPER GOVERNMENTAL DEPARTMENT!
THEN FATHER WILL NOT HAVE DIED IN VAIN!
YOUR FATHER AND YOU... AND MR. KING HERE... HAVE RENDERED A GREAT SERVICE TO CHINA, AND TO THE WORLD!
CAROL SLIPPED HER ARM IN MINE...
I REALLY DON'T KNOW HOW I CAN THANK YOU, GREGG!
DON'T TRY, CAROL!
BACK AT THE HOTEL, WE STOOD ON THE TERRACE AND LOOKED OUT OVER HONG KONG!
YOU KNOW, GREGG! FROM UP HERE IT DOESN'T LOOK HALF BAD!
H-M-M-M-M! NOW WHERE HAVE I HEARD THAT BEFORE?
THE END
7

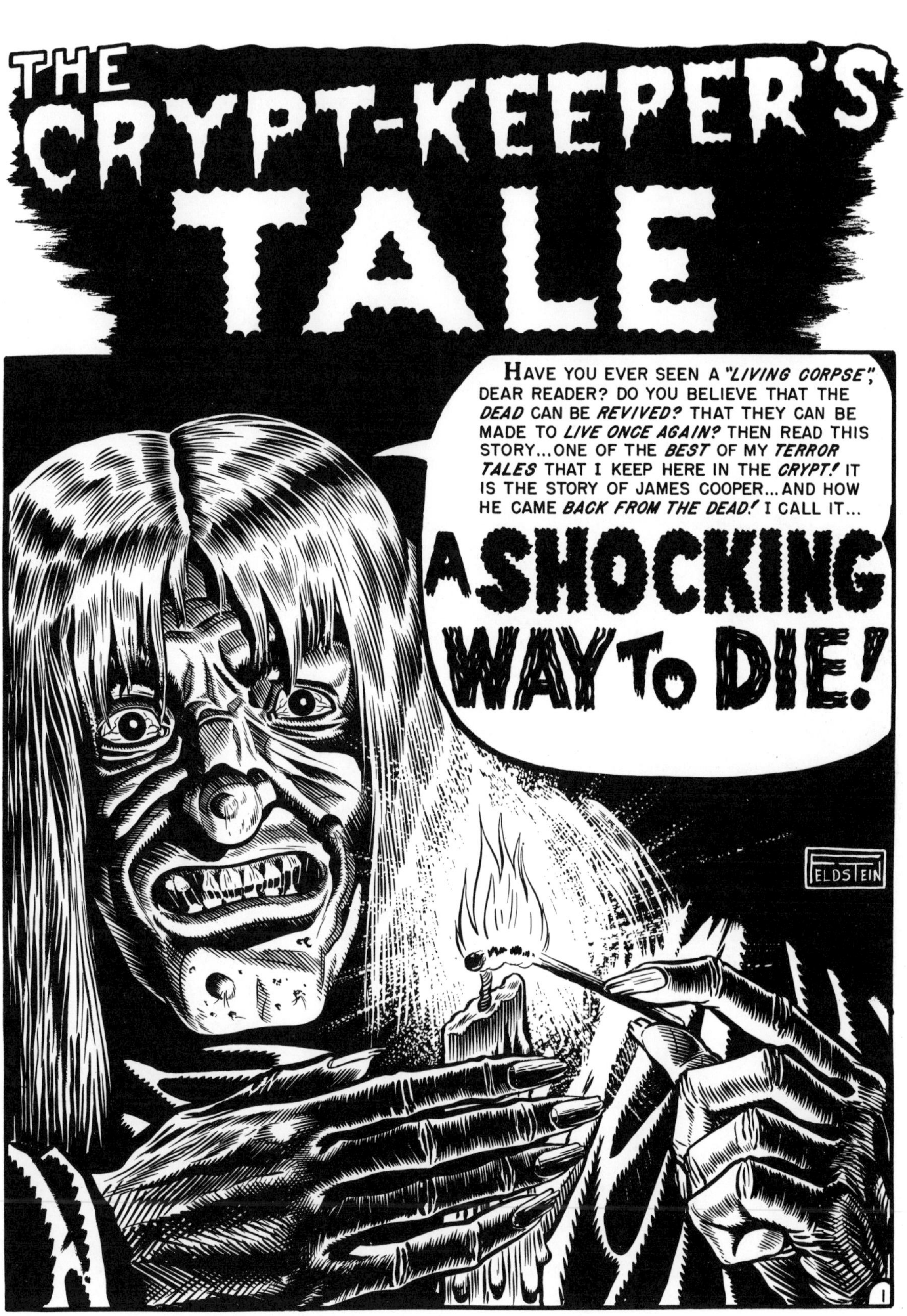
THE CRYPT-KEEPER'S TALE
HAVE YOU EVER SEEN A "LIVING CORPSE", DEAR READER? DO YOU BELIEVE THAT THE DEAD CAN BE REVIVED? THAT THEY CAN BE MADE TO LIVE ONCE AGAIN? THEN READ THIS STORY...ONE OF THE BEST OF MY TERROR TALES THAT I KEEP HERE IN THE CRYPT! IT IS THE STORY OF JAMES COOPER...AND HOW HE CAME BACK FROM THE DEAD! I CALL IT...
A SHOCKING WAY TO DIE!
FELDSTEIN
1

A SHOCKING WAY TO DIE!

Panel 1: My story begins in a courtroom, crowded with the curious who have come to watch a convicted murderer be sentenced to death...
"...And it is the judgment of this court, James Cooper, that you be sent to state prison, and there be electrocuted on the night of November 7th... and may the Lord have mercy on your soul!"
"No... no!"

Panel 2: "I've been *framed!* You're all *against* me! But... *I'll get even!* I'll come *back*... and I'll *get you*... *all* of you! I'll have *revenge!* You'll see! I..."
"Let's go, Cooper!"

Panel 3: The evening papers carried blaring headlines of James Cooper's threat...
EVENING BU[GLE]
CONVICTED MURDERER SWEARS REVENGE!!
TO RETURN FROM THE DEAD!
JURY MEMBERS AMUSED!
COOPER TO DIE NIGHT OF NOV. 7TH.
CONVICTED KILL[ER]

Panel 4: But a few nights later, in a ramshackle house outside of town...
"For the *right price*, gentlemen, I can *bring* James Cooper back from the *dead*... revive him *after* he has been *electrocuted!*"
"What? You can... make him *live* again?"

Panel 5: "That is *correct!* I have been experimenting on electrocution deaths for many years and have been *successful* with *animals!* I have longed to experiment on a human... that is why I've contacted you!"

Panel 6: And so... a few days before James Cooper was to die in the electric chair... he had a visitor in the death house...
"What do you think, Jimmy? Want to chance it?"
"*Of course,* you fool! What have I got to *lose?* Pay him his money!"

Panel 7: The deal was made, and on the night of November 7th, at the appointed hour...
"All right, Cooper! Let's go!"
"Sure, guard! Sure!"

2

260

A SHOCKING WAY TO DIE!

Panel 1: DOWN THE LONG CORRIDOR TO THE LITTLE GREEN DOOR, THE CONVICTED MAN... FLANKED BY THE WARDEN AND A GUARD... SLOWLY MADE HIS WAY... DOWN THE "LAST MILE"...

Panel 2: THE HEAVY DOOR SWUNG OPEN! INSIDE SAT REPORTERS ASSIGNED TO COVER THE EXECUTION...
- LOOK, JOE! THE JERK'S *SMILING!*
- WAIT! HE'LL *CRACK!* THEY ALWAYS *DO!*

Panel 3: OUTSIDE THE DARK GREY WALLS IN THE PRISON YARD STOOD A BLACK HEARSE! A FACE PEERED OUT FROM BEHIND DRAWN CURTAINS...

Panel 4: WHILE WITHIN, THE PRISONER WAS BEING STRAPPED INTO THE LETHAL CHAIR...
- HE DOESN'T SEEM TO BE AFRAID!
- I DON'T GET IT!

Panel 5: ELECTRODES WERE FASTENED INTO PLACE...
- ALL SET, WARDEN!
- ALL RIGHT, MR. EXECUTIONER!

Panel 6: A SMALL MAN STEPPED TO A CONTROL PANEL AND PULLED A SWITCH...

Panel 7: THE STENCH OF BURNING FLESH AND SINGED HAIR FILLED THE ROOM AS THE LIGHTS DIMMED! AFTER A FEW MOMENTS, A DOCTOR STEPPED FORWARD AND PLACED HIS STETHOSCOPE ON JAMES COOPER'S HEART...
- THIS MAN IS DEAD!

A SHOCKING WAY TO DIE!

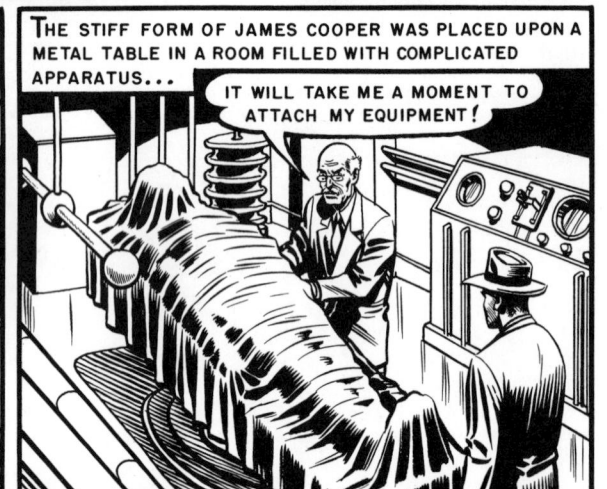

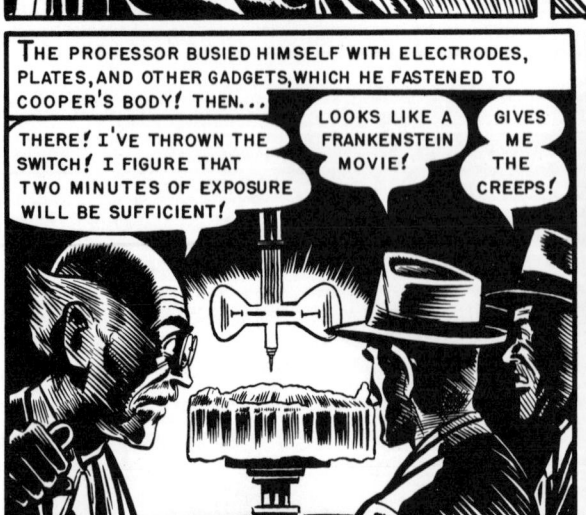

Panel 1: A guard stepped forward...
"His relatives are here to claim his body, sir!"
"They may come in!"

Panel 2: The doors to the black hearse swung open, and the covered body of James Cooper was lifted in...
"Hurry!"
"Okay, Prof!"

Panel 3: The huge gates to the prison parted, and the hearse...with its odious prize...roared through...
"Quick! We haven't a moment to lose!"
"Step on it, Looey!"

Panel 4: In a matter of minutes, the black car pulled up before the professor's house...
"Careful! I've given him THREE hypodermics! Do not JAR him!"
"Don't worry, Prof! We'll handle him like a BABY!"

Panel 5: The stiff form of James Cooper was placed upon a metal table in a room filled with complicated apparatus...
"It will take me a moment to attach my equipment!"

Panel 6: The professor busied himself with electrodes, plates, and other gadgets, which he fastened to Cooper's body! Then...
"There! I've thrown the switch! I figure that two minutes of exposure will be sufficient!"
"Looks like a Frankenstein movie!"
"Gives me the creeps!"

Panel 7: After the two minutes had passed, the apparatus was turned off! All eyes watched the still form! The seconds ticked off...ten...twenty...then...
"Look! His hand! It MOVED!"
"He's ALIVE!"

A SHOCKING WAY TO DIE!

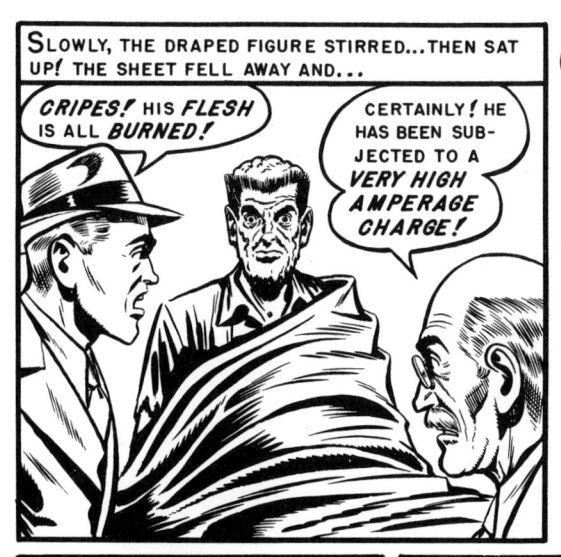

YOU SHOULDN'T HAVE DONE THAT, JIMMY! HE WAS GONNA FIX UP YOUR BURNS!
DON'T NEED IT! NOW... I'M GONNA GET THAT JURY!
WAIT, JIMMY! DON'T DO NOTHING FOOLISH! FORGET THE JURY! THEY JUST DID THEIR DUTY!
I SWORE REVENGE! NOW I'M GOING TO GET IT!
HE...HE'S DIFFERENT! HE DOESN'T SEEM TO BE ALL THERE!
MAYBE...WHAT THE PROF SAID... ABOUT HIS BRAIN BEING DAMAGED...
LATE THE NEXT NIGHT, ON A DARK STREET...
ALL RIGHT, JUROR NUMBER ONE... HERE'S WHERE YOU GET YOURS!
WHA..? WHO IS IT? I...NO...NO! COOPER...
AND THE NEXT MORNING...
THE MORNING
STAR—COMET—PRESS
JUROR IN COOPER CASE FOUND MURDERED! FEARED VICTIM OF GANGLAND RETALIATION...
STRANGE MARKS ON THROAT SAID TO BE BURNED FLESH PRINTS!
MEANWHILE, AT THE COOPER GANG'S HIDEOUT...
IT'S THE BOSS!
GOOD LORD! LOOK AT HIM!
HE LOOKS WORSE THAN YESTERDAY!
WHAT ARE YOU STARING AT?
6

A SHOCKING WAY TO DIE!

IT WAS TRUE! JAMES COOPER'S BURNED AND SEARED BODY *DID* LOOK WORSE! IT SEEMED TO BE... *ROTTING*?

YOU SHOULDN'T HAVE *DONE* IT, JIMMY! THEY'VE TURNED THE *HEAT* ON...

WHO CARES? I'LL *GET* THEM! EVERY *LAST ONE* OF THEM!

AGAIN THAT NIGHT, JAMES COOPER STALKED A VICTIM...

THAT TAKES CARE OF *YOU*, JUROR NUMBER TWO!

AND THE PAPERS PLAYED IT UP...

STAR NEWS
SECOND JUROR FOUND MURDERED!
POLICE ROUNDING UP EVERY KNOWN MEMBER OF COOPER GANG!
COURTROOM PROMISE TO RETURN IS RECALLED!

THE POLICE GRILLED SUSPECT AFTER SUSPECT! MEANWHILE, THE OTHER JURORS WERE GIVEN POLICE PROTECTION...

ALL RIGHT! ALL RIGHT! I'LL TALK... I'LL TALK! IT'S *COOPER*! HE'S ALIVE!

YOU'RE *LYING*!

YEAH? THEN WHY DON'T YOU LOOK IN HIS GRAVE FOR HIS BODY?

HOGAN! GET THE NECESSARY PAPERS! WE'LL TAKE THIS STOOLIE'S SUGGESTION!

BY COURT ORDER, THE GRAVE OF JAMES COOPER WAS OPENED...

OKAY, BOYS! PRY OPEN THE COFFIN!

IT... IT'S *EMPTY*!

HE *IS* ALIVE!

IT *CAN'T* BE! I WOULDN'T BELIEVE IT IF I HADN'T SEEN IT WITH MY OWN EYES!

A SHOCKING WAY TO DIE!

That night, James Cooper again roamed the city, being careful to keep out of sight! He was a ghastly thing to see! His flesh had almost completely decayed from his body!

While the cops are guarding the jurors, I'll get the judge that sentenced me...

His hideous face peered into the study of Judge Warren Hawley...

Good! He's alone!

Slowly he opened the French doors and entered...

Cooper! Good Lord! What... what you LOOK like...

I...I've come to... to kill you... Judge!

The judge snatched a poker from the nearby fireplace... and as Cooper advanced toward him...

Keep away, Cooper... KEEP AWAY! All right! You FORCE me to...

YAAAAAAH!

The blow from the heavy iron poker caught Cooper across the face, and the remaining flesh fell away!...Then...

He...he collapsed into a heap of bones... and decayed rot!

Later, after the coroner had examined Cooper's remains...

I don't know what to make of it, Judge! You say he TALKED and WALKED? According to my tests, he's been DEAD since NOVEMBER 7TH!

DEAD? But he LIVED... I SAW him...

Yes, Judge! Cooper LIVED! At least he moved... and talked! But he was a living CORPSE! And his body CONTINUED TO DECAY, as ALL dead bodies do! Soon, he had decayed to such a point that even the 'life' that the poor old professor had given him slipped away! Too bad, though! He was getting to look REAL PRETTY! Didn't YOU think so? Well... for more spine-tingling tales, READ ON... if you DARE! Just don't GO TO PIECES like poor old Jimmy!

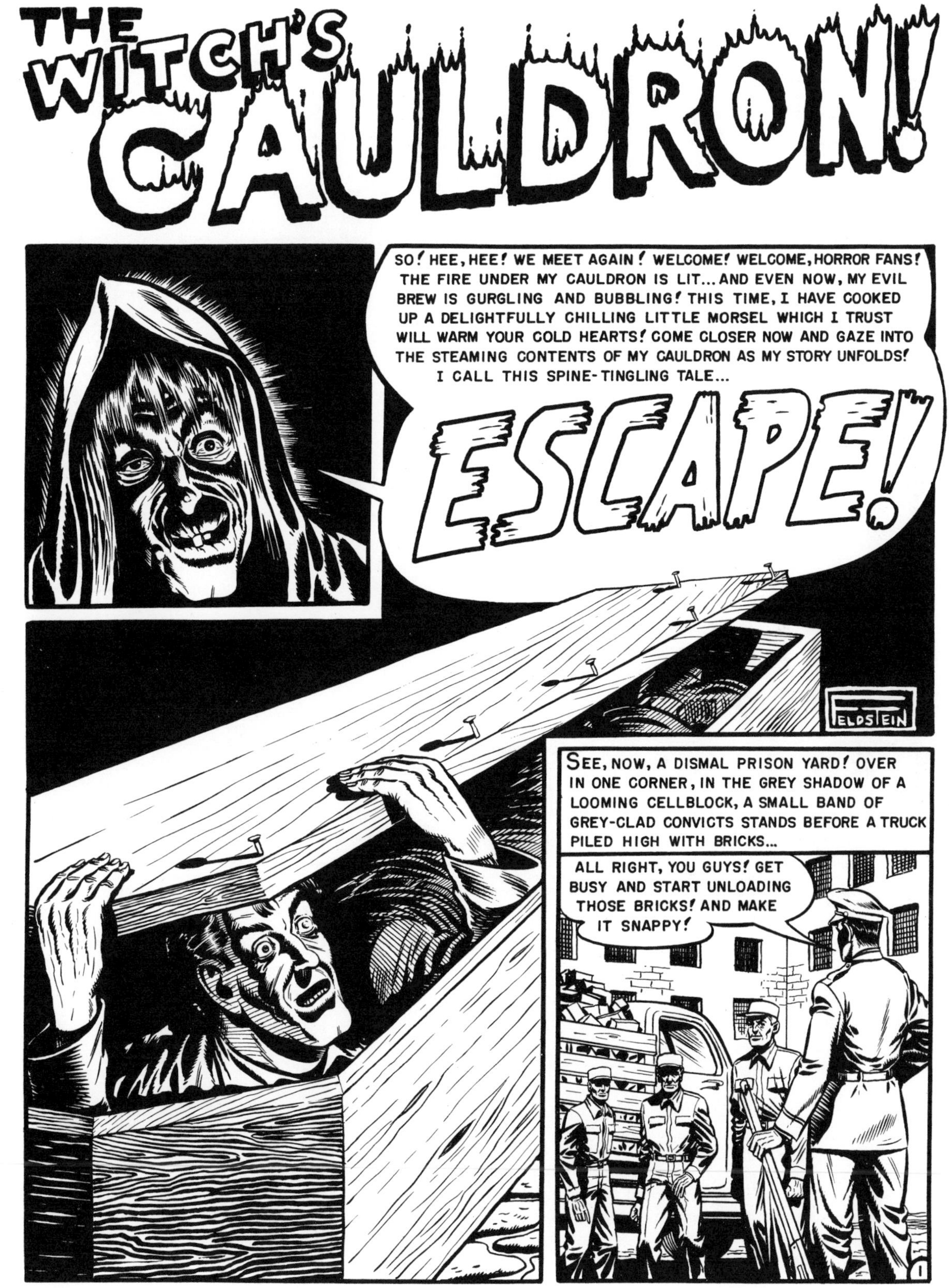
THE WITCH'S CAULDRON!
SO! HEE, HEE! WE MEET AGAIN! WELCOME! WELCOME, HORROR FANS! THE FIRE UNDER MY CAULDRON IS LIT... AND EVEN NOW, MY EVIL BREW IS GURGLING AND BUBBLING! THIS TIME, I HAVE COOKED UP A DELIGHTFULLY CHILLING LITTLE MORSEL WHICH I TRUST WILL WARM YOUR COLD HEARTS! COME CLOSER NOW AND GAZE INTO THE STEAMING CONTENTS OF MY CAULDRON AS MY STORY UNFOLDS! I CALL THIS SPINE-TINGLING TALE...
ESCAPE!
FELDSTEIN
SEE, NOW, A DISMAL PRISON YARD! OVER IN ONE CORNER, IN THE GREY SHADOW OF A LOOMING CELLBLOCK, A SMALL BAND OF GREY-CLAD CONVICTS STANDS BEFORE A TRUCK PILED HIGH WITH BRICKS...
ALL RIGHT, YOU GUYS! GET BUSY AND START UNLOADING THOSE BRICKS! AND MAKE IT SNAPPY!
1

THE GRUMBLING CONVICTS SET TO WORK AT THE BACKBREAKING TASK OF REMOVING THE HUGE PILE OF BRICKS FROM THE TRUCK...
LET'S GO, LUGER!
OKAY! OKAY!
RELUCTANTLY, ONE OF THE MEMBERS OF THE GREY-CLAD GROUP ROLLS HIS WHEELBARROW UP TO THE TRUCK...
HAW! IF THE BOYS BACK IN THE CITY COULD SEE YOU NOW, LUGER...
SHADDUP, CREEP!
PETE LUGER HAD ONCE BEEN THE KING OF A NATIONWIDE CRIME SYNDICATE...
CREEP, HUH? DON'T BE SURPRISED IF YOU GET A PICKAXE IN YOUR SKULL ONE OF THESE DAYS, LUGER!
CUT IT, YOU GUYS! THE GUARD'S EYEIN' YOU!
AND SO, THE DAY PASSED... AND THE BRICKS WERE ALL UNLOADED AND STACKED NEATLY BESIDE THE CELLBLOCK...
WHEW! I'M BEAT...
S'MATTER, LUGER? YUH SOIL YER LILY-WHITE HANDS?
OKAY, MEN! LINE UP!
THE RAGGED GROUP, THEIR SHIRTS SOAKED WITH SWEAT, LINED UP FOR THE MARCH BACK TO THEIR CELLS...
ANOTHER CRACK LIKE THAT, BONEHEAD, AND YOU'LL BE CHEWIN' ONE OF THOSE BRICKS...
HEY, LOOK!
A HEARSE!
SLOWLY, THE OMINOUS BLACK TRUCK PULLED UP BEFORE A SMALL DOOR...
WHAT'S THAT PLACE?
THE PRISON MORGUE!
SOME YARDBIRD MUSTA CROAKED!
THE DOOR OPENED, AND A SIMPLE PINE BOX WAS CARRIED OUT...
THEY TAKE HIM INTO TOWN AND BURY THE POOR JOE IN 'POTTER'S FIELD'!
UNLESS HIS FAMILY WANTS HIM...
...AND WHOSE WOULD?
2

ESCAPE!

ESCAPE!

GET SOME TOOLS FROM CARPENTRY AND GET BUSY ON A COFFIN!
OKAY, GUARD! RIGHT AWAY!
THAT NIGHT, LUGER SCRIBBLED A HASTY NOTE TO THE BOYS ON THE OUTSIDE...
...COME VISIT ME. I'M LONELY. PETE
ON THE FOLLOWING VISITING DAY, PETE LUGER'S OLD LIEUTENANT PAID A CALL...
WHAT'S UP, PETE?
I'M BREAKIN' OUT! I GOT A PLAN... AND YOU GUYS GOTTA HELP!
EVER WARY OF THE GUARDS THAT PACED THE VISITING ROOM, PETE UNFOLDED HIS PLAN...
...AND WHEN THE HEARSE PULLS OUT OF THE PRISON YARD, YOU TRAIL IT! AT A SAFE SPOT...TAKE OVER! I'LL BE IN THE COFFIN...
IN THE COFFIN?
YEAH! DON'T ASK QUESTIONS! JUST FOLLOW MY INSTRUCTIONS! TOMORROW! KEEP A SHARP WATCH FOR THE HEARSE...
OKAY, LUGER! TIME'S UP!
PETE LUGER WENT BACK TO THE MORGUE AND GAZED OUT OF THE WINDOW...
HMMMM! THEY'VE ALMOST COMPLETED WHATEVER IT IS THEY'RE BUILDING! LOOKS LIKE A CHIMNEY!
PRISON MORGUE
SUCKERS! HAULIN' THOSE BRICKS WHILE I SIT AROUND HERE! AND TOMORROW...HAH... I GET OUT!
5

ESCAPE!

Panel 1: THE NEXT DAY...
"GET GREYSON INTO HIS COFFIN, LUGER! TWO MEN WILL BE HERE TO PICK HIM UP AT TWO O'CLOCK SHARP!"
"O.K., GUARD! TWO O'CLOCK!"

Panel 2: PETE MOVED THE CRUDELY MADE COFFIN INTO THE CENTER OF THE ROOM...
"THEY'LL NEVER FIND WHAT'S LEFT OF GREYSON..."

Panel 3: AND THEN... HE CLIMBED IN...
"WHAT A PLAN! BRILLIANT! BRILLIANT!"

Panel 4: AT TWO O'CLOCK, TWO CONVICTS ENTERED...
"HEY, LUGER! WE..."
"HE AIN'T AROUND!"

Panel 5: "MUSTA WENT TO CHOW! WELL! GRAB AN END!"
"WAIT! LOOK! THE COFFIN..."

Panel 6: "S'MATTER!"
"IT AIN'T NAILED DOWN!"

ESCAPE!

QUICKLY, THE CONVICT REACHED FOR THE HAMMER AND NAILS...
LEAVE IT TO LUGER TO LEAVE A JOB UNFINISHED...THE *CRUMB!*

OKAY, JAKE! LET'S GO! GRAB AN END!
YEAH! ONLY A FEW MORE MINUTES...

...THEN... FREEDOM!
Y'KNOW, I ALWAYS WONDERED WHAT THAT WAS WE WERE BUILDIN' WITH THOSE BRICKS...

YEAH! SO DID I!

THE HEAVY IRON DOOR SLAMMED SHUT! THE ROAR OF THE FLAMES MUFFLED LUGER'S FRENZIED CRIES...
A *CREMATORIUM!* WHO'DA THUNK IT?
YEAH! I *NEVER* FIGURED IT...

HEH...HEH! WELL, KIDDIES! NEITHER DID PETE LUGER! HE WAS *SURE* HE HAD A *HOT* IDEA! I'LL BET HE'S *ALL BURNED UP* ABOUT IT NOW, THOUGH! WELL, IT ONLY GOES TO SHOW...DON'T COUNT YOUR BRICKS BEFORE THE BUILDING IS MADE...OR IT MIGHT *BACKFIRE*...HEE-HEE... AS IT *DID* ON POOR PETER! I HOPE MY LITTLE TALE FOR THIS ISSUE *SCORCHED* YOU! I'LL TRY TO HAVE ANOTHER *HEARTWARMER* NEXT ISSUE! BYE, NOW...AND DON'T FORGET TO WRITE TO THE *VAULT-KEEPER* AND LET HIM KNOW WHAT YOU THINK OF...AHEM... *OUR* BOOK...HEE, HEE!

ADDRESS YOUR LETTERS TO...THE VAULT-KEEPER, ROOM 706, DEPT. 16, 225 LAFAYETTE STREET, N.Y.C., 12, N.Y.

7

THE CRYPT OF TERROR

HEH, HEH! WELL! SO WE MEET AGAIN, DEAR FRIENDS! WELCOME! WELCOME ONCE MORE TO THE *CRYPT OF TERROR!* THIS TIME I HAVE A REALLY CHILLING TALE FROM MY COLLECTION OF SPINE-TINGLERS TO RELATE TO YOU! NOW, LIE BACK IN YOUR CASKETS! TUCK YOURSELVES IN WITH YOUR SHROUDS! COMFY? GOOD! THEN I'LL BEGIN! I CALL THIS STORY...

THE THING FROM THE GRAVE!

JAMES BARRY AND WILLIAM FERTH WERE BOTH IN LOVE WITH THE SAME GIRL, LAURA MASON! JIM WAS KIND... CONSIDERATE... A GENTLEMAN! BILL WAS BRAZEN... FUN-LOVING... AND AT TIMES, LAURA WAS ALMOST AFRAID OF HIM! AND SO WHEN JIM ASKED THE INEVITABLE QUESTION. . .
MARRY ME, LAURA? I KNOW I CAN MAKE YOU HAPPY!
BUT, JIM! WHAT ABOUT BILL? I...I'M AFRAID OF WHAT HE'LL DO WHEN HE FINDS OUT!
DON'T WORRY, LAURA! BILL WILL HAVE TO TAKE IT LIKE A MAN! ALL'S FAIR IN LOVE AND WAR, Y'KNOW!
YES! BUT BILL ISN'T THE TYPE TO GIVE UP EASILY!
LAURA DIDN'T KNOW HOW RIGHT SHE WAS WHEN SHE SPOKE THOSE WORDS! YES! BILL WAS NOT THE TYPE TO GIVE UP SO EASILY! HE WANTED LAURA!
...AND I'LL HAVE HER, TOO! EVEN IF I HAVE TO KILL YOU, JAMES BARRY!
SOON, LAURA AND JIM WERE MARRIED! THEY WERE VERY HAPPY THOSE FIRST FEW WEEKS...BUT THEN, BUSINESS CALLED JIM OUT OF TOWN FOR A FEW DAYS...
I'LL BE BACK THURSDAY NIGHT, DEAREST!
OH, JIM! I'M AFRAID! I DON'T WANT TO BE LEFT ALONE! BILL MIGHT...
BILL WON'T DO ANYTHING TO YOU, LAURA! BUT, IF YOU EVER ARE IN DANGER, NO MATTER WHERE I AM, SOMEHOW, I'LL GET TO YOU... AND SAVE YOU!
YOU'RE JOKING WITH ME, JAMES BARRY... BUT I'VE BEEN SERIOUS!
SO HAVE I, LAURA! SO HAVE I! 'BYE!
'BYE, JIM! HURRY BACK!
2

THE THING FROM THE GRAVE!

JIM'S CAR SPED ALONG A DARK COUNTRY ROAD TOWARDS THE MAIN HIGHWAY! THE HEADLIGHTS, KNIFING THROUGH THE VELVETY BLACKNESS, SUDDENLY FELL UPON...

A *MAN!* STANDING IN THE ROAD...

JIM PRESSED HARD ON HIS BRAKES, AND THE CAR SCREECHED TO A STOP...

CRAZY FOOL! I COULD HAVE KILLED YOU! WHO ARE YOU... ANYWAY?

BILL! IT'S *ME*... BILL!

THE SHADOWY FIGURE MOVED TOWARDS THE CAR... AND AS HE PASSED THE HEADLIGHT, A GLINT OF SHINY STEEL CAUGHT JIM'S EYE...

HE... HE'S GOT A KNIFE! HE'S... GOING TO *KILL* ME!

THE SOUND OF A STRUGGLE SHATTERED THE SILENCE HANGING OVER THE DESERTED ROAD AND THE HEAVY WOODS FLANKING IT! THEN THERE WAS A THUD AND A PIERCING SHRIEK...

...AND NOW, LAURA WILL BE *MINE!* ALL MINE!

BILL FERTH PICKED UP THE BODY OF THE MURDERED JAMES BARRY AND DRAGGED IT INTO THE WOODS...

...GOT TO GET RID OF THE BODY SO NO ONE WILL EVER FIND IT! GOT TO *BURY* IT *DEEP* IN THESE WOODS!

AGAIN THE THICK SILENCE OF THE WOODS WAS BROKEN! THIS TIME BY THE SOUND OF A SPADE STRIKING THE SOFT EARTH BELOW TOWERING TREES...

SORRY TO GIVE YOU SUCH A CRUDE BURIAL, JIM OL' BOY, BUT IT'S THE BEST I CAN DO UNDER THE CIRCUMSTANCES!

SOON, A GAPING HOLE WAS OPENED, AND THE STIFF BODY OF JAMES BARRY WAS DROPPED INTO IT...
NOW TO COVER IT UP, DITCH THE CAR, AND GET BACK HOME! THEN ALL I DO IS WAIT! IF I PLAY MY CARDS RIGHT, SHE'LL BE MINE!
A LITTLE LATER, THE SLEEK FORM OF JAMES BARRY'S AUTOMOBILE HURTLED OVER A CLIFF INTO A DEEP LAKE...
THEY'LL NEVER FIND THE CAR! IT'LL SINK INTO THE MUD AT THE BOTTOM OF THE LAKE!
AND SO THE JOB WAS DONE! BILL FERTH HAD PLANNED EVERYTHING CAREFULLY! THE WEEKS WENT BY, AND THEN THE TIME CAME FOR HIM TO GO AND SEE LAURA...
YES, LAURA! BUT IT'S OVER A MONTH NOW! HE'S LEFT YOU! HE'S PROBABLY FOUND ANOTHER WOMAN!
I CAN'T BELIEVE THAT, BILL! SOMETHING'S HAPPENED TO HIM! I KNOW IT! I FEEL IT!
BILL COULD WAIT! HE HAD PLENTY OF TIME! SHE'D COME AROUND! HE WAS SURE! AFTER ANOTHER MONTH...
IF ANYTHING HAD HAPPENED TO HIM, YOU WOULD HAVE KNOWN BY NOW, LAURA! CAN'T YOU SEE? HE'S LEFT YOU... DESERTED YOU!
I'LL WAIT FOR HIM... TO COME BACK!
HE'LL NEVER COME BACK! NEVER!
THEN I'LL WAIT FOR HIM FOREVER! I'LL NEVER STOP LOVING HIM, BILL! JIM WAS MY LIFE! WITHOUT HIM...
THEN... IT'S ALL WASTED! THE PLANNING... THE WORK... THE WAITING... WASTED!
WHAT DO YOU MEAN? WHAT ARE YOU SAYING?
4

YES! I KILLED HIM! HE'S DEAD! I WANTED YOU, LAURA, AND HE STOOD IN MY WAY!
Y-YOU K-KILLED JIM? I HATE YOU...YOU...YOU MANIAC! HATE YOU... HATE...
NOW... I'VE GOT TO KILL YOU, LAURA! IF I CAN'T HAVE YOU, NO ONE ELSE WILL EITHER! I'LL MAKE SURE OF THAT!
YOU...YOU'RE MAD... A RAVING MADMAN!
BILL FERTH FORCED LAURA INTO HIS CAR AND DROVE HER TO A DESERTED CABIN... DEEP IN THE WOODS NEAR WHERE HE HAD KILLED JIM...
THIS ROOM HAS NO WINDOWS...SO WHEN I LOCK YOU IN, YOU WON'T BE ABLE TO ESCAPE!
W...WHAT ARE YOU GOING TO DO TO ME?
I'M GOING TO SET FIRE TO THE CABIN! THEY'LL NEVER FIND WHAT'S LEFT OF YOU...NEVER! IT'LL BE ASHES...ALL ASHES!
FACED WITH THE HORROR OF BEING BURNED ALIVE BY THIS MADMAN, LAURA SCREAMED FOR HELP..
IT WAS AN EAR-SPLITTING SCREAM THAT SHOT THROUGH THE WOODS, REVERBERATING FROM TREE TO TREE ... ROCK TO ROCK...
AND SOMEWHERE OUT THERE, UNDER THE SOFT EARTH THAT COVERED IT... SOMETHING STIRRED...THEN PUSHED ITS DECAYED AND ROTTED HAND UP.. UP... THROUGH THE BLACK DIRT INTO THE BLACK NIGHT...
EEEEEEEAAAAGGHH
5

THE THING FROM THE GRAVE!

SLOWLY, THE EARTH GAVE WAY, AS THE THING PUSHED UPWARD, CLAWING! THE CLEAN FRESH AIR SEEPED DOWN INTO ITS SHALLOW GRAVE...

IT GOT TO ITS FEET CLUMSILY... STOOD ERECT IN THE MOONLIGHT! IT LIFTED ITS HEAD... LISTENING! IT HAD HEARD A SCREAM... A SCREAM THAT HAD MADE IT SEEK THE OPEN AIR...

IT MOVED FORWARD AT A STUMBLING GAIT! ITS ROTTED LEGS... ITS SIGHTLESS EYES... THE DECAYED FLESH THAT CLUNG HERE AND THERE TO WHITENED BONE... MOVED THROUGH THE UNDERBRUSH...

BACK AT THE CABIN, BILL POURED THE CAN OF KEROSENE AROUND THE OUTSIDE WALLS...

EEEEEEEEEEE

GO AHEAD... SCREAM, YOU FOOL! NO ONE WILL HEAR YOU!

BUT OUT IN THE DEEP SHADOWS OF THE WOODS, THE THING HEARD THE SCREAM... AND STUMBLED FORWARD... TOWARDS IT...

THE CABIN WAS ON FIRE NOW! INSIDE, LAURA CRINGED AGAINST THE DOOR AS THE FLAMES LICKED AT HER... WHITE... HOT...

OH... SAVE ME, JIM! WHEREVER YOU ARE... YOU PROMISED... OOOOH!

OUTSIDE, BILL WATCHED AS THE FLAMES LEAPED HIGHER AND HIGHER! THEN, FROM THE FRINGE OF THE TREES, HE SAW THE THING COMING... STUMBLING... STAGGERING...

GOOD LORD!

THE THING FROM THE GRAVE!

THE THING DID NOT SEE BILL! IT WAS LOOKING AT THE BURNING CABIN! BILL PUT HIS HAND OVER HIS MOUTH! HE WAS SICK! HE WHIMPERED...

J-JIM...

THE THING WENT INTO THE FIRE! IT DID NOT FEEL THE FLAMES LICKING AT ITS TATTERED CLOTHES...ITS ROTTED FLESH! IT WAS DEAD! IT COULD FEEL NOTHING...

AFTER A FEW MOMENTS, IT CAME OUT! ITS HAIR WAS SINGED! ITS DECAYED FLESH WAS CHARRED! WHERE THE FIRE HAD TOUCHED THE BONE, IT WAS BLACK AND SCORCHED! IT CARRIED THE GIRL...

BILL WAS SCREAMING NOW! HE BEGAN TO RUN WILDLY INTO THE WOODS...SCREAMING...SCREAMING.

A-A-A-A-A-A-H

THE THING PUT LAURA DOWN ON THE COOL GRASS FAR FROM THE BURNING CABIN! SHE WAS UNCONSCIOUS! SHE HAD FAINTED BEFORE THE THING HAD REACHED HER! SHE HAD NOT SEEN IT...

THEN THE THING TURNED...TOWARDS THE HYSTERICAL SHRIEKING THAT CAME FROM THE NEARBY WOODS...

SLOWLY IT SHAMBLED TOWARDS THE SCREAMING BILL AS HE CRASHED MADLY THROUGH THE THICK UNDERGROWTH...

HE'S COMING ...AFTER ME!

SUDDENLY, BILL STUMBLED INTO A YAWNING BLACK HOLE...
GOOD GOD! HIS GRAVE! JIM'S GRAVE... WHERE I BURIED HIM!
THE THING WAS COMING NOW! BILL TRIED TO STAND, BUT HE COULDN'T! THE PAIN! HE HAD BROKEN HIS LEG! HE TRIED TO DRAG HIMSELF FROM THE SHALLOW PIT... BUT THEN...
NO... NO!
THE THING WAS ON TOP OF HIM, PINNING HIM DOWN! HE TRIED TO STRUGGLE, BUT THE THING WAS STRONG! IT HELD HIM EASILY...
LET ME GO! LET ME GO! YOU'RE DEAD! DEAD!
AND THEN THE THING BEGAN, WITH ONE ROTTED AND DECAYED HAND, TO FILL THE GRAVE AGAIN... BURYING THEM...
NO... NO! YOU CAN'T BURY ME! I'M ALIVE... ALIVE!
IT DIDN'T TAKE LONG TO FILL THE GRAVE! THE DIRT WAS GETTING TO BILL'S EYES... HIS MOUTH! HIS SCREAMING WAS WILDER NOW... HYSTERICAL, MAD, TERRORIZED SCREAMING...
Y-I-I-E-E-E-E
AND THEN... AFTER A WHILE... THE SCREAMING STOPPED...
AND THAT'S MY STORY, DEAR READER! JIM CERTAINLY KEPT HIS PROMISE TO LAURA, DIDN'T HE? LUCKY FOR HER SHE FAINTED BEFORE HE GOT THERE, THOUGH! SHE'LL ALWAYS REMEMBER HIM IN A NICE WAY, NOW! AND POOR BILL! NOW JIM'S GOT HIM FOR COMPANY ... DOWN THERE WHERE IT'S COLD AND BLACK! WELL, THEY CAN ALWAYS HOLD GRAVE CONVERSATIONS TOGETHER! HEH, HEH! NOW, IF YOU'RE NOT TOO BROKEN UP OVER THIS TALE... WHY NOT READ ON? MORE CHILLS AWAIT YOU!

THE CRYPT OF TERROR

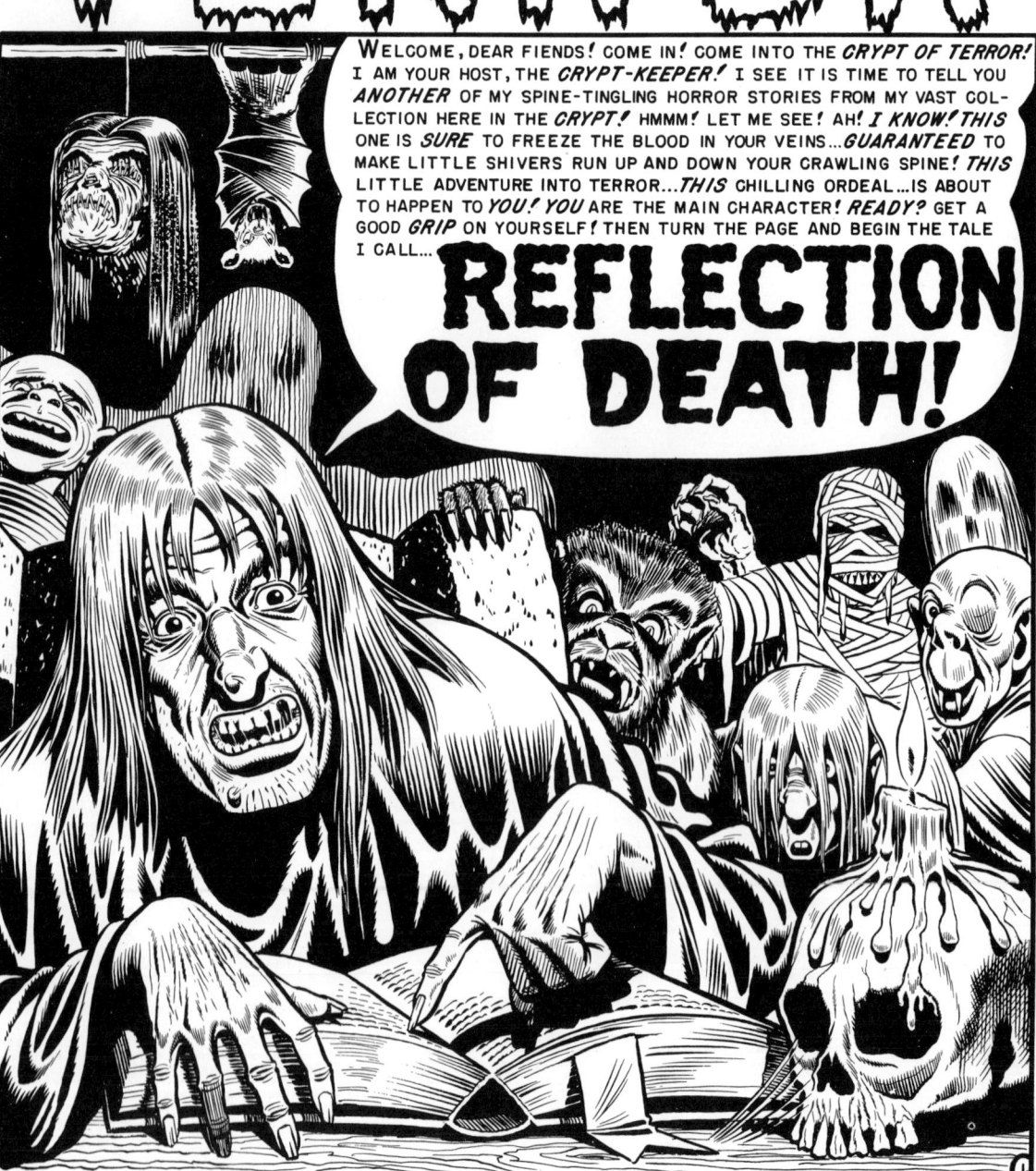

WELCOME, DEAR FIENDS! COME IN! COME INTO THE *CRYPT OF TERROR!* I AM YOUR HOST, THE *CRYPT-KEEPER!* I SEE IT IS TIME TO TELL YOU *ANOTHER* OF MY SPINE-TINGLING HORROR STORIES FROM MY VAST COLLECTION HERE IN THE *CRYPT!* HMMM! LET ME SEE! AH! *I KNOW! THIS* ONE IS *SURE* TO FREEZE THE BLOOD IN YOUR VEINS... *GUARANTEED* TO MAKE LITTLE SHIVERS RUN UP AND DOWN YOUR CRAWLING SPINE! *THIS* LITTLE ADVENTURE INTO TERROR... *THIS* CHILLING ORDEAL... IS ABOUT TO HAPPEN TO *YOU! YOU* ARE THE MAIN CHARACTER! READY? GET A GOOD *GRIP* ON YOURSELF! THEN TURN THE PAGE AND BEGIN THE TALE I CALL... **REFLECTION OF DEATH!**

REFLECTION OF DEATH!

AHEAD OF YOU, THE WHITE LINE THAT DIVIDES THE ROAD STRETCHES INTO THE DARKNESS BEYOND YOUR HEADLIGHT BEAM! BESIDE YOU, CARL SITS PUFFING ON A CIGARETTE...

"GETTING PRETTY COLD, ISN'T IT, CARL?"

"YEAH! AND THE HEATER'S ON THE FRITZ, TOO! IT'S GOOD WE WORE WARM CLOTHES!"

YOU'RE AT THE WHEEL! YOU AND CARL HAVE BEEN DRIVING SINCE DAYBREAK! IN TWO MORE HOURS, YOU'LL BE HOME! YOU'RE TIRED, NOW! THE STRAIN OF DRIVING THROUGHOUT THE DAY AND INTO THE NIGHT IS BEGINNING TO HAVE ITS EFFECT! YOUR EYELIDS ARE *HEAVY*... THEY KEEP *CLOSING*...

"YOU'D BETTER TAKE OVER, CARL! I'M GETTING TIRED! I'D HATE TO FALL ASLEEP AT THE WHEEL!"

"OKAY, AL! PULL OVER AND WE'LL SWITCH!"

YOU STOP THE CAR, AND CARL GETS OUT! YOU SLIDE ACROSS THE SEAT, AND CARL SLIPS BEHIND THE WHEEL...

"WHY DON'T YOU TAKE A SNOOZE, AL? I'LL WAKE YOU UP WHEN WE GET TO TOWN!"

"MAYBE... MAYBE I WILL, CARL!"

YOU DRAW YOUR COAT UP TIGHT AROUND YOU... PULL YOUR HAT DOWN... REACH INTO YOUR POCKET FOR YOUR GLOVES...

YOU STARE OUT THROUGH THE WINDSHIELD! THE ROAD COMES OUT OF THE DARKNESS AT YOU AND SLIDES BENEATH THE CAR... UNENDING... FASTER... FASTER! CARL BEGINS TO WHISTLE AN OFF-KEY TUNE! THE MOTOR PURRS... THE ROAD COMES ON... ON...

YOUR HEAD BEGINS TO NOD! CARL'S WHISTLING CONTINUES... FLAT... UNMELODIC! SUDDENLY HE GASPS! YOU LOOK UP! A PAIR OF HEADLIGHTS... BRIGHT... BLINDING... HURTLES AT YOU FROM THE DARKNESS! CARL SHOUTS! YOU TRY TO SCREAM, BUT IT CHOKES UP IN YOUR THROAT... A RATTLING COUGH...

"LOOK OUT... AL... WE'RE GOING TO HIT..."

THERE IS A SPLINTERING SHRIEKING CRASH OF METAL AND GLASS AND SQUEALING BRAKES...

YOU FEEL YOURSELF FLYING FORWARD... A BLASTING LIGHT... THE PAIN... THE COLD... AND THEN THE VELVET NIGHT CLOSES IN! ALL IS QUIET, EXCEPT FOR A DISTANT... FAR AWAY... WHIMPERING...

②

REFLECTION OF DEATH!

The blackness is empty... eternal! You float in it... turning... twisting... falling... then rising again! The pain is gone... everything is gone... only the darkness... on... on... dark... black... empty...

You open your eyes! Tiny pinpoints of light blink bright and dim before you! A leaf flutters... then glides at you! You are on your back... gazing up at the night sky...

You raise your head and look about! You are lying at the edge of a road! You remember now! The headlights... the crash... there must have been a collision! But the wreck... there's no sign of it...

You get to your feet! Your clothes are torn and dirty! There is a smell... a sickening smell! You look up and down the road! No smashed glass! No twisted metal! Nothing! Just a road... clean... white... reaching into the night...

A car is coming! You stumble out onto the concrete! You raise your gloved hand as the car bears down upon you! Its wailing brakes bring it to a stop...

"CRAZY FOOL! DO YOU WANT TO GET YOURSELF KILLED? I... I..."

You step close to him! You begin to ask him if he'll drive you into town... that there's been a wreck! Suddenly you see the wild look in his eyes! A look of *STARK TERROR!* He stares at you and *SHRIEKS*...

"YAAAAAAAAAH!"

The car meshes gears and roars away! You can hear him screaming! You cannot understand! Then you laugh to yourself! Of course! You must have been cut in the accident! Maybe the sight of blood scared him! You start down the road... toward town... toward home...

REFLECTION OF DEATH!

REFLECTION OF DEATH!

Panel 1: YOU ARE ABOUT TO TELL HER NOT TO BE AFRAID... THAT YOU MEAN NO HARM! BUT THERE IS NO TIME! SHE LOOKS AT YOU... HER EYES ROLL... SHE GURGLES A FAINT GROAN AND FAINTS...
U-U-U-G-H-H!

Panel 2: YOU GET INTO HER CAR! YOU DRIVE IT INTO THE OUTSKIRTS OF TOWN AND LEAVE IT... THE WOMAN UNCONSCIOUS BEHIND THE WHEEL! YOU MAKE YOUR WAY HOME... *HOME!* BUT WHEN YOU REACH IT...

Panel 3: THE WINDOWS ARE BOARDED UP! YOU CANNOT UNDERSTAND! THERE IS A SIGN TACKED TO THE HOUSE! YOU MOVE CLOSER... TO READ IT...

NO TRESPASSING BY ORDER OF THE SHERIFF! THIS PROPERTY BELONGS TO THE PEOPLES BANK AND TRUST COMPANY FORECLOSED JANUARY 15, 1951 FOR INFORMATION CONCERNING THIS PROPERTY...

Panel 4: FORECLOSED! ON JANUARY 15, 1951! BUT TODAY IS... OR IS IT? THE NEWSPAPER YOU FOUND! REMEMBER? HAVE YOU BEEN UNCONSCIOUS FOR ALMOST *TWO MONTHS?* YOU TURN AWAY FROM THE HOUSE! A LONE FIGURE APPROACHES ON THE DESERTED DARK STREET...

Panel 5: YOU WALK TOWARD HIM! YOU WANT TO ASK HIM THE DATE! HE COMES CLOSER! THEN HE SEES YOU...
GOOD LORD...

Panel 6: HE BEGINS TO RUN FROM YOU! YOU RUN AFTER HIM! YOU ONLY WANT TO ASK HIM A *QUESTION!* WHY DOES EVERYONE STARE AT YOU *WIDE-EYED... FAINT... SCREAM... RUN* FROM YOU? *WHY?* CARL'S HOUSE! YOU'RE IN FRONT OF CARL'S HOUSE NOW! CARL... WHO WAS WITH YOU... WHEN THE ACCIDENT HAPPENED! YOU GO UP THE STEPS... STAND BEFORE THE DOOR... RING THE BELL...

Panel 7: HEAVY FOOTSTEPS APPROACH! THE DOOR OPENS! CARL STARES OUT AT YOU! YOU WAIT FOR HIM TO SCREAM... TO RUN... WAIT FOR THAT LOOK OF HORROR... BUT NOTHING HAPPENS...
CARL! LET ME COME IN! YOU'VE GOT TO HELP ME!
I... I... DON'T...

5

REFLECTION OF DEATH!

You rush into his apartment! It is dark! Carl objects! You tell him the story! You blurt it out... everything! The crash... how you woke up... the people that screamed when they saw you! Except Carl... *Carl* did not scream! Carl... your *friend*...

"You joke with me... whoever you are..."

He stares at you, blankly! There is no recognition! 'Don't you know me, Carl? Don't you recognize your old friend... Al?', you say! He shakes his head and turns away...

"You're fooling! This is some sort of a gag! Surely you know that Al and I were in an accident almost two months ago... that Al was killed... *horribly mangled*..."

"...and I lost my sight! That I am totally blind!"

You, *dead!* You gasp! You look around! A mirror! You get up... stagger toward it...

...and look in!

You scream! You open your *rotted, torn, decomposed mouth* and *scream!*

Carl is at your side shaking you... shaking you...

"Al... *Al... Al...!*"

6

REFLECTION OF DEATH!

WAKE UP, AL! YOU'RE HAVING A NIGHTMARE!

HUH? WHA...?

YOU LOOK AROUND! YOU'RE IN THE CAR! CARL IS DRIVING! YOU'VE BEEN DREAMING... *DREAMING* THE WHOLE *HORRIBLE EXPERIENCE*...

THANK GOD! THANK GOD!

FOR WHAT, AL?

MY NIGHTMARE! I DREAMED I WAS DEAD! EVERYTHING WAS SO REAL! THANK GOD IT WAS ONLY A DREAM!

OH! YEAH! YEAH!

YOU WATCH THE ROAD AS IT UNFOLDS BEYOND THE HEADLIGHT GLOW AND RUSHES TOWARD YOU AND UNDER THE SPINNING WHEELS! YOU WONDER IF YOU SHOULD TELL CARL ABOUT YOUR DREAM...

WE'LL BE HOME SOON, AL!

YOU STARE OUT OF THE WINDSHIELD! FAR AWAY, THE HEADLIGHTS OF AN APPROACHING CAR KNIFE THROUGH THE DARKNESS! ICY FINGERS GRIP YOUR HAMMERING HEART! THEY'RE COMING AT YOU NOW... FAST...

CARL! YOU...THAT CAR...

YOU TRY TO MOVE! YOU'RE PARALYZED! THE DREAM! IT'S SO MUCH LIKE THE DREAM! YOU TRY TO SCREAM BUT NOTHING COMES OUT! CARL GASPS...THEN SHOUTS...

LOOK OUT...AL...WE'RE GOING TO HIT...

THERE IS A SQUEAL OF BRAKES...AND THE IMPACT OF TEARING METAL AND SHATTERING GLASS...

REFLECTION OF DEATH!

YOU FEEL YOURSELF THROWN FORWARD... A BLINDING LIGHT... A SHOOTING PAIN! THEN THE DARKNESS CLOSES IN... AND YOU'RE FLOATING IN A SEA OF VELVET BLACK...

YOU OPEN YOUR EYES! YOU CAN SEE THE STARS... ABOVE YOU... TWINKLING! A LEAF FLOATS FROM THE TREE OVERHEAD TO EARTH! YOU ARE LYING AT THE SIDE OF THE ROAD...

YOU LIFT YOUR HEAD AND GAZE DOWN TOWARD YOUR FEET! THE DREAM... SO MUCH LIKE THE DREAM...

YOU STRUGGLE TO YOUR FEET! THE ROAD IS BARE! THERE IS NO SIGN OF THE WRECK! FROM FAR OFF... THE SOUND OF A MOTOR TELLS YOU OF AN APPROACHING CAR! YOU STEP OUT INTO THE ROAD...

THE SMELL... THE SICKENING SMELL OF ROTTED FLESH BURNS YOUR NOSTRILS! SO MUCH LIKE THE DREAM... ONLY NOW YOU *KNOW* WHAT THE STENCH IS! THE CAR STOPS! YOU MOVE TOWARD IT...

CRAZY FOOL! DO YOU WANT TO GET YOURSELF KILLED?

THE DREAM IS *REAL!* YOU *KNOW* WHAT'S ABOUT TO HAPPEN! HE SEES YOUR FACE! YOU STEEL YOURSELF FOR HIS REACTION! IT COMES! A *HAUNTING TERRIFIED SCREAM*...

E-E-A-A-A-A-H!

YOU'RE *DEAD!* YOU *KNOW* IT, *NOW! DEAD!* AND *THIS* TIME, IT *ISN'T* A *DREAM*...

THE END

HEH, HEH! WELL, KIDDIES! THAT'S IT! LIKE IT? LIKE BEING A *CORPSE?* WELL, YOU MIGHT AS WELL GET *USED* TO IT! IT'S *BOUND* TO *HAPPEN... EVENTUALLY.* OH, COME, COME! WHY THE *GRAVE* LOOK? YOU'VE GOT TIME! HEH, HEH! MAYBE YOU'LL KNOW IT'S COMING BY HAVING A DREAM LIKE POOR AL IN THIS STORY! IF YOU DO, YOU'LL HAVE SOMETHING TO LOOK FORWARD TO! IN THE MEANTIME, YOU CAN LOOK FORWARD TO SOME MORE CHILLING TALES IN THIS BOOK! COMPOSE YOURSELF! READY? O.K. THEN, I'LL TURN YOU OVER TO *THE OLD WITCH!*

WIGGLING HER WAY THRU THE TEST TUBES, MARSHA CAME TOWARD ME, WEARING A GLISTENING KNITTING NEEDLE CLUTCHED IN HER HAND-ARRGH!-I CHOKED WITH ANTICIPATION...
ANTICIPATION BY MICKEY SPILLANE A NOVEL
MCCARTHY AND YOU

STEVE RINGGENBERG

AL FELDSTEIN

"We just took to each other. Within a year, he was writing and drawing all of his own material, and then, shortly after that, he was an editor. Soon after this, he was writing everyone's material. ... We almost know what the other's thinking after all these years."

— William Gaines *EC Lives!*, 1972

If publisher William M. Gaines was the heart and soul of EC Comics, editor/writer/artist Al Feldstein was the company's intellect. A prolific, reliable professional, Feldstein edited more comics and wrote more scripts for EC than anyone. He also drew 66 comics stories and 76 covers for the company.

Feldstein was born October 25, 1925 in Brooklyn, New York and began working in comics at the age of 15 at the Eisner and Iger Studio. He graduated from the High School of Music and Art, as did other EC and *Mad* stalwarts, including Harvey Kurtzman, Will Elder, and Al Jaffee.

He attended classes at Brooklyn College and the Art Students League before entering the Air Corps during World War II. While in the Special Forces, he drew a comic strip called *Baffy* for the Blytheville, Arkansas, base newspaper, designed posters, and painted murals. After the war, he worked for Iger again before moving on to Fox Feature Syndicate.

At Fox, Feldstein wrote and drew *Meet Corliss Archer* (a "good girl" comic based on the long-running situation comedy radio show), and *Junior* and *Sunny*, two "good girl" teen humor titles.

One day, freelance letterer Jim Wroten (the hand behind EC's distinctive Leroy Lettering even then), informed Feldstein that their mutual employer, the sleazy and exploitive Victor ("I'm the King of Comics!") Fox, was having financial difficulties that might interfere with Feldstein's income.

So, just before Valentine's Day, 1948, Feldstein presented samples of his work to Bill Gaines in the hope of doing comics for EC like the ones he'd been packaging for Fox and other publishers. Gaines was glad to see the talented young artist because at that point he had been running EC for not quite six months, following the unexpected death of his father, and he needed to build up his staff.

Feldstein's samples, loaded with buxom young women, impressed Gaines enough to assign the young artist to write and draw a new teen comic, *Going Steady With Peggy*. But Gaines changed his mind, telling Feldstein that sales of such material had tanked, and he pulled the plug

---

OPPOSITE: Marie Severin drew this caricature of Al Feldstein for the 1952 EC Christmas party.

291

on the project before Feldstein could do more than pencil the first story and a cover. Gaines offered to pay Feldstein for his work, even though Gaines had no use for it, but Feldstein demurred, which made a great impression on Gaines.

Feldstein was a good fit for EC, and he and Gaines got along well from the beginning. Even though Gaines was only three years older than Feldstein, Gaines took a paternalistic role in their relationship, setting a style that he fostered with most of his employees until the day he died.

Feldstein already had plenty of experience as an artist, and he got right to work, churning out stories for *Saddle Justice*, *Gunfighter*, *Crime Patrol*, and *War Against Crime*. For the first two months or so, he worked from scripts by veteran comics writers such as Ivan Klapper and Gardner Fox. But, sensing an opportunity to make extra money and find more creative satisfaction, Feldstein asked Gaines if he could write his own scripts. Gaines agreed.

Initially, Feldstein only wrote scripts for the stories that he illustrated, but he covered all of EC's bases at the time: Western, crime, and romance. Before long, he was scripting stories for other EC artists. It was only the beginning.

Gaines had been resistant to taking over his father's business and had played only a desultory role at first, but he came to fall in love with comics and was eager to move beyond his business role as publisher and be involved creatively in his comic books. He and Feldstein became fast friends and collaborators.

In 1950, Gaines and Feldstein launched new horror, crime, suspense, and science fiction comics titles. This "New Trend" boosted the company's sales and shook up the comics industry. Their explicitly gory, yet tongue-in-cheek horror titles spawned countless imitations.

Their newfound success brought with it the need for Feldstein to write a script every day, Monday through Thursday. On Fridays, he attended to other editorial duties.

Gaines and Feldstein began plotting stories together, and Gaines loved nothing more than the almost daily back-and-forth of working out a story with Feldstein. Feldstein enjoyed it, too, and took special pride in turning in a fully scripted story that Gaines liked.

Feldstein recalled it this way to Frank Jacobs in *The Mad World of William M. Gaines* (1972): "When I wrote a script, my first and foremost motivation was for Bill to read it and enjoy it. Bill supplied my need for a father. For this, I did all I could to earn his love."

Gaines made Feldstein an assistant editor and, later, an editor. But it wasn't Feldstein's title that mattered. It was the personal and professional relationship that he and Gaines shared — a unique creative symbiosis that developed a remarkable way of working together to turn out a complete comic book every week, as required by EC's schedule. It was, by the accounts of both men, a hectic, joyful, and creatively satisfying partnership.

Gaines saw it as his job to be the "springboard man." He was taking prescription amphetamines at the time in an effort to curb his appetite and lose weight. He suffered insomnia as an unfortunate side effect, so he spent his sleepless nights reading horror and science fiction stories. A lot of them.

As he read, he'd jot down "springboards" — short, one- or two-sentence story ideas that he could pitch to Feldstein in the morning. As Gaines humorously recounted in *EC Lives!*, the program book for the 1972 EC Fan-Addict convention, "after he [Feldstein] had rejected the first 33 on general principles, he *might* show a little interest in number 34. I'd then give him the hard sell [...] He would normally write the story in three hours, breaking it down as he wrote it right onto [the art boards]. Meanwhile, I'd sit there ... with a nervous stomach because I never knew if and when Al would come bursting back in and say, 'I can't write that goddamn plot!'"

Feldstein remembered it this way: "I used to drive him nuts because we would plot these together, and I would say, "No, no, no, Bill, that just doesn't work.""

Still, it must have worked most of the time, because Feldstein wrote four scripts a week for more than four years, becoming, in the process, EC's most prolific scriptwriter. The demands of his editorial and writing duties, however, forced Feldstein to forego drawing stories around the middle of 1951. He continued to draw covers, though, for EC's science fiction titles, *Weird Science*, *Weird Fantasy*, and their combined successor, *Weird Science-Fantasy*.

(An artist with relatively little art training, Feldstein always claimed he was not inspired by other comic book artists, but in his cover work, the influences of famed science fiction pulp illustrator Frank R. Paul and astronomical illustrator Chesley Bonestell are evident to the discerning eye.)

Since Gaines didn't always tell Feldstein what he was reading, Feldstein often unknowingly adapted short stories by famous writers including Katherine Kurtz, H.P. Lovecraft, and Ray Bradbury. Bradbury, however, caught their unauthorized use of two of his stories "Kaleidoscope" and "The Rocket Man," whose plots Gaines and Feldstein had amalgamated into the story "Home to Stay" (not in this volume). Bradbury wrote Gaines a letter politely demanding payment.

Bradbury liked the adaptation, however, and, in a postscript, suggested that EC adapt stories from his collections *Dark Carnival*, *The Illustrated Man*, and *The Martian Chronicles*.

Gaines immediately paid Bradbury for the use of his plots, then struck a deal to adapt more, at $25 each.

Bradbury's work proved an enormous source of inspiration for Feldstein. As Feldstein recalled in his interview with Grant Geissman in *Tales of Terror!* (Fantagraphics Books and Gemstone Publishing, 2000), "This became the love of my life, adapting Ray Bradbury into comics. I did *The Martian Chronicles*, *Golden Apples of the Sun*, and for the horror, I was doing *The Dark Carnival*. And I just loved it. That was where I think my writing really started to improve, because I was immersed in his writing — much to the detriment of the artists. The old joke was that I got to write such heavy captions and balloons that all the characters had to be drawn with a hunchback ... He was my idol as a writer, and I kind of aped him. See, I was never a writer."

In all, Feldstein ended up scripting 26 Bradbury adaptations for *Weird Fantasy*, *Weird Science*, *Weird Science-Fantasy*, *Shock SuspenStories*, *Tales From the Crypt*, *Vault of Horror*, and *Haunt of Fear*. Johnny Craig provided his own adaptation for a 27th Bradbury tale, "Touch and Go" (later known as "The Fruit at the Bottom of the Bowl" — see *Fall Guy For Murder And Other Stories*, Volume 5 in this series). (For other EC Bradbury adaptations, see *50 Girls 50*, *Sucker Bait*, *Zero Hour*, *Judgment Day*, *Forty Whacks*, *The High Cost of Dying*, *The Living Mummy*, *The Million Year Picnic*, *The Thing From The Grave*, *Daddy Lost His Head*, *Master Race*, and *Doctor of Horror*, in this series).

Despite his claim not to be a writer, Feldstein went on to produce more than 650 scripts for EC before the burden of it all became too much. EC began hiring outside writers, including Carl Wessler, Jack Oleck, Otto ("Adam Link") Binder, and Daniel (*Flowers for Algernon*) Keyes, among others.

When Bill Gaines pulled the plug on EC Comics in 1956 due to slumping sales, he was forced to let Feldstein go, along with all the other EC freelancers who weren't working with Harvey Kurtzman on *Mad* magazine.

Feldstein was at liberty for a few months, freelancing scripts for *The Yellow Claw* for Stan Lee at Marvel, but then Kurtzman, in an effort to ensure total editorial control over *Mad*, demanded a 51% ownership stake in the company. Gaines told Kurtzman to go to hell.

Kurtzman had orchestrated a successful transition from *Mad* the comic book to *Mad* the black-and-white magazine, but he left immediately, with the latest issue unfinished, and he took the art staff, excepting only Wallace Wood, with him.

Gaines still had an ace in the hole, even though he may not have realized it immediately. On the advice of Lyle Stuart, his friend and business manager, and after talking it over with his wife, Nancy, Bill Gaines decided to reach out to Al Feldstein.

Feldstein was the logical choice, of course, because he had never had the kind of deadline problems the temperamental Kurtzman always ran into. Feldstein had also edited *Panic*, EC's homegrown imitation of *Mad*.

Although he claimed not to have much of a feel for humor, Feldstein had written about half of the *Panic* scripts before his workload had gotten too heavy, and he'd had to pass the writing on to Jack Mendelsohn and Nick Meglin.

Gaines drove out to the Long Island Railroad station where Al Feldstein was returning home after a fruitless day of pounding the pavement for freelance work. *In The Mad World of William M. Gaines*, author Frank Jacobs reconstructed their momentous reunion:

"Al, Harvey's left, and I'd like you to come back. I don't know if we'll continue with *Mad*, but we'll do something."

"We should do *Mad*," Feldstein said.

"Well, whatever we do, you'll go all the way with me."

Feldstein agreed and guided *Mad* from 1956 until he retired in 1985. In the process,

OPPOSITE: Al Feldstein drew this self-caricature for the 1951 EC Christmas party.

he turned it into one of the most successful humor magazines of the 20th century, with a peak circulation of 2.4 million copies. Unlike Kurtzman, Feldstein was able to negotiate a non-ownership percentage deal with Gaines that resulted in Feldstein becoming one of the highest paid magazine editors in the world.

After moving to Jackson Hole, Wyoming, he fulfilled his lifelong dream of becoming a fine artist, completing more than 300 canvases. In 1999, he received an honorary Doctorate of the Arts degree from Rocky Mountain College in Billings, Montana. He and his third wife, Michelle, retired to a 270-acre ranch in Montana that they operated as a refuge for injured animals and where he painted award-winning wildlife and Western scenes and re-creations of some of his favorite covers from EC Comics. He remained a popular and much-beloved figure appearing from time to time at comics and horror conventions. He died at home, April 29, 2014.

In 2013, Futurism/IDW published a biography, *FELDSTEIN: The MAD Life and Fantastic Art of Al Feldstein!* by Grant Geissman. Al Feldstein was inducted into the Will Eisner Comic Book Hall of Fame in 2003. In 2011, he received the Bram Stoker Award for Lifetime Achievement from the Horror Writers Association.

Michelle Feldstein continues their animal rescue work at the ranch they named Deer Haven.

S.C. "STEVE" RINGGENBERG *has been an EC Comics fan since his early teens and has had the good fortune to interview many EC contributors, including publisher William Gaines, editors Al Feldstein and Harvey Kurtzman, and artists John Severin, George Evans, Jack Davis, Jack Kamen, Al Williamson, Angelo Torres, and Frank Frazetta. He has written comics scripts for DC, Marvel, Bongo,* Heavy Metal, *Red Circle, and Americomics. He has authored six young adult novels and co-authored* Al Williamson: Hidden Lands. *He recently published a short story collection,* Zombie Gundown and Other Tales, *and has completed a science fiction novel.*

ASSOCIATE EDITOR!

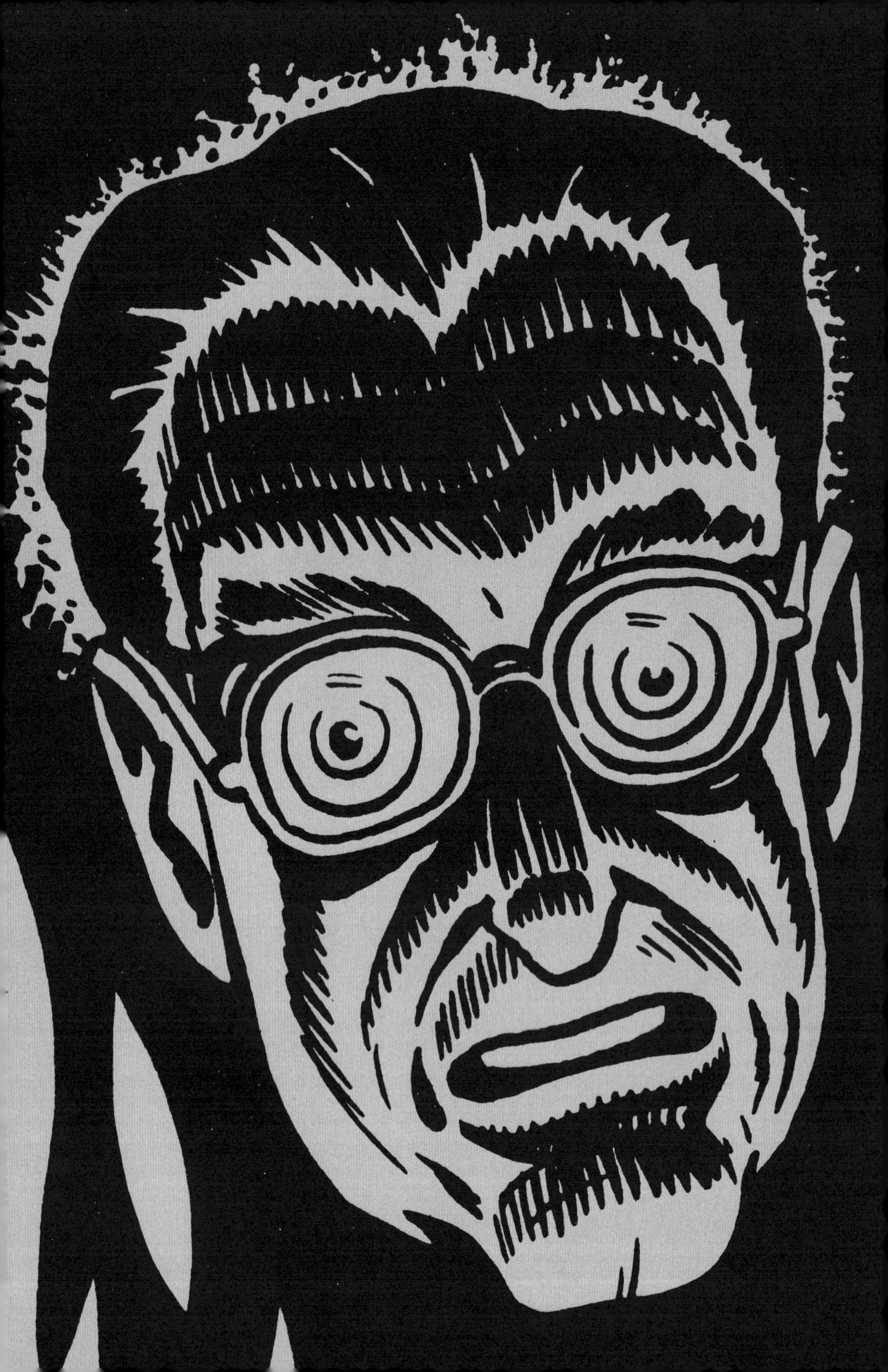

JOHN ALTON (b. and d. unknown) was a Canadian comic book artist who worked primarily on humor strips for the Canadian publisher Bell Features during World War II, especially "Doodlebugs," which appeared in *Joke Comics*, and which he co-created with a family member. Following the post-war collapse of that market, he moved to the United States in 1946 where he found work with several publishers, including American Comics Group, Fox Feature Syndicate, and EC Comics.

At EC, he drew the humor strip "Tumbles" in *Dandy* and earned the distinction of being the only artist to span the M.C. Gaines and Bill Gaines eras. When Bill Gaines became publisher, Alton switched to drawing crime, war, and Western comics.

He returned to Canada around 1953 where his only known subsequent credit is illustrating a science textbook for juveniles in 1961. Researcher Arthur Lortie notes that "John Alton" may be a pen name, and that the artist's real name might be Edward E. Alton.

GARDNER F. FOX (1911–1986) was a prolific comic book writer and novelist, best known for the many superhero characters he created for Detective Comics, Inc. (DC Comics) and others. In 1937, Fox began writing and developing features for DC Comics. By 1940, he was also writing for Maxwell C. Gaines's All-American Publications.

By 1947, Gaines had a new company, Entertaining Comics (EC Comics), where Fox developed a team of crimefighters from World War II's Allied powers for EC's *International Comics*. Shortly before Gaines's death in a boating accident that year, Fox introduced Moon Girl, an exotic alien princess living on Earth. Moon Girl artist and co-creator Sheldon Moldoff modeled her on the part-Indian Merle Oberon.

Fox wrote sporadically for EC's New Trend horror, crime, and science fiction titles until late 1950. Two outstanding stories are "The Man Who Was Death" (*The Crypt of Terror* #17) and "Man from the Grave" (*Came The Dawn And Other Stories*, Volume 2 in this series). He continued working for DC Comics after EC. Fox and other freelance writers left DC in 1968 when the company refused to provide them with health care and other benefits.

Fox also wrote novels and worked for other comics publishers, including Dell, Marvel, Warren, and Eclipse. He received multiple Alley Awards in the 1960s and was given the Jules Verne Award for Lifetime Achievement in 1982. Posthumously, he was inducted into the Jack Kirby Hall of Fame and the Will Eisner Award Hall of Fame. He was honored with the Bill Finger Award for Excellence in Comic Book Writing in 2007. Gardner Fox died in December 1986 at the age of 75.

WILLIAM MAXWELL GAINES (1922–1992, b. New York City) was the son of M.C. Gaines, the founder of EC Comics. Bill Gaines was studying chemistry at New York University when his father died in 1947, leaving him to run the family business. Bill moved to re-invigorate the company by breaking from the educational, humor, kiddy, Western, and romance titles that EC was then known for.

Under Bill Gaines, EC became known for its popular horror, crime, war, and science fiction comics, such as *Tales From the Crypt*, *Crime SuspenStories*, *Two-Fisted Tales*, and *Weird Science* — and, of course, *Mad*, which created its own category.

By 1956, EC had dropped all of its titles except *Mad*. Gaines remained publisher of *Mad* until his death in 1992. He was inducted into the Will Eisner Hall of Fame in 1993 and the Jack Kirby Hall of Fame in 1997.

IVAN KLAPPER (1922–2003) was an EC editor and writer, originally hired by M.C. Gaines to work on the company's crime titles.

His stories at EC centered on the occult and precognition, and it was the latter that earned him his position as technical consultant on *One Step Beyond* (ABC-TV, 1959–1961).

He also collaborated with Will Eisner on Eisner's cartoon guides and at *PS, The Preventive Maintenance Monthly*. Later in life, Klapper, proud owner of a bulldog, was involved in dog shows.

BILL MASON, **JANICE LEE** *and* **ARTHUR LORTIE**
contributed to these profiles.

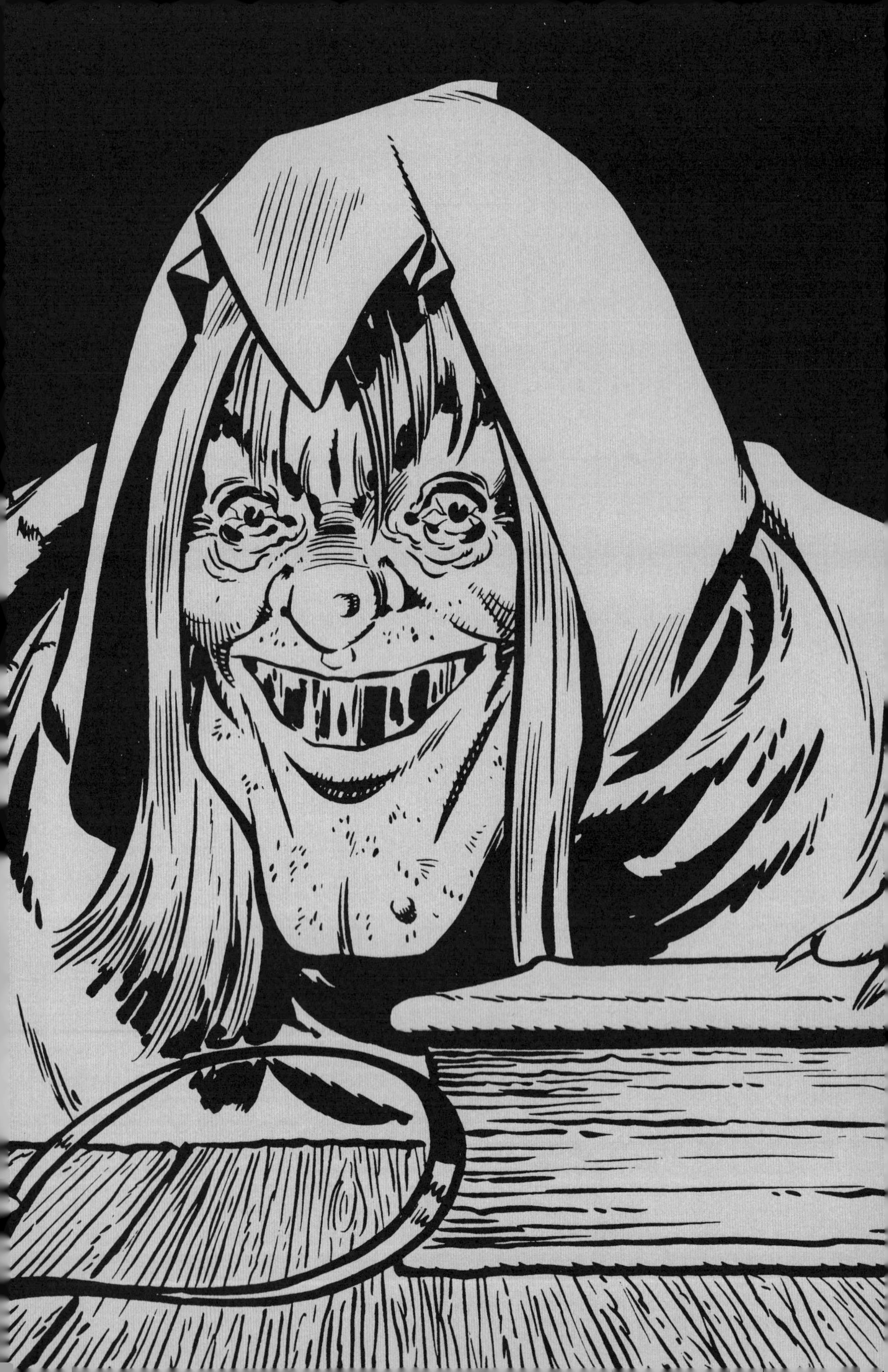

TED WHITE

Crime, Horror, Terror, Gore, Depravity, Disrespect For Established Authority— And Science Fiction, Too!

THE UPS AND DOWNS OF EC COMICS

M.C. Gaines was both a practical man, credited with inventing the comic book as we know it (although comic strips had been reprinted in book form for decades prior to his 1933 *Funnies on Parade*), and a visionary.

In the late 1930s, he formed a partnership with the owners of Detective Comics, Inc. (subsequently best known as DC Comics) and began publishing a series of superhero titles: *All-American Comics* (which featured the Green Lantern), *Flash Comics* (the Flash), *Sensation Comics* (Wonder Woman), *All-Star Comics* (The Justice Society of America), and *Comic Cavalcade* (a fatter 15¢ anthology of his superheroes).

But these were conventional commercial comic books of their day and, in essence, copies of DC's *Action Comics* (Superman), *Detective Comics* (Batman), and *World's Finest* (15¢ anthology), identical in formatting. Although successful, none (perhaps excepting Wonder Woman's titles) matched the success of DC's Superman and Batman titles. All were published under the DC imprint, and the children who read them probably saw little difference among them.

These comics were forthrightly aimed at kids — theoretically 8-year-olds. Although comics were hugely popular and widely read by World War II and Korean War GIs, the fiction was maintained throughout the 1950s that the average comic book reader was still only 8 years old.

From their inception, comic books were looked down upon by much of American society. They cost only 10¢ and were often thrown away after reading. Many teachers regarded comic book reading as a detriment to genuine literacy. The theory was that kids who read comic books would never go on to read "real" literature — they would demand pictures with their prose.

Gaines thought that the comic book medium could be much more than just throwaway entertainment, and he set out to prove it, first with *Picture Stories From the Bible*. It was earnestly done and intended to be educational rather than entertaining. Despite the best intentions of Gaines and his editors, writers, and artist (Don Cameron), it was pretty dull going for a comic book. But Gaines believed in it and pushed it.

Other matters were transpiring behind the scenes, and Gaines parted ways with DC in 1945, selling them all his titles except *Picture Stories From the Bible*.

Gaines began a new publishing imprint for his *Picture Stories* comics — Educational Comics, or "EC." In addition to *Picture Stories From the Bible*, he published *Picture Stories From American History*, *Picture Stories From Science*, and *Pictures Stories From World History*.

These were clearly intended to be sold in or through schools, and to be used with appropriate curricula. They were an idealistic venture, akin to *Classics Illustrated*, designed to prove that the lowly comic book could attain loftier goals of enlightenment.

But, like *Classics Illustrated*, they made no dent on academia. To teachers and other figures of authority over children, they were still "just comic books" and dismissed out of hand. And to the kids — their putative audience — they were dull stuff, lacking the excitement and panache of any superhero comic. They were not a commercial success.

When Gaines had left DC to found EC, he took one DC employee with him to be his business manager — Sol Cohen, whose first job as a teenager had been for DC, checking Manhattan comic book racks for sales movement during Superman's launch in 1938. Cohen had worked his way up through sales and distribution (DC and Independent News, an increasingly important distributor, had interlinking ownership), and he had a promising career at DC. But when Gaines asked Cohen to join him in his fledgling new company, Cohen accepted.

This proved to be a significant move for a reason no one anticipated. Because in 1947, M.C. Gaines and a friend, Sam Irwin, lost their lives in a boating accident on Lake Placid in New York. Gaines's final act was to save the life of his friend's 8-year-old son by throwing the boy to safety.

Gaines's son, William M. Gaines, inherited the company. But Bill was distant from his father, didn't care for comics, and was attending New York University with plans to become a chemistry teacher. Although entreated by his mother to take over the reins at EC, Bill was reluctant and for the first year did little but show up at the office periodically to sign checks.

Into this vacuum stepped Sol Cohen, EC's business manager. As he told me, years later, "the company was going down the toilet. The *Picture Stories* comics weren't selling and neither were the kiddy comics. I had to do something just to save my job."

His first act was to change "Educational Comics" to "Entertaining Comics."

"'Educational' was a word no comic-buying kid wanted to see. It was a kiss of death on any comic book," he told me.

His second act was to dump the *Picture Stories* titles and change the kiddy titles to crime, romance, and Western titles. (Due to postal regulations concerning second class mailing privileges — crucial for distribution purposes — it was financially wiser to change titles, continuing the previous numbering, than to drop one title and start a new one.)

1947 was a decisive turning point, although most of Cohen's changes occurred in 1948. In the late summer of 1947, *Moon Girl and the Prince* was launched. Moon Girl appears to have been a Wonder Woman copy. It went through two title changes before becoming *A Moon, A Girl, Romance*.

By then, Bill Gaines was the editor. In early 1948, EC launched *War Against Crime!*

By 1949, Bill Gaines had become interested in comic books. Sol Cohen moved on (to Avon Books), and Bill fully took over the company. He began bringing in the artists and editor/writers who would become known for their subsequent EC work.

Al Feldstein was brought in as a romance artist, although his first work for EC was for the Western title *Saddle Justice* in 1948.

Johnny Craig may have preceded Feldstein with work in the first *Gunfighter*, which also used Graham Ingels.

Harry Harrison and Wallace Wood (as collaborators) made their first appearance at EC in two Western titles that appeared at the end of 1949, *Gunfighter* and *Saddle Romances* (where Harrison, solo, had appeared in a previous issue).

The evolution of EC from 1947 to 1950 is one full of hints of the forthcoming "New Trend" titles. But fans of the latter titles may not find a lot to like in the earlier comics from EC. The quality was spotty, and there was not yet any focus on a unique style or approach to comics.

1950 was the year it all came together for EC. That spring saw the transformation of *War Against Crime!* into *The Vault of Horror*, *Crime Patrol* into *The Crypt of Terror* (later to become *Tales From the Crypt*), and *Gunfighter* into *The Haunt of Fear*, thus successfully establishing EC's horror title trio.

The same month *Haunt of Fear* made its debut so did two science fiction titles, *Weird Science* (with #12, previously *Saddle Romances*), and *Weird Fantasy* (with #13, previously *A Moon, A Girl, Romance*).

In the fall of 1950, *Two-Fisted Tales* made its debut, taking over the numbering of *Haunt of Fear*, so its first issue was designated #18. This was done to satisfy — or dodge — those postal regulations. *Haunt of Fear* itself continued, renumbered, with #4. It confused the fans but made the business office happy. *Crime SuspenStories* premiered about the same time (starting with #1), thus setting in place EC's basic New Trend stable of titles.

Two-Fisted Tales was Harvey Kurtzman's first title, and it brought a sense of realism, irony, and anti-romance to war stories. *Frontline Combat* would join it half a year later.

Crime SuspenStories was Johnny Craig's title (as was, to a lesser degree, *Vault of Horror*; Al Feldstein was the overall SF and horror editor).

By 1951, the classic EC lineup was almost in place, lacking only *Shock SuspenStories* (1952) and *Mad* (1952).

The first half of the 1950s was EC's glory time — for better and for worse. For us comics fans, it was the best of times — crowned by superlative art and provocative stories — while for those who watched sternly over us, tut-tutting, it was the worst of times — a triumph of gore and disgust.

The basic "crime" of EC was that it did not edit its comics for those 8-year-old kids. The editors aimed higher, at a somewhat older, more mature reader. (13-year-olds, perhaps — I was 13 when I discovered ECs, and I had by then mostly given up on other comics.)

The naysayers won, in the short term. There were state and federal inquiries (inquisitions?), local comic book bonfires, and ultimately *Seduction of the Innocent* and the Comics Code. The New Trend comics were shelved in favor of a "New Direction" and new titles — horror and crime conspicuous by their absence.

But the tide had turned against EC. Its competitors wanted it put out of business (and many claim the Comics Code Authority was formed for that purpose).

In 1956, Bill Gaines gave up a losing fight and folded all his titles except *Mad* — which outlived him and continued its reliable formula through several corporate mergers through 2019, when, after 67 years, it went all-reprint.

However, in the long term, EC has survived. There have been countless reprints of the comics themselves, as both comic books and as hardcover books. There have been TV shows and movies based on *Tales From the Crypt*. And now there are these new collections from Fantagraphics, showcasing for the first time the individual artists whose works personified EC.

Theirs was a magical time — a time when young, ambitious artists decided for themselves to take comic book art to heights never previously dreamed of, heights that equaled the best work of the greatest of the newspaper strip artists of the 20th century.

Some of them went on to major successes in commercial art — book covers, movie posters, *TV Guide* covers — while others lived and eventually died in poverty.

No one told them then that what they were doing was a waste of time and ambition. We are all better off for their accomplishments, and we celebrate their work here.

TED WHITE *has been a comics fan for most of his life and, with Larry Stark, Bhob Stewart, and Fred von Bernewitz, was a seminal EC fan in the early 1950s. He has been a (still-quoted) jazz critic, a science fiction writer and editor, and a radio deejay. He wrote the Captain America novel* The Great Gold Steal *in 1966 and edited* Heavy Metal *in 1980.*

THE FANTAGRAPHICS EC ARTISTS' LIBRARY

Corpse On The Imjin And Other Stories
(*Harvey Kurtzman*)

Came The Dawn And Other Stories
(*Wallace Wood*)

50 Girls 50 And Other Stories
(*Al Williamson*)

'Tain't The Meat ... It's The Humanity
And Other Stories
(*Jack Davis*)

Fall Guy For Murder And Other Stories
(*Johnny Craig*)

Child Of Tomorrow And Other Stories
(*Al Feldstein*)

Sucker Bait And Other Stories
(*Graham Ingels*)

Zero Hour And Other Stories
(*Jack Kamen*)

Judgment Day And Other Stories
(*Joe Orlando*)

Bomb Run And Other Stories
(*John Severin*)

Aces High
(*George Evans*)

Spawn Of Mars And Other Stories
(*Wallace Wood*)

Grave Business And Other Stories
(*Graham Ingels*)

Forty Whacks And Other Stories
(*Jack Kamen*)

The High Cost of Dying And Other Stories
(*Reed Crandall*)

The Living Mummy And Other Stories
(*Jack Davis*)

Voodoo Vengeance And Other Stories
(*Johnny Craig*)

The Million Year Picnic And Other Stories
(*Will Elder*)

The Thing From The Grave And Other Stories
(*Joe Orlando*)

Daddy Lost His Head And Other Stories
(*Jack Kamen*)

Master Race And Other Stories
(*Bernard Krigstein*)

Death Stand And Other Stories
(*Jack Davis*)

Doctor of Horror And Other Stories
(*Graham Ingels*)

The Martian Monster And Other Stories
(*Jack Kamen*)

The Woman Who Loved Life
And Other Stories
(*Johnny Craig*)

Atom Bomb And Other Stories
(*Wallace Wood*)

Man And Superman And Other Stories
(*Harvey Kurtzman*)

Terror Train And Other Stories
(*Al Feldstein*)

COMING SOON

Accidents And Old Lace And Other Stories
(*Graham Ingels*)

www.fantagraphics.com/ec